Ending the Era

of

Elitism

Spiritualizing the World, vol 11

Ending the Era

of

Elitism

KIM MICHAELS

MORE TO LIFE PUBLISHING

www.morepublish.com

For foreign and translation rights,

contact: info@ morepublish.com

ISBN: 978-87-93297-72-2

Cover art by Sandra Singer

For more information: *www.ascendedmasterlight.com and*
www.transcendencetoolbox.com

Content

INTRODUCTION

This book belongs to the series *Spiritualizing the World*. The books in this series are given by the ascended masters as workbooks that provide the knowledge and practical tools we need in order to make a contribution to solving concrete world problems. This book contains the knowledge and the tools we need in order to end the era where elitism and various power elite groups have such a dominant influence on earth. These books do not contain foundational knowledge about ascended masters and their teachings. In order to make the most efficient use of this book, you need to have a general knowledge of the following topics:

- You need to know who the ascended masters are, how they give their teachings and how you can make the best use of them on a personal and planetary level. You can find extensive teachings on this in the books: *How You Can Help Change the World* and *The Power of Self*.

- You need to know how the earth functions as a cosmic schoolroom. You need to know your own role and the authority you have as a spiritual being in embodiment. You need to know the role of the ascended masters and how only we who are in embodiment can give them the authority to use their unlimited power to affect change on earth. You can find more on these topics in the first book in this series: *How You Can Help Change the World*.

• You need to know how to use the practical tools given by the ascended masters. You can find more on this topic in: *How You Can Help Change the World* and on the website: *www.transcendencetoolbox.com*.

• You need to know about the existence and methods of the dark forces who are ultimately responsible for creating problems on earth. You can find foundational teachings on this in: *Cosmology of Evil*.

How to use this book

There is no one way of using the teachings and tools in this book. However, if you want to make a significant contribution to solving world problems, it is suggested that you start by following this program:

• You read one of the chapters in the book completely in order to increase your understanding of the topic.

• You give the invocation associated with that chapter once a day for nine days while studying the same chapter again.

The reasoning behind this program is that the chapters in the book form a progression. As you give an invocation for one chapter, you are also clearing your own consciousness from certain energies and illusions. This makes it easier for you to absorb and apply the teachings from the next chapter.

You can of course also read the book all the way through and then select one or more invocation(s) that you give several times. It is always more powerful to give an invocation once a day for nine or 33 days.

Because some of the invocations in this book are quite long, they have been divided into two or more parts. It takes about 15-20 minutes to give each part. If you prefer, you can give all of the parts for one invocation in succession. In that case, you do not need to give the sealing after the first invocation or the preamble to the next. You give a preamble in the beginning, continue through the parts and give a sealing in the end.

1 | THE STAGES OF THE SPIRITUAL PATH

NOTE This talk was given by Kim Michaels at the conference in Washington, D.C. where the dictations in this book were also delivered. It is included here because Mother Mary refers to it in the first dictation.

Listening to all of you earlier, I realized that we all have, all of us, certain similarities in our paths and how we found the teachings and the masters, and I just wanted to say a few things about that.

I guess we could say, if we want to be very linear and systematic, that there are three stages of the spiritual path. First, you are running away from something, the next stage you are running towards something and the third stage you stop running. You can look at yourselves and see where you are at on that. I think it is not everybody, but many people I have met started the spiritual path because they had some kind of problem. For many it could be a health issue. They started looking into diet and alternative medicine and eventually spirituality as a way to heal a physical problem. It could also be a specific outer problem they had, for many people a lack of money and they got into some kind of teaching with positive mental attitude and how to manifest things. For others, it was a difficult childhood, difficult upbringing, psychological problems or various issues.

What I am saying is that you have a specific problem that you want to get away from and there is nothing wrong with that. I am not trying to say there is anything wrong with this, we all have to start somewhere.

I have met many, many people on the spiritual path who had a very difficult childhood and that was one of their prime motivators for why they started looking into something new, something different. In many cases, the church they grew up in did not help them deal with that difficult childhood and maybe even made the problem worse and so, it is a very necessary phase to go through.

What eventually happens to many people is that they find some kind of healing or there is some kind of resolution to the issue so that it's not so dominant in their consciousness anymore. Then, they move into that next phase where, now instead of getting away from a problem, they see a positive goal. They shift and now they see that the spiritual path offers you a positive goal that you can run towards, and it can be in many different ways that people see this. It can be a higher state of consciousness, it can be peace of mind, freedom from many issues, psychological issues.

We are running towards something and for me, I was blessed by not having a difficult childhood. I had a much easier childhood than most people I've met on the spiritual path. I was not really running away from something, but when I found Yogananda's book *Autobiography of a Yogi* when I was 18, it gave me a positive vision that there is something to strive for and there is a higher state of consciousness that we human beings can attain. That was my primary motivation for engaging in the spiritual path.

From the outer to the inner path

For the first many years on my path, I was running towards that goal of a higher state of consciousness. In the beginning, I was, even though I saw my goal was a higher state of consciousness, I really had no idea what it was, what it meant, or how to get there. I was very much on the outer path, as I call it, because I thought it was a matter of studying an outer teaching, practicing a technique and doing these outer things. If I did enough outer things, then eventually someday: click, I would be there. In a meditation movement I was in, it was that you do meditation, in Yogananda they had the Kriya Yoga technique and of course, when I found the ascended master teachings, it was giving decrees.

Looking back at it, in the beginning, I thought, because that was just the culture in the ascended master movement, if you give enough degrees, especially violet flame, you will have transmuted all your karma, all your substance in your psychology and one day you will just sort of be there.

There were people who thought that if they gave enough decrees for the rest of their lives, they would automatically ascend after that lifetime.

I came to a point where I started questioning that because there was actually a point in the late 80s and the beginning of the 90s where the masters started talking about the need to resolve psychology. I think I always had a certain understanding that I needed to change myself in order to make progress, but in the beginning I had not connected the two. I still thought that if I kept doing the decrees (and I was very, very conscientious about decrees, I would decree for hours a day for many years) that would give me some automatic progress. I am not saying it doesn't, because as the masters say we have two aspects of the limitations in our psychology and one is just energy that is accumulated. And when you give decrees, you are transforming that energy so, it does have an effect.

The other aspect of the limitations in our psychology is some kind of belief, or as the masters call it now, some kind of self or internal spirit and that internal spirit is based on, it started with, a decision we made in a past life where we experienced something, a trauma. It could be, as the *My Lives* book said, the first embodiment where we encountered earth or the fallen beings. When we experienced that trauma, we made a decision. We made a decision that created the self that is programmed to uphold that decision, and until we see that decision consciously and change it, we will not be free of it.

There is, in my view, absolutely no technique out there ever invented, that will automatically bring you to a higher state of consciousness. Anybody who says so, I just think they are lying, or they do not know what they're talking about. The reason for this is that I have come to a much greater understanding of free will than I had when I started the spiritual path. We made a decision and until we consciously see that decision and say: "I no longer want that decision to dominate my life," until we do that, we are not free of it. If you really understand free will, once you have made a choice, the only thing that is going to override that is you making another choice.

There was a point where I started shifting and I started realizing there is an inner path and that it isn't enough to do these outer things, but I actually need to look at my psychology. That happened for me in the early 1990s where I started realizing that in my ascended master movement, we gave hours and hours of decrees and decree services for world conditions. The motto we had was: "We are changing the world for Saint Germain." I am not saying that was invalid, but you had a Sunday service that started in the morning and went to the afternoon. Then, you had a Wednesday night healing service. You had a Friday night ascension service that could be four hours. You had a Saturday night Saint Germain service that was four hours and then at one point, they also came up with a Tuesday night El Morya service. Almost every night, you could go to one of these services and decree for three or four hours. On top of that, we had other things. There was a point where we had these labors of Hercules we had to decree for, and we could have decree services where we decreed at high volume for seven-eight hours.

I came to a point where I recognized in myself that I had used this goal of saving the world for Saint Germain as an excuse for not looking at my own psychology. So I started looking at my own psychology, went to a psychologist, did various kinds of therapy, inner child, Gestalt, EMDR, all kinds of therapies. That was where I started to go more on the inner path because I started to look more at myself and I started to decree more on my personal issues. Still, I understood it was about changing myself, but I did not understand what it involved. I did not understand what I just said that it's about me seeing a decision I made and consciously changing it. So, I was still running towards a goal, but I did not really have a vision of what the goal was and I did not really know how to get there.

Overcoming the gap

That's what the masters have talked about a little bit in the last couple of years. Master MORE gave a profound dictation about it. There's a gap. When I look at many of the spiritual teachings I have studied or been involved in myself, I can see the pattern. You find it in traditional churches as well. They define a goal for you and they define certain methods that you are supposed to do, certain things you are supposed to do. But there's a gap so even if you do all of those things, you are never going to get there. You are never going to cross the gap.

If you look at the many, many people in the world today who are atheists, agnostics or angry with Christianity, it's because for several lifetimes, they have believed in the Christian promotional line that if you are a good Christian and you believe in the Bible and you follow the outer rules of the church, you'll go to heaven after this lifetime. So, they live a whole lifetime believing this, then they make the transition and instead of meeting St. Peter who was saying: "Here is the door," they meet some other master who says: "You are going to have to go back down to earth." When you have done that several times, you might get a little annoyed and you might come in with a certain mistrust of the Christian religion.

It's the same thing with many spiritual teachings: there's simply a gap. There is simply a gap between the goal, that is to find enlightenment, a higher state of consciousness, and the method they give you for reaching it. It is always tempting to say, but now we have all of these teachings the masters have given, starting with the *My Lives* book and *Healing your Spiritual Traumas* and the other books. So now we have the methods for crossing the gap. I do believe that we have the methods that can work for *some* people, but I do not allow myself to believe it could work for *all* people, because people are very different.

There are different things they need and the reason why I am saying this is that I still do not think that if you read the *My Lives* book and you started with *Healing your Spiritual Traumas* and you studied those dictations and gave the invocations and did that for all of the five books, I still do not think you would *automatically* have healed your traumas. It will not happen automatically, no matter how good of a teaching you have, no matter how good of a technique you have. So what I am hoping to convey here is that there is no automatic path, neither this nor anything else.

There can be tools that can be good, but in the end it is about us seeing something that we have not seen before. So the question is, what is going to trigger that for each one of us? I can see in myself its been many, many different things. All of the things I have done in my life have helped me as I can hear from many of you that you have also been helped. You were in a certain teaching, you studied it, it took you to a certain level and then you needed something else to get to another level.

That is why I will never claim that this is the highest possible teaching, it can heal all your problems because it's so individual. What it really is a matter of is coming to that realization: There's something I need to see that I have not seen and in order to see what I have not seen, I have to do something different. I have to think differently. Because with the approach I have taken so far, if that approach could have shown it to me, I would have seen it, but I have not seen it. It is Einstein again, if you keep doing the same thing and expect different results—you know.

Looking at our reactions

So again, we are all different, but for me, it has helped me tremendously, first of all, to be aware of this and also look at my own reactions. There came a point where I realized that when I react to other people, it does not show me something about them and their faults. It actually shows me something about myself, my own mechanism that is keeping me trapped. *That* has helped me look at my reaction and there came a point where I realized that it was such a powerful story for me to read about Gautama Buddha. Here he is, he is ready to go into Nirvana and he is sitting under this Bo tree, which is just a tree, where he is sitting there meditating and there is one final initiation he has to go through. It is that he has to sit there and watch as all the demons of Mara, all the demons in the world, are parading before him. In Buddhism when they tell the story, they just make it seem like it was an easy initiation for him, he was the Buddha ready to go into Nirvana. But it actually was not because what I realized, and I felt I got this from Gautama intuitively, was that this was his temptation. It was not a temptation like you normally talk about temptation, to drink or eat another piece of chocolate or whatever. It was "his" temptation. Could they come up with something in this world that he would react to? Was there some reaction in him, or like Jesus said: "The prince of this world comes and has nothing in me."

So, Gautama Buddha is sitting there and the demons of Mara can do anything they want. They can come up with absolutely anything. Could they come up with something that could make him react? We are not just talking about a negative reaction, it could be something as subtle as, here are some people, you could help them, you could help them change. Or here is something you have not finished that you could do and you are the only one who could do it. It could be any kind of temptation. So, if there was anything in this world that he was attached to, that he felt he was not done with, they could have gotten him to react and he would not have been able to go into Nirvana.

How do you go into Nirvana? Again with the ascended master movement, they had some requirements for the ascension: balance 51% of your karma, fulfill your Divine plan and your sacred labor. Well, what exactly does that mean? What does it mean to fulfill your Divine plan and your sacred labor, what is that? For that matter, how are you going to ascend with 51% of your karma? Are there ascended masters up there with 51% of their karma and unresolved psychology?

When I pondered this, I saw intuitively that there comes a point, and this was before I knew about the 144 levels, but I still saw there comes a point where you are standing here, and here is a gate and it leads to the ascended realm. Before you can walk through that gate, you have to turn around and look at earth. You have to look at this planet and everything on it, and is there anything that pulls you back here? Anything you feel you want to do, you want to experience, you have not finished? Is there anything that pulls you back here? Then, you are not ready to walk through that gate and ascend because what is the ascension? It is that you are *permanently* and *forever* leaving the earth behind. You are saying: "I'm done with earth! There is nothing I want to do here, nothing I want to experience. I am completely done."

In the ascended master movement, it was almost portrayed like you just give enough violet flame and you "pop up there" and you are an ascended master looking down on earth. But why did you come to earth in the first place? You made choices, right? So, aren't you going to have to make a choice to leave? Yeah, and it's the choice that there is nothing left for you to do or experience on earth. I realized that the goal of Buddhahood is non-attachment and it's the same with the ascension. Non-attachment means again, there is nothing on earth that's pulling on you, that you have to do. I also realized that it was my reactionary patterns that made me want to do something on earth or feel like there was something I had to do, that it was all my reactions. So, I started pondering this a long time ago. I started really looking at this, what am I attached to, what are my attachments? This has followed me ever since. It's been a long process. I am not trying to in any way say that this can be done in five minutes. The spiritual path to me is not a quick fix. It is not an instant gratification. It is a lifelong process.

Coming to grips with free will

I think I probably realized these things in the early 2000s. So far it has been 19 years that I have been working on this, looking at my attachments. Everything I have gone through has been a great opportunity for that. When I separated from my second wife and she started accusing me on the internet about all of these things, even personal things, I realized I had an attachment to being seen as a good person by other people because I always saw myself as good person. I know I am a good person,

I never intentionally hurt anybody. But I had an attachment to being seen as a good person. I realized it is an attachment, it has to go because, and here is the real issue, if you really understand what the ascension is about, and what spiritual growth is about, it all depends on your choices. It is all a matter of *you* making choices, not somebody else. But we have all been brought up, conditioned, programmed and brainwashed over many lifetimes to have all of these reactionary patterns where we think: "I cannot make this choice because of..." some condition outside of yourself, such as other people, humanity as a whole, your family or society, or even your own spiritual path, what you want to do.

I realized that I could not allow myself to have my choices be dependent on, controlled by or directed by the choices of other people. It was a long process of actually coming to grips with free will. I can look back at my life and I can see that I have always been very, very, reluctant to influence other people, to force other people, manipulate people. I have been very reluctant to do it. I have been so afraid of doing it, that it has in parts of my life made me very passive where I did not really dare to be assertive, I did not really recognize my own feelings, my own desires, what I wanted to do. It was more about what I felt I *should* do, what was expected of me or what other people wanted. I would tend to be so afraid of manipulating other people that I did not dare to do anything or say anything, make any demands, or even recognize my own desires.

What I realized was that I respected other people's free will but I did not respect my own free will the same way. I had more respect for other people's free will than my own. I realized this is unbalanced, this is completely unbalanced, and it came to a point where I realized I have absolute respect for other people's free will but I have the same respect for my own free will.

And what does that mean? That means I have a right to make my choices independently of the choices other people make because that's what free will is. It's that you can make *your* choices and other people can make *their* choices but you are not making your choices dependent on their choices. You are not adjusting to them. Of course, we are adjusting to each other when we live together and we are in a group, or whatever, it is not that, but what I was talking about is not the outer actions to accommodate other people. It was actually more inside of myself, how I saw myself, what I thought I could do, or what I could not do. It's again these attachments.

As an example, I started doing the Ask Real Jesus website in 2002 and in the beginning, I really had the thought or the attitude, the belief that I should be able to help. I knew I could not help everybody, but I should be able to help as many people as possible. It should be so that if people came to the teachings or came to a conference, I wouldn't scare them away by being the person I am. So, I should be as accommodating and as open, as patient as possible. I felt I could not allow myself to define "who am I" as a teacher, what am I about. I couldn't allow myself to put any demands on people. I was just there to give them something, offer them something but not put any demands on them.

So, in the early years, I would have some people, for example, who would come and talk to me, or sometimes even in a group setting like here, there would be somebody who would monopolize the conversation and talk for half an hour. I am not kidding. Some people would come to me and they would talk for hours and hours and hours and I would feel that I should listen to them and be kind and this and that.

But after some years I realized that I was not really helping people by doing that. I was, if anything, just enabling them to stay in that mode because most of these people, they weren't looking at themselves and they were not really talking to me. I realized they were not talking to me because they wanted me to help them. They were talking to me because they saw me as having a position so they felt that they were building a status by talking to me and that was what it was about. They were playing a game so I came to a point where I decided: "I cannot help these people. I do not want to help these people. That is not the kind of teacher I am." This was back in 2013-14 and since then hardly anybody like that comes to a conference anymore, or calls me or emails me. It is mostly people that are serious about the spiritual path and that want a different perspective. They want me to help them see something they cannot see and that sometimes, by the grace of God, I can do.

Daring to be ourselves

But that really did not shift until *I* shifted. I started realizing that everything in my outer situation is connected to what is going on inside myself. If I look at myself and see that throughout my life, I have had a certain pattern, there is a certain kind of people that I have run into again and again and they bother me, I react to them, I have a reactionary pattern. If I see that and then instead of thinking, how can I avoid these people, how can I deal with them, how can I change them, how can I save them, which is even worse, which I had a tendency to do. I was thinking: "Oh, I should be able to help that person, I really should be able to make them see what they can't see." But if instead, I look at myself and say: "Why do I have that reactionary pattern? Why am I reacting to them? What belief do I have that makes me think that when I am around a person like that, I have to behave a certain way?"

I started realizing that I was so accommodating that when I met a person, I was trying to tune in and behind me were all of these like costumes in the theater where they can have these stands with the costumes hanging on. And all these were there and I was trying to know what costume you want me to put on and then I jump into it. I was so willing to do this that I was not true to who I am. I did not really know who I am. I never dared to define who I am or even look at it.

I realized that I just had enough of that. I came to a point where it felt I'd had enough of it and from that moment on there was a certain type of people, I do not really need them because I am not willing to play the role and so they just go elsewhere. They go and find somebody who is willing to play the role that they have assigned to a spiritual teacher.

That was a pattern I had. That was a pattern I had at my consciousness and I think we all have the same thing because we have over lifetimes been in certain situations, we have been around certain types of people, where just in order to survive, or in order to be around these people and not have a big fight or a big blow-out all the time, we have taken on a certain costume, taken on a certain role, so we can get along with these people.

That is what I mean with: "You are running towards something, but you do not really know what it takes to get there." You are running towards higher states of consciousness, enlightenment, whatever it is, but you do not see that you are carrying along with you all of these roles and costumes and reactionary patterns.

You think that when you get to enlightenment, they will all melt away. But the reality is that the only way to get to enlightenment is to see them and dismiss them. You have to realize that you are playing a role and then you have to decide consciously: "I no longer want to play this role. I am done with it. I do not want to play this role anymore." Then, you have to look at the belief. What was the belief that made you think you have to do this? When you see that belief, and can consciously let it go, then you are free of it. That is the process described with the separate selves because these costumes could just as easily be called separate selves. You are literally stepping into a different kind of personality in certain situations.

So many of the teachings out there, they portray it that way. There is a goal, enlightenment, here is the path you need to follow to get there and you do not have to look at your psychology because once you get to enlightenment, it all falls away. But you are not going to get there. The way to get there is to see these selves and dismiss them because what is enlightenment? It is freedom from any reactionary pattern on earth. *That* is enlightenment.

The enlightenment industry

I was thinking about this one day years ago, because there is a whole industry, there is the enlightenment industry out there, where the goal is enlightenment and there are all these spiritual teachers and all these courses and all these books. I thought: "There's something wrong." I could not put my finger on what it was. There is something wrong there. There is even something wrong in the concept of enlightenment.

Then, I realized these organizations out there where they have a leader and they are all going around saying: "Oh, he is enlightened." He may not be saying it himself. I am not sure Eckhart Tolle says he is enlightened, but a lot of people say he is. It hit me one day: "If you were enlightened, would you say it?" Because see, what is enlightenment? It is freedom from all of these roles, but what do the roles do? When you are in a certain role you are labeling everything. You are seeing life through that filter and that means the role defines certain labels for how you are supposed to be, including, for example, how you are supposed to be as a spiritual teacher. So, if you come out and say: "I am enlightened," not only are you putting a label on yourself, but you are reinforcing the label that all of those people who believe you have, and therefore, you are not helping set them free. You are actually helping them stay in the role where they are the follower and you are the leader.

Enlightenment is when you stop labeling anything, at least yourself. You would never say it, because once you are there it does not matter anymore. It just doesn't matter. It fades away. I came to the conclusion that what I really wanted was not to be enlightened or to have any particular high level of consciousness, what I actually wanted was freedom. Freedom in my own mind to choose my reactions.

This again came back to my deeper and deeper understanding of free will, where I realized that you can have the concept, like Buddha had the concept of the demons of Mara, Jesus had the concept of the prince of this world. You can look at it that there is a certain force in this world who is trying to pull you to stay in this world, to prevent you from getting free where you can move beyond the earth. It does this by trying to pull you into these reactionary patterns that make you believe in certain lies. But how do you really get free of it? You do it by coming to that point where you do not have the reactionary patterns, and for me it was very important to realize that there is a lie that this force has been promoting for millennia about free will.

Denying free will is a prison

There are people who deny that we have free will. There is a man who is called Sam Harris, who has written a whole book where he basically denies free will. My reaction to that book is: "Why should I believe your arguments when you don't believe in them yourself?" Why do I say that? Because he has written a whole book where he is trying to convince me to accept his arguments for why I do not have free will. Which faculty would allow me to accept his arguments over what I believe right now? If I did not have free will, how could I choose to accept his arguments? So, he must believe I have free will, otherwise why write the book?

So, the same thing again, we do not realize, because there is such a force in the world and it is religion and it is Scientific Materialism that says: "We do not really have freedom of choice." Many spiritual movements reinforce it because they say: "You have karma. You made karma in past lives. You cannot just choose to do anything you want. You have to admit that you did something bad in a past life and this limits you now." I came to a point where I started asking myself: "Why? If I really have free will, if God has given me free will, why should I be bound by my past? Why should I be bound by my past choices? If God has given me free will, why would he want me to be bound by my past choices?"

I started processing this in my mind, and I actually started realizing that God or the ascended masters are not putting any limitations on what choices I can make right now. The same goes for each one of you. You can make any choice that you want to make right now—*if* you can over-come the mechanism in your own mind that made you make the previous choices. Why did you make the choices you made in the past? Because you had created this self and you saw the world through that self. When you see the world through that self, you think: "I cannot do anything I want, there are only these or these options I have." Whenever you hear people who have gotten into some kind of trouble, whatever it is, they so often say: "I had no other choice" or "I had no choice" "I couldn't help it" "I had to kill this guy" or "I had to do this. I had no choice." But why did they not have a choice? Because they could not see that there were other options, the self that they saw life through excluded all the other options but one or two. The force of this world, the prince of this world, always wants to manipulate us into situations where we think we have only one or two choices and they are both bad. Pest or cholera.

I realized that the reason I made a bad choice in the past was not that I am a bad person. It was that I had a self that I saw life through and that caused me to make that choice. As long as I am dragging that self with me, it is true that I cannot make any choice I want. But if I overcome that self, I am free, at least from *that* self, and suddenly I can make choices that I did not think I could make before. When I get to a point where all of the selves are gone, I can make any choice I want, there is absolutely nothing I *have* to do. For me that came full circle when I was doing the invocations for the book *Healing Your Spiritual Traumas*. They talk about the primal self and I was working on this. I was really asking the masters to help me see this and what came to me at that point, I have since gotten other insights, but what came to me at that point was that when I came to earth as an avatar, I came here because I saw the suffering and I wanted to help people overcome that suffering. The whole dynamic of why I came to earth was: I want to help change other people.

Why we came to earth

So, by the very way that I chose to came to earth, the mindset I had when I came to earth, I had put myself in a situation where my choices on earth depended on the choices of other people. I was not here because I wanted to be here and experience and do what we can do on earth. No, I was, in my mind, just here to help other people. I was always in this mode of how can I help other people.

Well, I cannot help them if they reject me, if they will not listen to me. How do I need to change myself so I can get people to listen to me? That was my basic modus operandi, in terms of planet earth. No, I could not allow myself to enjoy life, because I was here to help other people. I could not allow myself to say: "Well, who am I and how do I want to be?" Because what if that offended somebody so they would not listen to me? When I came to see that, I woke up at four o'clock in the morning. My body was not even awake, but mentally I was there and I just saw this in a vision. I saw this whole scenario of how I put myself in this frame of mind of wanting to help other people and therefore, I could not be a certain way. Because there was something I had to do here on earth, and I felt I just *had* to do it. That was the only reason I was here and if I did not do it, there was no point in me being here. It was pointless to be here. It was ridiculous that I have been here for 2 million years, if I could not accomplish what I came for. How stupid can you be to come to a planet and you have no chance of accomplishing what you came for? No, you *have* to. You have to do this.

I saw it and it was like, all of a sudden, something just broke inside of me and I just let it go. I felt at that point, I could not have gotten out of bed. My body was so relaxed, so soft. I could not have gotten out of bed. I think I actually fell back to sleep and two or three hours later, I woke up, but for three days, my body was so soft I could not really do anything. I could not lift anything. I could not have done any physical work and my mind, I just felt so relaxed, so at peace, so free, because I realized that I kept repeating to myself: "There's nothing I *have* to do on earth."

So, what was I left with? What do you *want* to do on earth? Is there something you want to do? And all of a sudden, instead of feeling that everything I did on this planet was something I *had* to do, now I could start saying: "What do I *choose* to do? What do I *want* to do?"

Setting yourself and other people free

That was just such a shift. I have never experienced such a shift in my whole lifetime. All the shifts I have had on the spiritual path, nothing compares to this because I realized if I really respect other people's free will, I cannot try to change anybody. I cannot look at somebody, I cannot allow myself to look at somebody and say: "Oh, he's really suffering." We were walking to lunch today and there was this bronze statue up here of this man with a contorted face and he had no arms and no legs, so that's probably why he was screaming, but I looked at it, I said: "That's the epitome of suffering there." But I can't even allow myself to look at somebody and say: "That person is suffering and he shouldn't be suffering so therefore, I should change that person so he's not suffering." I have to accept that if people are suffering, it's a result of choices they have made, perhaps for many, many lifetimes, and who am I to tell them they should choose otherwise? Who am I to even have an opinion about what they should choose or what they shouldn't choose? So, if I do not have an opinion about what choices they should make, why should I have an opinion about the consequences of those choices? There are certain choices you make here on earth, they will lead to suffering, there's no question about it. But why should I think suffering is wrong, and people should not be suffering? If God gave them free will, and if they have made the choice, and the consequence of that choice is suffering, why should I judge it? That is what I was doing before and that is what I did before I came to earth and that's what brought me here and so, that was just a tremendous liberation.

I think many spiritual people have this because why are we on earth? We see there's so many things wrong here. We are here because we have compassion, we want to help other people. But it's almost impossible on a planet like this, where there's so much suffering, to not look at this suffering and judge that it's wrong. If people are suffering and the only way to get out of suffering is that they change, then we are almost ready to force them to change so they won't suffer anymore. But then we are going right into the same mindset as the fallen beings, who have been trying to force people. They have been trying to force people into suffering and here we are claiming to be better than them, but we are trying to force them out of suffering. Makes no sense whatsoever. It is still force. Because what is the basic law of the universe? Free will.

Now, the fallen beings have created a lot of philosophies that do not respect free will and it ties in with the topic of the conference, elitism. There's always an elite that do not respect the free will of the people and therefore, they want to force and control the people into doing this or that. How can we be spiritual people if we do the same thing? We may say: "But we have the good intentions," but look at how many people are trying to force people, and they also think they have good intentions. What's the road to hell paved with? So, we have got to step up. We have got to step up and realize that's not why we are here.

What are we here for? The masters said it in one of the later books in the series: "We are here to experience ourselves in this environment." You can experience your selves, your outer selves, in this environment, or you can experience yourself as you really are in this environment. As long as we are looking at earth through these outer selves, even the outer selves we had with us when we came, we are running towards a goal. The only way to stop running, is to get rid of these selves, because then we can just be who we are.

I am not going to stop writing books or taking dictations, or speaking, because I came to this realization that there is nothing I *have* to do. But it's just a whole different way of doing it, because I do not *have* to, I am not *forced* to, I am not *compelled*. I do it because I choose to do it and it's a world of difference. I think it's not even a process that's over with. I think we could all eventually come to that point where we say: "What do I really want to do here on earth?" If we do not want to do anything, maybe we are ready to ascend. But there could still be things we say from a positive: "I do not *have* to do it. But this is what I *want* to do, this is what I *choose* to do." It gives us just a whole other approach to life.

Question: I was wondering, how does the collective consciousness impact free will? Because we live in society, and we are swayed by the collective consciousness in one way or the other and it seems like it's difficult to maintain your free will at all times.

Kim: Oh, it is, absolutely. You could say that the people who say we do not have free will, in a way are right. But I would say that the real question to ask is not: "Do we have free will?," but: "How free is it?" The many people that are so overpowered by the collective consciousness that they are not really making free choices, they are just doing what they are supposed to do and what they see people around them do. But as spiritual people, just the fact that we go away from mainstream religion and find a spiritual teaching, we've already demonstrated that we are in the process of raising ourselves above the collective consciousness. Some of you describe how you found the path and all of a sudden you became very eager to study the teachings and to practice, give decrees and invocations, I did the same thing. I think it was valid for me for many, many years to do all those hours of decrees because it helped pull myself above the mass consciousness.

You could divide it up and say, the first stage of the spiritual path is where you are pulling yourself above the mass consciousness so your choices are not propelled by the mass consciousness. Once you get to that point, that's when you then start needing to go on the inner path, because now you need to realize that you no longer have so many external forces that are forcing your will, but you have all the internal forces, the selves, the internal spirits and this and that. That is the next phase where you pull yourself above that, and that's when you can then start feeling free and at peace.

I can look back at my own path and I can see that when I first found ascended master teachings, I had a certain dynamic in my psychology and actually, I think I have seen it in many other people. We grow up, we are spiritual people, and we feel like outsiders because we cannot talk to anybody about our spiritual beliefs. Nobody wants to listen to it, whether it's our family or whatever and so we feel like we are outsiders, we feel like we are possibly even put down by many people. Certainly, we *are* put down by both the established religions and materialistic science because just look how we spiritual people are portrayed in movies and TV shows: crazed cult members who are mindlessly following some kind of leader, or talking about stupid things like chakras and this and that. Always portrayed in a negative way, like kind of stupid people.

I think when I found the ascended master teachings, I had an inferiority complex because I knew I was different. You find ascended master teachings and you have these organizations that have a very high barrier of entry. You have to go through a lot of things to become a member, you have to make a lot of choices, you have to go through a certain process. The more hoops you have to jump through, the more special you end up feeling, compared to all those people out there who have not done it. Many of us, we come in with an inferiority complex, we switch to a superiority complex and we have to get to the point where we no longer have any complexes.

When I first started doing the work I am doing with the websites and I started doing conferences, because I was in this reactionary pattern, I was very aware of people's reactions, very sensitive to it. I also had a certain insecurity in myself where I wanted to do the best job, I did not want to make any mistakes and I did not want people to reject me or be angry with me or whatever. I had a certain insecurity in myself about what I was doing and that gave me a certain tension and maybe most people could not see it, but I felt it myself.

Again, I came to a point where that just faded away and I am just saying: "Well, I am who I am, I am the kind of person I am. I have a certain background. I grew up in a certain culture. But I also have a certain history as a being on earth, and I am deciding who I want to be and what kind of a spiritual teacher I want to be." I am not trying to force anybody or manipulate or persuade anybody to follow me. If they do not want to, they should go find a teacher that resonates with them. But I do not want to change myself to accommodate people and I do not care how many people I attract or do not attract anymore. I did 15 years ago. But today I do not, because it's not about that. I am not needing the recognition from anybody or the validation by having 1000 people or selling 100,000 books or whatever. I do not need that. What I get out of the work today is the joy of seeing that the teachings are in the physical where people can find them and of course the joy and interacting with people who've been helped by the teachings. But it's not like I need to build up something in myself to cover up any insecurity in myself. It is a joy to see that it works, it's a joy to see that it helps people. It is a joy that I have seen people that I have known for years, and I can see how much they have changed, just like I have changed. I do not need the outer stuff and I think that is when we start becoming free of both the external factors that pull on our free will and the internal factors that pull on our free will.

Question: If I go into something negative and see it and you can say: "Oh, there's a self." You see something that is completely opposite to what you do, and you can see it now, and your reaction and you are like, wow, it's not me. But you can see that self and then separate yourself from it.

Kim: Yeah, you can. The first many, many years I was on the spiritual path, especially after I found an ascended master teaching, I was in what I call "deficit mode." In the ascended master teachings I found, the culture was that, the masters were so high, perfect, up there. In order to be worthy to be their student, you had to live up to a certain standard and that was defined by the culture as an outer standard. You had to behave a certain way, look a certain way and did not wear orange or black or whatever. If you lived up to these outer rules, you could feel that you were a "good chela," as the saying was. But the problem was that the standard of what you were supposed to live up to, there were certain outer rules, but there was also a more subtle standard. You were supposed to be perfect somehow. Which did not really make any sense, because if there is such a thing as perfection, then the ascended masters would be the only ones that would qualify.

I do not think any of us, as long as we are in embodiment, are going to qualify. But I think there was that dream in the organization (and that dream is there in many spiritual movements and many religions) that you can actually become perfect. That is also why you have these teachers who are seen as enlightened, it maintains that dream: "Oh, that person is perfect, maybe we can eventually become like that," and so you have this dream. It was actually a very big relief for me to give that up and say: "You know, I do not even want to worry about this anymore. I am going to accept that I am going to be imperfect for as long as I am in embodiment. For the rest of my life I am going to still have things in my psychology that I need to see and resolve. I am not going to feel that I am supposed to live up to some superhuman standard."

I had it when I was a student in my first organization, and then when I became a messenger I had another standard for how I was supposed to be as a spiritual teacher. I came to a point where I just saw that and I thought: "Do I want to live this way for the rest of my life? Absolutely not. I do not want to live this way." Again, I realized it was just a self, but it is more than that. It is true that there can be a self that pulls you into a certain reactionary pattern and you need to resolve the self. But what I am saying is that even resolving a self does not necessarily mean that you automatically shift, because there are some times we have to make a decision to shift. I went to a point where I realized, I had to make a decision to shift out of this deficit approach and shift to a positive approach where I just accepted: "I am good enough, I am acceptable as I am right now."

The masters have given dictations over the last couple years where they have said several times: "Please do not think that we are like the fallen beings. Please do not think that we are looking at you as imperfect beings and we are ready to condemn you anytime you make a mistake. Please do not think that we think that because you have made a mistake here on earth, you will never be worthy again."

That is another lie about free will: You can make one choice and then you are doomed forever. What nonsense. I came to a point where I just decided I was going to accept I am okay. I am acceptable. It does not mean I was going to stop growing. I am still growing. I am growing faster than I was before because I am not trying to maintain an outer image anymore and therefore tying up my mental and emotional energies in maintaining some outer image. So, I am actually much more free in awareness to look at whatever I have left that is unresolved.

The other thing that was very, very important for me was that when I made that shift, I suddenly saw, that in all the time I had been in ascended master teachings, there had been almost like a division in my mind. There are certain limitations I could have that were okay to see that I had, because they were not the bad, dangerous limitations. For certain aspects of the ego, it was okay to see that and get over it. But there were certain things that I did not want to see in myself because I thought if I had those, the masters would condemn me, so I would rather not see them, because then I could maintain the illusion that I was not so bad. I realized the masters are not going to condemn me, because to them, it is just all unreality anyway and how is one aspect of unreality worse than another aspect? It all has to go. Then, I could get rid of that self that had resisted looking at myself. Even though I was always willing to look at myself in a certain way, there was certain things I was not willing to look at because I did not want to admit that I could have had that particular issue.

When I got rid of that, it was another big liberation. I could just start looking at whatever is there, and I could look at it neutrally. I did not have to condemn myself for it. I could just look at it and say, okay, it has got to go. I see you. You are just another self. You are not me, I am not you. I do not want you anymore in my life experience and then you die. I do not know that that formula works for everybody, but it has worked tremendously for me.

2 | MOST PEOPLE ARE NOT INHERENTLY EVIL

I am the Ascended Master Mother Mary. It is my great joy to open this conference, as I have now opened many of these ascended master conferences. This topic of elitism is in a sense the essential challenge facing earth at least at the present moment. Of course, it has been facing earth for a very, very long time, especially since the fallen beings were allowed to incarnate on this planet. They of course brought with them a certain mindset of clearly seeing themselves as superior to any other beings on earth specifically, but even to any other beings in this unascended sphere.

Naturally, we do not expect the general public to come to accept ascended master teachings or the concept of fallen beings, but it is necessary for you, as ascended master students, to know about this. You simply cannot understand elitism, if you are not aware that there is a certain group of beings in embodiment on earth (and even in the three higher octaves of earth), who have this quintessential elitist attitude. You cannot understand where elitism comes from on earth, unless you know that there are these beings.

Behavior that is not human nature

Now, you will see of course that there is a growing awareness of this even in the public, even in the collective consciousness. There is much talk about sociopaths, narcissists and so on. This is of course something that we have gradually built up over a very long time, by working with the people in the field of psychology, self-help and spirituality to bring forth these concepts. We have been working to get it to a point where these ideas can spread, and people can begin to see that it is necessary to look at human behavior and see that there is a certain type of behavior that just is not human. It *is* not human. What this can eventually lead to, and which is beginning to break through (at least in the mental realm), is an acceptance that not everything human beings do is human or human nature.

You look at many of the atrocities that have taken place, such as the Holocaust. You will see how there are certain writers, philosophers, psychologists, scientists, even religious people who have taken these events, these atrocities, and they have said: "Oh, this is just human nature." You even have a formerly quite known religious person, Mother Teresa, who said: "We all have a little Hitler inside of us." This shows you how these ideas have been spread for a very long time, which says that any human being has the potential to do these evil acts, these atrocious acts.

This is what you need to realize is a complete and utter lie, created by the fallen beings specifically to camouflage themselves. Why? As their primary modus operandi, they do not want to be identified for what and who they are. They do not want human beings to see them for what and who they are. Therefore, they have tried to create this myth that "it's just human nature to do evil," that any human being could potentially perform such acts. It is a total and absolute lie. It is not in *human* nature, it is in *fallen* nature.

God did not create evil

Of course, nobody was created by God as a fallen being. The implication of the philosophy of religious people, if you look at it in a consistent manner, is that God must have created human nature so that human beings have a propensity for evil. God did not create people (human beings or any other beings) with a propensity for evil. God gave self-aware beings free will and free will implies that they can choose to commit any act that they can imagine. They can also choose to label these acts as good or evil. God has not labelled any acts as good or evil. The concept of good and evil (as we have now explained many, many times through the ideas of duality and the duality consciousness) did not come from God.

God gave you free will. God looks at anything you do in a completely neutral manner. God, the ascended masters, we do not judge in terms of good and evil. Who created the concept of good and evil? The fallen beings did. Why did they do it? Well, partly to manipulate human beings, by defining certain things as good and other things as evil. Once you define for a certain culture or society what is seen as good and evil, what have you done? You have instantly set yourself up as the elite for that society. You are defining what an entire society, an entire civilization, defines as good and evil. Thereby, you can manipulate people in a myriad of ways. You can manipulate them into doing what is defined as good, seeking to avoid what is defined as evil.

What if there is another group of people who are doing what your group defines as evil? Well, in order to prevent some greater evil, you might start thinking it is justified to kill that other group of people. Even though killing is actually in your own definition defined as "evil," in order to avoid this bigger evil, it is okay for you to do this smaller evil. Suddenly, the fallen beings can manipulate societies into going to war with each other and committing these horrendous atrocities, while somehow thinking that they are doing something "good," perhaps even something that was approved by God and will earn them entry into heaven and seventy virgins or whatever they see as the Promised Land.

There is no human nature

You see here that talking about "human nature" is a meaningless concept because human nature implies that people are created with a certain nature. They are endowed with this, either by God or by nature and there is nothing you can do about it. The fallen beings want human beings to think that you are either inherently bad, you are sinners by nature, or you have the potential to do evil, the potential that you see in the world. You see my beloved, you do not have a little Hitler inside of you. *Hitler* had a "little Hitler" inside of him and it became big and did what it did. Only the fallen beings have a Hitler or a Stalin, or a Mao inside of them. Human beings who are not fallen, do not.

Now, many people will object to this and say: "But look: The guards in Auschwitz who pushed people into the gas chambers and poured those pellets down that released the gas, they were committing evil acts." Yes my beloved, but did they decide to build Auschwitz? Did they come up with the idea for the final solution and decide to implement it? Nay, they did not. They were manipulated into a situation. No excuse for it, it was not right or good what they did but it was not by their own initiative that they did this. It was by the initiative of the fallen beings that they were manipulated into doing this. So yes, the fallen beings can manipulate human beings into doing evil acts, but it is only the fallen beings who are the originators of evil.

This is something that is very, very important, *essentially* important, for you who are ascended master students to contemplate and make calls on. You have the teaching that allows you to look back throughout human history, even beyond known history, and see how there is this very old programming of making all people on earth feel guilty for the actions of the fallen beings and feel that you could have potentially done something like this. Let me just assure you, my beloved, none of you could have initiated this kind of evil. None of you ever have in any of your embodiments or you would not be open to this teaching.

The guilt trip put upon people

Therefore, you need to look at yourselves and recognize that throughout your long history of being in embodiment on this earth, it is very likely that you have embodied in one of these cultures where they have attempted to put this guilt trip on human beings. The fallen beings have attempted to make you feel guilty and partly responsible for the evils that they initiated. You need to look at these selves that you might have created in reaction to this, you need to see they are only selves. They have no reality to them. You need to come to the point where you can identify that there is a self in you (whatever your background is) that believes that you should feel responsible for these evils you have seen in history. You may even have a self that makes you feel that you were part of this and therefore you should condemn yourself, put yourself down and feel responsible for something that happened in the near or distant past. I need you to contemplate this and ask for my guidance, ask for my help, to see if you have such selves. Then, come to the point where you can see the belief that the self is based on, where you came to accept some sense of responsibility for these evils initiated by the fallen beings. Then, I need to you to consciously dismiss that self, let go of that decision and stop taking responsibility for what is not your responsibility.

I do not care if you were one of the prison guards at Auschwitz in a past life. You were responsible for what you did and for your state of mind that made you do it (and by the way, I am not saying that any of you *were* a prison guard at Auschwitz) but you are not responsible for the greater evil, the entire context in which this happened. I am not telling you that you should think you never did anything evil in your previous lifetimes. I am not telling you that you should not take responsibility for anything. But I *am* telling you, in connection with the messenger's talk, not to take responsibility for what is not your responsibility. The evils perpetrated by the fallen beings on this planet are not your personal responsibility. They never have been, they never *will* be and you will not help raise the earth into the Golden Age by accepting responsibility for what is not your responsibility. *Do you hear me?* [Audience answers: "Yes."] I need you to hear me because the selves that you have will never hear me. You need to separate yourselves from those selves and see them for what they are.

A deficit attitude to life

It very much ties in with what the messenger said. You can make a conscious decision to step away from a deficit attitude to the spiritual path. Now, the messenger did not even mention this in his talk because he has not seen it. He has not had this issue in this lifetime. He did not grow up in this kind of culture. But there are some of you that have grown up in this culture of wanting you to feel guilty, feeling ashamed, feeling you are sinners, that you are not worthy and all of these programmings of the fallen beings that are aimed at putting you down so that you have a deficit attitude to life. You think you have to compensate for something.

Some of you, when you first found the spiritual path, you thought that by giving, for example, decrees or other spiritual techniques, you could compensate for this deficit you felt in yourself. You were a sinner, you had done something bad, you were not worthy, whatever it may be for you individually. You were seeking to compensate for it. Do you see my beloved, this is another programming of the fallen beings? They pull you into one of their big schemes, whether it is a war or the Holocaust, or the

Inquisition or the crusades or whatever. They fool you into thinking that in order to accomplish a worthy end, you have to do what you actually know is wrong, you have to kill other human beings.

Almost all of you have in past lives been pulled into participating in some kind of war, some kind of other fight that resulted in you killing another human being or even several. It is almost impossible to have been embodied for a long time on this planet without being pulled into these schemes. Even if you did not do it directly, you were surely supporting it in some way. So many of you carry this with you as a subconscious memory because after you did kill somebody, you had that moment of realization that regardless of all the nonsense of how this was necessary for the greater good, you knew inside that it was not right to kill another human being. You experienced this. So, in order to deal with this, you created this self. In many cases, it is this self that is not based on any God reality, it is based on the fallen beings where they first trapped you into doing something that you know is wrong. Then, they offer you a way out by saying you can compensate for this by giving so many Hail Mary's, lighting candles, giving hours of decrees, doing good deeds, doing penance and all of this stuff.

You have carried with you for many lifetimes this idea that you have done something wrong, you have done something bad and you need to get out of it by compensating. So you have both the self that condemns you for having done something bad and another self that always wants to compensate. As a result, you end up *over*compensating. But my beloved, what I am telling you is this: The idea that you need to compensate for anything is created by the fallen beings, it does not come from God and the ascended masters.

What did the messenger say? "You can change your choices at any time. But you can only do it by overcoming the selves that made you make those choices." Once you overcome those selves, there is no power of God that wants to hold you back from growing, from being free. Therefore, you need to come to the point where you see these selves. You see the self that makes you feel guilty, you see the self that makes you feel that you could do something evil, that you could *be* evil. You see the selves that want you to compensate and you dismiss them. You let them go, you say: "Enough with this, I have played this game for so long, I do not want to do it anymore. I have just had enough."

The messenger said: "There is nothing I *have* to do on this earth." Yes! That was to release him from the idea he had before he came. So many people have, after they came here and encountered the fallen beings and were pulled into the schemes of the fallen beings, they have come to the belief that they need to compensate for something on earth. I say to you: "There is nothing you have to compensate for on earth."

No need to compensate

Why did you make a mistake in a past life? Why did you potentially kill somebody or do something else you might label as wrong or evil? Because you were doing through a separate self. So now you see that you have done something evil, now you are creating another separate self and you are saying: "Oh, I can overcome the first evil by doing through another separate self." This will never happen. *Do you hear me?* [Audience responds: "Yes."] It will never, *ever* work! Why? Because God loves you unconditionally, has given you free will and has no desire to use your past choices against you, or to hold you back from growing and coming back to that sense of Oneness with your Creator. God has no desire to limit his own creation. Why would he? You are out of God's own Being and consciousness. Why would God want to limit itself? You do not need to compensate for anything for God's sake or for my sake. There is no mechanism, regardless of what teachings you may hear about sin or karma, there is no mechanism created by God or any higher spiritual authority that requires you to compensate for what you did.

You made a choice. Why? Because you saw life through a separate self that gave you a limited view of life and your options. You saw only a limited number of options, you chose one of those options, they created certain consequences, but what are the consequences? What have we said about karma now several times? You take an action. You are sending an energy impulse into the four levels of the material universe. That energy impulse cycles through those four levels and at some point in the future it descends again through your identity body, your mental body, your emotional body and then into the physical. When it descends into the physical, it may precipitate a certain event. If you killed somebody in a past life, you may be killed in order to experience what it is like. When the impulse starts descending, it can only descend if there is something in your identity body that reinforces it and sends it to the mental body. Only if there is something in the mental body that reinforces it, will it be sent on to the emotional body. And only if there is something in the emotional body, will it be sent on to the physical.

This is because when you have made a choice, you are given a grace period, a delayed return of your karma so to speak, so that you have the opportunity to change your consciousness. When the impulse comes back, it does not descend further than the identity body. Or maybe you have not cleared your identity body and it will descend into the mental. Maybe you have not cleared your mental and identity body and it will descend into the emotional. If you have cleared your emotional body, it will not descend into the physical. Of course it is difficult to clear the emotional without clearing the mental and identity but nevertheless my point is this: If you have cleared part of that consciousness that caused you to make the original choice or the original karma, your karma does not have to become physical. The only point in it becoming physical is to teach you something that you have not learned in the three higher bodies. Therefore, you need to see it outpictured in the physical where you cannot ignore it. Many times it is because people have not been willing to look at themselves. *That* is the only reason things become physical for them because then they cannot really ignore that something has happened.

The real way to balance karma

So here you are, you have somehow accepted a limited self in direct reaction to the fallen beings. You do something that creates an energy impulse. Then, you feel it was wrong what you did. Now, you create another self. You have to compensate for this and what are you doing by creating this compensation self? You are thinking, as many religious people are thinking, as many spiritual people are thinking: "I don't need to look at myself and my psychology. I just do this outer thing that compensates for what I did wrong and then I will be free of my karma." Do you see how many people (how many spiritual people who acknowledge karma or even sin), they think that: "If I just do these outer things to compensate, I won't have a physical return, a punishment by God or a return of my karma. I can avoid it by doing these outer things."

How can you avoid what is in your three higher bodies? You cannot because that is the Law of Free Will. What you send out, *will* come back to you. When it comes back to you, it will either be magnified if the same thing is still in your three higher bodies, or it will be dissolved if you have resolved it in your three higher bodies. That is the law of karma and therefore, no amount of compensation will prevent the physical return. Only resolution of the beliefs and the selves will prevent the physical return.

There is no human nature

Human nature is not evil. But what is human nature? There is no such thing as human nature. It is a figment of the fallen imagination. Why? Because you were all created as individual beings with free will. Therefore, the nature that you have as an individual in this lifetime was not created by God, was not defined by some natural law, it is not the result of your genetic make-up. It is the result of choices you have made in many past lifetimes. These are the individual choices. You each have a personal nature but there is no such thing as *human* nature. Well of course, you can look at certain groups of people, you can talk about a mass consciousness and you can say that *that* nature is shared by a large number of people. It still is not *human* nature in the sense that human beings are inherently evil or have the potential to commit evil.

There is no predefined elite

What does this lead on to? It leads on to the realization that if there is no predefined human nature, there cannot be a predefined elite that is above other human beings. What is the essence of elitism? It is that there are certain people who are by nature, whether it is as a result of God's creation or a natural phenomenon, but by nature they are superior to other human beings. Therefore, they are the elite and they should be allowed to rule because they know best. What am I telling you? This is all nonsense, a complete lie, complete fantasy. All beings were created with a point-like sense of identity. There are no beings that were created inferior or superior. It is a meaningless concept, but it goes to the original self-aware beings that were created, whether it was in this sphere or in a previous sphere.

The fallen beings, even if they were created in the fourth sphere, were not created superior to you. You may say, but was not the fourth sphere lighter, of a higher vibration? Well yes, but why did the fallen beings fall?

Because they could not follow the ascension of their sphere. So they were not created superior to you. They may appear to have a certain superiority for the simple reason that they have been in embodiment for so long that they have learned to manipulate other people to a degree that those who are created in this sphere simply cannot do. If you define that as being superior, then of course you can say they are superior. That is a definition *you* have created, that the fallen beings have created. It is not a definition that comes from God. The ability to manipulate others is not a God quality here. There is no God flame of manipulation.

No natural inequality

You realize here that elitism is based on an essential lie. It says in the Declaration of Independence: "All men are created equal." That is true but not if you look at this lifetime. They were *created* equal, not alike but of equal value, in the sense that all have infinite value or no value, because value is a meaningless concept when it comes to self-aware beings. This is again a product of the duality consciousness. So all are created equal originally, but all have had many lifetimes to make choices and to build a certain outer personality. That outer personality is comprised of a number of selves. What makes one person have a certain ability, such as being a leader of business? Why is it that one person is the CEO and many other people are the workers? Well, it is not because the CEO was created by nature or by God to be superior but because that person, that lifestream, has had more lifetimes to build this outer personality that allows it to manipulate others.

What am I saying here? There is no elite that is superior in any positive quality except their ability to manipulate. Now, of course many people will immediately object to this and say: "But surely there are people, such as the great scientists, or the great humanitarians and writers, who have abilities that are beyond the normal population and they are not manipulating people. They are just expressing their abilities and coming up with new ideas." Well yes, but the question is: Do these people see themselves as superior to others, because if they do, they will see themselves as part of the elite. If they see themselves as part of the elite, they *are* manipulating other people. The very idea, the very concept, that there is an elite that is superior to the general population, that very concept is manipulative by nature because it was created to be manipulative. It was created to establish the position of the elite by making all of those who are not in the elite accept the existence of the elite, the necessity of an elite, accept their own inferiority and accept that they need to have an elite, or that they can do nothing about the elite. The very concept of elitism is manipulative, is one big manipulation. It cannot be any other way because God did not create an elite.

Nothing is predefined

These are very important concepts. I do not expect that the general public will accept what I have said here but you who are the spiritual students can come to accept them. The reason we are starting out by giving you this teaching, is that if you do not accept this, you cannot actually make use of the rest of this conference, the teachings we will give here, the invocations that will be created and the book that will come out. You cannot make use of this if you are not clear in your own mind that there is no elite that was created by God or by nature. Everything is a result of choices. The attainment, the abilities that people have or do not have is a result of choices they have made over many lifetimes, not anything that was predefined. You may say that if a person is born in a highly abusive home or in a very poor home in some third world country, then those situations, those conditions were given afore-hand in this lifetime but they are still the result of choices made over many past lifetimes. There is still the potential that the person could become conscious of this and desire to raise itself above it.

What have you all done by finding the spiritual path? You have raised yourself above the track that your life was set on by your outer conditions and your upbringing. Look back at your lives and see that if you had done what your parents and your siblings have done, your life would have been locked on a track from childhood. You would not be anywhere near where you are today. You have proven that people can raise themselves above their outer circumstances. Some of you have had very difficult circumstances in childhood and you have raised yourself above them, or at least you are in the process of doing so. You have already proven that you can get beyond it.

There is no benevolent elite

Therefore, you can also get beyond this programming of the elitist mindset, the belief in a certain elite and of course, my beloved, of course this revolves around your own path as well. There is an aspect of this that requires you to look at the fact that many spiritual organizations and teachings have an elitist element because they set their members apart from the public. You are the few chosen individuals who have accepted this sophisticated teaching and this sophisticated guru and therefore, surely you are above the general population. Surely you belong to a spiritual elite and therefore is it not possible that there could be a benevolent elite, an elite that is doing good, that is helping to raise the consciousness of humankind, raise planet earth out of all of the atrocities, raise it into the Golden Age or the fifth dimension or whatever you have?

In other words, is there such a thing as a positive or benevolent elite? My beloved, there is not. All of the spiritual and religious people, or all of the materialists or the communists or whatever you have, all of the people who believe that they belong to a benevolent elite, they are all believing a lie. Why? Because what does it truly mean to raise your consciousness? It means to raise your consciousness so you can see beyond the dualistic illusions. You attain the Christ consciousness. What do you see when you attain the Christ consciousness? You see beyond outer appearances and you see that despite the fact that people appear to be very, very different, possibly even at different levels of consciousness, they all came from the same source. You see Oneness behind diversity, you see union behind division. *That* is the Christ consciousness.

There are many, many people (I know this very well), even in ascended master teachings who think that when you attain Christ consciousness, you become part of the elite but you do not see yourself as an elite if you attain the Christ consciousness. Did Gautama Buddha consider himself superior to other people? Did he think that he was the leader of an elite group? I can assure you he did not, despite what millions of Buddhists believe.

Did Jesus see himself as being superior to other people? Did he think that he was creating an elitist organization that was a benevolent elite that was better than everybody else? No, he did not. If he did, why would he have said: "He who would be greatest among you, let him be the servant of all." This is a completely anti-elitist statement. It is also completely realistic. When you attain Christ consciousness, you do not see yourself as better or superior to others because you see the underlying oneness of all. Therefore, you seek to raise the All because you know that this is how you raise yourself.

Raising the All is anti-elitist

There is a point on the spiritual path where you are seeking to raise yourself as an individual because you have to raise yourself above the pull of the mass consciousness. If you think that you are, for the rest of your path, going to raise yourself as an individual and become more and more superior, then you are on the left-handed path. This is what can happen even up to the 96th level. Some people at the 96th level feel they have done so much work, they have served so hard, that surely they must have attainment now above and beyond others and they do not want to let go of that feeling of superiority. So they keep trying to build onto it but they never go beyond the 96th level and they very quickly go below it, even if they do not see it. The only way to go above the 96th level is to make that shift and start striving to be the servant of all, striving to overcome any sense of separation. Only in separation can there be superiority and inferiority, only in separation can there be value judgments.

So this might be (if you want something to go to sleep on), the thought to go to sleep on. He who would be greatest among you, let him be the servant of all. She who would be greatest among you, let her be the servant of all. Truly, that is how we all ascended, serving the All with no concern for raising ourselves as individuals. You do not become an ascended master by raising yourself as an individual. Even though from a certain viewpoint, you *are* raising yourself as an individual because you ascend as an individual and you raise your consciousness to the 144th level. You are not seeing that by doing this you are becoming superior to others. Superiority and inferiority, they fade away and you are focused on serving the All. This is also, as the messenger was seeking to explain, an incredible freedom when you are not concerned about maintaining the image of superiority.

Consider how many spiritual movements are completely enveloped in this game of seeking to maintain an image of superiority and how that game prevents them from being the servants of all. If you want to be superior, you cannot be the servant of all. It is impossible. It is not impossible to make that shift and become focused on serving the All. Not that you make it instantly, but that you make it consciously and thereby you start noticing in yourself when there is a reactionary pattern, when there is a self that seeks to suddenly pull you back into feeling superior. Then, you can let it go, you can just let it go.

You can actually (as the messenger was also explaining) come to that point where now you accept that even though you are not perfect, you do not have to feel bad about it because you do not have to be perfect! If you do not have to be superior, my beloved, what goes when you drop the desire to be superior? What goes is the idea that you should be perfect. When you no longer think that you have to be perfect, you can accept yourself for who you are. Therefore, your path is not in a deficit. You are not seeking to compensate for inferiority by putting on an outer facade, an image of being such a spiritual person. You can allow yourself to accept yourself for who you are right now. You can allow yourself to accept that I accept you for who you are right now.

My acceptance of you is not based on the outer selves that you still have left. It is based on who you are and I am fully capable of accepting you for who you are right now because you are who you are right now regardless of the outer selves that you have. You may see yourself as being these outer selves, or rather, you see yourself through the filter of the outer selves, but I am not inside your outer selves. I see you for who you are and I accept you for who you are. You can make that switch—it is not impossible. It may require you to wrestle with some selves and dismiss them but you can make that switch and accept yourself as I accept you.

That my beloved, I truly desire for all of you because it is such a liberation that you can scarcely believe it. It is such a freedom and when you have that freedom, how could you not want that for others, and *that* is the basis for becoming the servant of all. You have become free of these selves. You have become free of the superiority and inferiority selves. Therefore, you want the same thing for everybody else, and that is what you are focused on and that is what you are working on.

With this, my beloved, you realize that just as the messenger said, we all have so much to say and so much to share with you that it is hard for us sometimes to restrain ourselves. I will choose to now let you go to your rest and hopefully I have given you something to sleep on.

3 | INVOKING FREEDOM FROM THE LIE OF SUPERIORITY (PART 1)

In the name of the I AM THAT I AM, Jesus Christ, I use the authority that I have as a being in embodiment on earth to call upon Mother Mary to reinforce my calls and use my chakras to project the statements in this invocation into the collective consciousness and awaken people to the need to overcome all sense that some people are superior to others. Awaken people to the reality that we are spiritual beings and that we can co-create a new future by working with the ascended masters. I especially call for …

[Make your own calls here.]

Part 1

1. Mother Mary, shatter the energetic matrix that prevents people from seeing that elitism is the essential challenge facing earth at this time.

> O blessed Mary, Mother mine,
> there is no greater love than thine,

as we are one in heart and mind,
my place in hierarchy I find.

**O Mother Mary, generate,
the song that does accelerate,
the earth into a higher state,
all matter does now scintillate.**

2. Mother Mary, shatter the energetic matrix that prevents people from seeing that elitism springs from a specific group of narcissistic beings who have the mindset of seeing themselves as superior to any other beings on earth.

I came to earth from heaven sent,
as I am in embodiment,
I use Divine authority,
commanding you to set earth free.

**O Mother Mary, generate,
the song that does accelerate,
the earth into a higher state,
all matter does now scintillate.**

3. Mother Mary, shatter the energetic matrix that prevents people from seeing that we cannot understand elitism if we are not aware that there is a certain group of narcissistic beings who have this quintessential elitist attitude.

I call now in God's sacred name,
for you to use your Mother Flame,
to burn all fear-based energy,
restoring sacred harmony.

**O Mother Mary, generate,
the song that does accelerate,
the earth into a higher state,
all matter does now scintillate.**

4. Mother Mary, shatter the energetic matrix that prevents people from seeing that it is necessary to look at human behavior and see that there is a certain type of behavior that is not human. Not everything human beings do is human or human nature.

> Your sacred name I hereby praise,
> collective consciousness you raise,
> no more of fear and doubt and shame,
> consume it with your Mother Flame.

> **O Mother Mary, generate,**
> **the song that does accelerate,**
> **the earth into a higher state,**
> **all matter does now scintillate.**

5. Mother Mary, shatter the energetic matrix that prevents people from seeing that certain writers, philosophers, psychologists, scientists, even religious people have taken atrocities, such as the Holocaust, and they have said: "Oh, this is just human nature."

> All darkness from the earth you purge,
> your light moves as a mighty surge,
> no force of darkness can now stop,
> the spiral that goes only up.

> **O Mother Mary, generate,**
> **the song that does accelerate,**
> **the earth into a higher state,**
> **all matter does now scintillate.**

6. Mother Mary, shatter the energetic matrix that prevents people from seeing that for a long time, ideas have been spread that say any human being has the potential to do these evil acts, these atrocious acts.

> All elemental life you bless,
> removing from them man-made stress,
> the nature spirits are now free,
> outpicturing Divine decree.

> **O Mother Mary, generate,**
> **the song that does accelerate,**
> **the earth into a higher state,**
> **all matter does now scintillate.**

7. Mother Mary, shatter the energetic matrix that prevents people from seeing that this is a complete and utter lie, created by narcissistic beings specifically to camouflage themselves.

> I raise my voice and take my stand,
> a stop to war I do command,
> no more shall warring scar the earth,
> a golden age is given birth.

> **O Mother Mary, generate,**
> **the song that does accelerate,**
> **the earth into a higher state,**
> **all matter does now scintillate.**

8. Mother Mary, shatter the energetic matrix that prevents people from seeing that the primary modus operandi of these narcissistic beings is that they do not want to be identified for what and who they are. They do not want human beings to see them as a power elite.

> As Mother Earth is free at last,
> disasters belong to the past,
> your Mother Light is so intense,
> that matter is now far less dense.

> **O Mother Mary, generate,**
> **the song that does accelerate,**
> **the earth into a higher state,**
> **all matter does now scintillate.**

9. Mother Mary, shatter the energetic matrix that prevents people from seeing that the narcissistic beings have tried to create the myth that "it's just human nature to do evil," that any human being could potentially perform such acts.

In Mother Light the earth is pure,
the upward spiral will endure,
prosperity is now the norm,
God's vision manifest as form.

**O Mother Mary, generate,
the song that does accelerate,
the earth into a higher state,
all matter does now scintillate.**

Part 2

1. Mother Mary, shatter the energetic matrix that prevents people from seeing that nobody was created by God as an evil being. God did not create human nature so that human beings have a propensity for evil.

O blessed Mary, Mother mine,
there is no greater love than thine,
as we are one in heart and mind,
my place in hierarchy I find.

**O Mother Mary, generate,
the song that does accelerate,
the earth into a higher state,
all matter does now scintillate.**

2. Mother Mary, shatter the energetic matrix that prevents people from seeing that God gave self-aware beings free will, and free will implies that we can choose to commit any act that we can imagine.

I came to earth from heaven sent,
as I am in embodiment,
I use Divine authority,
commanding you to set earth free.

**O Mother Mary, generate,
the song that does accelerate,**

the earth into a higher state,
all matter does now scintillate.

3. Mother Mary, shatter the energetic matrix that prevents people from seeing that we can also choose to label these acts as good or evil. God has not labelled any act as good or evil. The concept of good and evil did not come from God.

I call now in God's sacred name,
for you to use your Mother Flame,
to burn all fear-based energy,
restoring sacred harmony.

O Mother Mary, generate,
the song that does accelerate,
the earth into a higher state,
all matter does now scintillate.

4. Mother Mary, shatter the energetic matrix that prevents people from seeing that God gave us free will. God looks at anything we do in a completely neutral manner. God and the ascended masters do not judge in terms of good and evil.

Your sacred name I hereby praise,
collective consciousness you raise,
no more of fear and doubt and shame,
consume it with your Mother Flame.

O Mother Mary, generate,
the song that does accelerate,
the earth into a higher state,
all matter does now scintillate.

5. Mother Mary, shatter the energetic matrix that prevents people from seeing that the narcissistic beings created the concept of good and evil. They did this in order to manipulate human beings, by defining certain things as good and other things as evil.

All darkness from the earth you purge,
your light moves as a mighty surge,
no force of darkness can now stop,
the spiral that goes only up.

O Mother Mary, generate,
the song that does accelerate,
the earth into a higher state,
all matter does now scintillate.

6. Mother Mary, shatter the energetic matrix that prevents people from seeing that once you define for a certain culture or society what is seen as good and evil, you have instantly set yourself up as a power elite for that society.

All elemental life you bless,
removing from them man-made stress,
the nature spirits are now free,
outpicturing Divine decree.

O Mother Mary, generate,
the song that does accelerate,
the earth into a higher state,
all matter does now scintillate.

7. Mother Mary, shatter the energetic matrix that prevents people from seeing that the power elite is defining what an entire society, an entire civilization, defines as good and evil. Thereby, the elite can manipulate people into doing what is defined as good, seeking to avoid or destroy what is defined as evil.

I raise my voice and take my stand,
a stop to war I do command,
no more shall warring scar the earth,
a golden age is given birth.

O Mother Mary, generate,
the song that does accelerate,

the earth into a higher state,
all matter does now scintillate.

8. Mother Mary, shatter the energetic matrix that prevents people from seeing that if another group of people are doing what the power elite defines as evil, people start thinking it is justified to kill that other group of people.

As Mother Earth is free at last,
disasters belong to the past,
your Mother Light is so intense,
that matter is now far less dense.

O Mother Mary, generate,
the song that does accelerate,
the earth into a higher state,
all matter does now scintillate.

9. Mother Mary, shatter the energetic matrix that prevents people from seeing how the power elite has manipulated people into thinking that even though killing is defined as "evil," in order to avoid this bigger evil, it is necessary to do this smaller evil.

In Mother Light the earth is pure,
the upward spiral will endure,
prosperity is now the norm,
God's vision manifest as form.

O Mother Mary, generate,
the song that does accelerate,
the earth into a higher state,
all matter does now scintillate.

Part 3

1. Mother Mary, shatter the energetic matrix that prevents people from seeing that power elites can manipulate societies into going to war with

each other and committing horrendous atrocities, while people are thinking that they are doing something "good."

> O blessed Mary, Mother mine,
> there is no greater love than thine,
> as we are one in heart and mind,
> my place in hierarchy I find.

> **O Mother Mary, generate,**
> **the song that does accelerate,**
> **the earth into a higher state,**
> **all matter does now scintillate.**

2. Mother Mary, shatter the energetic matrix that prevents people from seeing that "human nature" is a meaningless concept because human nature implies that we are created with a certain nature. We are endowed with this, either by God or by nature and there is nothing we can do about it.

> I came to earth from heaven sent,
> as I am in embodiment,
> I use Divine authority,
> commanding you to set earth free.

> **O Mother Mary, generate,**
> **the song that does accelerate,**
> **the earth into a higher state,**
> **all matter does now scintillate.**

3. Mother Mary, shatter the energetic matrix that prevents people from seeing that the power elite wants human beings to think that we are either inherently bad, we are sinners by nature, or we have the potential to do evil, the potential that we see in the world.

> I call now in God's sacred name,
> for you to use your Mother Flame,
> to burn all fear-based energy,
> restoring sacred harmony.

O Mother Mary, generate,
the song that does accelerate,
the earth into a higher state,
all matter does now scintillate.

4. Mother Mary, shatter the energetic matrix that prevents people from seeing that we do not have a little Hitler inside of us. Hitler had a "little Hitler" inside of him and it became big and did what it did. Only the narcissistic beings in the power elite have a Hitler, Stalin or Mao inside of them. Human beings who are not narcissists do not.

Your sacred name I hereby praise,
collective consciousness you raise,
no more of fear and doubt and shame,
consume it with your Mother Flame.

O Mother Mary, generate,
the song that does accelerate,
the earth into a higher state,
all matter does now scintillate.

5. Mother Mary, shatter the energetic matrix that prevents people from seeing that human beings can be manipulated into doing evil acts, but they did not decide to build Auschwitz.

All darkness from the earth you purge,
your light moves as a mighty surge,
no force of darkness can now stop,
the spiral that goes only up.

O Mother Mary, generate,
the song that does accelerate,
the earth into a higher state,
all matter does now scintillate.

6. Mother Mary, shatter the energetic matrix that prevents people from seeing that it was by the initiative of the narcissistic beings that people were manipulated into doing evil. It is the narcissistic beings who are the originators of evil.

All elemental life you bless,
removing from them man-made stress,
the nature spirits are now free,
outpicturing Divine decree.

**O Mother Mary, generate,
the song that does accelerate,
the earth into a higher state,
all matter does now scintillate.**

7. Mother Mary, shatter the energetic matrix that prevents people from seeing that there is this very old programming of making all people on earth feel guilty for the actions of the narcissistic beings and feel that we could have potentially done something like this.

I raise my voice and take my stand,
a stop to war I do command,
no more shall warring scar the earth,
a golden age is given birth.

**O Mother Mary, generate,
the song that does accelerate,
the earth into a higher state,
all matter does now scintillate.**

8. Mother Mary, shatter the energetic matrix that prevents people from seeing that the narcissistic beings have attempted to make us feel guilty and partly responsible for the evils that they initiated.

As Mother Earth is free at last,
disasters belong to the past,
your Mother Light is so intense,
that matter is now far less dense.

**O Mother Mary, generate,
the song that does accelerate,
the earth into a higher state,
all matter does now scintillate.**

9. Mother Mary, shatter the energetic matrix that prevents people from seeing that we have come to accept some sense of responsibility for these evils initiated by the narcissistic beings. Help people consciously let go of that decision and stop taking responsibility for what is not our responsibility.

> In Mother Light the earth is pure,
> the upward spiral will endure,
> prosperity is now the norm,
> God's vision manifest as form.

> **O Mother Mary, generate,**
> **the song that does accelerate,**
> **the earth into a higher state,**
> **all matter does now scintillate.**

Part 4

1. Mother Mary, shatter the energetic matrix that prevents people from seeing that the evils perpetrated by the narcissistic beings on this planet are not our personal responsibility. They never have been, they never will be.

> O blessed Mary, Mother mine,
> there is no greater love than thine,
> as we are one in heart and mind,
> my place in hierarchy I find.

> **O Mother Mary, generate,**
> **the song that does accelerate,**
> **the earth into a higher state,**
> **all matter does now scintillate.**

2. Mother Mary, shatter the energetic matrix that prevents people from seeing that we will not help raise the earth into the Golden Age by accepting responsibility for what is not our responsibility.

> I came to earth from heaven sent,
> as I am in embodiment,

I use Divine authority,
commanding you to set earth free.

O Mother Mary, generate,
the song that does accelerate,
the earth into a higher state,
all matter does now scintillate.

3. Mother Mary, shatter the energetic matrix that prevents people from making a conscious decision to step away from a deficit attitude to life and the spiritual path.

I call now in God's sacred name,
for you to use your Mother Flame,
to burn all fear-based energy,
restoring sacred harmony.

O Mother Mary, generate,
the song that does accelerate,
the earth into a higher state,
all matter does now scintillate.

4. Mother Mary, shatter the energetic matrix that prevents people from seeing that we grew up in a culture of wanting us to feel guilty, feeling ashamed, feeling we are sinners, that we are not worthy. These are the programmings of the narcissistic beings that are aimed at putting us down so that we have a deficit attitude to life. We think we have to compensate for something.

Your sacred name I hereby praise,
collective consciousness you raise,
no more of fear and doubt and shame,
consume it with your Mother Flame.

O Mother Mary, generate,
the song that does accelerate,
the earth into a higher state,
all matter does now scintillate.

5. Mother Mary, shatter the energetic matrix that prevents people from seeing that the narcissistic beings pull us into one of their schemes, whether it is a war, the Holocaust, the Inquisition or the crusades, by fooling us into thinking that in order to accomplish a worthy end, we have to do what we actually know is wrong, we have to kill other human beings.

> All darkness from the earth you purge,
> your light moves as a mighty surge,
> no force of darkness can now stop,
> the spiral that goes only up.

> **O Mother Mary, generate,**
> **the song that does accelerate,**
> **the earth into a higher state,**
> **all matter does now scintillate.**

6. Mother Mary, shatter the energetic matrix that prevents people from seeing that many of us carry this with us as a subconscious memory because after we did kill somebody, we had a moment of realization that regardless of all the nonsense of how this was necessary for the greater good, we knew inside that it was not right to kill another human being.

> All elemental life you bless,
> removing from them man-made stress,
> the nature spirits are now free,
> outpicturing Divine decree.

> **O Mother Mary, generate,**
> **the song that does accelerate,**
> **the earth into a higher state,**
> **all matter does now scintillate.**

7. Mother Mary, shatter the energetic matrix that prevents people from seeing that the narcissistic beings first trap us into doing something that we know is wrong. Then, they offer us a way out by saying we can compensate for this by doing specific things.

> I raise my voice and take my stand,
> a stop to war I do command,

no more shall warring scar the earth,
a golden age is given birth.

O Mother Mary, generate,
the song that does accelerate,
the earth into a higher state,
all matter does now scintillate.

8. Mother Mary, shatter the energetic matrix that prevents people from seeing that we have carried for many lifetimes this idea that we have done something wrong, and we need to get out of it by compensating.

As Mother Earth is free at last,
disasters belong to the past,
your Mother Light is so intense,
that matter is now far less dense.

O Mother Mary, generate,
the song that does accelerate,
the earth into a higher state,
all matter does now scintillate.

9. Mother Mary, shatter the energetic matrix that prevents people from seeing that we condemn ourselves for having done something bad, we want to compensate, so we end up overcompensating.

In Mother Light the earth is pure,
the upward spiral will endure,
prosperity is now the norm,
God's vision manifest as form.

O Mother Mary, generate,
the song that does accelerate,
the earth into a higher state,
all matter does now scintillate.

Sealing

In the name of the I AM THAT I AM, I accept that Archangel Michael, Astrea and Shiva form an impenetrable shield around myself and all constructive people, sealing us from all fear-based energies in all four octaves. I accept that the Light of God is consuming and transforming all fear-based energies that make up the dark forces working against ending the era of elitism on earth!

4 | INVOKING FREEDOM FROM THE LIE OF SUPERIORITY (PART 2)

In the name of the I AM THAT I AM, Jesus Christ, I use the authority that I have as a being in embodiment on earth to call upon Mother Mary to reinforce my calls and use my chakras to project the statements in this invocation into the collective consciousness and awaken people to the need to overcome all sense that some people are superior to others. Awaken people to the reality that we are spiritual beings and that we can co-create a new future by working with the ascended masters. I especially call for …

[Make your own calls here.]

Part 1

1. Mother Mary, shatter the energetic matrix that prevents people from seeing that the idea that we need to compensate for anything is created by the narcissistic beings, it does not come from God and the ascended masters.

O blessed Mary, Mother mine,
there is no greater love than thine,
as we are one in heart and mind,
my place in hierarchy I find.

O Mother Mary, generate,
the song that does accelerate,
the earth into a higher state,
all matter does now scintillate.

2. Mother Mary, shatter the energetic matrix that prevents people from seeing that we can change our choices at any time, but we can only do it by overcoming the consciousness or selves that made us make those choices.

I came to earth from heaven sent,
as I am in embodiment,
I use Divine authority,
commanding you to set earth free.

O Mother Mary, generate,
the song that does accelerate,
the earth into a higher state,
all matter does now scintillate.

3. Mother Mary, shatter the energetic matrix that prevents people from seeing that once we overcome the selves, there is no power of God that wants to hold us back from growing.

I call now in God's sacred name,
for you to use your Mother Flame,
to burn all fear-based energy,
restoring sacred harmony.

O Mother Mary, generate,
the song that does accelerate,
the earth into a higher state,
all matter does now scintillate.

4. Mother Mary, shatter the energetic matrix that prevents people from seeing that God loves us unconditionally, has given us free will and has no desire to use our past choices against us, or to hold us back from growing and coming back to the sense of Oneness with our Creator.

Your sacred name I hereby praise,
collective consciousness you raise,
no more of fear and doubt and shame,
consume it with your Mother Flame.

O Mother Mary, generate,
the song that does accelerate,
the earth into a higher state,
all matter does now scintillate.

5. Mother Mary, shatter the energetic matrix that prevents people from seeing that God has no desire to limit his own creation. We do not need to compensate for anything for God's sake or for your sake. There is no mechanism created by God or any higher spiritual authority that requires us to compensate for what we did.

All darkness from the earth you purge,
your light moves as a mighty surge,
no force of darkness can now stop,
the spiral that goes only up.

O Mother Mary, generate,
the song that does accelerate,
the earth into a higher state,
all matter does now scintillate.

6. Mother Mary, shatter the energetic matrix that prevents people from seeing that we made choices because we saw life through a separate self that gave us a limited view of life and our options. We sent an energy impulse into the four levels of the material universe.

All elemental life you bless,
removing from them man-made stress,

the nature spirits are now free,
outpicturing Divine decree.

O Mother Mary, generate,
the song that does accelerate,
the earth into a higher state,
all matter does now scintillate.

7. Mother Mary, shatter the energetic matrix that prevents people from seeing that the energy impulse eventually descends again through the identity, mental and emotional body and then into the physical.

I raise my voice and take my stand,
a stop to war I do command,
no more shall warring scar the earth,
a golden age is given birth.

O Mother Mary, generate,
the song that does accelerate,
the earth into a higher state,
all matter does now scintillate.

8. Mother Mary, shatter the energetic matrix that prevents people from seeing that only if there is something in the identity, mental and emotional body that reinforces it, will the impulse be sent on to the physical.

As Mother Earth is free at last,
disasters belong to the past,
your Mother Light is so intense,
that matter is now far less dense.

O Mother Mary, generate,
the song that does accelerate,
the earth into a higher state,
all matter does now scintillate.

9. Mother Mary, shatter the energetic matrix that prevents people from seeing that when we have made a choice, we are given a grace period, a delayed return of our karma, so that we have the opportunity to change

our consciousness. If we do, the impulse does not descend to the physical level.

In Mother Light the earth is pure,
the upward spiral will endure,
prosperity is now the norm,
God's vision manifest as form.

O Mother Mary, generate,
the song that does accelerate,
the earth into a higher state,
all matter does now scintillate.

Part 2

1. Mother Mary, shatter the energetic matrix that prevents people from seeing that if we have cleared part of the consciousness that caused us to make the original choice or the original karma, our karma does not have to become physical.

O blessed Mary, Mother mine,
there is no greater love than thine,
as we are one in heart and mind,
my place in hierarchy I find.

O Mother Mary, generate,
the song that does accelerate,
the earth into a higher state,
all matter does now scintillate.

2. Mother Mary, shatter the energetic matrix that prevents people from seeing that the only point in karma becoming physical is to teach us something we have not learned in the three higher bodies. Therefore, we need to see it outpictured in the physical where we cannot ignore it.

I came to earth from heaven sent,
as I am in embodiment,

I use Divine authority,
commanding you to set earth free.

O Mother Mary, generate,
the song that does accelerate,
the earth into a higher state,
all matter does now scintillate.

3. Mother Mary, shatter the energetic matrix that prevents people from seeing that many religious and spiritual people are thinking: "I don't need to look at myself and my psychology. I just do this outer thing that compensates for what I did wrong and then I will be free of my karma or sin."

I call now in God's sacred name,
for you to use your Mother Flame,
to burn all fear-based energy,
restoring sacred harmony.

O Mother Mary, generate,
the song that does accelerate,
the earth into a higher state,
all matter does now scintillate.

4. Mother Mary, shatter the energetic matrix that prevents people from seeing that we cannot avoid what is in our three higher bodies. What we send out *will* come back to us. When it comes back, it will either be magnified if the same self is still in our three higher bodies, or it will be dissolved if we have resolved it in our three higher bodies.

Your sacred name I hereby praise,
collective consciousness you raise,
no more of fear and doubt and shame,
consume it with your Mother Flame.

O Mother Mary, generate,
the song that does accelerate,
the earth into a higher state,
all matter does now scintillate.

5. Mother Mary, shatter the energetic matrix that prevents people from seeing that this is the law of karma, and no amount of compensation will prevent the physical return. Only resolution of the beliefs and the selves will prevent the physical return.

All darkness from the earth you purge,
your light moves as a mighty surge,
no force of darkness can now stop,
the spiral that goes only up.

O Mother Mary, generate,
the song that does accelerate,
the earth into a higher state,
all matter does now scintillate.

6. Mother Mary, shatter the energetic matrix that prevents people from seeing that there is no such thing as human nature. It is a figment of the fallen imagination. We were all created as individual beings with free will.

All elemental life you bless,
removing from them man-made stress,
the nature spirits are now free,
outpicturing Divine decree.

O Mother Mary, generate,
the song that does accelerate,
the earth into a higher state,
all matter does now scintillate.

7. Mother Mary, shatter the energetic matrix that prevents people from seeing that the nature we have as an individual in this lifetime was not created by God, was not defined by some natural law, it is not the result of our genetic make-up. It is the result of choices we have made in many past lifetimes.

I raise my voice and take my stand,
a stop to war I do command,
no more shall warring scar the earth,
a golden age is given birth.

O Mother Mary, generate,
the song that does accelerate,
the earth into a higher state,
all matter does now scintillate.

8. Mother Mary, shatter the energetic matrix that prevents people from seeing that we each have a personal nature but there is no such thing as *human* nature. There is a mass consciousness but human beings are not inherently evil.

As Mother Earth is free at last,
disasters belong to the past,
your Mother Light is so intense,
that matter is now far less dense.

O Mother Mary, generate,
the song that does accelerate,
the earth into a higher state,
all matter does now scintillate.

9. Mother Mary, shatter the energetic matrix that prevents people from seeing that if there is no predefined human nature, there cannot be a predefined elite that is above other human beings.

In Mother Light the earth is pure,
the upward spiral will endure,
prosperity is now the norm,
God's vision manifest as form.

O Mother Mary, generate,
the song that does accelerate,
the earth into a higher state,
all matter does now scintillate.

Part 3

1. Mother Mary, shatter the energetic matrix that prevents people from seeing that the essence of elitism is that there are certain people who are by nature, whether it is as a result of God's creation or a natural phenomenon, superior to other human beings. Therefore, they are the elite and they should be allowed to rule because they know best.

> O blessed Mary, Mother mine,
> there is no greater love than thine,
> as we are one in heart and mind,
> my place in hierarchy I find.

> **O Mother Mary, generate,**
> **the song that does accelerate,**
> **the earth into a higher state,**
> **all matter does now scintillate.**

2. Mother Mary, shatter the energetic matrix that prevents people from seeing that this is a complete lie, a complete fantasy. All beings were created with a point-like sense of identity. There are no beings that were created inferior or superior. It is a meaningless concept.

> I came to earth from heaven sent,
> as I am in embodiment,
> I use Divine authority,
> commanding you to set earth free.

> **O Mother Mary, generate,**
> **the song that does accelerate,**
> **the earth into a higher state,**
> **all matter does now scintillate.**

3. Mother Mary, shatter the energetic matrix that prevents people from seeing that the narcissistic beings may appear to have a certain superiority for the simple reason that they have been in embodiment for so long that they have learned to manipulate other people.

I call now in God's sacred name,
for you to use your Mother Flame,
to burn all fear-based energy,
restoring sacred harmony.

O Mother Mary, generate,
the song that does accelerate,
the earth into a higher state,
all matter does now scintillate.

4. Mother Mary, shatter the energetic matrix that prevents people from seeing that this is not a definition that comes from God. The ability to manipulate others is not a God quality. There is no God flame of manipulation.

Your sacred name I hereby praise,
collective consciousness you raise,
no more of fear and doubt and shame,
consume it with your Mother Flame.

O Mother Mary, generate,
the song that does accelerate,
the earth into a higher state,
all matter does now scintillate.

5. Mother Mary, shatter the energetic matrix that prevents people from seeing that all humans were *created* equal, not alike but of equal value, in the sense that all have infinite value or no value, because value is a meaningless concept when it comes to self-aware beings. Value is a product of the duality consciousness.

All darkness from the earth you purge,
your light moves as a mighty surge,
no force of darkness can now stop,
the spiral that goes only up.

O Mother Mary, generate,
the song that does accelerate,
the earth into a higher state,
all matter does now scintillate.

6. Mother Mary, shatter the energetic matrix that prevents people from seeing that all are created equal originally, but all have had many lifetimes to make choices and to build a certain outer personality. That outer personality is comprised of a number of selves. What makes one person have a certain ability is that the person has had more lifetimes to build this outer personality that allows it to manipulate others.

All elemental life you bless,
removing from them man-made stress,
the nature spirits are now free,
outpicturing Divine decree.

O Mother Mary, generate,
the song that does accelerate,
the earth into a higher state,
all matter does now scintillate.

7. Mother Mary, shatter the energetic matrix that prevents people from seeing that there is no elite that is superior in any positive quality. The idea that there is an elite that is superior to the general population, is manipulative by nature because it was created to be manipulative.

I raise my voice and take my stand,
a stop to war I do command,
no more shall warring scar the earth,
a golden age is given birth.

O Mother Mary, generate,
the song that does accelerate,
the earth into a higher state,
all matter does now scintillate.

8. Mother Mary, shatter the energetic matrix that prevents people from seeing that elitism was created to establish the position of the elite by making all of those who are not in the elite accept the existence of the elite, the necessity of the elite, accept their own inferiority and accept that they need the elite.

As Mother Earth is free at last,
disasters belong to the past,
your Mother Light is so intense,
that matter is now far less dense.

**O Mother Mary, generate,
the song that does accelerate,
the earth into a higher state,
all matter does now scintillate.**

9. Mother Mary, shatter the energetic matrix that prevents people from seeing that the very concept of elitism is manipulative, is one big manipulation. It cannot be any other way because God did not create an elite.

In Mother Light the earth is pure,
the upward spiral will endure,
prosperity is now the norm,
God's vision manifest as form.

**O Mother Mary, generate,
the song that does accelerate,
the earth into a higher state,
all matter does now scintillate.**

Part 4

1. Mother Mary, shatter the energetic matrix that prevents people from seeing that the attainment and abilities that people have or do not have is a result of choices they have made over many lifetimes, not anything that was predefined.

O blessed Mary, Mother mine,
there is no greater love than thine,
as we are one in heart and mind,
my place in hierarchy I find.

O Mother Mary, generate,
the song that does accelerate,
the earth into a higher state,
all matter does now scintillate.

2. Mother Mary, shatter the energetic matrix that prevents people from seeing that when people are born in very difficult situations, those conditions were given afore-hand in this lifetime but they are still the result of choices made over many past lifetimes. There is the potential that the person could become conscious of this and raise itself above it.

I came to earth from heaven sent,
as I am in embodiment,
I use Divine authority,
commanding you to set earth free.

O Mother Mary, generate,
the song that does accelerate,
the earth into a higher state,
all matter does now scintillate.

3. Mother Mary, shatter the energetic matrix that prevents people from seeing that many spiritual organizations and teachings have an elitist element because they set their members apart from the public.

I call now in God's sacred name,
for you to use your Mother Flame,
to burn all fear-based energy,
restoring sacred harmony.

O Mother Mary, generate,
the song that does accelerate,
the earth into a higher state,
all matter does now scintillate.

4. Mother Mary, shatter the energetic matrix that prevents people from seeing that if we think we belong to a spiritual elite, we also think there could be a benevolent elite, an elite that is doing good and is helping to raise the consciousness of humankind.

Your sacred name I hereby praise,
collective consciousness you raise,
no more of fear and doubt and shame,
consume it with your Mother Flame.

O Mother Mary, generate,
the song that does accelerate,
the earth into a higher state,
all matter does now scintillate.

5. Mother Mary, shatter the energetic matrix that prevents people from seeing that there is no such thing as a positive or benevolent elite. All of the well-meaning people who believe that they belong to a benevolent elite, they are all believing a lie.

All darkness from the earth you purge,
your light moves as a mighty surge,
no force of darkness can now stop,
the spiral that goes only up.

O Mother Mary, generate,
the song that does accelerate,
the earth into a higher state,
all matter does now scintillate.

6. Mother Mary, shatter the energetic matrix that prevents people from seeing that what it truly means to raise our consciousness is to go beyond the dualistic illusions and attain the Christ consciousness.

All elemental life you bless,
removing from them man-made stress,
the nature spirits are now free,
outpicturing Divine decree.

O Mother Mary, generate,
the song that does accelerate,
the earth into a higher state,
all matter does now scintillate.

7. Mother Mary, shatter the energetic matrix that prevents people from seeing that when we attain the Christ consciousness, we see beyond outer appearances and we see that despite the fact that people appear to be different, we all came from the same source. We see Oneness behind diversity, we see union behind division. *That* is the Christ consciousness.

I raise my voice and take my stand,
a stop to war I do command,
no more shall warring scar the earth,
a golden age is given birth.

O Mother Mary, generate,
the song that does accelerate,
the earth into a higher state,
all matter does now scintillate.

8. Mother Mary, shatter the energetic matrix that prevents people from seeing that it is an illusion to think that when we attain Christ consciousness, we become part of the elite. We do not see ourselves as an elite if we attain the Christ consciousness.

As Mother Earth is free at last,
disasters belong to the past,
your Mother Light is so intense,
that matter is now far less dense.

O Mother Mary, generate,
the song that does accelerate,
the earth into a higher state,
all matter does now scintillate.

9. Mother Mary, shatter the energetic matrix that prevents people from seeing that when we attain Christ consciousness, we do not see ourselves as better or superior to others because we see the underlying oneness of all. We seek to raise the All because we know that this is how we raise ourselves.

In Mother Light the earth is pure,
the upward spiral will endure,

prosperity is now the norm,
God's vision manifest as form.

O Mother Mary, generate,
the song that does accelerate,
the earth into a higher state,
all matter does now scintillate.

Part 5

1. Mother Mary, shatter the energetic matrix that prevents people from seeing that there is a point on the spiritual path where we are seeking to raise ourselves as individuals, because we have to raise ourselves above the pull of the mass consciousness.

O blessed Mary, Mother mine,
there is no greater love than thine,
as we are one in heart and mind,
my place in hierarchy I find.

O Mother Mary, generate,
the song that does accelerate,
the earth into a higher state,
all matter does now scintillate.

2. Mother Mary, shatter the energetic matrix that prevents people from seeing that if we think we are going to continue to raise ourselves as individuals and become more and more superior, then we are on the left-handed path.

I came to earth from heaven sent,
as I am in embodiment,
I use Divine authority,
commanding you to set earth free.

O Mother Mary, generate,
the song that does accelerate,

the earth into a higher state,
all matter does now scintillate.

3. Mother Mary, shatter the energetic matrix that prevents people from seeing that the only way to go above a certain level is to make a shift and start striving to be the servant of all, striving to overcome any sense of separation. Only in separation can there be superiority and inferiority, only in separation can there be value judgments.

I call now in God's sacred name,
for you to use your Mother Flame,
to burn all fear-based energy,
restoring sacred harmony.

O Mother Mary, generate,
the song that does accelerate,
the earth into a higher state,
all matter does now scintillate.

4. Mother Mary, shatter the energetic matrix that prevents people from seeing that many spiritual movements are completely enveloped in this game of seeking to maintain an image of superiority. That game prevents them from being the servants of all.

Your sacred name I hereby praise,
collective consciousness you raise,
no more of fear and doubt and shame,
consume it with your Mother Flame.

O Mother Mary, generate,
the song that does accelerate,
the earth into a higher state,
all matter does now scintillate.

5. Mother Mary, shatter the energetic matrix that prevents people from making that shift and becoming focused on serving the All. Help people see that superiority and inferiority is a prison created by the elite, so that they can just let it all go.

All darkness from the earth you purge,
your light moves as a mighty surge,
no force of darkness can now stop,
the spiral that goes only up.

O Mother Mary, generate,
the song that does accelerate,
the earth into a higher state,
all matter does now scintillate.

6. Mother Mary, shatter the energetic matrix that prevents people from accepting that even though we are not perfect, we do not have to feel bad about it because we do not have to be perfect! If we do not have to be superior, we do not have to be perfect.

All elemental life you bless,
removing from them man-made stress,
the nature spirits are now free,
outpicturing Divine decree.

O Mother Mary, generate,
the song that does accelerate,
the earth into a higher state,
all matter does now scintillate.

7. Mother Mary, shatter the energetic matrix that prevents people from seeing that when we no longer think we have to be perfect, we can accept ourselves for who we are. Our path is not in a deficit, we are not seeking to compensate for inferiority by putting on an outer facade of being a spiritual person.

I raise my voice and take my stand,
a stop to war I do command,
no more shall warring scar the earth,
a golden age is given birth.

O Mother Mary, generate,
the song that does accelerate,

the earth into a higher state,
all matter does now scintillate.

8. Mother Mary, shatter the energetic matrix that prevents people from seeing that we can allow ourselves to accept ourselves for who we are right now. We can allow ourselves to accept that the ascended masters accept us for who we are right now.

As Mother Earth is free at last,
disasters belong to the past,
your Mother Light is so intense,
that matter is now far less dense.

O Mother Mary, generate,
the song that does accelerate,
the earth into a higher state,
all matter does now scintillate.

9. Mother Mary, shatter the energetic matrix that prevents people from seeing that the greatest freedom is to accept ourselves for who we are. When we become free of the superiority and inferiority selves, we want the same thing for everybody else, and that is when we can focus on raising the All.

In Mother Light the earth is pure,
the upward spiral will endure,
prosperity is now the norm,
God's vision manifest as form.

O Mother Mary, generate,
the song that does accelerate,
the earth into a higher state,
all matter does now scintillate.

Sealing

In the name of the I AM THAT I AM, I accept that Archangel Michael, Astrea and Shiva form an impenetrable shield around myself and all constructive people, sealing us from all fear-based energies in all four octaves. I accept that the Light of God is consuming and transforming all fear-based energies that make up the dark forces working against ending the era of elitism on earth!

5 | ELITISM IS INCOMPATIBLE WITH DEMOCRACY

I AM the Ascended Master MORE, or as I was known in the past, El Morya. What does Morya stand for? More to You All. So why not just MORE? For MORE I am, and what else could I be dedicated to than becoming MORE myself, and helping all people on earth become MORE? For as Mother Mary said – as Mother MORE said – you come to a point on the path where you connect to that basic humanity, or basic spirituality, the basic identity, the sense that we all came from the same source, and therefore you want to raise up all. You want all to experience what you have experienced, of overcoming all of these limitations that are burdening people, that are keeping them trapped in all of these patterns that they are trapped in, that constantly cause them suffering.

Let us take a look at planet earth, and let us confine ourselves to known history. You go back and you see that there was a time when there were only primitive societies: hunter-gatherers, small groups of agricultural communities here and there. But then, at a certain point, at least in some parts of the world, there emerged what we call a civilization that had a greater level of organization, and a greater level of a centralized command structure, a centralized leadership. As soon as you see the formation of such societies, you also see the formation of an elite. You may have had the beginnings of elites even in the hunter-gatherer cultures, as you can see in some native peoples where they had a leadership structure, but it was not really until you saw these more organized civilizations that you see a very clear division of the population into two classes: a ruling class, and a class that is being ruled, that is following the leaders.

Is an elite necessary?

What is the basis for this formation of an elite? Is it really necessary? Well, if you ask that question of many people in today's world, they would say: "Yes, it is necessary that there is an elite that rules the majority of the people because the majority of the people cannot rule themselves." This is what many, many people here in Washington, D.C., both those who are elected representatives and those who work in the bureaucracy, will say: "The people are not capable of ruling themselves."

Let us examine that statement. Is it true that the people cannot rule themselves? Or do people believe this because for millennia they have been conditioned to believe this? This is the question very rarely, if ever, asked by anybody who is involved with society, or who is a philosopher or writer. The reason this question is not asked is of course that most people have been programmed by this belief. They have been programmed to accept this belief, not only in this lifetime but over many, many lifetimes on this earth where they have lived in societies where there was a ruling elite. There was an elite that had power and that exercised power over the population, therefore there was a power elite. It is not difficult for people to see that there is a power elite today, and that there always was, at least from these more organized societies and forward. There was a power elite ruling the population.

The philosopher king

You go back even to the ancient Greek philosophers, such as Plato, whose ideal was the philosopher king. Well, at Plato's time, 2,500 years ago or so, it was not necessarily that he was wrong in coming up with this concept. At the time, society was so programmed to think that there had to be an elite that was ruling. The question is: If you have a society where there must be a leader, a supreme leader, would it not be better to have the kind of leader that Plato described as the philosopher king? The ideal for the philosopher king described by Plato would be that it was a person who had overcome so much of his ego that he was not an egomaniac, he was not a narcissist, but he was actually an intuitive person who had good intentions and had some intuitive attunement with the ascended masters. This was, at Plato's time, an important ideal to put out there. You can ask ourselves whether it was ever achieved, either before or after Plato, but nevertheless it was important to put out the ideal that there could be a leader who had some higher guidance.

You also saw, in the whole myth that was created around King Arthur, that there was also that ideal of the philosopher king who had pure intentions and had some guidance, whether through Merlin or through his own inner guidance. Of course, this was a myth. There was never – and let me state this unequivocally – there was *never* a physical King Arthur and a physical Camelot, regardless of what some of our students of previous dispensations like to believe. It was a mythological kingdom. This does not make it any less important because at the time when the myth or the legend of King Arthur was created, society was very different. People did not have the linear, analytical mindset that you have today. It is very difficult for you today to actually understand how people were thinking 1,500 years ago or so because they were much more into symbols. They also did not take the Bible as literally as many people do today. So, raising up this symbol of a king that had some higher purpose than the kings people saw around them was important.

Now, of course the fallen beings are always quick to take any idea and abuse it. They very quickly created the idea that you see through the feudal societies and medieval times of a king that was anointed by God, that was appointed by God, and that was approved of by God's representatives on earth, namely the Catholic church and its hierarchy. Therefore, you saw that fusion of church and state where the king gained part of his authority from the church, in return for therefore also supporting the church. You can look at these kind of societies, and you can actually ask yourself a relatively simple question, which of course most people out there are not capable of asking. The question is: "Why was it necessary to create this idea that validated the power of the king and the church?" Why was it necessary? The king had the raw force to suppress the population. Why not just create a rule based on raw force?

Power elites always use ideas

This is where you can then begin to help people see that there must be a certain element of the power elite that recognize the limitations of raw force, and therefore always seeks to come up with some kind of idea to support their existence and their power over the population. There are examples of societies that have been ruled by a power elite that based their rule exclusively on power, but they are relatively few, and in most cases they were short-lived. When you actually look back at various civilizations (and you can go back, as an example, to the ancient Egyptians), you see that they also had the idea that the king either was a god or was supported by the gods, was working with the gods, was representing the gods on earth. Thereby, you see that there was always a need to create some kind of idea (a religion, an ideology, a thought system) that makes the population accept that they need an elite. It gives legitimacy and authority to the elite.

Why is it important to recognize this? Because when you recognize that a power elite always, or at least in most cases, supports its existence and power by an idea, you can begin to critically examine the ideas that the power elites of history have used. If you begin by looking back in time, you can see that very few people today would believe that the Roman emperor was a literal god on earth, that he was God in embodiment. Or that some of the Egyptian pharaohs were God in embodiment. Or the Sumerian leaders, or the leaders of the ancient Vedic Indian societies, or other societies in East Asia where you also find this belief that some people are either gods in embodiment, or God's representatives, are anointed by God, have been given authority from God. You find this over and over and over again. When you see that you do not accept the claims made in these ancient civilizations, how difficult is it then to zoom up through history and see that even today, you look back at medieval times (even as recently as 1500s, 1600s in some areas) and you see that the divine right of kings is not something you accept today in the modern democracies.

Can you not then also take that leap and say: "What are the ideas that the power elite today is using to support its existence?" Can we not then examine those ideas and see: Do they actually make sense? Are they consistent? Or are they an expression of cognitive dissonance? Are they contradictory? Do they make any kind of sense to us, really, or is it just something we have been brought up to accept and never really question?

The divine rights of kings

Let us look at some of these ideas. You have the religious tradition, which states that God has appointed or anointed certain leaders to rule. There are royal houses in Europe today where (even though they do not advertise this too often) they have a certain belief that through their legacy, through their family, they have been chosen and anointed by God to be the kings or the queens. Even though they have no political power, they still believe that they have some legitimacy from a higher authority.

Even though Mother Mary has already said this is an illusion, let us examine the belief. If it is true that God has anointed certain leaders of society, it would mean that God has created people in distinctly different categories. In other words, God has created some people to be in the category of leaders, and most of the population are created in the category of followers. Some are created superior by God, with superior leadership abilities, and most people are not.

Now, if you take this belief and compare it to the democratic constitutions seen around the world, you will see that it is in complete contradiction to the foundational ideas of democracy. You take the American Declaration of Independence: "all men are created equal." And of course that includes women, which the writers of the Declaration might not have agreed with, but that is beside the point because most people agree with this today.

If all people are created equal by their creator, then God could not have created different classes: a ruling class and a following class. If God has not done so, then what is the validity of the claim that kings have divine right and are appointed by God? It makes no sense. There is a cognitive dissonance between the royal houses of Europe and their democratic constitutions, or at least the foundations for those constitutions. The very cornerstone of democracy, modern democracy, is precisely that all men have the same (all human beings have the same) potential: the potential to grow.

You go back to the first democracy seen in Athens, and you will see that we make a distinction between that and modern democracy because the Greek democracy was not based on the concept of equality. Women were not allowed to vote. Slaves and other types of "inferior" citizens were not allowed to vote. So it was not an equal democracy. It was not based on equality. It was not based on the recognition that you all have an essential humanity. The essential humanity is the foundation (even if that word is not used) for all modern democracies. It is also the foundation for the teachings of the Buddha, who said that all people have the potential to attain Buddhahood. It is also the foundation for the teachings of Jesus who said that the kingdom of God is within you and that you can do what he did.

You see here that when you go to the core of it, it makes no sense that God should have created two different classes of people. God could not have done so. God created all with the same potential. But as Mother Mary said, this can only really be accepted when you also accept reincarnation, because this explains why not all people are born with the same abilities in this lifetime. They have made choices in many past lifetimes, and some have attained a higher ability in a certain area than others. You see here that God did not create an elite and a big part of the population that is inferior. That means God did not create elitism. He did not create or mandate that on earth there should be elitist societies. That idea does not come from God. As Mother Mary said, it comes from the fallen beings, but the general public can come to understand that it could not have come from God.

Materialism and democracy

Now, we look at the other thought system that is dominating modern democracies: Scientific Materialism. Its idea is that nature is a process of competition and that this competition selects out those who are not as fit, and therefore only the fittest survive. Now, if you examine this idea, you must ask yourself: "How did the majority of the human population then survive?" Most of the proponents of Materialism are actually elitists. They do believe, because this is their Darwinian background, that the reason why there is a ruling elite in society is that nature simply selected them because they were more fit to rule, and they were more fit to survive. But how then did the rest of humanity survive if they are not fit?

Then, you look at animal species. Is there any animal species that has a ruling elite? I know that you have a Disney cartoon, a very subtle piece of propaganda work by the elite, called The Lion King. The king of the lions. But has it any basis in reality? Of course not. There is no hierarchy of rulers in the animal world. This is what human beings project onto it in order to sell the idea of elitism among humans. We have at previous conferences talked about evolutionary theory and the fact that what you really see, if you look at the evolution of species, is that it is not the most competitive who survive, but those who can cooperate. It is cooperation, adaptation, that ensures survival, not actually competition.

What you must say is that the whole idea of survival of the fittest has been used to create a philosophy, even something beyond a philosophy, a very widespread set of ideas that are found in many different contexts, many different sciences, philosophies and writings. Their only purpose is to support the existence of an elite by making it seem as if nature itself created a ruling elite. Therefore, if you believe in God, you must think that God created the elite. If you believe there is no God, you must think that nature created the elite. Regardless of what you believe or do not believe, you believe there must be an elite.

Materialism and elitism

Do you see that if you go back to medieval society, it is easy to see that this was a completely elitist society? Anybody who looks at it can see it. You cannot fail to see that this was a clearly elitist society with a king and a noble class ruling the population. The population was stuck and had very little ability to improve their situation. Here comes Scientific Materialism and it claims to set people free from the superstition of religion. But what was it really that suppressed the population? Was it the superstition of religion or was it the power elite that used religion to suppress the people? Materialism claims to have freed people from the superstitious ideas of religion. But instead of freeing them from the power elite, they have just created another power elite that now rules, not because they are appointed by God, but because they are appointed by nature to rule.

Is this progress? I am putting this question into the collective consciousness. Is this progress? Of course, it is not. The other question that needs to be asked is: "Is this democratic? Is it in accordance with democratic ideals?" Of course, it is not. What is then the cognitive dissonance here? What people fail to see is that in a democratic society there cannot be an elite because democracy and elitism are incompatible. There is a fundamental, you might say, conflict or contradiction between an elite and democracy. Of course, you can look at any democracy in the world today and you can see that they do have, they all have, elites. In every nation there are elites.

Elitism and democracy are incompatible

What has been building very gradually in the collective consciousness for a long time is this tension. Many, many people are ready to just snap out of the blindness they were brought up with and see that it is not logically consistent that we claim to have a democratic society, but we still allow this society to be ruled and dominated by a small elite. This is not democracy. You look at the fact that a majority of Americans believe that they belong to the underclass, the non-elite that is being ruled by an elite. They believe that they have very little influence on the political process. Most Americans can also see that wealth is being concentrated in the hands of fewer and fewer people. Some people have so much money that it is quite frankly ridiculous that an individual could accumulate that much money. How will they ever spend it on personal consumption? What good does it do you to have these numbers on your bank account?

There is the potential right now for you, when you make the shift and when you make the calls, to help bring about this shift where people wake up and see that elitism and democracy are fundamentally different. You cannot have a fully functioning democracy if you have an elite. It simply is not compatible. Therefore, the existence of elites is undemocratic by its very nature. There is no discussion about this.

The claim that people cannot rule themselves

Of course, there is discussion about it in society and the elites will come up with all kinds of subtle arguments. They are all based on the same idea: "The people cannot rule themselves. If you allow the people to rule, it will be disaster." They will rail against populism. They will rail against direct democracy and say: "If we allow the people to rule, it will be one disaster after another."

The simple response to that line of argumentation is: "How do you know? Show me an example where the people have been allowed to rule without being dominated by an elite. Show me a society where that has happened." They will say: "Well, they elected Donald Trump." But are you saying that the United States is a society not dominated by an elite? Because I do not see it that way. Others will point to Brexit and other societies. But the fact is that you do not have a society in known history that was not dominated by an elite. How do you know that the people, if they were allowed to make their own choices, would create disaster after disaster? What evidence do you have? You have none whatsoever.

Now, let us look at what evidence there is available. Look at history. Look at the atrocities and the disasters created in history. Who created them? Who precipitated the Second World War, the Holocaust, the Soviet Union, the First World War, all of the wars you saw during the Middle Ages, the crusades, the Inquisition? Who precipitated this? Was that the population who voted on it? No! It was an elite, a power elite. Behind every atrocity you see in known history, you see a power elite. Sometimes you see two power elites that were rivaling against each other, that were fighting about who should be the dominant elite. But it was in no case the people who created the wars and the atrocities. They may have participated because they were pulled into it, but they did not initiate it.

When you look at empirical evidence, historical evidence, if you are not completely blind, you must conclude that elites have created enormous amounts of atrocities and suffering. Look at some of the rulers of the Roman Empire or the medieval kings of Europe and the momentous mistakes they made because one person had the position where his word was law and any decision he made was carried out. Look what Stalin precipitated out of his paranoia. Look at Mao who was so in love with his own ideas that he thought the Cultural Revolution would bring a new society. The cost of killing dozens of millions of people was not even a concern for him because the idea was more important than the people. If you look at this honestly, you must say: "How could the people do worse than the elite? How could they possibly do worse than all the nonsense you see in history?" If you look at it just from a probability standpoint, it is highly probable that the people could not possibly do worse than the elites have done. What basis do you have for saying that the people could not rule?

The reality is, as we have said before, that the people *can* rule. When all of the people are heard, they will balance each other out and they will come up with a solution that is an expression of that basic humanity. The basic humanity is a thing that can change over time. As the collective consciousness is raised, the basic sense of humanity is raised also. At any given time, in any society, there is a certain basic humanity, and that basic humanity is very simple. People want to live a good, personal life. They want to have security in their personal lives. This means that the people will not start a war. Because anytime you start a war, you do not know what the outcome will be. You are generating a basic insecurity that most people will see as a threat, and therefore, they will not vote to go to war.

Have the people supported wars in the past? Of course, they have, but why did they do this? Because they were seduced by the power elite with the rationale that the end can justify the means and that it is necessary to go to war for whatever reasons. This was not something that the people would have initiated without the elite. Therefore, if you allow the people to rule, you can forget about wars. All wars in history have been started by elites of various kinds, often two elites that were fighting for domination. The people do not do this. They do not need domination. They want security in their daily lives.

What do they also want? They want a reasonable standard of living, not an affluent, luxurious standard of living. They want a good standard of living where they can take care of their children and put them in a good way in life. Who is it that wants this affluent lifestyle? Who is it that wants more than they need in order to give themselves and their children a good material life? Only the power elite wants this. What would the people vote for? Would they ever create an economy that was driven by greed that led to these fanciful financial instruments that caused the crash of 1929 or the crash of 2008? Would they create this economy with the ups and downs, with inflation? The people would never create this kind of economy. They would create an economy that is based on letting the people who do the work reap the financial reward so that all of the people could have a reasonable standard of living.

The poor are getting poorer

You look at the United States today. You can see that there is a growing number of people who have a very low standard of living. Now, I know you can compare it to third world countries and say they are still much better off. But when you look just at the United States, you see that there is a growing number of people (and you see the same in other modern democracies) who are called the working poor. They are working a job, they may even be working two jobs, but they have a hard time making ends meet, taking care of their children.

You see a middle class who in past ages were doing quite well, but who are actually having their lifestyle, their standard of living, eroded. Then, you see an upper class that has more money than anybody could ever need. You see a growing number of people in this upper class, but you also see that there are a few people at the top of this upper class who control the vast majority of the money. Now, if you took the money that is available in the United States' economy and distributed it more evenly, then all people in the United States could have a good, secure standard of living. I can guarantee you that if you allowed the American population to vote on this, there would be an overwhelming majority who would vote to have exactly that kind of economy, where all people had a good standard of living. They could accept that there were still a few who had above the average, but very few of them would accept a ruling class that had so much more money than they could ever need.

Would it be a detriment to the United States' economy if the people were allowed to rule: "This is the kind of economy we want?" What would happen to the economy? The elite will say, oh, it would crash. But I can tell you that the opposite would happen. You would create an economy that was free from the risk of crashing because it is not based on greed. It is not based on trying to maximize the outcome regardless of the consequences. It is based on creating a sustainable economy that is tied (where the value of money, the value of stocks) is tied to something that has real value. *That* is the kind of economy that the people would want if they were educated a little bit better and if they were allowed to vote.

What would happen if you instituted that kind of an economy? Well, as we have said before, how many luxury yachts could you possible need? If you distributed the income more evenly among the people, this would mean that all of the people who today do not have enough would suddenly have enough, and what would they do? They would buy, they would buy a bigger house, they would buy a bigger car, they would buy new refrigerator, they would buy this, they would buy that. What would that do to the economy? Raise the entire economy of the country to a much higher level than it is today.

Who could not like this? Well, of course the elite will not like it. What would be the detriment of creating that kind of a people's economy? It would only be a detriment to the elite. Well, my beloved, if a country has an economy that is entirely designed to enrich the elite and keep the people poor, can you really say that that country is a democracy? Is it functioning according to democratic principles? Whether you call it a republic or something else, is it functioning according to democratic principles, the greatest good for the greatest number of people? Of course it is not. It is functioning entirely to allow the elite to become richer and richer, to have more and more control.

Greed creates an impossible quest

Therefore, again I say, who created the crash of 1929 and the crash of 2008 and all of the many ups and downs in the economy since then? The elite created it all. The people did not have the means to create it, and they would not have created it even if they had the means because they do not have the greed. This boundless insatiable greed that you must be able to see in the upper class. Anybody who looks at this can see that they have a greed that could never be satisfied. You are creating an entire society that is based on greed that could never be satisfied. It is an impossible quest. You would never create a society where the elite felt that they had enough—enough power, enough security, enough money. They will never have enough. It is quite within the range of where the collective consciousness is at, that people could make that switch and come to see: We are allowing our entire society to function to concentrate wealth, power, money in the hands of a small elite of people who will never be satisfied anyway. It will never be enough for them.

Why are we doing this? Why are we allowing this to happen? There must be a better way. There must be more than our current status, our current society. This cannot be what America is about. You may say, it cannot be what the founding fathers envisioned, but truth be told, most of the founding fathers were elitists. If you had asked Jefferson, even Washington to some degree, they would have believed that the people were not able to rule themselves. That is not to say that they were fallen beings, but they had come to believe in the philosophy of the fallen beings because they had been conditioned over so many lifetimes to believe this.

That is the conclusion of my address: That there has been created this overlay, this consciousness. We have called it beasts in the collective consciousness that is blinding people so they cannot see that the emperor has nothing on. They simply cannot see the fallacy of elitism. They cannot see the fallacy of these justifications for elitism. You have the religious justification, the materialist justification and the pragmatic justification that the people could not rule themselves. They are all based on illusions but people cannot see it.

My beloved, by you making the calls and by many other people around the world considering these ideas, there can come that breakthrough, that shift, where suddenly they see it: "Why have we been believing this for so long? Why? And why should we continue to believe this when really the power elite has nothing on?" This is a realistic shift to happen within a relatively short period of time.

The potential for change in America

If you actually look back at history, you must ask yourself: If democracy is really the antithesis of elitism, how could democracy ever arise? How could the elite ever allow this to happen? You can look at outer factors but the real reason for this is that, as the collective consciousness is raised, people no longer believe in the ideas that used to support elitism and people come to accept new ideas. When that happens, the ideological foundation for the elite's rule crumbles, and when it crumbles, the elite must give way. They have historically and they will, they *must*, do it again. When the collective consciousness shifts, when there is an opening in the clouds and people suddenly see it, then the entire equation of society will change. It *will* change.

You may look at America, you may look at other modern democracies, but especially America, and you may see that it seems to be so far away that this could happen. It seems to be almost impossible that people would come to see this. You would have said the same thing when those fifty people signed the Declaration of Independence. It is not far-fetched that people can come to see that what we really need independence from is from the power elite, not the British king, even though he was part of the power elite. We need independence from the power elite that has been created in this country. When people come to see this, you need to recognize here that the equation is fundamentally different than it was in 1776. Regardless of what you think about American society, it is not ruled by military force. If enough people decide to stand up to the power elite, the power elite cannot send the Army or the National Guard or Special Forces to start killing the people. It cannot happen. It *will* not happen.

The same thing with the press and media, if enough people start speaking about this, the press cannot ignore it. They cannot suppress it. The same thing with the politicians. They cannot ignore it if they sense that the people are united. Not all, but a critical mass of people are united. They cannot ignore it. I can assure you, there are many, many people in the political apparatus (among elected representatives at all levels of American government and in the bureaucracy) who have, to use a euphemism, their hearts in the right place. There are many people who have some attunement to Saint Germain and his Golden Age ideas. There are many, many people who sense that there is something missing, there is something not right, in America but they cannot always put their finger on it. And many of them do not dare to speak out about it.

There is a cone of silence where people think they cannot speak out about it. But if that shift happens where the people begin to speak out and demand it, many, many people in the government apparatus will actually say: "That is exactly what I've been waiting for. Now I can come forward. Now I can do something that could not be done when the popular backing wasn't there." You can see that the tension is there, the potential is there. It just takes that little spark to ignite the fuse that will blow up the rule of the power elite, that will blow up this cone of ideas, this cloud of ignorance that is blinding the people right now. It does not take that much to shatter it so that the people will wake up and more and more people will wake up. A critical mass of people can ignite this, and then so many more people will support it and say: "This is what we need. This is what we want. We couldn't put words on it but there it is. Now we see it and we want it because this is our right."

What is your rights in America? Life, liberty and the pursuit of happiness. Is that not what I talked about, that most people want a good life for themselves? They want a right to live. They want to be free to pursue creating a better life for themselves. They want to pursue happiness as they see it, which is not anywhere near how the power elite sees it. When you allow the people those rights, because right now they do not have those rights in full measure, then it will create a country that has a sustainable economy that is not seeking to police the world and create wars here and there so that the military-industrial complex can make a bigger profit. Because that is not what the people want. They want the good life and there is nothing wrong with the people wanting the good life. It is far better to have a society that is based on the *people's* definition of the good life rather than the *power elite's* definition of the good life.

With this, I thank you for your attention, for your willingness to come together, to come together to recognize that essential humanity, which you call the essential spirituality, but nevertheless, it is the essential humanity because all people are spiritual beings. That is how they were created and that is why they were created equal by their Creator. Because you are spiritual beings, you are not defined by these outer conditions on earth that can so easily be used to create that sense of superiority and inferiority.

You are spiritual beings and therefore the outer things do not define you. That is what you know, that is what you practice in your lives. That is why you are becoming more with Master MORE and the other ascended masters who are happy to guide you and experience your growth with you, as we indeed do. We find great joy in seeing your growth, seeing you overcome those limitations, shed those snake skins of the human consciousness and realize: "I am more. I am more than this previous identity that I saw myself as. I'm even more than this primal self that has been controlling my relationship to this planet for so long. I'm even more than the self that I had when I came here as an avatar, thinking I could do good and change the people on the earth or perhaps even change the fallen beings."

You *can*, but you cannot do it by changing *them*. You can only do it by changing *yourself* and thereby giving them an example and pulling them up. Not by taking direct action to change others. That is the subtle difference that no previous ascended master dispensation has grasped. We are happy to see that so many of you are grasping this essential difference and beginning to live it.

With this, I seal you in the intensely pink love of the First Ray, for I am indeed not anywhere near this strict disciplinarian that I have been portrayed to be in previous ascended master dispensations. I love you with a love that is unconditional because I see beyond the conditions to who you really are underneath it all. My only desire is that you come to see who you really are underneath all of the outer things. So my love, my love, my love for each and every one of you, as you are right now and as you are in the process of becoming.

6 | INVOKING AN AWAKENING OF THE PEOPLE (PART 1)

In the name of the I AM THAT I AM, Jesus Christ, I use the authority that I have as a being in embodiment on earth to call upon Master MORE to reinforce my calls and use my chakras to project the statements in this invocation into the collective consciousness and awaken people to the fact that we do not need an elite to rule the population. Awaken people to the reality that we are spiritual beings and that we can co-create a new future by working with the ascended masters. I especially call for …

[Make your own calls here.]

Part 1

1. Master MORE, shatter the energetic matrix that prevents people from seeing that as soon as we had civilizations with a greater level of organization, and a greater level of a centralized leadership, we also see the formation of an elite.

Master MORE, come to the fore,
we will absorb your flame of MORE.
Master MORE, our will so strong,
our power centers cleared by song.

**Master MORE, your Sacred Heart,
from this we will no more depart,
we are forever in your flow,
of Diamond Will that you bestow.**

2. Master MORE, shatter the energetic matrix that prevents people from seeing that when there emerged more organized civilizations, we see a clear division of the population into two classes: a ruling class, and a class that is being ruled, that is following the leaders.

Master MORE, your wisdom flows,
as our attunement ever grows.
Master MORE, we have a tie,
that helps us see through Serpent's lie.

**Master MORE, your Sacred Heart,
from this we will no more depart,
we are forever in your flow,
of Diamond Will that you bestow.**

3. Master MORE, shatter the energetic matrix that prevents people from seeing that many would say it is necessary that there is an elite that rules the majority of the people because the majority of the people cannot rule themselves.

Master MORE, your love so pink,
there is no purer love, we think.
Master MORE, you set us free,
from all conditionality.

**Master MORE, your Sacred Heart,
from this we will no more depart,
we are forever in your flow,
of Diamond Will that you bestow.**

4. Master MORE, shatter the energetic matrix that prevents people from seeing that we only believe this because for millennia we have been conditioned to believe this.

> Master MORE, we will endure,
> your discipline that makes us pure.
> Master MORE, intentions true,
> as we are always one with you.

> **Master MORE, your Sacred Heart,**
> **from this we will no more depart,**
> **we are forever in your flow,**
> **of Diamond Will that you bestow.**

5. Master MORE, shatter the energetic matrix that prevents people from seeing that we have been programmed to accept this belief, not only in this lifetime but over many lifetimes, where we have lived in societies with an elite that had power, meaning a power elite.

> Master MORE, our vision raised,
> the will of God is always praised.
> Master MORE, creative will,
> raising all life higher still.

> **Master MORE, your Sacred Heart,**
> **from this we will no more depart,**
> **we are forever in your flow,**
> **of Diamond Will that you bestow.**

6. Master MORE, shatter the energetic matrix that prevents people from seeing that there is a power elite today, and that there always was, at least from these more organized societies and forward. There was a power elite ruling the population.

> Master MORE, your peace is power,
> the demons of war it will devour.
> Master MORE, we serve all life,
> our flames consuming war and strife.

**Master MORE, your Sacred Heart,
from this we will no more depart,
we are forever in your flow,
of Diamond Will that you bestow.**

7. Master MORE, shatter the energetic matrix that prevents people from seeing that Plato's ideal of a philosopher king is not suited for the higher collective consciousness we have today.

Master MORE, we are so free,
eternal bond from you we see.
Master MORE, we find rebirth,
in flow of your eternal mirth.

**Master MORE, your Sacred Heart,
from this we will no more depart,
we are forever in your flow,
of Diamond Will that you bestow.**

8. Master MORE, shatter the energetic matrix that prevents people from seeing that the fallen beings used the idea of a philosopher king to create the feudal societies with a king that was anointed by God, and that was approved of by God's representatives on earth, namely the Catholic church and its hierarchy.

Master MORE, you balance all,
the seven rays upon our call.
Master MORE, forever MORE,
we are the Spirit's open door.

**Master MORE, your Sacred Heart,
from this we will no more depart,
we are forever in your flow,
of Diamond Will that you bestow.**

9. Master MORE, shatter the energetic matrix that prevents people from seeing that this created the fusion of church and state, where the king gained part of his authority from the church, in return for supporting the church.

Master MORE, your Presence here,
filling up the inner sphere.
Life is now a sacred flow,
God Power we on all bestow.

**Master MORE, your Sacred Heart,
from this we will no more depart,
we are forever in your flow,
of Diamond Will that you bestow.**

Part 2

1. Master MORE, shatter the energetic matrix that prevents people from seeing that there is a certain element of the power elite that recognizes the limitations of raw force, and therefore always seeks to come up with some kind of idea to support their existence and their power over the population.

Master MORE, come to the fore,
we will absorb your flame of MORE.
Master MORE, our will so strong,
our power centers cleared by song.

**Master MORE, your Sacred Heart,
from this we will no more depart,
we are forever in your flow,
of Diamond Will that you bestow.**

2. Master MORE, shatter the energetic matrix that prevents people from seeing that in most societies they had the idea that the king either was a god or was supported by the gods, was working with the gods, was representing the gods on earth.

Master MORE, your wisdom flows,
as our attunement ever grows.
Master MORE, we have a tie,
that helps us see through Serpent's lie.

Master MORE, your Sacred Heart,
from this we will no more depart,
we are forever in your flow,
of Diamond Will that you bestow.

3. Master MORE, shatter the energetic matrix that prevents people from seeing that there was always a need to create some kind of idea (a religion, an ideology, a thought system) that makes the population accept that we need an elite. It gives legitimacy and authority to the elite.

Master MORE, your love so pink,
there is no purer love, we think.
Master MORE, you set us free,
from all conditionality.

Master MORE, your Sacred Heart,
from this we will no more depart,
we are forever in your flow,
of Diamond Will that you bestow.

4. Master MORE, shatter the energetic matrix that prevents people from seeing that when we recognize that a power elite supports its existence and power by an idea, we can begin to critically examine the ideas that the power elites of history have used.

Master MORE, we will endure,
your discipline that makes us pure.
Master MORE, intentions true,
as we are always one with you.

Master MORE, your Sacred Heart,
from this we will no more depart,
we are forever in your flow,
of Diamond Will that you bestow.

5. Master MORE, shatter the energetic matrix that prevents people from seeing that we do not accept the claims made in ancient civilizations, so we need to look at the ideas that the power elite is using to support its existence today. We need to ask whether they make sense to us or whether

is it just something we have been brought up to accept and never really question.

Master MORE, our vision raised,
the will of God is always praised.
Master MORE, creative will,
raising all life higher still.

**Master MORE, your Sacred Heart,
from this we will no more depart,
we are forever in your flow,
of Diamond Will that you bestow.**

6. Master MORE, shatter the energetic matrix that prevents people from seeing that if it was true that God had anointed certain leaders of society, it would mean that God had created people in distinctly different categories. God had created some people to be in the category of leaders, and most of the population were created in the category of followers.

Master MORE, your peace is power,
the demons of war it will devour.
Master MORE, we serve all life,
our flames consuming war and strife.

**Master MORE, your Sacred Heart,
from this we will no more depart,
we are forever in your flow,
of Diamond Will that you bestow.**

7. Master MORE, shatter the energetic matrix that prevents people from seeing that if we compare this idea to the democratic constitutions, it is in complete contradiction to the foundational ideas of democracy.

Master MORE, we are so free,
eternal bond from you we see.
Master MORE, we find rebirth,
in flow of your eternal mirth.

**Master MORE, your Sacred Heart,
from this we will no more depart,
we are forever in your flow,
of Diamond Will that you bestow.**

8. Master MORE, shatter the energetic matrix that prevents people from seeing that if all people are created equal by their creator, then God could not have created different classes: a ruling class and a following class.

Master MORE, you balance all,
the seven rays upon our call.
Master MORE, forever MORE,
we are the Spirit's open door.

**Master MORE, your Sacred Heart,
from this we will no more depart,
we are forever in your flow,
of Diamond Will that you bestow.**

9. Master MORE, shatter the energetic matrix that prevents people from seeing that if God has not done so, then what is the validity of the claim that kings have divine rights and are appointed by God? There is a cognitive dissonance between the royal houses of Europe and the foundations for their constitutions.

Master MORE, your Presence here,
filling up the inner sphere.
Life is now a sacred flow,
God Power we on all bestow.

**Master MORE, your Sacred Heart,
from this we will no more depart,
we are forever in your flow,
of Diamond Will that you bestow.**

Part 3

1. Master MORE, shatter the energetic matrix that prevents people from seeing that the very cornerstone of modern democracy is precisely that all human beings have the same potential: the potential to grow.

> Master MORE, come to the fore,
> we will absorb your flame of MORE.
> Master MORE, our will so strong,
> our power centers cleared by song.

> **Master MORE, your Sacred Heart,**
> **from this we will no more depart,**
> **we are forever in your flow,**
> **of Diamond Will that you bestow.**

2. Master MORE, shatter the energetic matrix that prevents people from seeing that our essential humanity is the foundation for all modern democracies. It is also the foundation for the teachings of the Buddha and the teachings of Jesus.

> Master MORE, your wisdom flows,
> as our attunement ever grows.
> Master MORE, we have a tie,
> that helps us see through Serpent's lie.

> **Master MORE, your Sacred Heart,**
> **from this we will no more depart,**
> **we are forever in your flow,**
> **of Diamond Will that you bestow.**

3. Master MORE, shatter the energetic matrix that prevents people from seeing that it makes no sense that God should have created two different classes of people. God created all with the same potential, but this can only be accepted when we also accept reincarnation, because this explains why not all people are born with the same abilities in this lifetime.

Master MORE, your love so pink,
there is no purer love, we think.
Master MORE, you set us free,
from all conditionality.

**Master MORE, your Sacred Heart,
from this we will no more depart,
we are forever in your flow,
of Diamond Will that you bestow.**

4. Master MORE, shatter the energetic matrix that prevents people from seeing that we have made choices in many past lifetimes, and some people have attained a higher ability in a certain area than others.

Master MORE, we will endure,
your discipline that makes us pure.
Master MORE, intentions true,
as we are always one with you.

**Master MORE, your Sacred Heart,
from this we will no more depart,
we are forever in your flow,
of Diamond Will that you bestow.**

5. Master MORE, shatter the energetic matrix that prevents people from seeing that God did not create an elite and a big part of the population that is inferior.

Master MORE, our vision raised,
the will of God is always praised.
Master MORE, creative will,
raising all life higher still.

**Master MORE, your Sacred Heart,
from this we will no more depart,
we are forever in your flow,
of Diamond Will that you bestow.**

6. Master MORE, shatter the energetic matrix that prevents people from seeing that God did not create elitism. He did not create or mandate that on earth there should be elitist societies. That idea does not come from God, it comes from the narcissistic beings.

Master MORE, your peace is power,
the demons of war it will devour.
Master MORE, we serve all life,
our flames consuming war and strife.

**Master MORE, your Sacred Heart,
from this we will no more depart,
we are forever in your flow,
of Diamond Will that you bestow.**

7. Master MORE, shatter the energetic matrix that prevents people from seeing that Scientific Materialism promotes the idea that nature is a process of competition and that it selects out those who are not as fit, and therefore only the fittest survive. How did the majority of the human population then survive?

Master MORE, we are so free,
eternal bond from you we see.
Master MORE, we find rebirth,
in flow of your eternal mirth.

**Master MORE, your Sacred Heart,
from this we will no more depart,
we are forever in your flow,
of Diamond Will that you bestow.**

8. Master MORE, shatter the energetic matrix that prevents people from seeing that most of the proponents of Materialism are elitists. They believe there is a ruling elite in society because nature selected them and they were more fit to rule, even more fit to survive. But how then did the rest of humanity survive if we are not fit?

Master MORE, you balance all,
the seven rays upon our call.

Master MORE, forever MORE,
we are the Spirit's open door.

Master MORE, your Sacred Heart,
from this we will no more depart,
we are forever in your flow,
of Diamond Will that you bestow.

9. Master MORE, shatter the energetic matrix that prevents people from seeing that no animal species has a ruling elite. This is what human beings project in order to sell the idea of elitism among humans. In reality, it is not the most competitive who survive, but those who can cooperate.

Master MORE, your Presence here,
filling up the inner sphere.
Life is now a sacred flow,
God Power we on all bestow.

Master MORE, your Sacred Heart,
from this we will no more depart,
we are forever in your flow,
of Diamond Will that you bestow.

Part 4

1. Master MORE, shatter the energetic matrix that prevents people from seeing that the idea of survival of the fittest has been used to create a philosophy, a set of ideas that are found in many different contexts, many different sciences, philosophies and writings.

Master MORE, come to the fore,
we will absorb your flame of MORE.
Master MORE, our will so strong,
our power centers cleared by song.

Master MORE, your Sacred Heart,
from this we will no more depart,

we are forever in your flow,
of Diamond Will that you bestow.

2. Master MORE, shatter the energetic matrix that prevents people from seeing that their only purpose is to support the existence of an elite by making it seem as if nature itself created a ruling elite.

Master MORE, your wisdom flows,
as our attunement ever grows.
Master MORE, we have a tie,
that helps us see through Serpent's lie.

Master MORE, your Sacred Heart,
from this we will no more depart,
we are forever in your flow,
of Diamond Will that you bestow.

3. Master MORE, shatter the energetic matrix that prevents people from seeing that if we believe in God, we must think that God created the elite. If we believe there is no God, we must think that nature created the elite. Regardless of what we believe or do not believe, we must believe there is an elite.

Master MORE, your love so pink,
there is no purer love, we think.
Master MORE, you set us free,
from all conditionality.

Master MORE, your Sacred Heart,
from this we will no more depart,
we are forever in your flow,
of Diamond Will that you bestow.

4. Master MORE, shatter the energetic matrix that prevents people from seeing that Scientific Materialism claims to set people free from the superstition of religion. Yet what really suppressed the population was the power elite that used religion to suppress the people.

Master MORE, we will endure,
your discipline that makes us pure.
Master MORE, intentions true,
as we are always one with you.

Master MORE, your Sacred Heart,
from this we will no more depart,
we are forever in your flow,
of Diamond Will that you bestow.

5. Master MORE, shatter the energetic matrix that prevents people from seeing that Materialism claims to have freed people from the superstition of religion. Instead of freeing them from the power elite, they have just created another power elite that now rules, not because they are appointed by God, but because they are appointed by nature.

Master MORE, our vision raised,
the will of God is always praised.
Master MORE, creative will,
raising all life higher still.

Master MORE, your Sacred Heart,
from this we will no more depart,
we are forever in your flow,
of Diamond Will that you bestow.

6. Master MORE, shatter the energetic matrix that prevents people from seeing that this is not progress. Neither is it democratic. It is contrary to democratic ideals.

Master MORE, your peace is power,
the demons of war it will devour.
Master MORE, we serve all life,
our flames consuming war and strife.

Master MORE, your Sacred Heart,
from this we will no more depart,
we are forever in your flow,
of Diamond Will that you bestow.

7. Master MORE, shatter the energetic matrix that prevents people from seeing that the cognitive dissonance is that in a democratic society, there cannot be an elite because democracy and elitism are incompatible. There is a fundamental contradiction between an elite and democracy.

Master MORE, we are so free,
eternal bond from you we see.
Master MORE, we find rebirth,
in flow of your eternal mirth.

**Master MORE, your Sacred Heart,
from this we will no more depart,
we are forever in your flow,
of Diamond Will that you bestow.**

8. Master MORE, shatter the energetic matrix that prevents people from snapping out of the blindness we were brought up with, so we see that it is not logically consistent that we claim to have a democratic society, but we still allow this society to be ruled and dominated by a small elite. This is not democracy.

Master MORE, you balance all,
the seven rays upon our call.
Master MORE, forever MORE,
we are the Spirit's open door.

**Master MORE, your Sacred Heart,
from this we will no more depart,
we are forever in your flow,
of Diamond Will that you bestow.**

9. Master MORE, shatter the energetic matrix that prevents people from making the shift and seeing that elitism and democracy are fundamentally different. We cannot have a fully functioning democracy if we have an elite. It simply is not compatible. The existence of elites is undemocratic by its very nature.

Master MORE, your Presence here,
filling up the inner sphere.

Life is now a sacred flow,
God Power we on all bestow.

**Master MORE, your Sacred Heart,
from this we will no more depart,
we are forever in your flow,
of Diamond Will that you bestow.**

Part 5

1. Master MORE, shatter the energetic matrix that prevents people from seeing that the power elite will always say that the people cannot rule themselves. If we allow the people to rule, it will be disaster.

Master MORE, come to the fore,
we will absorb your flame of MORE.
Master MORE, our will so strong,
our power centers cleared by song.

**Master MORE, your Sacred Heart,
from this we will no more depart,
we are forever in your flow,
of Diamond Will that you bestow.**

2. Master MORE, shatter the energetic matrix that prevents people from seeing that the power elite will say that direct democracy cannot work because if we allow the people to rule, it will be one disaster after another. But how do they know?

Master MORE, your wisdom flows,
as our attunement ever grows.
Master MORE, we have a tie,
that helps us see through Serpent's lie.

**Master MORE, your Sacred Heart,
from this we will no more depart,**

we are forever in your flow,
of Diamond Will that you bestow.

3. Master MORE, shatter the energetic matrix that prevents people from seeing that there is no example where the people have been allowed to rule without being dominated by an elite. We do not have a society in known history that was not dominated by an elite.

Master MORE, your love so pink,
there is no purer love, we think.
Master MORE, you set us free,
from all conditionality.

Master MORE, your Sacred Heart,
from this we will no more depart,
we are forever in your flow,
of Diamond Will that you bestow.

4. Master MORE, shatter the energetic matrix that prevents people from seeing that the atrocities and the disasters created in history were not created because the population voted on it. Behind every atrocity we see in history, there is a power elite.

Master MORE, we will endure,
your discipline that makes us pure.
Master MORE, intentions true,
as we are always one with you.

Master MORE, your Sacred Heart,
from this we will no more depart,
we are forever in your flow,
of Diamond Will that you bestow.

5. Master MORE, shatter the energetic matrix that prevents people from seeing that sometimes we see two power elites that were rivaling against each other, that were fighting about who should be the dominant elite. But it was in no case the people who created the wars and the atrocities.

Master MORE, our vision raised,
the will of God is always praised.
Master MORE, creative will,
raising all life higher still.

**Master MORE, your Sacred Heart,
from this we will no more depart,
we are forever in your flow,
of Diamond Will that you bestow.**

6. Master MORE, shatter the energetic matrix that prevents people from seeing that when we look at empirical evidence, historical evidence, we must conclude that elites have created enormous amounts of atrocities and suffering.

Master MORE, your peace is power,
the demons of war it will devour.
Master MORE, we serve all life,
our flames consuming war and strife.

**Master MORE, your Sacred Heart,
from this we will no more depart,
we are forever in your flow,
of Diamond Will that you bestow.**

7. Master MORE, shatter the energetic matrix that prevents people from seeing that narcissistic leaders are so in love with their own ideas that the cost of killing dozens of millions of people is not even a concern for them, because the ideas are more important than the people.

Master MORE, we are so free,
eternal bond from you we see.
Master MORE, we find rebirth,
in flow of your eternal mirth.

**Master MORE, your Sacred Heart,
from this we will no more depart,
we are forever in your flow,
of Diamond Will that you bestow.**

8. Master MORE, shatter the energetic matrix that prevents people from seeing that if we look at this honestly, we must conclude that the people could not possibly do worse than the elite. They could not possibly do worse than all of the nonsense we see in history.

> Master MORE, you balance all,
> the seven rays upon our call.
> Master MORE, forever MORE,
> we are the Spirit's open door.

> **Master MORE, your Sacred Heart,**
> **from this we will no more depart,**
> **we are forever in your flow,**
> **of Diamond Will that you bestow.**

9. Master MORE, shatter the energetic matrix that prevents people from seeing that from a probability standpoint, it is highly probable that the people could not possibly do worse than the elites have done. So what basis do we have for saying that the people could not rule?

> Master MORE, your Presence here,
> filling up the inner sphere.
> Life is now a sacred flow,
> God Power we on all bestow.

> **Master MORE, your Sacred Heart,**
> **from this we will no more depart,**
> **we are forever in your flow,**
> **of Diamond Will that you bestow.**

Sealing

In the name of the I AM THAT I AM, I accept that Archangel Michael, Astrea and Shiva form an impenetrable shield around myself and all constructive people, sealing us from all fear-based energies in all four octaves. I accept that the Light of God is consuming and transforming all fear-based energies that make up the dark forces working against ending the era of elitism on earth!

7 | INVOKING AN AWAKENING OF THE PEOPLE (PART 2)

In the name of the I AM THAT I AM, Jesus Christ, I use the authority that I have as a being in embodiment on earth to call upon Master MORE to reinforce my calls and use my chakras to project the statements in this invocation into the collective consciousness and awaken people to the fact that we do not need an elite to rule the population. Awaken people to the reality that we are spiritual beings and that we can co-create a new future by working with the ascended masters. I especially call for …

[Make your own calls here.]

Part 1

1. Master MORE, shatter the energetic matrix that prevents people from seeing the reality that the people *can* rule. When all of the people are heard, we will balance each other out, and we will come up with a solution that is an expression of our basic humanity.

Master MORE, come to the fore,
we will absorb your flame of MORE.
Master MORE, our will so strong,
our power centers cleared by song.

**Master MORE, your Sacred Heart,
from this we will no more depart,
we are forever in your flow,
of Diamond Will that you bestow.**

2. Master MORE, shatter the energetic matrix that prevents people from seeing that the basic humanity can change over time, because as the collective consciousness is raised, the basic sense of humanity is raised also.

Master MORE, your wisdom flows,
as our attunement ever grows.
Master MORE, we have a tie,
that helps us see through Serpent's lie.

**Master MORE, your Sacred Heart,
from this we will no more depart,
we are forever in your flow,
of Diamond Will that you bestow.**

3. Master MORE, shatter the energetic matrix that prevents people from seeing that at any given time, in any society, there is a certain basic humanity, and it is that people want to live a good personal life. They want to have security in their personal lives.

Master MORE, your love so pink,
there is no purer love, we think.
Master MORE, you set us free,
from all conditionality.

**Master MORE, your Sacred Heart,
from this we will no more depart,
we are forever in your flow,
of Diamond Will that you bestow.**

4. Master MORE, shatter the energetic matrix that prevents people from seeing that this means that the people will not start a war. Anytime we start a war, we do not know what the outcome will be. We are generating a basic insecurity that most people will see as a threat, and therefore, they will not vote to go to war.

Master MORE, we will endure,
your discipline that makes us pure.
Master MORE, intentions true,
as we are always one with you.

**Master MORE, your Sacred Heart,
from this we will no more depart,
we are forever in your flow,
of Diamond Will that you bestow.**

5. Master MORE, shatter the energetic matrix that prevents people from seeing that the people support wars only when they are seduced by the power elite with the rationale that the end can justify the means, and that it is necessary to go to war for some greater good.

Master MORE, our vision raised,
the will of God is always praised.
Master MORE, creative will,
raising all life higher still.

**Master MORE, your Sacred Heart,
from this we will no more depart,
we are forever in your flow,
of Diamond Will that you bestow.**

6. Master MORE, shatter the energetic matrix that prevents people from seeing that war is not something that the people would initiate without the elite. If we allow the people to rule, we can forget about wars.

Master MORE, your peace is power,
the demons of war it will devour.
Master MORE, we serve all life,
our flames consuming war and strife.

> **Master MORE, your Sacred Heart,**
> **from this we will no more depart,**
> **we are forever in your flow,**
> **of Diamond Will that you bestow.**

7. Master MORE, shatter the energetic matrix that prevents people from seeing that all wars in history have been started by elites of various kinds, often two elites that were fighting for domination. The people do not do this. We do not need domination. We want security in our daily lives.

> Master MORE, we are so free,
> eternal bond from you we see.
> Master MORE, we find rebirth,
> in flow of your eternal mirth.

> **Master MORE, your Sacred Heart,**
> **from this we will no more depart,**
> **we are forever in your flow,**
> **of Diamond Will that you bestow.**

8. Master MORE, shatter the energetic matrix that prevents people from seeing that people want a reasonable standard of living, where we can take care of our children and put them in a good way in life.

> Master MORE, you balance all,
> the seven rays upon our call.
> Master MORE, forever MORE,
> we are the Spirit's open door.

> **Master MORE, your Sacred Heart,**
> **from this we will no more depart,**
> **we are forever in your flow,**
> **of Diamond Will that you bestow.**

9. Master MORE, shatter the energetic matrix that prevents people from seeing that only the elite want an affluent lifestyle. The elite wants more than they need in order to give themselves and their children a good material life. They can never have enough.

Master MORE, your Presence here,
filling up the inner sphere.
Life is now a sacred flow,
God Power we on all bestow.

Master MORE, your Sacred Heart,
from this we will no more depart,
we are forever in your flow,
of Diamond Will that you bestow.

Part 2

1. Master MORE, shatter the energetic matrix that prevents people from seeing that the people would never create an economy that was driven by greed, and that led to these fanciful financial instruments that caused the crash of 1929 or the crash of 2008.

Master MORE, come to the fore,
we will absorb your flame of MORE.
Master MORE, our will so strong,
our power centers cleared by song.

Master MORE, your Sacred Heart,
from this we will no more depart,
we are forever in your flow,
of Diamond Will that you bestow.

2. Master MORE, shatter the energetic matrix that prevents people from seeing that the people would never create an economy with the ups and downs, with inflation. The people would create an economy that is based on letting the people who do the work reap the financial reward so that all of the people could have a reasonable standard of living.

Master MORE, your wisdom flows,
as our attunement ever grows.
Master MORE, we have a tie,
that helps us see through Serpent's lie.

> **Master MORE, your Sacred Heart,**
> **from this we will no more depart,**
> **we are forever in your flow,**
> **of Diamond Will that you bestow.**

3. Master MORE, shatter the energetic matrix that prevents people from seeing that in the United States today, there is a growing number of people who have a very low standard of living. The middle class is having their standard of living eroded. There is a growing number of people in the upper class, but only a few people at the top control the vast majority of the money.

> Master MORE, your love so pink,
> there is no purer love, we think.
> Master MORE, you set us free,
> from all conditionality.

> **Master MORE, your Sacred Heart,**
> **from this we will no more depart,**
> **we are forever in your flow,**
> **of Diamond Will that you bestow.**

4. Master MORE, shatter the energetic matrix that prevents people from seeing that if we took the money that is available in the United States' economy and distributed it more evenly, then all people in the United States could have a good, secure standard of living.

> Master MORE, we will endure,
> your discipline that makes us pure.
> Master MORE, intentions true,
> as we are always one with you.

> **Master MORE, your Sacred Heart,**
> **from this we will no more depart,**
> **we are forever in your flow,**
> **of Diamond Will that you bestow.**

5. Master MORE, shatter the energetic matrix that prevents people from seeing that if we allowed the American population to vote on this, an

overwhelming majority would vote to have the kind of economy, where all people have a good standard of living and where there is no ruling class that has more money than they could ever need.

Master MORE, our vision raised,
the will of God is always praised.
Master MORE, creative will,
raising all life higher still.

**Master MORE, your Sacred Heart,
from this we will no more depart,
we are forever in your flow,
of Diamond Will that you bestow.**

6. Master MORE, shatter the energetic matrix that prevents people from seeing that the elite will say this kind of economy would crash. In reality, the economy would be free from the risk of crashing because it is not based on greed. It is not based on trying to maximize the outcome regardless of the consequences.

Master MORE, your peace is power,
the demons of war it will devour.
Master MORE, we serve all life,
our flames consuming war and strife.

**Master MORE, your Sacred Heart,
from this we will no more depart,
we are forever in your flow,
of Diamond Will that you bestow.**

7. Master MORE, shatter the energetic matrix that prevents people from seeing that we want a sustainable economy where the value of money, the value of stocks is tied to something that has real value. *That* is the kind of economy that the people would want, if we were educated better and if we were allowed to vote.

Master MORE, we are so free,
eternal bond from you we see.

Master MORE, we find rebirth,
in flow of your eternal mirth.

Master MORE, your Sacred Heart,
from this we will no more depart,
we are forever in your flow,
of Diamond Will that you bestow.

8. Master MORE, shatter the energetic matrix that prevents people from seeing that if we distributed the income more evenly among the people, they would spend the money and that would raise the entire economy to a much higher level than it is today.

Master MORE, you balance all,
the seven rays upon our call.
Master MORE, forever MORE,
we are the Spirit's open door.

Master MORE, your Sacred Heart,
from this we will no more depart,
we are forever in your flow,
of Diamond Will that you bestow.

9. Master MORE, shatter the energetic matrix that prevents people from seeing that the only people who could not like this is the elite who do not want to lose their privileged position. If a country has an economy that is entirely designed to enrich the elite and keep the people poor, can we really say that this country is a democracy?

Master MORE, your Presence here,
filling up the inner sphere.
Life is now a sacred flow,
God Power we on all bestow.

Master MORE, your Sacred Heart,
from this we will no more depart,
we are forever in your flow,
of Diamond Will that you bestow.

Part 3

1. Master MORE, shatter the energetic matrix that prevents people from seeing that a country with an elite is not functioning according to democratic principles of the greatest good for the greatest number of people. It is functioning entirely to allow the elite to become richer and richer, to have more and more control.

> Master MORE, come to the fore,
> we will absorb your flame of MORE.
> Master MORE, our will so strong,
> our power centers cleared by song.
>
> **Master MORE, your Sacred Heart,**
> **from this we will no more depart,**
> **we are forever in your flow,**
> **of Diamond Will that you bestow.**

2. Master MORE, shatter the energetic matrix that prevents people from seeing that the elite created the crash of 1929 and the crash of 2008 and all of the many ups and downs in the economy since then. The people did not have the means to create it, and we would not have created it even if we had the means because we do not have the greed.

> Master MORE, your wisdom flows,
> as our attunement ever grows.
> Master MORE, we have a tie,
> that helps us see through Serpent's lie.
>
> **Master MORE, your Sacred Heart,**
> **from this we will no more depart,**
> **we are forever in your flow,**
> **of Diamond Will that you bestow.**

3. Master MORE, shatter the energetic matrix that prevents people from seeing that a person must have a boundless insatiable greed in order to be in the upper class. Members of the elite have a greed that could never be satisfied.

Master MORE, your love so pink,
there is no purer love, we think.
Master MORE, you set us free,
from all conditionality.

**Master MORE, your Sacred Heart,
from this we will no more depart,
we are forever in your flow,
of Diamond Will that you bestow.**

4. Master MORE, shatter the energetic matrix that prevents people from seeing that we are creating an entire society that is based on greed that could never be satisfied. It is an impossible quest.

Master MORE, we will endure,
your discipline that makes us pure.
Master MORE, intentions true,
as we are always one with you.

**Master MORE, your Sacred Heart,
from this we will no more depart,
we are forever in your flow,
of Diamond Will that you bestow.**

5. Master MORE, shatter the energetic matrix that prevents people from seeing that we could never create a society where the elite felt that they had enough power, enough security, enough money. They will never have enough.

Master MORE, our vision raised,
the will of God is always praised.
Master MORE, creative will,
raising all life higher still.

**Master MORE, your Sacred Heart,
from this we will no more depart,
we are forever in your flow,
of Diamond Will that you bestow.**

6. Master MORE, shatter the energetic matrix that prevents people from seeing that we are allowing our entire society to function in order to concentrate wealth, power, money in the hands of a small elite of people who will never be satisfied anyway. It will never be enough for them.

> Master MORE, your peace is power,
> the demons of war it will devour.
> Master MORE, we serve all life,
> our flames consuming war and strife.

> **Master MORE, your Sacred Heart,**
> **from this we will no more depart,**
> **we are forever in your flow,**
> **of Diamond Will that you bestow.**

7. Master MORE, shatter the energetic matrix that prevents people from asking: Why are we doing this? Why are we allowing this to happen? There must be a better way. There must be more than our current status, our current society. This cannot be what democracy is about.

> Master MORE, we are so free,
> eternal bond from you we see.
> Master MORE, we find rebirth,
> in flow of your eternal mirth.

> **Master MORE, your Sacred Heart,**
> **from this we will no more depart,**
> **we are forever in your flow,**
> **of Diamond Will that you bestow.**

8. Master MORE, shatter the energetic matrix that prevents people from seeing that there has been created this overlay, this consciousness, that is blinding people so we cannot see that the emperor has nothing on. We simply cannot see the fallacy of elitism. We cannot see the fallacy of these justifications for elitism.

> Master MORE, you balance all,
> the seven rays upon our call.

Master MORE, forever MORE,
we are the Spirit's open door.

**Master MORE, your Sacred Heart,
from this we will no more depart,
we are forever in your flow,
of Diamond Will that you bestow.**

9. Master MORE, shatter the energetic matrix that prevents people from seeing that we have the religious justification, the materialist justification and the pragmatic justification that the people could not rule themselves. They are all based on illusions but we cannot see it.

Master MORE, your Presence here,
filling up the inner sphere.
Life is now a sacred flow,
God Power we on all bestow.

**Master MORE, your Sacred Heart,
from this we will no more depart,
we are forever in your flow,
of Diamond Will that you bestow.**

Part 4

1. Master MORE, shatter the energetic matrix that prevents people from having a breakthrough and suddenly seeing: Why have we been believing this for so long? Why should we continue to believe this when really the power elite has nothing on?

Master MORE, come to the fore,
we will absorb your flame of MORE.
Master MORE, our will so strong,
our power centers cleared by song.

**Master MORE, your Sacred Heart,
from this we will no more depart,**

we are forever in your flow,
of Diamond Will that you bestow.

2. Master MORE, shatter the energetic matrix that prevents people from seeing that if democracy is the antithesis of elitism, how could democracy ever arise? How could the elite ever allow this to happen? The real reason is that, as the collective consciousness is raised, people no longer believe in the ideas that used to support elitism and we come to accept new ideas.

Master MORE, your wisdom flows,
as our attunement ever grows.
Master MORE, we have a tie,
that helps us see through Serpent's lie.

Master MORE, your Sacred Heart,
from this we will no more depart,
we are forever in your flow,
of Diamond Will that you bestow.

3. Master MORE, shatter the energetic matrix that prevents people from seeing that when we accept new ideas, the ideological foundation for the elite's rule crumbles, and when it crumbles, the elite must give way. They have historically and they *must* do it again.

Master MORE, your love so pink,
there is no purer love, we think.
Master MORE, you set us free,
from all conditionality.

Master MORE, your Sacred Heart,
from this we will no more depart,
we are forever in your flow,
of Diamond Will that you bestow.

4. Master MORE, shatter the energetic matrix that prevents people from seeing that when the collective consciousness shifts, when there is an opening in the clouds and people suddenly see it, then the entire equation of society will change. It *will* change.

Master MORE, we will endure,
your discipline that makes us pure.
Master MORE, intentions true,
as we are always one with you.

**Master MORE, your Sacred Heart,
from this we will no more depart,
we are forever in your flow,
of Diamond Will that you bestow.**

5. Master MORE, shatter the energetic matrix that prevents people from seeing that if enough of us decide to stand up to the power elite, the power elite cannot send the army to start killing us. It cannot happen. It *will* not happen.

Master MORE, our vision raised,
the will of God is always praised.
Master MORE, creative will,
raising all life higher still.

**Master MORE, your Sacred Heart,
from this we will no more depart,
we are forever in your flow,
of Diamond Will that you bestow.**

6. Master MORE, shatter the energetic matrix that prevents people from seeing that if enough people start speaking about this, the press cannot ignore it. They cannot suppress it. The politicians cannot ignore it if they sense that a critical mass of us are united.

Master MORE, your peace is power,
the demons of war it will devour.
Master MORE, we serve all life,
our flames consuming war and strife.

**Master MORE, your Sacred Heart,
from this we will no more depart,
we are forever in your flow,
of Diamond Will that you bestow.**

7. Master MORE, shatter the energetic matrix that prevents people from seeing that there are many people in the political apparatus who have some attunement to Saint Germain and his Golden Age ideas. There are many people who sense that there is something missing, there is something not right, but they cannot put their finger on it or dare to speak out about it.

Master MORE, we are so free,
eternal bond from you we see.
Master MORE, we find rebirth,
in flow of your eternal mirth.

**Master MORE, your Sacred Heart,
from this we will no more depart,
we are forever in your flow,
of Diamond Will that you bestow.**

8. Master MORE, shatter the energetic matrix that prevents people from seeing that there is a cone of silence where people think they cannot speak out about it. If we begin to speak out, many people in the government apparatus will say: "That is exactly what I've been waiting for. Now I can come forward. Now I can do something that could not be done when the popular backing wasn't there."

Master MORE, you balance all,
the seven rays upon our call.
Master MORE, forever MORE,
we are the Spirit's open door.

**Master MORE, your Sacred Heart,
from this we will no more depart,
we are forever in your flow,
of Diamond Will that you bestow.**

9. Master MORE, shatter the energetic matrix that prevents people from seeing that the tension is there, the potential is there. It just takes a little spark to ignite the fuse that will blow up the rule of the power elite, that will blow up this cone of ideas, this cloud of ignorance that is blinding the people.

Master MORE, your Presence here,
filling up the inner sphere.
Life is now a sacred flow,
God Power we on all bestow.

**Master MORE, your Sacred Heart,
from this we will no more depart,
we are forever in your flow,
of Diamond Will that you bestow.**

Part 5

1. Master MORE, shatter the energetic matrix so that the people will wake up and say: "This is what we need. This is what we want. We couldn't put words on it but there it is. Now we see it and we want it because this is our right."

Master MORE, come to the fore,
we will absorb your flame of MORE.
Master MORE, our will so strong,
our power centers cleared by song.

**Master MORE, your Sacred Heart,
from this we will no more depart,
we are forever in your flow,
of Diamond Will that you bestow.**

2. Master MORE, shatter the energetic matrix that prevents people from seeing that the rights to life, liberty and the pursuit of happiness is precisely that most people want a good life for themselves.

Master MORE, your wisdom flows,
as our attunement ever grows.
Master MORE, we have a tie,
that helps us see through Serpent's lie.

**Master MORE, your Sacred Heart,
from this we will no more depart,
we are forever in your flow,
of Diamond Will that you bestow.**

3. Master MORE, shatter the energetic matrix that prevents people from seeing that when we allow the people those rights, then it will create a country that has a sustainable economy that is not seeking to police the world and create wars, so that the military-industrial complex can make a bigger profit. Because that is not what the people want.

Master MORE, your love so pink,
there is no purer love, we think.
Master MORE, you set us free,
from all conditionality.

**Master MORE, your Sacred Heart,
from this we will no more depart,
we are forever in your flow,
of Diamond Will that you bestow.**

4. Master MORE, shatter the energetic matrix that prevents people from seeing that people want the good life and there is nothing wrong with the people wanting the good life. It is far better to have a society that is based on the people's definition of the good life, rather than the power elite's definition of the good life.

Master MORE, we will endure,
your discipline that makes us pure.
Master MORE, intentions true,
as we are always one with you.

**Master MORE, your Sacred Heart,
from this we will no more depart,
we are forever in your flow,
of Diamond Will that you bestow.**

5. Master MORE, shatter the energetic matrix that prevents people from recognizing our essential humanity, which is really our essential spirituality.

We are spiritual beings, and we are not defined by these outer conditions on earth that can so easily be used to create the sense of superiority and inferiority.

Master MORE, our vision raised,
the will of God is always praised.
Master MORE, creative will,
raising all life higher still.

**Master MORE, your Sacred Heart,
from this we will no more depart,
we are forever in your flow,
of Diamond Will that you bestow.**

6. Master MORE, shatter the energetic matrix that prevents people from seeing that we are spiritual beings and therefore the outer things do not define us.

Master MORE, your peace is power,
the demons of war it will devour.
Master MORE, we serve all life,
our flames consuming war and strife.

**Master MORE, your Sacred Heart,
from this we will no more depart,
we are forever in your flow,
of Diamond Will that you bestow.**

7. Master MORE, shatter the energetic matrix that prevents people from seeing that: "I am more. I am more than this previous identity that I saw myself as. I'm even more than this self that has been controlling my relationship to this planet for so long. I'm even more than the self that I had when I came here as an avatar, thinking I could do good and change the people on earth or perhaps even change the fallen beings."

Master MORE, we are so free,
eternal bond from you we see.
Master MORE, we find rebirth,
in flow of your eternal mirth.

Master MORE, your Sacred Heart,
from this we will no more depart,
we are forever in your flow,
of Diamond Will that you bestow.

8. Master MORE, shatter the energetic matrix that prevents people from seeing that we cannot do anything by changing others. We can only do something by changing ourselves and thereby giving them an example and pulling them up.

Master MORE, you balance all,
the seven rays upon our call.
Master MORE, forever MORE,
we are the Spirit's open door.

Master MORE, your Sacred Heart,
from this we will no more depart,
we are forever in your flow,
of Diamond Will that you bestow.

9. Master MORE, I accept the intensely pink love of the First Ray. I accept your love that is unconditional because you see beyond the conditions to who we really are underneath it all. Help us come to see who we really are underneath all of the outer things.

Master MORE, your Presence here,
filling up the inner sphere.
Life is now a sacred flow,
God Power we on all bestow.

Master MORE, your Sacred Heart,
from this we will no more depart,
we are forever in your flow,
of Diamond Will that you bestow.

Sealing

In the name of the I AM THAT I AM, I accept that Archangel Michael, Astrea and Shiva form an impenetrable shield around myself and all constructive people, sealing us from all fear-based energies in all four octaves. I accept that the Light of God is consuming and transforming all fear-based energies that make up the dark forces working against ending the era of elitism on earth!

8 | THE MESSAGE OF CHRIST IS ANTI-ELITIST

I AM the Ascended Master Jesus Christ. My contribution to this conference is to give you the perspective on how Christianity has been used by the power elite to further the cause of the power elite.

Many people are ready to see this, although they are not aware that they are ready. But if we looked at what people are aware of, we might as well have abandoned this planet and gone somewhere else. We are the optimists. We are also in a sense realists because we see that even though people are not aware of something at the conscious level, they can become aware. They can be jolted into awareness. This is of course what I attempted to do 2,000 years ago by many of the statements I made that were meant to be shocking, to be provocative.

The genesis of fanaticism

Let us begin by looking at the Bible. Although we do not quote the Bible much and do not encourage you to take it literally, there are of course certain lessons that can be learned there. Let us go to the very beginning of Genesis where it talks about Adam and Eve in the Garden of Eden. As we have said before, this is a symbol for the state that humankind was in before the descent into the consciousness of duality. What was it that caused Adam and Eve to fall, to fall below the innocence of the non-dualistic state of consciousness and fall into the dualistic state of consciousness? Was it not the serpent? Then, what is the serpent a symbol for? In the widest sense, the power elite. As Master MORE and Mother Mary have said, it is not natural, it is not in human nature, for people to create war. When you look at history and see how people have been tricked into going to war and killing each other, it has always happened because they were misled by a power elite, or several power elites that were fighting for ultimate dominion.

The way to understand the serpent in the Garden of Eden is to understand that this was, in its broadest sense, the power elite. We have of course given more specific teachings about the fallen beings, and these teachings are important because you cannot look at the biblical story as it is given right now and understand it. Most Christians have no understanding of what it truly means because they miss those key ingredients. First of all, you need to understand that the Garden of Eden portrayed in Genesis was not a heavenly realm where the supreme God of the universe walked and talked with Adam and Eve in the cool of the evening. It was a symbol for a state of consciousness in which humankind had contact with their spiritual teachers, direct contact with their spiritual teachers, because they were not in duality. Therefore, they had not become as gods, defining what is good and evil.

You also need to understand that there could be no serpent in a heavenly realm. That is one of the most confusing aspects of the Genesis story, and so many people wonder: How could there be a serpent in this Garden of Eden? Did God create the serpent? Where did the serpent come from? Many, many people, not only Christians but anyone who reads the Old Testament, have been confused about this. Of course, we have given the explanation that this was the fallen beings and it was not a higher realm that they were in, but it was a state of consciousness. In a more specific sense, the serpent is a symbol for the dualistic state of consciousness. It is a state of consciousness where you have separated yourself from your source. When you separate yourself from your source, which is your higher self, your I AM Presence, you lose sight of your own basic humanity or spirituality. Therefore, you cannot see it in other people either. This gives rise to the illusion that you are separated from God, separated from other people.

The separation from your source means that you do not have a frame of reference for knowing a truth, a reality that is universal, valid, not individualized, not subjectivized. You might even call it objective. When you lose that frame of reference, you so easily become seduced by the serpentine state of mind into thinking that you can define what is good and evil based on your current state of consciousness. You think that you are capable of defining what is good and evil internally in your current state of consciousness, without having that frame of reference from something that is beyond your state of consciousness.

This is of course what the fallen beings have been doing since they fell or even before, and they have seduced most human beings on earth into believing in this very lie. Not necessarily that many people believe that they themselves are capable of defining good and evil, but they believe that someone on earth, some earthly authority, is capable of defining it, and they are able to recognize it. They are able to recognize that authority.

Christ is the alternative to duality

What did I come to do 2,000 years ago? What is the very essence of what I came to do? It was to show people that there is an alternative to the serpentine state of mind, the dualistic state of consciousness, where you define good and evil and your definition is entirely relative and subjective. You, or at least the authority figure you follow, elevate it to the status of being absolute—absolute truth and objective truth that cannot or should not be gainsaid. I came to free people from this state of consciousness, and I did it in various ways.

One of the ways I did it was to make certain statements that were calculated to shock people out of that serpentine mindset, that serpentine logic, where they could perhaps come to question what they had taken for granted. I also did it through my example, by demonstrating that there is a higher state of consciousness, which we can call the Christ consciousness, or a neutral state of consciousness that allows you to see beyond the serpentine illusions. You can actually see through the serpentine logic, see the cognitive dissonance, the contradictions, the unanswered questions of the serpentine logic. Therefore, you can begin to reach for a frame of reference that is beyond your own mind, but even beyond the serpentine mind and the collective mind of humankind.

This was what I came to offer people: a way out of duality. I offered to set people free, or give them the tools that could set them free, from the serpents who have misled humanity. They are of course the very ones who form the power elite and have formed it in all eras since they first came here. What has actually been lost in the process of creating Christianity, and has remained lost to this day by most Christian churches, is that the essence of my mission was anti-elitist. I was here to set people free from the elite, ultimately of the fallen beings, the real serpents, but also of all who were part of the power elite that had been seduced by the serpents into thinking that they had some special quality that allowed them to be the leaders of the people because they knew better than the people.

There was a clear division in the society that you saw in Judea or Israel at the time. A clear division between those who knew or thought they knew, namely, the religious leaders of various groups, and then the people. It was considered that the people did not know and could not know what was true, that they needed the leaders. This of course is exactly why that power elite (that was there in that society) had me killed when I started to become a threat. How did I become a threat? By offering people that frame of reference where they could find the kingdom of God within them and they themselves could attain that discernment of Christ, that mind of Christ. They could put on the mind of Christ and see through the lies that the elite was using to keep them in bondage. This was the very essence of my mission, and I challenge you to go out there and find a Christian church that preaches that message.

Killing the messenger, then the message

How did that message become lost? First of all, you need to recognize that the fallen beings did to me what they have done to many others who spoke a higher perspective, a higher truth. They killed me. This is characteristic of the power elite. When someone takes a stand for truth or brings forth a higher perspective, they will first attempt to ignore the person and hope that he or she does not gain any followers. If that fails, they will kill that person, thinking, as has indeed happened in many cases, that this will kill that particular threat, it will destroy the threat. They killed me, and they attempted to kill some of my early followers, and then they thought that would take care of the problem.

Over time, gradually, more and more people started following the teachings as they were able to do and as the teachings were presented to them. There emerged a more coherent Christian movement. This then became seen as a threat by the power elite of the Roman Empire. It led to the persecution of the Christians in Rome and elsewhere, where they again attempted to kill the people who were bringing forth an alternative. Then, of course there came that point where some among the power elite realized that it was indeed difficult to kill all of the Christians. They switched their strategy as they have done in many other cases. They used the motto: "If you can't beat them, join them."

The fallen beings in the higher octaves used their tool, the emperor Constantine, to suddenly turn Christianity into the state religion of the Roman Empire. This was from the very beginning an entirely political move. In Constantine's mind, it was his way of trying to reestablish control over the Roman Empire by unifying the people in a religion that he considered could be made more appealing than the old religion and the old gods. But for this purpose he needed of course a religion with a strong God and a strong prophet. Very quickly, there was created this idolatrous version of Christianity that elevated Christianity to promoting the superior God of the universe, the one and only God. Whereas the Romans had many gods for specific areas, here was only one God, although of course he had three aspects, which nobody could really explain.

They also elevated me to being the Son of God. Oh, no, I was not just the Son of God. No, I was created at the same time as the Father. In fact, I was not created. I had always existed because I was of the same substance as the Father. Still in the Nicene Creed that is the basis for the Catholic church, still something that nobody can really explain. You can go out there and look at the explanations that people have come up with. You can see how artificial and intellectual and in fact serpentine they are. The entire purpose was to elevate me to a status that first of all gave the Romans the illusion that I could do for them what the old gods could not do because they were inferior to me.

This was where the collective consciousness was at. You had gods because you wanted them to do something practical for you in your daily life. It was not about raising your consciousness. It was not even about being saved. It was about having a wish-fulfilling God, a kind of Santa Claus, that could come and do what you needed in your everyday life. If you happened to be the emperor of the Roman Empire, then that God could come and solidify your position and slay your enemies and unify your empire under your rule.

What was the effect of this? It was that whereas the early Christian religion had been somewhat diversified, the Catholic church from the very beginning was an entirely elitist institution. It was never, ever about raising the whole, about raising all of the people to a higher state of consciousness.

It was always about creating a society that had a very clear division between the ruling elite and all of the people who were just followers. Nay, they were not just followers. They were sinners by nature through the original sin of Adam and Eve. This guilt trip has continued to be reinforced by the Catholic church ever since. I dare you to find a Protestant or other non-Catholic church that actually has thoroughly challenged that guilt trip.

The Christ can be born in all people

You see how, from the very beginning, the Catholic church was an entirely elitist institution. It reinforced the already existing mindset that there is an elite that rules and a majority that follows or that submits to the rule. But this was not what I said. This was not what I preached. What did I preach? The kingdom of God is within you—and you, and you, and you, and you. It is within *all* of you. You all have the potential to put on the mind of Christ. When you put on the mind of Christ, what happens? You do not need an authority on earth to tell you what to do, what to believe, what you can know and what you cannot know. You have access to a source that is beyond earth.

That is the miracle of the Christ consciousness. The Christ can be born in all people. That is the importance of the symbolism that I was born in a manger, born to humble people. I was not born as part of the elite of my society at the time. Many, many people who were in the elite rejected me precisely because of my humble birth. This is the symbol for the fact that the Christ, the Christ consciousness, can be born in all people because all people have the potential to put on the mind of Christ. When a critical mass of people put on the mind of Christ, why do you need an elite to tell you what is true or what is good and what is evil? Why do you need an earthly authority when you have the authority that is beyond earth, namely the Christ mind? The question is what do you submit to: an authority on earth, or an authority beyond earth, the mind of Christ? The mind of the serpent or the mind of Christ. Who is your master?

You look at the scriptures about my life, you look at my words, as imperfectly as they are portrayed in those scriptures, and see how many times I challenged the power elite of my time. "Ye are of your father the devil." "Scribes and Pharisees, hypocrites." I talked about those who appear beautiful outwardly, but inwardly they are whitened sepulchers, filled with dead men's bones. Many other statements like this that were meant to provoke and shock people into realizing that the Christ has no respect for earthly authority, that Christ has no respect for an earthly elite. The Christ sees the reality that all came from the same source, and all have the potential to rise. When you put on the mind of Christ, there is no superiority or inferiority. There is no high or low. All are one in Christ, in that Christ mind. *That* was the message that I actually preached.

Look at what the Catholic church did with it. Look how, instead of seeing me as an example, it elevated me to be something that nobody could emulate. Ask yourself why this happened. The answer is of course simple. The power elite does not want anyone to do what I did. Anyone who does what I did cannot be controlled by the power elite, as I could not be controlled.

The world could have been very different

Just look with this perspective at the historical developments of the past 2,000 years. Just consider if it was *that* message that had been passed on from the beginning. Just consider if that message had been spread, if people had heeded it, taking it seriously and if a critical mass of people had put on that mind of Christ. Where would the world be today if that had happened?

I can tell you that the world would have been so different that most people cannot even imagine it. First of all, as you discussed earlier, if a critical mass of people had applied the teachings I gave, had put on that mind of Christ, had reconnected to the kingdom of God within them, then by now there would not have been war on earth. The First and the Second World Wars could have been avoided if enough people had put on the mind of Christ. Then, the power elite, the serpents, could not have misled people into starting these massive wars and committing these massive atrocities. It simply could not have happened because people would not have submitted to the elite. They would not have believed in the lies and the illusions of the elite that made it seem like these wars were beneficial, necessary or unavoidable.

Just consider how many people today look at war as something that just happens. Nobody really understands why. It just happens, or maybe it is always those other bad people who are creating war, and we have to fight them to avoid them destroying us. How many people understand that war is not natural, it is not in human nature? It is artificially created by the power elite. How many people understand the duality consciousness and how the power elite uses the duality consciousness to seduce people into going to war and supporting their wars?

This could have been understood through the mind of Christ in these past 2,000 years. It is something that can be understood very quickly as more and more people raise their consciousness, whether they follow this teaching, that teaching or the next teaching. Millions of people around the world are raising their consciousness in these years and decades. We are getting close to that point where people can begin to break through and see that war is not a natural occurrence. It is not in human nature to create war. It is only something that can happen when people are manipulated by those who are in a specific state of consciousness and have absolutely no empathy, no sense of essential humanity, and they do not care how many millions of people are killed as long as they can further whatever they see as their end.

When people see that these emperors of war have nothing on, then they will also see that these justifications that are given have no reality to them whatsoever. So, in a sense, you could say that my teachings were entirely anti-war. I am not saying that I consciously in my outer mind was able to see the potential for what could happen over these 2,000 years when I was embodiment. Before I came into embodiment, I was of course in councils with the ascended masters that I was working with. They very clearly showed me the potential for what could happen at the end of the Piscean Age if people did not get that message that there is an alternative to the relativistic definition of good and evil. If people continued to think that there were those in embodiment who are as gods, who can define good and evil, and that there are many more who can recognize these gods as they walk among them, then what could happen was indeed what *has* happened.

Even worse things could have happened. There could have been a more severe war, a war that would have ended all wars because it would have ended humanity as we know it through nuclear weapons. We could say that the worst has been avoided, but the highest potential is very, very far from having been manifest.

The Christ potential today

Yet, even saying this, you recognize that this does not mean that I consider these last 2,000 years to be a complete failure. Far from it. The reason for this is very simple. The Christ consciousness wants to raise people up, to see beyond the dualistic vision. As we have said, this can happen in two ways: It can happen by people connecting to the Christ within themselves, often helped by an external teacher or teaching, or it can happen through the School of Hard Knocks. It can happen through direct experience. What we can say is that the inner process of people attaining Christhood did not come to fruition, at least not in sufficient numbers. That is why you have seen the wars. But precisely because you have seen all of these atrocities, there is, both on the individual level and in the collective consciousness, that very clear, undeniable vision of how bad things can go.

It is a tension that has been building in the collective consciousness and therefore, again, with you raising your consciousness, with you making the calls, there can be that breakthrough where people begin to see the lesson that they were meant to see during the Piscean Age. They can come to see it very quickly so that, instead of a gradual shift of consciousness, there can be a faster shift of consciousness. People begin to see precisely that it is not in human nature to create war. It is only certain people, a certain class of people, that create war. Those kinds of people are in a special state of consciousness. You may call it narcissist, psychopath, sociopath, whatever there may be, but they are in a special state of consciousness, and most human beings are not anywhere near that state of consciousness. It is only because people can be seduced by these very subtle, very persuasive lies, the lie that there is always some epic cause that must be fulfilled in order to avoid an epic calamity. In order to avoid this calamity that would be so bad, we have to kill those people who are opposing God's work. The calamity of killing those people is less than the calamity that would ensue if they continue to do their evil deeds.

It is very close that a very large number of people can come to see the fallacy of this and see how this pattern has repeated itself so many times. Even going into modern times, even going into how George Bush invaded

Iraq in order to avoid some epic evil, some "axis of evil," and spread free-dom and democracy through force. Very quickly people can come to see this and see the hollowness of this serpentine lie. When people begin to see this and see that it is the elite that has created war, then that will be a major step towards building this determination in people that says: "We have to do something about elitism. We have to free ourselves from this elite that has created war after war, atrocity after atrocity. We have to look at ourselves and see how we were seduced into believing not only what was the agenda of the elite, but even believing in the necessity, the legitimacy, perhaps even the authority, of such an elite. Why were we seduced into thinking that we cannot know a higher truth on our own, but that we need an elite to define for us what is good and evil? Why do we need to follow those who think they are gods on earth and can define good and evil? Why do we think that we can recognize them and should follow them? Why should we believe that killing other people is doing God's work, or even the work of Christ?"

There are millions of people who have been embodied in Christian societies for many, many lifetimes. Many have been embodied almost continuously throughout the Piscean Age. They have experienced directly how either they were persecuted and killed by Christians in the crusades, the witch hunts, the Inquisition and so on. Or they were pulled into either performing these acts, or at least supporting them. Again, the fallen beings have no willingness to look at themselves, to tune in to anything. A fallen being can go through an embodiment where it kills thousands of people, not necessarily personally, but is instrumental in the killing of thousands or millions of people, and it can go out of embodiment without having any need or willingness to look at itself, to evaluate itself. But human beings who are not fallen cannot participate in the killing of others (whether they do it themselves or they support it) without reflecting on it after they go out of embodiment.

When you have done this for a certain number of lifetimes, you come into your next embodiment with an inner sense that this just is not right. You may come in with a sense of being very negative towards the religion, such as Christianity, that seduced you into thinking this was right. These are the people who are right now in the state of consciousness where they could begin to consciously acknowledge what they had learned before they came into this embodiment. They can begin to connect to what they already know in their hearts and see why this was such a lie that they have come to believe in. They can see why elitism is based on a fundamental lie, why war is based on a fundamental lie, why war never serves that epic cause because of course God never wanted war. God never created war. God never encouraged people to go to war. And the real God never told the Israelites to go into the Promised Land and commit genocide.

Jesus was entirely non-violent

These are the false gods, whether they are in or out of embodiment, who are in the fallen consciousness. You can look at the teachings of Christ, and many people are ready to have that sudden switch where it is not a matter of argumentation. It is not even a matter of the reasoning process that I have given in this release. It is a matter of them making a switch and they suddenly see: "But the teachings of Jesus were entirely non-violent. It is a complete illusion and manipulation that his teachings were used to justify all of this violence over these many centuries." It can suddenly click, and it can hit them as if the scales fall from their eyes. They can have an experience much like Paul on the road to Damascus where they suddenly see this. It is beyond argumentation. It is not a matter of convincing them. Their eyes are opened and they see the fallacy. But they also see beyond it and see that it is not just a matter of criticizing or tearing down the Christian churches. It is a matter of recognizing that there is a group of people, the power elite, that was behind this and that they used a specific state of consciousness to make this seem like something that was approved by Christ.

This is the real problem on earth. It is this very consciousness that we need to free ourselves from. That is what the mission of Jesus was all about, and that is what the Christ consciousness is all about, us seeing through the serpentine lies and realizing that there is a higher reality. This is what I preached 2,000 years ago, not as clearly as I have done today, whether in this release or many of my other dictations and books through this messenger and even previous messengers. But it was preached as it could be done, given the level of the collective consciousness as it was 2,000 years ago.

What is the real tragedy of the creation of the Catholic church? It was that they took the teaching that was released back then, based on the state of the collective consciousness as it was, and they froze it in time. Well, actually they also distorted it. It would have been better if they had just frozen it as it was given, but they also distorted it. Even freezing it in time is limiting what the message can do because naturally, as the collective consciousness is raised, more can be given. Where can that more come from? Well, where did the original teachings come from? They came from the mind of Christ individualized in me. As I ascended, I could have continued to give new and more advanced perspectives and teachings through that mind of Christ for those who were able to use the teachings to open themselves up to it. There could have been a process of continual progressive revelation directly from me to various people over these past 2,000 years.

The message of Christ is always outside the elite

How could that process have happened? How did I give my teachings 2,000 years ago? Was I born into one of the important families? Was I accepted as one of the Jewish leaders? Did I stand inside the temple and give my message? No, I stood outside of the elite and gave my message. So who could have received my progressive revelation over these past 2,000 years? Well, certainly not the elite. Where was the elite? They were the leaders of all of the Christian churches, the Catholic church and all of the others. Who would have been able in those churches to receive the progressive revelation of Jesus Christ? None. Because they were not willing. So where could I have given it? Well, only outside, but what did the power elite do? Well, first of all they distorted the teaching so none dared follow my example, or very few. Then, they set up a power apparatus that would instantly kill anybody who dared to speak the truth of Christ. Look at the many women who were tuned in to a higher reality, who had a more intuitive vision but were labeled and burned as witches. There could have been a feminist revolution in the 1400s and 1500s if it had not been for the witch hunts, but they did everything they could to squash it.

This cannot and will not happen anymore. We have passed the point where they can suppress the true teachings of Christ. They will be given through this messenger, through many other people who can receive elements of the teaching, ideas of the teaching. You who are ascended master students should all count yourselves among these people. This does not mean you have to do what the messenger is doing and take a dictation like this. But you should all consider that you can tune in to the mind of Christ. You can put on the mind of Christ, and you can receive ideas directly from me or another ascended master.

You can share those ideas, even often without having to say where they came from. You can share the ideas and let the ideas do their work. Where can you do this? You may have heard of this recent development called the Internet. What a tool! What a tool for sharing your presence. Look what the messenger has said: He has overcome this personal ambition of wanting to change others. In a sense, at the higher levels of Christhood you are not seeking to change other people. You are just giving them an alternative to the serpentine state of consciousness. You are all able to do this. I am not talking to just those of you who are here, but anybody who has sincerely studied ascended master teachings or any other valid spiritual teaching. You are all able to do this.

I acknowledge that when I stood there at the wedding at Cana, I hesitated. I felt paralyzed. I acknowledge that many of you feel that too. But it is because you still have some separate selves that go all the way back to your primal self, where you, as Nada coined the phrase, were hammered down by the fallen beings. Have we not attempted to give you tools and teachings so you can free yourself from that primal self and therefore come to the point where you do not need Mother Mary to push you forward: "They have no wine." "What have I to do with you, woman? Do you think I am a bartender?" You can overcome that hesitancy when you overcome that need to feel validated, to not be rejected, to produce some kind of result. You can realize that what you are really on this planet for is to share yourself, share who you are, share your Presence. You are not trying to change other people. You are just showing and telling them how you have changed yourself, and that is enough. That is enough. It will work for some people. As Gautama realized, *some* will understand. *Some* will understand.

How do you know that is true? Have *you* not understood? If *you* can understand, why not others? You are not really *that* smart, my beloved.

9 | INVOKING AWARENESS OF HOW THE ELITE CREATES WAR (PART 1)

In the name of the I AM THAT I AM, Jesus Christ, I use the authority that I have as a being in embodiment on earth to call upon Jesus to reinforce my calls and use my chakras to project the statements in this invocation into the collective consciousness and awaken people to the methods used by the elite to create wars. Awaken people to the reality that we are spiritual beings and that we can co-create a new future by working with the ascended masters. I especially call for …

[Make your own calls here.]

Part 1

1. Jesus, shatter the energetic matrix that prevents people from seeing how Christianity has been used by the power elite to further the cause of elitism.

O Jesus, blessed brother mine,
I walk the path that you outline,

a great example to us all,
I follow now your inner call.

**O Jesus, let the Fire of Joy,
consume the devil's subtle ploy,
transfigured is our planet earth,
the golden age is given birth.**

2. Jesus, shatter the energetic matrix that prevents people from seeing that the Garden of Eden is a symbol for the state that humankind was in before the descent into the consciousness of duality.

O Jesus, open inner sight,
the ego wants to prove it's right,
but this I will no longer do,
I want to be all one with you.

**O Jesus, let the Fire of Joy,
consume the devil's subtle ploy,
transfigured is our planet earth,
the golden age is given birth.**

3. Jesus, shatter the energetic matrix that prevents people from seeing that what caused Adam and Eve to fall below the innocence of the non-dualistic state of consciousness, and fall into the dualistic state of consciousness, was the serpent.

O Jesus, I now clearly see,
the Key of Knowledge given me,
my Christ self I hereby embrace,
as you fill up my inner space.

**O Jesus, let the Fire of Joy,
consume the devil's subtle ploy,
transfigured is our planet earth,
the golden age is given birth.**

4. Jesus, shatter the energetic matrix that prevents people from seeing that the serpent is a symbol for the power elite.

O Jesus, show me serpent's lie,
expose the beam in my own eye,
as Christ discernment you me give,
in oneness I forever live.

O Jesus, let the Fire of Joy,
consume the devil's subtle ploy,
transfigured is our planet earth,
the golden age is given birth.

5. Jesus, shatter the energetic matrix that prevents people from seeing that it is not natural, it is not in human nature, for people to create war. People have been tricked into going to war and killing each other, but it has always happened because they were misled by a power elite.

O Jesus, I am truly meek,
and thus I turn the other cheek,
when the accuser attacks me,
I go within and merge with thee.

O Jesus, let the Fire of Joy,
consume the devil's subtle ploy,
transfigured is our planet earth,
the golden age is given birth.

6. Jesus, shatter the energetic matrix that prevents people from seeing that the Garden of Eden was not a heavenly realm where the supreme God of the universe walked and talked with Adam and Eve.

O Jesus, ego I let die,
surrender ev'ry earthly tie,
the dead can bury what is dead,
I choose to walk with you instead.

O Jesus, let the Fire of Joy,
consume the devil's subtle ploy,
transfigured is our planet earth,
the golden age is given birth.

7. Jesus, shatter the energetic matrix that prevents people from seeing that it was a symbol for a state of consciousness in which humankind had direct contact with our spiritual teachers, because we were not in duality. We had not become as gods, defining what is good and evil.

O Jesus, help me rise above,
the devil's test through higher love,
show me separate self unreal,
my formless self you do reveal.

O Jesus, let the Fire of Joy,
consume the devil's subtle ploy,
transfigured is our planet earth,
the golden age is given birth.

8. Jesus, shatter the energetic matrix that prevents people from seeing that God did not create the serpent because in a more specific sense, the serpent is a symbol for the dualistic state of consciousness.

O Jesus, what is that to me,
I just let go and follow thee,
with this I do pass ev'ry test,
to find with you eternal rest.

O Jesus, let the Fire of Joy,
consume the devil's subtle ploy,
transfigured is our planet earth,
the golden age is given birth.

9. Jesus, shatter the energetic matrix that prevents people from seeing that this is a state of consciousness where we have separated ourselves from our source, our higher selves. This gives rise to the illusion that we are separated from God, separated from other people.

O Jesus, fiery master mine,
my heart now melting into thine,
I love with heart and mind and soul,
the God who is my highest goal.

**O Jesus, let the Fire of Joy,
consume the devil's subtle ploy,
transfigured is our planet earth,
the golden age is given birth.**

Part 2

1. Jesus, shatter the energetic matrix that prevents people from seeing that the separation from our source means we do not have a frame of reference for knowing a truth, a reality that is universal, not individualized, not subjectivized.

O Jesus, blessed brother mine,
I walk the path that you outline,
a great example to us all,
I follow now your inner call.

**O Jesus, let the Fire of Joy,
consume the devil's subtle ploy,
transfigured is our planet earth,
the golden age is given birth.**

2. Jesus, shatter the energetic matrix that prevents people from seeing that when we lose that frame of reference, we so easily become seduced by the serpentine state of mind into thinking that we can define what is good and evil based on our current state of consciousness.

O Jesus, open inner sight,
the ego wants to prove it's right,
but this I will no longer do,
I want to be all one with you.

**O Jesus, let the Fire of Joy,
consume the devil's subtle ploy,
transfigured is our planet earth,
the golden age is given birth.**

3. Jesus, shatter the energetic matrix that prevents people from seeing that we think that we are capable of defining what is good and evil internally in our current state of consciousness, without having that frame of reference from something that is beyond our state of consciousness.

O Jesus, I now clearly see,
the Key of Knowledge given me,
my Christ self I hereby embrace,
as you fill up my inner space.

**O Jesus, let the Fire of Joy,
consume the devil's subtle ploy,
transfigured is our planet earth,
the golden age is given birth.**

4. Jesus, shatter the energetic matrix that prevents people from seeing that this is what the narcissistic beings have been doing since they fell into duality. They have seduced most human beings into believing in this very lie.

O Jesus, show me serpent's lie,
expose the beam in my own eye,
as Christ discernment you me give,
in oneness I forever live.

**O Jesus, let the Fire of Joy,
consume the devil's subtle ploy,
transfigured is our planet earth,
the golden age is given birth.**

5. Jesus, shatter the energetic matrix that prevents people from seeing that so many people believe that someone on earth, some earthly authority, is capable of defining good and evil, and they are able to recognize that authority.

O Jesus, I am truly meek,
and thus I turn the other cheek,
when the accuser attacks me,
I go within and merge with thee.

**O Jesus, let the Fire of Joy,
consume the devil's subtle ploy,
transfigured is our planet earth,
the golden age is given birth.**

6. Jesus, shatter the energetic matrix that prevents people from seeing that the very essence of what you came to do was to show people that there is an alternative to the serpentine state of mind, the dualistic state of consciousness, where we define good and evil and our definition is entirely relative and subjective.

O Jesus, ego I let die,
surrender ev'ry earthly tie,
the dead can bury what is dead,
I choose to walk with you instead.

**O Jesus, let the Fire of Joy,
consume the devil's subtle ploy,
transfigured is our planet earth,
the golden age is given birth.**

7. Jesus, shatter the energetic matrix that prevents people from seeing that we define good and evil and we, or at least the authority figure we follow, elevate it to the status of being absolute—absolute truth and objective truth that cannot or should not be gainsaid. You came to free people from this state of consciousness.

O Jesus, help me rise above,
the devil's test through higher love,
show me separate self unreal,
my formless self you do reveal.

**O Jesus, let the Fire of Joy,
consume the devil's subtle ploy,
transfigured is our planet earth,
the golden age is given birth.**

8. Jesus, shatter the energetic matrix that prevents people from seeing that you made certain statements that were calculated to shock people out of

the serpentine mindset, so they could question what they had taken for granted.

> O Jesus, what is that to me,
> I just let go and follow thee,
> with this I do pass ev'ry test,
> to find with you eternal rest.

> **O Jesus, let the Fire of Joy,**
> **consume the devil's subtle ploy,**
> **transfigured is our planet earth,**
> **the golden age is given birth.**

9. Jesus, shatter the energetic matrix that prevents people from seeing that you also gave us an example by demonstrating that there is a higher state of consciousness, which is the Christ consciousness that allows us to see beyond the serpentine illusions.

> O Jesus, fiery master mine,
> my heart now melting into thine,
> I love with heart and mind and soul,
> the God who is my highest goal.

> **O Jesus, let the Fire of Joy,**
> **consume the devil's subtle ploy,**
> **transfigured is our planet earth,**
> **the golden age is given birth.**

Part 3

1. Jesus, shatter the energetic matrix that prevents people from seeing that through the Christ consciousness we can see through the serpentine logic, see the cognitive dissonance, the contradictions, the unanswered questions of the serpentine logic. We can reach for a frame of reference that is beyond our own mind, but even beyond the serpentine mind and the collective mind of humankind.

O Jesus, blessed brother mine,
I walk the path that you outline,
a great example to us all,
I follow now your inner call.

O Jesus, let the Fire of Joy,
consume the devil's subtle ploy,
transfigured is our planet earth,
the golden age is given birth.

2. Jesus, shatter the energetic matrix that prevents people from seeing that you came to offer us a way out of duality. You offered to set us free or give us the tools that could set us free from the serpents who have misled humanity.

O Jesus, open inner sight,
the ego wants to prove it's right,
but this I will no longer do,
I want to be all one with you.

O Jesus, let the Fire of Joy,
consume the devil's subtle ploy,
transfigured is our planet earth,
the golden age is given birth.

3. Jesus, shatter the energetic matrix that prevents people from seeing that the serpents are the very ones who form the power elite and have formed it in all eras since they first came here.

O Jesus, I now clearly see,
the Key of Knowledge given me,
my Christ self I hereby embrace,
as you fill up my inner space.

O Jesus, let the Fire of Joy,
consume the devil's subtle ploy,
transfigured is our planet earth,
the golden age is given birth.

4. Jesus, shatter the energetic matrix that prevents people from seeing that what has been lost in the process of creating Christianity, and has remained lost to this day by most Christian churches, is that the essence of your mission was anti-elitist.

O Jesus, show me serpent's lie,
expose the beam in my own eye,
as Christ discernment you me give,
in oneness I forever live.

**O Jesus, let the Fire of Joy,
consume the devil's subtle ploy,
transfigured is our planet earth,
the golden age is given birth.**

5. Jesus, shatter the energetic matrix that prevents people from seeing that you came to set people free from the elite, ultimately of the fallen beings, the real serpents, but also of all who were part of the power elite. These are the people who had been seduced by the serpents into thinking that they had some special quality that allowed them to be the leaders of the people because they knew better than the people.

O Jesus, I am truly meek,
and thus I turn the other cheek,
when the accuser attacks me,
I go within and merge with thee.

**O Jesus, let the Fire of Joy,
consume the devil's subtle ploy,
transfigured is our planet earth,
the golden age is given birth.**

6. Jesus, shatter the energetic matrix that prevents people from seeing that there was a clear division in the society of Israel at your time, a clear division between those who knew or thought they knew, namely, the religious leaders of various groups, and then the people.

O Jesus, ego I let die,
surrender ev'ry earthly tie,

the dead can bury what is dead,
I choose to walk with you instead.

O Jesus, let the Fire of Joy,
consume the devil's subtle ploy,
transfigured is our planet earth,
the golden age is given birth.

7. Jesus, shatter the energetic matrix that prevents people from seeing that it was considered that the people did not know and could not know what was true, that is why they needed the leaders. The power elite had you killed when you started to challenge this illusion.

O Jesus, help me rise above,
the devil's test through higher love,
show me separate self unreal,
my formless self you do reveal.

O Jesus, let the Fire of Joy,
consume the devil's subtle ploy,
transfigured is our planet earth,
the golden age is given birth.

8. Jesus, shatter the energetic matrix that prevents people from seeing that you became a threat by offering people a frame of reference where they could find the kingdom of God within them, and they themselves could attain that discernment of Christ, that mind of Christ.

O Jesus, what is that to me,
I just let go and follow thee,
with this I do pass ev'ry test,
to find with you eternal rest.

O Jesus, let the Fire of Joy,
consume the devil's subtle ploy,
transfigured is our planet earth,
the golden age is given birth.

9. Jesus, shatter the energetic matrix that prevents people from seeing that you came to show us that we can put on the mind of Christ and see through the lies that the elite is using to keep us in bondage. This was the very essence of your mission, and there is no Christian church that preaches that message.

O Jesus, fiery master mine,
my heart now melting into thine,
I love with heart and mind and soul,
the God who is my highest goal.

**O Jesus, let the Fire of Joy,
consume the devil's subtle ploy,
transfigured is our planet earth,
the golden age is given birth.**

Part 4

1. Jesus, shatter the energetic matrix that prevents people from seeing that the fallen beings did to you what they have done to many others who spoke a higher perspective, a higher truth. They killed you.

O Jesus, blessed brother mine,
I walk the path that you outline,
a great example to us all,
I follow now your inner call.

**O Jesus, let the Fire of Joy,
consume the devil's subtle ploy,
transfigured is our planet earth,
the golden age is given birth.**

2. Jesus, shatter the energetic matrix that prevents people from seeing that it is characteristic of the power elite that when someone takes a stand for truth or brings forth a higher perspective, they will first attempt to ignore the person and hope that he or she does not gain any followers. If that fails, they will kill that person, thinking this will destroy the threat.

O Jesus, open inner sight,
the ego wants to prove it's right,
but this I will no longer do,
I want to be all one with you.

**O Jesus, let the Fire of Joy,
consume the devil's subtle ploy,
transfigured is our planet earth,
the golden age is given birth.**

3. Jesus, shatter the energetic matrix that prevents people from seeing that as more people started following your teachings, there emerged a more coherent Christian movement. This became seen as the threat by the power elite of the Roman Empire and led to the persecution of Christians.

O Jesus, I now clearly see,
the Key of Knowledge given me,
my Christ self I hereby embrace,
as you fill up my inner space.

**O Jesus, let the Fire of Joy,
consume the devil's subtle ploy,
transfigured is our planet earth,
the golden age is given birth.**

4. Jesus, shatter the energetic matrix that prevents people from seeing that there came a point where some among the power elite realized that it was difficult to kill all of the Christians. They switched their strategy as they have done in many other cases. They used the motto: "If you can't beat them, join them."

O Jesus, show me serpent's lie,
expose the beam in my own eye,
as Christ discernment you me give,
in oneness I forever live.

**O Jesus, let the Fire of Joy,
consume the devil's subtle ploy,**

transfigured is our planet earth,
the golden age is given birth.

5. Jesus, shatter the energetic matrix that prevents people from seeing that
the fallen beings in the higher octaves used their tool, the emperor Constantine, to turn Christianity into the state religion of the Roman Empire.
This was from the very beginning an entirely political move.

O Jesus, I am truly meek,
and thus I turn the other cheek,
when the accuser attacks me,
I go within and merge with thee.

O Jesus, let the Fire of Joy,
consume the devil's subtle ploy,
transfigured is our planet earth,
the golden age is given birth.

6. Jesus, shatter the energetic matrix that prevents people from seeing that
in Constantine's mind, it was his way of trying to reestablish control over
the Roman Empire by unifying the people in a religion that was more
appealing than the old religion and the old gods.

O Jesus, ego I let die,
surrender ev'ry earthly tie,
the dead can bury what is dead,
I choose to walk with you instead.

O Jesus, let the Fire of Joy,
consume the devil's subtle ploy,
transfigured is our planet earth,
the golden age is given birth.

7. Jesus, shatter the energetic matrix that prevents people from seeing that
for this purpose, he needed a religion with a strong God and a strong
prophet. There was created this idolatrous version of Christianity that elevated Christianity to promoting the superior God of the universe, the one
and only God.

O Jesus, help me rise above,
the devil's test through higher love,
show me separate self unreal,
my formless self you do reveal.

O Jesus, let the Fire of Joy,
consume the devil's subtle ploy,
transfigured is our planet earth,
the golden age is given birth.

8. Jesus, shatter the energetic matrix that prevents people from seeing that they also elevated you to being the Son of God. They even said you were not created, you had always existed because you were of the same substance as the Father.

O Jesus, what is that to me,
I just let go and follow thee,
with this I do pass ev'ry test,
to find with you eternal rest.

O Jesus, let the Fire of Joy,
consume the devil's subtle ploy,
transfigured is our planet earth,
the golden age is given birth.

9. Jesus, shatter the energetic matrix that prevents people from seeing that the purpose was to elevate you to a status that gave the Romans the illusion that you could do for them what the old gods could not do because they were inferior to you.

O Jesus, fiery master mine,
my heart now melting into thine,
I love with heart and mind and soul,
the God who is my highest goal.

O Jesus, let the Fire of Joy,
consume the devil's subtle ploy,
transfigured is our planet earth,
the golden age is given birth.

Part 5

1. Jesus, shatter the energetic matrix that prevents people from seeing that the collective consciousness was so low that people had gods because they wanted them to do something practical for them in daily life.

> O Jesus, blessed brother mine,
> I walk the path that you outline,
> a great example to us all,
> I follow now your inner call.

> **O Jesus, let the Fire of Joy,**
> **consume the devil's subtle ploy,**
> **transfigured is our planet earth,**
> **the golden age is given birth.**

2. Jesus, shatter the energetic matrix that prevents people from seeing that it was not about raising consciousness or being saved. It was about having a wish-fulfilling God, a kind of Santa Claus, that could do what people needed in everyday life.

> O Jesus, open inner sight,
> the ego wants to prove it's right,
> but this I will no longer do,
> I want to be all one with you.

> **O Jesus, let the Fire of Joy,**
> **consume the devil's subtle ploy,**
> **transfigured is our planet earth,**
> **the golden age is given birth.**

3. Jesus, shatter the energetic matrix that prevents people from seeing that the effect was that whereas the early Christian religion had been somewhat diversified, the Catholic church from the very beginning was an entirely elitist institution.

> O Jesus, I now clearly see,
> the Key of Knowledge given me,

my Christ self I hereby embrace,
as you fill up my inner space.

**O Jesus, let the Fire of Joy,
consume the devil's subtle ploy,
transfigured is our planet earth,
the golden age is given birth.**

4. Jesus, shatter the energetic matrix that prevents people from seeing that for the Catholic church, it was never about raising the whole, about raising all of the people to a higher state of consciousness. It was always about creating a society that had a clear division between the ruling elite and all of the people who were just followers.

O Jesus, show me serpent's lie,
expose the beam in my own eye,
as Christ discernment you me give,
in oneness I forever live.

**O Jesus, let the Fire of Joy,
consume the devil's subtle ploy,
transfigured is our planet earth,
the golden age is given birth.**

5. Jesus, shatter the energetic matrix that prevents people from seeing that to the Catholic church, people were not just followers. They were sinners by nature through the original sin of Adam and Eve.

O Jesus, I am truly meek,
and thus I turn the other cheek,
when the accuser attacks me,
I go within and merge with thee.

**O Jesus, let the Fire of Joy,
consume the devil's subtle ploy,
transfigured is our planet earth,
the golden age is given birth.**

6. Jesus, shatter the energetic matrix that prevents people from seeing that this guilt trip has continued to be reinforced by the Catholic church ever since. Hardly any Protestant or other non-Catholic church has thoroughly challenged this guilt trip.

O Jesus, ego I let die,
surrender ev'ry earthly tie,
the dead can bury what is dead,
I choose to walk with you instead.

O Jesus, let the Fire of Joy,
consume the devil's subtle ploy,
transfigured is our planet earth,
the golden age is given birth.

7. Jesus, shatter the energetic matrix that prevents people from seeing that from the very beginning, the Catholic church was an entirely elitist institution. It reinforced the already existing mindset that there is an elite that rules and a majority that follows or that submits to the rule.

O Jesus, help me rise above,
the devil's test through higher love,
show me separate self unreal,
my formless self you do reveal.

O Jesus, let the Fire of Joy,
consume the devil's subtle ploy,
transfigured is our planet earth,
the golden age is given birth.

8. Jesus, shatter the energetic matrix that prevents people from seeing that this was not what you preached. You preached that the kingdom of God is within us—all of us. We all have the potential to put on the mind of Christ.

O Jesus, what is that to me,
I just let go and follow thee,
with this I do pass ev'ry test,
to find with you eternal rest.

O Jesus, let the Fire of Joy,
consume the devil's subtle ploy,
transfigured is our planet earth,
the golden age is given birth.

9. Jesus, shatter the energetic matrix that prevents people from seeing that when we put on the mind of Christ, we do not need an authority on earth to tell us what to do, what to believe, what we can know and what we cannot know. We have access to a source that is beyond earth.

O Jesus, fiery master mine,
my heart now melting into thine,
I love with heart and mind and soul,
the God who is my highest goal.

O Jesus, let the Fire of Joy,
consume the devil's subtle ploy,
transfigured is our planet earth,
the golden age is given birth.

Sealing

In the name of the I AM THAT I AM, I accept that Archangel Michael, Astrea and Shiva form an impenetrable shield around myself and all constructive people, sealing us from all fear-based energies in all four octaves. I accept that the Light of God is consuming and transforming all fear-based energies that make up the dark forces working against ending the era of elitism on earth!

10 | INVOKING AWARENESS OF HOW THE ELITE CREATES WAR (PART 2)

In the name of the I AM THAT I AM, Jesus Christ, I use the authority that I have as a being in embodiment on earth to call upon Jesus to reinforce my calls and use my chakras to project the statements in this invocation into the collective consciousness and awaken people to the methods used by the elite to create wars. Awaken people to the reality that we are spiritual beings and that we can co-create a new future by working with the ascended masters. I especially call for …

[Make your own calls here.]

Part 1

1. Jesus, shatter the energetic matrix that prevents people from seeing that the miracle of the Christ consciousness is that the Christ can be born in all people. That is the importance of the symbolism that you were born in a manger, born to humble people. You were not born as part of the elite.

O Jesus, blessed brother mine,
I walk the path that you outline,
a great example to us all,
I follow now your inner call.

O Jesus, let the Fire of Joy,
consume the devil's subtle ploy,
transfigured is our planet earth,
the golden age is given birth.

2. Jesus, shatter the energetic matrix that prevents people from seeing that many people in the elite rejected you precisely because of your humble birth. This is a symbol for the fact that the Christ, the Christ consciousness, can be born in all people because all people have the potential to put on the mind of Christ.

O Jesus, open inner sight,
the ego wants to prove it's right,
but this I will no longer do,
I want to be all one with you.

O Jesus, let the Fire of Joy,
consume the devil's subtle ploy,
transfigured is our planet earth,
the golden age is given birth.

3. Jesus, shatter the energetic matrix that prevents people from seeing that when a critical mass of people put on the mind of Christ, why do we need an elite to tell us what is true or what is good? Why do we need an earthly authority when we have the authority that is beyond earth, namely the Christ mind?

O Jesus, I now clearly see,
the Key of Knowledge given me,
my Christ self I hereby embrace,
as you fill up my inner space.

O Jesus, let the Fire of Joy,
consume the devil's subtle ploy,

transfigured is our planet earth,
the golden age is given birth.

4. Jesus, shatter the energetic matrix that prevents people from seeing that the question is what we submit to: an authority on earth, or an authority beyond earth, the mind of Christ? The mind of the serpent or the mind of Christ. Who is our master?

O Jesus, show me serpent's lie,
expose the beam in my own eye,
as Christ discernment you me give,
in oneness I forever live.

O Jesus, let the Fire of Joy,
consume the devil's subtle ploy,
transfigured is our planet earth,
the golden age is given birth.

5. Jesus, shatter the energetic matrix that prevents people from seeing that you many times challenged the power elite of your time. "Ye are of your father the devil." "Scribes and Pharisees, hypocrites."

O Jesus, I am truly meek,
and thus I turn the other cheek,
when the accuser attacks me,
I go within and merge with thee.

O Jesus, let the Fire of Joy,
consume the devil's subtle ploy,
transfigured is our planet earth,
the golden age is given birth.

6. Jesus, shatter the energetic matrix that prevents people from seeing that you talked about those who appear beautiful outwardly, but inwardly they are whitened sepulchers, filled with dead men's bones.

O Jesus, ego I let die,
surrender ev'ry earthly tie,

the dead can bury what is dead,
I choose to walk with you instead.

O Jesus, let the Fire of Joy,
consume the devil's subtle ploy,
transfigured is our planet earth,
the golden age is given birth.

7. Jesus, shatter the energetic matrix that prevents people from seeing that many of your statements were meant to provoke and shock people into realizing that the Christ has no respect for earthly authority, that Christ has no respect for an earthly elite.

O Jesus, help me rise above,
the devil's test through higher love,
show me separate self unreal,
my formless self you do reveal.

O Jesus, let the Fire of Joy,
consume the devil's subtle ploy,
transfigured is our planet earth,
the golden age is given birth.

8. Jesus, shatter the energetic matrix that prevents people from seeing that the Christ sees the reality that all came from the same source, and all have the potential to rise. When we put on the mind of Christ, there is no superiority or inferiority. There is no high or low. All are one in Christ, in that Christ mind. This was the message that you actually preached.

O Jesus, what is that to me,
I just let go and follow thee,
with this I do pass ev'ry test,
to find with you eternal rest.

O Jesus, let the Fire of Joy,
consume the devil's subtle ploy,
transfigured is our planet earth,
the golden age is given birth.

9. Jesus, shatter the energetic matrix that prevents people from seeing that instead of seeing you as an example, the Catholic church elevated you to be something that nobody could emulate. The power elite does not want anyone to do what you did. Anyone who does what you did cannot be controlled by the power elite, as you could not be controlled.

> O Jesus, fiery master mine,
> my heart now melting into thine,
> I love with heart and mind and soul,
> the God who is my highest goal.

> **O Jesus, let the Fire of Joy,**
> **consume the devil's subtle ploy,**
> **transfigured is our planet earth,**
> **the golden age is given birth.**

Part 2

1. Jesus, shatter the energetic matrix that prevents people from seeing that if your true message had been passed on from the beginning, if people had heeded it, if a critical mass of people had put on that mind of Christ, the world would have been so different that most people cannot even imagine it.

> O Jesus, blessed brother mine,
> I walk the path that you outline,
> a great example to us all,
> I follow now your inner call.

> **O Jesus, let the Fire of Joy,**
> **consume the devil's subtle ploy,**
> **transfigured is our planet earth,**
> **the golden age is given birth.**

2. Jesus, shatter the energetic matrix that prevents people from seeing that if a critical mass of people had applied the teachings you gave and put on that mind of Christ, by now there would not have been war on earth.

O Jesus, open inner sight,
the ego wants to prove it's right,
but this I will no longer do,
I want to be all one with you.

**O Jesus, let the Fire of Joy,
consume the devil's subtle ploy,
transfigured is our planet earth,
the golden age is given birth.**

3. Jesus, shatter the energetic matrix that prevents people from seeing that
the First and the Second World Wars could have been avoided if enough
people had put on the mind of Christ.

O Jesus, I now clearly see,
the Key of Knowledge given me,
my Christ self I hereby embrace,
as you fill up my inner space.

**O Jesus, let the Fire of Joy,
consume the devil's subtle ploy,
transfigured is our planet earth,
the golden age is given birth.**

4. Jesus, shatter the energetic matrix that prevents people from seeing that
the power elite, the serpents, could not have misled people into starting
these massive wars and committing these massive atrocities.

O Jesus, show me serpent's lie,
expose the beam in my own eye,
as Christ discernment you me give,
in oneness I forever live.

**O Jesus, let the Fire of Joy,
consume the devil's subtle ploy,
transfigured is our planet earth,
the golden age is given birth.**

5. Jesus, shatter the energetic matrix that prevents people from seeing that people would not have submitted to the elite. They would not have believed in the lies and the illusions of the elite that made it seem like these wars were beneficial, necessary or unavoidable.

> O Jesus, I am truly meek,
> and thus I turn the other cheek,
> when the accuser attacks me,
> I go within and merge with thee.

> **O Jesus, let the Fire of Joy,**
> **consume the devil's subtle ploy,**
> **transfigured is our planet earth,**
> **the golden age is given birth.**

6. Jesus, shatter the energetic matrix that prevents people from seeing that too many look at war as something that just happens. Nobody really understands why. It just happens, or maybe it is always those other bad people who are creating war, and we have to fight them to avoid them destroying us.

> O Jesus, ego I let die,
> surrender ev'ry earthly tie,
> the dead can bury what is dead,
> I choose to walk with you instead.

> **O Jesus, let the Fire of Joy,**
> **consume the devil's subtle ploy,**
> **transfigured is our planet earth,**
> **the golden age is given birth.**

7. Jesus, shatter the energetic matrix that prevents people from seeing that war is not natural, it is not in human nature. It is artificially created by the power elite. The power elite uses the duality consciousness to seduce people into going to war and supporting their wars.

> O Jesus, help me rise above,
> the devil's test through higher love,

show me separate self unreal,
my formless self you do reveal.

O Jesus, let the Fire of Joy,
consume the devil's subtle ploy,
transfigured is our planet earth,
the golden age is given birth.

8. Jesus, shatter the energetic matrix that prevents people from seeing that this could have been understood through the mind of Christ in these past 2,000 years. It is something that can be understood very quickly as more and more people raise their consciousness.

O Jesus, what is that to me,
I just let go and follow thee,
with this I do pass ev'ry test,
to find with you eternal rest.

O Jesus, let the Fire of Joy,
consume the devil's subtle ploy,
transfigured is our planet earth,
the golden age is given birth.

9. Jesus, shatter the energetic matrix that prevents people from seeing that war is not a natural occurrence. It is not in human nature to create war. It is only something that can happen when people are manipulated by those who are in a specific state of consciousness and have absolutely no empathy, no sense of essential humanity. They do not care how many millions of people are killed as long as they can further whatever they see as their end.

O Jesus, fiery master mine,
my heart now melting into thine,
I love with heart and mind and soul,
the God who is my highest goal.

O Jesus, let the Fire of Joy,
consume the devil's subtle ploy,

transfigured is our planet earth,
the golden age is given birth.

Part 3

1. Jesus, shatter the energetic matrix that prevents people from seeing that the emperors of war have nothing on, and the justifications that are given have no reality to them whatsoever.

O Jesus, blessed brother mine,
I walk the path that you outline,
a great example to us all,
I follow now your inner call.

O Jesus, let the Fire of Joy,
consume the devil's subtle ploy,
transfigured is our planet earth,
the golden age is given birth.

2. Jesus, shatter the energetic matrix that prevents people from seeing that your teachings were entirely anti-war. You came to help us see that there is an alternative to the relativistic definition of good and evil.

O Jesus, open inner sight,
the ego wants to prove it's right,
but this I will no longer do,
I want to be all one with you.

O Jesus, let the Fire of Joy,
consume the devil's subtle ploy,
transfigured is our planet earth,
the golden age is given birth.

3. Jesus, shatter the energetic matrix that prevents people from seeing that the atrocities of the past 2,000 years happened because we continued to think that there were those in embodiment who are as gods, who can

define good and evil, and that we can recognize these gods as they walk among us.

> O Jesus, I now clearly see,
> the Key of Knowledge given me,
> my Christ self I hereby embrace,
> as you fill up my inner space.

> **O Jesus, let the Fire of Joy,**
> **consume the devil's subtle ploy,**
> **transfigured is our planet earth,**
> **the golden age is given birth.**

4. Jesus, shatter the energetic matrix that prevents people from seeing that you do not consider these last 2,000 years to be a complete failure. The Christ consciousness wants to raise people up to see beyond the dualistic vision.

> O Jesus, show me serpent's lie,
> expose the beam in my own eye,
> as Christ discernment you me give,
> in oneness I forever live.

> **O Jesus, let the Fire of Joy,**
> **consume the devil's subtle ploy,**
> **transfigured is our planet earth,**
> **the golden age is given birth.**

5. Jesus, shatter the energetic matrix that prevents people from seeing that this can happen in two ways: It can happen by people connecting to the Christ within themselves, often helped by an external teacher or teaching, or it can happen through the School of Hard Knocks. It can happen through direct experience.

> O Jesus, I am truly meek,
> and thus I turn the other cheek,
> when the accuser attacks me,
> I go within and merge with thee.

**O Jesus, let the Fire of Joy,
consume the devil's subtle ploy,
transfigured is our planet earth,
the golden age is given birth.**

6. Jesus, shatter the energetic matrix that prevents people from seeing that the inner process of people attaining Christhood did not come to fruition in sufficient numbers. That is why we have seen the wars. Precisely because we have seen all of these atrocities, there is both an individual and a collective vision of how bad things can go.

O Jesus, ego I let die,
surrender ev'ry earthly tie,
the dead can bury what is dead,
I choose to walk with you instead.

**O Jesus, let the Fire of Joy,
consume the devil's subtle ploy,
transfigured is our planet earth,
the golden age is given birth.**

7. Jesus, shatter the energetic matrix that prevents people from seeing the lesson that we were meant to see during the Piscean Age. I call forth an instant shift in consciousness so people begin to see that it is not in human nature to create war.

O Jesus, help me rise above,
the devil's test through higher love,
show me separate self unreal,
my formless self you do reveal.

**O Jesus, let the Fire of Joy,
consume the devil's subtle ploy,
transfigured is our planet earth,
the golden age is given birth.**

8. Jesus, shatter the energetic matrix that prevents people from seeing that it is only a certain class of people that create war. Those kinds of people

are in a special state of consciousness, and most human beings are not anywhere near that state of consciousness.

O Jesus, what is that to me,
I just let go and follow thee,
with this I do pass ev'ry test,
to find with you eternal rest.

**O Jesus, let the Fire of Joy,
consume the devil's subtle ploy,
transfigured is our planet earth,
the golden age is given birth.**

9. Jesus, shatter the energetic matrix that prevents people from seeing that we can be seduced by the lie that there is some epic cause that must be fulfilled in order to avoid an epic calamity. In order to avoid this calamity, we have to kill those people who are opposing God's work. The calamity of killing those people is less than the calamity that would ensue if they continue to do their evil deeds—so the lie says.

O Jesus, fiery master mine,
my heart now melting into thine,
I love with heart and mind and soul,
the God who is my highest goal.

**O Jesus, let the Fire of Joy,
consume the devil's subtle ploy,
transfigured is our planet earth,
the golden age is given birth.**

Part 4

1. Jesus, shatter the energetic matrix that prevents people from seeing the fallacy of this and how this pattern has repeated itself so many times.

O Jesus, blessed brother mine,
I walk the path that you outline,

a great example to us all,
I follow now your inner call.

O Jesus, let the Fire of Joy,
consume the devil's subtle ploy,
transfigured is our planet earth,
the golden age is given birth.

2. Jesus, shatter the energetic matrix that prevents people from seeing the hollowness of this serpentine lie, and therefore seeing that it is the elite that has created war.

O Jesus, open inner sight,
the ego wants to prove it's right,
but this I will no longer do,
I want to be all one with you.

O Jesus, let the Fire of Joy,
consume the devil's subtle ploy,
transfigured is our planet earth,
the golden age is given birth.

3. Jesus, shatter the energetic matrix that prevents people from building the determination that says: "We have to do something about elitism. We have to free ourselves from this elite that has created war after war, atrocity after atrocity.

O Jesus, I now clearly see,
the Key of Knowledge given me,
my Christ self I hereby embrace,
as you fill up my inner space.

O Jesus, let the Fire of Joy,
consume the devil's subtle ploy,
transfigured is our planet earth,
the golden age is given birth.

4. Jesus, shatter the energetic matrix that prevents people from saying: "We have to look at ourselves and see how we were seduced into believing

not only what was the agenda of the elite, but even believing in the necessity, the legitimacy, perhaps even the authority, of such an elite."

> O Jesus, show me serpent's lie,
> expose the beam in my own eye,
> as Christ discernment you me give,
> in oneness I forever live.

> **O Jesus, let the Fire of Joy,**
> **consume the devil's subtle ploy,**
> **transfigured is our planet earth,**
> **the golden age is given birth.**

5. Jesus, shatter the energetic matrix that prevents people from saying: "Why were we seduced into thinking that we cannot know a higher truth on our own, but that we need an elite to define for us what is good and evil? Why do we need to follow those who think they are gods on earth and can define good and evil? Why do we think that we can recognize them and should follow them? Why should we believe that killing other people is doing God's work, or even the work of Christ?"

> O Jesus, I am truly meek,
> and thus I turn the other cheek,
> when the accuser attacks me,
> I go within and merge with thee.

> **O Jesus, let the Fire of Joy,**
> **consume the devil's subtle ploy,**
> **transfigured is our planet earth,**
> **the golden age is given birth.**

6. Jesus, shatter the energetic matrix that prevents people from seeing that the fallen beings have no willingness to look at themselves. A fallen being can go through an embodiment where it kills thousands or millions of people, and it can go out of embodiment without having any need or willingness to look at itself.

> O Jesus, ego I let die,
> surrender ev'ry earthly tie,

the dead can bury what is dead,
I choose to walk with you instead.

O Jesus, let the Fire of Joy,
consume the devil's subtle ploy,
transfigured is our planet earth,
the golden age is given birth.

7. Jesus, shatter the energetic matrix that prevents people from seeing that human beings who are not fallen cannot participate in the killing of others, whether we do it ourselves or we support it, without reflecting on it after we go out of embodiment.

O Jesus, help me rise above,
the devil's test through higher love,
show me separate self unreal,
my formless self you do reveal.

O Jesus, let the Fire of Joy,
consume the devil's subtle ploy,
transfigured is our planet earth,
the golden age is given birth.

8. Jesus, shatter the energetic matrix that prevents people from acknowledging what we learned before we came into this embodiment, and therefore connecting to what we already know in our hearts, thereby seeing why elitism is based on a fundamental lie.

O Jesus, what is that to me,
I just let go and follow thee,
with this I do pass ev'ry test,
to find with you eternal rest.

O Jesus, let the Fire of Joy,
consume the devil's subtle ploy,
transfigured is our planet earth,
the golden age is given birth.

9. Jesus, shatter the energetic matrix that prevents people from seeing that war is based on a fundamental lie. War never serves an epic cause because God never wanted war. God never created war. God never encouraged people to go to war. The real God never told the Israelites to go into the Promised Land and commit genocide.

O Jesus, fiery master mine,
my heart now melting into thine,
I love with heart and mind and soul,
the God who is my highest goal.

**O Jesus, let the Fire of Joy,
consume the devil's subtle ploy,
transfigured is our planet earth,
the golden age is given birth.**

Part 5

1. Jesus, shatter the energetic matrix that prevents people from seeing that war was created by the false gods, whether they are in or out of embodiment, who are in the fallen consciousness.

O Jesus, blessed brother mine,
I walk the path that you outline,
a great example to us all,
I follow now your inner call.

**O Jesus, let the Fire of Joy,
consume the devil's subtle ploy,
transfigured is our planet earth,
the golden age is given birth.**

2. Jesus, shatter the energetic matrix that prevents people from seeing that your teachings were entirely non-violent. It is a complete illusion and manipulation that your teachings were used to justify all of this violence over these many centuries.

O Jesus, open inner sight,
the ego wants to prove it's right,
but this I will no longer do,
I want to be all one with you.

**O Jesus, let the Fire of Joy,
consume the devil's subtle ploy,
transfigured is our planet earth,
the golden age is given birth.**

3. Jesus, shatter the energetic matrix that prevents people from having the scales fall from our eyes and have an experience like Paul on the road to Damascus, where we suddenly see this.

O Jesus, I now clearly see,
the Key of Knowledge given me,
my Christ self I hereby embrace,
as you fill up my inner space.

**O Jesus, let the Fire of Joy,
consume the devil's subtle ploy,
transfigured is our planet earth,
the golden age is given birth.**

4. Jesus, shatter the energetic matrix that prevents people from having our eyes are opened and seeing the fallacy. Help us recognize that there is a group of people, the power elite, that was behind this and that they used a specific state of consciousness to make this seem like something that was approved by Christ.

O Jesus, show me serpent's lie,
expose the beam in my own eye,
as Christ discernment you me give,
in oneness I forever live.

**O Jesus, let the Fire of Joy,
consume the devil's subtle ploy,
transfigured is our planet earth,
the golden age is given birth.**

5. Jesus, shatter the energetic matrix that prevents people from seeing that the real problem on earth is the fallen consciousness. Your mission was all about helping us free ourselves from this. The Christ consciousness is all about helping us see through the serpentine lies and realizing that there is a higher reality.

> O Jesus, I am truly meek,
> and thus I turn the other cheek,
> when the accuser attacks me,
> I go within and merge with thee.

> **O Jesus, let the Fire of Joy,**
> **consume the devil's subtle ploy,**
> **transfigured is our planet earth,**
> **the golden age is given birth.**

6. Jesus, shatter the energetic matrix that prevents people from seeing that this is what you preached 2,000 years ago, not as clearly as you can do now, but it was preached as it could be done, given the level of the collective consciousness as it was back then.

> O Jesus, ego I let die,
> surrender ev'ry earthly tie,
> the dead can bury what is dead,
> I choose to walk with you instead.

> **O Jesus, let the Fire of Joy,**
> **consume the devil's subtle ploy,**
> **transfigured is our planet earth,**
> **the golden age is given birth.**

7. Jesus, shatter the energetic matrix that prevents people from seeing that the real tragedy of the creation of the Catholic church is that they took the teaching that was released back then, based on the state of the collective consciousness as it was, and they froze it in time and they also distorted it.

> O Jesus, help me rise above,
> the devil's test through higher love,

show me separate self unreal,
my formless self you do reveal.

**O Jesus, let the Fire of Joy,
consume the devil's subtle ploy,
transfigured is our planet earth,
the golden age is given birth.**

8. Jesus, shatter the energetic matrix that prevents people from seeing that this is limiting what the message can do, because as the collective consciousness is raised, more can be given, more teachings can come from the mind of Christ individualized in you.

O Jesus, what is that to me,
I just let go and follow thee,
with this I do pass ev'ry test,
to find with you eternal rest.

**O Jesus, let the Fire of Joy,
consume the devil's subtle ploy,
transfigured is our planet earth,
the golden age is given birth.**

9. Jesus, shatter the energetic matrix that prevents people from seeing that as you ascended, you could have continued to give new and more advanced perspectives and teachings through the mind of Christ for those who were able to use the teachings. There could have been a process of continual progressive revelation directly from you to various people over these past 2,000 years.

O Jesus, fiery master mine,
my heart now melting into thine,
I love with heart and mind and soul,
the God who is my highest goal.

**O Jesus, let the Fire of Joy,
consume the devil's subtle ploy,
transfigured is our planet earth,
the golden age is given birth.**

Part 6

1. Jesus, shatter the energetic matrix that prevents people from seeing that this process could only have happened outside of the elite. Those who could have received your progressive revelation over these past 2,000 years were not part of the elite.

> O Jesus, blessed brother mine,
> I walk the path that you outline,
> a great example to us all,
> I follow now your inner call.

> **O Jesus, let the Fire of Joy,**
> **consume the devil's subtle ploy,**
> **transfigured is our planet earth,**
> **the golden age is given birth.**

2. Jesus, shatter the energetic matrix that prevents people from seeing that the elite were the leaders of all of the Christian churches, the Catholic church and all of the others. None of them would have been able to receive the progressive revelation of Jesus Christ.

> O Jesus, open inner sight,
> the ego wants to prove it's right,
> but this I will no longer do,
> I want to be all one with you.

> **O Jesus, let the Fire of Joy,**
> **consume the devil's subtle ploy,**
> **transfigured is our planet earth,**
> **the golden age is given birth.**

3. Jesus, shatter the energetic matrix that prevents people from seeing that the elite was not willing. You could have given new revelation only outside the elite, but the power elite distorted the teaching so few dared follow your example.

O Jesus, I now clearly see,
the Key of Knowledge given me,
my Christ self I hereby embrace,
as you fill up my inner space.

**O Jesus, let the Fire of Joy,
consume the devil's subtle ploy,
transfigured is our planet earth,
the golden age is given birth.**

4. Jesus, shatter the energetic matrix that prevents people from seeing that the elite set up a power apparatus that would instantly kill anybody who dared to speak the truth of Christ.

O Jesus, show me serpent's lie,
expose the beam in my own eye,
as Christ discernment you me give,
in oneness I forever live.

**O Jesus, let the Fire of Joy,
consume the devil's subtle ploy,
transfigured is our planet earth,
the golden age is given birth.**

5. Jesus, shatter the energetic matrix that prevents people from seeing that many women were tuned in to a higher reality and had a more intuitive vision, but they were labeled and burned as witches. There could have been a feminist revolution in the 1400s and 1500s, if it had not been for the witch hunts, but the elite did everything they could to squash it.

O Jesus, I am truly meek,
and thus I turn the other cheek,
when the accuser attacks me,
I go within and merge with thee.

**O Jesus, let the Fire of Joy,
consume the devil's subtle ploy,
transfigured is our planet earth,
the golden age is given birth.**

6. Jesus, shatter the energetic matrix that prevents people from seeing that we have passed the point where the elite can suppress the true teachings of Christ. They will be given through many people who can receive elements of the teaching, ideas of the teaching.

> O Jesus, ego I let die,
> surrender ev'ry earthly tie,
> the dead can bury what is dead,
> I choose to walk with you instead.

> **O Jesus, let the Fire of Joy,**
> **consume the devil's subtle ploy,**
> **transfigured is our planet earth,**
> **the golden age is given birth.**

7. Jesus, shatter the energetic matrix that prevents people from seeing that all ascended master students should count ourselves among the people who can tune in to the mind of Christ and receive ideas directly from you or another ascended master.

> O Jesus, help me rise above,
> the devil's test through higher love,
> show me separate self unreal,
> my formless self you do reveal.

> **O Jesus, let the Fire of Joy,**
> **consume the devil's subtle ploy,**
> **transfigured is our planet earth,**
> **the golden age is given birth.**

8. Jesus, shatter the energetic matrix that prevents people from seeing that we can share these ideas on the Internet and give people an alternative to the serpentine state of consciousness. We are all able to do this. Anybody who has sincerely studied ascended master teachings or any other valid spiritual teaching is all able to do this.

> O Jesus, what is that to me,
> I just let go and follow thee,

with this I do pass ev'ry test,
to find with you eternal rest.

O Jesus, let the Fire of Joy,
consume the devil's subtle ploy,
transfigured is our planet earth,
the golden age is given birth.

9. Jesus, help me free myself from the primal self and overcome the need to feel validated, to not be rejected, to produce some kind of result. Help me realize that I am on this planet to share myself, share my Presence— and *some* will understand.

O Jesus, fiery master mine,
my heart now melting into thine,
I love with heart and mind and soul,
the God who is my highest goal.

O Jesus, let the Fire of Joy,
consume the devil's subtle ploy,
transfigured is our planet earth,
the golden age is given birth.

Sealing

In the name of the I AM THAT I AM, I accept that Archangel Michael, Astrea and Shiva form an impenetrable shield around myself and all constructive people, sealing us from all fear-based energies in all four octaves. I accept that the Light of God is consuming and transforming all fear-based energies that make up the dark forces working against ending the era of elitism on earth!

11 | THE REAL CONSPIRACY RUNNING THE WORLD

I AM the Ascended Master Saint Germain. I wish to give you a discourse that will in one sense shatter the conspiracy theories that are out there about elitism and the power elite, and in another sense give you a deeper perspective on what is truly going on. There are many, many theories out there that talk about conspiracies at the physical level where there are various power elite groups that meet in secrecy and plot to take over the world or whatever they plot. How much reality is there to it?

Well, certainly there are groups of people who think they belong to an elite and who think they have power and who attempt to meet both in secret and sometimes in public and create some kind of agenda or policy for how they can influence the world. Some of them have good intentions according to their own definition of what is good. The reality is that there is no single group, no clearly defined group in the physical octave, that is running the world. There is no secret conspiracy in the physical octave that is running the world.

Does that mean I am thereby saying there is no, quote-unquote, conspiracy running the world? No, but it is an *unconscious* conspiracy. It is an *unaware* conspiracy where the people are not deliberately conspiring and plotting. What is actually running the world is the mindset that is much more difficult to combat than an actual physical conspiracy, because you cannot single out individuals or groups and say: "They are the culprit, they are the ones who started it all"—at least not in the physical.

What has actually been going on now for a very long time, but even in known history for quite a long time, is that the fallen beings in the higher realms, especially in the identity and mental realms, have introduced a number of very subtle, very persuasive, ideas that have gradually become more and more accepted by, not a large group of people, but actually in numbers a relatively small group of people. But they are found in all nations and they believe in this elitist philosophy. This is the real conspiracy, so to speak, that is running the world.

The elitist mindset is running the world

There is a mindset, this set of beliefs, that has been developed over time. They all revolve around the division of humankind into at least two classes, and one is the elite that has special abilities, special powers, special wisdom, special insight, that allows them to know better than the population how a country or the world should be run. Now, as we have talked about, this has been legitimized by religion, by Materialism, by political philosophies. The Soviet Union (communism, Marxism) is an elitist philosophy because there are always the true revolutionaries, those in the party apparatus who know better than the people.

They even know better than historical necessity. That is why they cannot sit around and wait for the historical necessity to bring about the communist utopia. They must use violence to force it into the physical before time. That is why the religious people must use violence to combat the enemies of God. And that is why even the materialists must use some kind of force to combat religion, or use more subtle kinds of force to get people to come into the fold and accept the paradigm that is currently being used to rule the earth.

You see here that there is the outer justifications: religion, political philosophy, whether it is capitalism, whether it is communism, whether it is Materialism. There is an outer philosophical framework. But behind this is a much more subtle mindset and this mindset cannot be described as a clearly formulated philosophy. It is not like the Communist Manifesto, for example, that has ten planks. You could talk about ten planks in the elitist philosophy, but there is nobody who has ever clearly defined it, at least nobody in the physical. They have come to believe in it, and the basis for this belief is this very conviction they have that they are in a separate class of people that is superior to the general population.

Now, besides this belief that there is an elite that is superior to the population, there is also the belief that there are different groupings in that elite. There are those who are opposing our group, those who have a different agenda and therefore are a threat to our power. Therefore, they must be destroyed by all means possible, and that is why sometimes these outer justifications of religion or political philosophy are used as a justification to get the population to support one elite in going to war against another.

How did this mindset ever come to, so to speak, take over the world, or at least the minds of so many people in the world? Not only people who are members of the elite, but even many among the population, many among writers, philosophers, thinkers, the media people and so on. How did this mindset come to dominate? Well, it did so because you have created a self-reinforcing effect. With "you," I mean the fallen beings in the higher realms, have created this self-reinforcing effect. It is very, very simple in principle. You define a society where there is an elite that has special powers, special privileges and of course affluence beyond the general population.

There will be a certain amount of people who want to be part of such an elite. These are not all fallen beings in embodiment who want to be part of the elite. There are some among the people who also want to be part of the elite. These can be some of the original inhabitants of the earth who have attained some mastery, some self-discipline, some ability to do something out of the ordinary: to manifest things, to get things going, to organize things. In many cases it is also avatars who, as Jesus and I talked about previously, come into embodiment on earth with a sense that you are a unique individual, you are a special individual. Then, you encounter the fallen beings who make you believe that you cannot express your spiritual specialness on earth. Therefore, you attempt to compensate for this by building a sense of being special based on the ideas, the concepts and the actions that are available on earth. This is how avatars become susceptible to thinking that they are part of the elite and this makes you special.

Whether you are an avatar, one of the original inhabitants or a fallen being, you have this desire to be special and to perhaps do something that is important. What you have created, what the fallen beings have created, is a society where there is a clearly defined elite. They have special powers, privileges and affluence beyond the general population. What does it take to become part of this elite? It takes that you do not question the idea that there is such an elite, that it has some reality, that it was either created by God or created by nature. And that it, therefore, is valid that there is an elite, that the elite know how to rule the world or society and that the population do not. If you do not question these basic ideas, then you can become part of the elite.

Once you are in the elite, you can fulfill your desire that makes you feel special, whether it is to have power, whether it is to have privileges, to enjoy a certain lifestyle or whether it is to have money. The condition for gaining membership in the elite is that you accept the elitist mindset and that you do not question it. Of course, if the elite is currently legitimizing themselves by the Christian religion, as was the case for over a thousand years in Europe, then you do not question that either. If they are doing it by the communist ideology, you do not question that. If they are using Scientific Materialism and the survival of the fittest, well then you do not question that either.

The other thing is that, if there is a division in the elite, as there most often is, then you must choose one side or the other. It is difficult to be a member of the elite and be neutral. Some people manage to fly under the radar, but most people find it difficult to remain neutral. They must choose one grouping or the other. Therefore, they become pulled into fighting for whatever cause is defined, whatever epic struggle happens to be the one that is dominating the times. These are the conditions that you must fulfill in order to become part of the elite. It really is not very sophisticated at all. It really is not rocket science. It really is not beyond what the average person in the modern democracies can grasp, understand, see and accept.

The elite defines the parameters for the debate

Why haven't they come to that understanding? Why haven't they seen it? Why haven't they accepted it? Well, of course because the elite has created this self-reinforcing effect. They have created this cloud that prevents people from seeing. How do they do this? Because the elite are the ones who are dominating the institutions of society. The elite always attempt to dominate government and in most cases they do. They attempt to dominate the media. They attempt to dominate publishing, distribution of books, the publication of ideas. They attempt to dominate education. They of course attempt to dominate business. You see that the major institutions of society become dominated by the elite. In many societies the military plays a prominent role. In the modern democracies, at least when you exclude the

United States, the military plays a lesser role than it has done in previous ages. In the United States of course the military is still a very dominant force. Or rather the military connected with the industry that makes its profits off of the military. They form a very powerful force, as they also do in certain other nations, most obviously England, Russia and now to an increasing degree, China as well.

You see here that the power elite, without really consciously conspiring to do this, they have managed to define the parameters for what is being debated in society. They are defining which issues need to be talked about, which issues are important. Therefore, they are excluding anything that could threaten their dominance. They are not even doing this as a result of some conscious conspiracy where they are sitting there making a list of which ideas to suppress and which to promote. They are just doing this because the people who are part of the elite have one overriding characteristic, which can be captured in the old saying that: "You have to go along to get along." You have to go along with the basic mindset of the elite in order to become part of the elite. Once you are part of the elite, you have to continue to go along in order to remain in your position.

What you see here is that everyone who is part of the elite is willing to compromise. What are they willing to compromise? Well, basically anything, but primarily they are willing to compromise their own inner ability to know a higher truth, a higher reality, their intuitive sense of what is right from a higher perspective. They are willing to give that up. It is not necessarily that they, with a malicious intent, accept a false belief or a false definition of good and evil. They are not maliciously or deliberately or even consciously accepting what Jesus called the serpentine logic. But they are taking it on because they have that characteristic that they want to be part of the elite and they are willing to do whatever it takes to gain that power or that privilege or that money.

This is a characteristic that again is not in human nature. People in the general population have often been manipulated into accepting this mindset where they are willing to compromise their principles, what they know in their hearts is true. That is why they have been manipulated into going to war, for example, or going along with an elitist economy that they know actually is not serving their own interests. You see that it is not actually in human nature to compromise. Human beings, when they are not manipulated by the elite, they have some sense of what we have called the basic humanity. This is a frame of reference that allows people to evaluate their own behavior and the behavior of others based on this very, very simple rule: "Do unto others what you want them to do unto you." Why is it that every religion in the world teaches that particular axiom in some form or another? Well, it is because it is a universal principle that people are tuned in to when they are not manipulated by the serpentine mindset. They know in their hearts that it is in their own interest to treat other people fairly so that they will be treated fairly. People do have a sense that whatever they send out, will come back to them somehow. Whether they believe in sin or karma or this or that, people have this intuitive sense that there will be consequences to your actions and that the better you treat other people, the better you will be treated yourself. This is something that the general population knows when they are not manipulated by the elite. The elite no longer knows this. They knew it originally but they have given it up because they want their privilege or power or money so much that they are willing to set it aside in order to get these outer things. That is precisely why, if you let the people rule without being manipulated by the elite, the people will make far better decisions than the elite has been doing and is doing.

The self-reinforcing illusion of duality

The reality here that I want to convey to you, because you need to understand this as ascended master students, and of course you need to make the calls on it, but you cannot make the calls on it if you do not grasp it. The primary feature of the duality consciousness is that it puts people in a state of illusion and that state of illusion is self-reinforcing. There is no way to use the duality consciousness to escape the duality consciousness. Because once you have gone into this state of mind, where you think you are a god who can define good and evil based on your current level of consciousness, based on the outer self, the dualistic self, then your definition of good and evil will always be relative to your state of consciousness. There will be nothing objective, universal or absolute about it.

That is why, as Jesus said: Only through the Christ consciousness can you gain a frame of reference from beyond duality. Quite frankly, if you could free the population from the manipulation of the elite, they would have a certain level of Christ consciousness, Christ discernment. Because they would have that essential humanity, which is an element of the Christ consciousness. Once you step into the duality consciousness, you lose it because now everything is relative. There is no rock of Christ. You are basing your life, your mind, on the shifting sands of the serpentine mind and in this serpentine mind everything is relative. That is what you can actually see and what many, many people can come to see when you look at history, look at the various elites, look at what they have used to justify their position and their power.

Jesus gave a set of principles that were entirely nonviolent. But you see how the Catholic church has managed to pervert Jesus' teachings to the point where they could be used to seemingly legitimize extremely violent actions. This is a very, very clear example of how the serpentine logic makes everything relative. You can go back and look at the medieval popes and you can ask yourself: Do you agree with them that the crusades were necessary, beneficial? That they were doing God's work when they massacred men, women and children? Do you agree with the witch hunts, the burning of witches at the stake by a mere suspicion raised by someone who did not like that person? Do you agree with the Inquisition where people were tortured in order to supposedly save their souls?

If you agree with this of course, then you would not be an ascended master student. But many people who are not ascended master students also do not agree with this, if they actually look at it. They can come to see: "Well, what was it then? How is it possible that these medieval popes could take the teachings of Christ – turn the other cheek, love your enemies, do unto others – and use them to legitimize violence at this rather extreme scale?" Well, it can only be because they had made those teachings of Christ relative to their situation, their state of consciousness, their way of thinking and the outer political goals that they had. In other words, Jesus came to set people free, but they had used the teachings of Christ, a perverted version of them, to enslave people even more.

Many people were less free during the Christian era, or the era of Catholic dominance, than they were before and that they are now. This shows you how the power elite is entirely enveloped in this serpentine consciousness that makes everything relative. When everything is relative, that means that at any time, in any given society, in any given situation, there is always an elite who can use whatever philosophy is there to justify doing whatever they want to do. The elite can always justify what they want to do and they always have attempted to justify it.

They have used the teachings of Christ. They have used the teachings of Muhammad. They have even in rare cases used the teachings of the Buddha. They have used the teachings of Marx, the teachings of Adam Smith and the teachings of Darwin to justify doing what they want to do, which is either to dominate and enslave the population or to defeat and destroy that competing power elite that is threatening their position, that wants to take over their position. Or they have used some teaching to justify dethroning the established power elite and instead setting themselves up as the new elite, as you saw in the communist revolution, the French revolution and so on.

These are all ideas that many of you who are ascended master students are familiar with. The reason it is important to bring them out here and make the calls on them is that many, many people out there are ready to come to see these ideas. It does not mean they will suddenly acknowledge ascended master teachings but we do not need them to acknowledge our existence or our teachings. We need them to accept these ideas that will then allow them to suddenly see what the power elites of history have been doing. You who are the ascended master students can of course go beyond this and make the calls not just for the power elite in the physical but also for the power elite in the emotional, mental and identity realms. The fallen beings there, the demons, the entire structure in the emotional realm. Also, those very deceptive beings in the mental realm. And the more higher ranking fallen beings in the identity realm, such as the Dark Master that we have mentioned to you.

The invisible conspiracy

This is where there is a certain conspiracy. Not really in the emotional realm because they are too divided, too trapped in anger and other negative emotions, that they cannot really form a coherent conspiracy. Even in the mental realm there is not so much of a conspiracy because in the mental realm you actually have groups of fallen beings who are polarized towards the two extremes of the duality consciousness. They are using the analytical mind, the dualistic state of mind, to argue against each other. In the identity realm you find a smaller number of fallen beings that on earth have submitted themselves to the rule of the being we have called the Dark Master. Therefore, they are more unified and they are the ones who are, therefore, able to have some more coherent strategy. They are actually using the fallen beings in the mental realm, those in the emotional realm and those in physical embodiment, even those who are not fallen beings in physical embodiment, to further that agenda. If you want to talk about a real conspiracy, that is where you find it: in the identity realm.

Of course, what can you do about it as a human being in embodiment? Well, you can make the calls for the judgment of Christ that authorizes the ascended masters to step in. You can make the calls that people will be cut free from these lies promoted by these fallen beings. Because as long as a large number of people in embodiment accept these lies and believe they are beneficial and believe in the elitist mindset, well then they cannot actually be taken. Because people must then learn from the School of Hard Knocks by seeing a more extreme outplaying of what the elitist mindset will do. What will the elitist mindset do? Well, it will always create some kind of crisis, some kind of disaster.

This messenger was inspired to read a book about the global super elite before he came to the conference. The author of this book – even though he is relatively positive because he actually believes the elitist lie – was actually able to see that when you look at the power elites of history, they all repeated the same pattern. Whatever philosophy they had, whatever agenda they had, they could never stop in time. They always took it so far that it created some kind of crisis, some kind of conflict, that eventually led them to lose their position so that another elite would take over.

This shows you the fact that here is an author who has no spiritual background whatsoever, who is actually positive towards elites and believes that many members of the elite are superior to the general population in intelligence and other qualities. Nevertheless, he was still able to see that historically, the elites have created one disaster, one crisis after another. This is exactly what we have told you over and over again for years, of how the School of Hard Knocks works that way so that the elites will always take things too far. They always go too far, they cannot stop in time. That is what eventually will overturn their dominance, perhaps causing another elite to spring up, but also in the long run, causing more and more people to question elitism.

Questioning elitism led to democracy

Why do you have democracies today? Because a certain number of people started to question elitism. They at least started to question elitism in the form you saw it in with the kings and the noblemen and the clergy of Europe. You saw that even though the founding fathers of America were still very much in an elitist mindset, they did see the fallacy of the elites of King George in England, the Catholic church and the noble class of

Europe. They did see the need to create a society that was not dominated by that form of elitism. Many people in the modern world have also started to question at least that form of elitism.

What I am telling you with this dictation is that many people in the world – even though they are not spiritual and do not need to know about ascended masters – they are still ready to question the elitist mindset itself and come to some awareness that there is a mindset behind the physical elite. And that it is this mindset that needs to be questioned in order for the modern democracies to actually become true democracies that are not dominated by an elite. You cannot, as we have said, have a true democracy that has a power elite that dominates the population. It is an antithesis to democracy. You can only then have a token democracy, a democracy by name, a democracy of pretending to be a free democratic society when it truly is not.

"Of course, of course," they will all say: "But isn't the United States more free than was the Soviet Union? Or England during the Middle Ages?" Well, is it? Is America more free? Do you actually have freedom if you have political freedom, but not psychological freedom? If you are still trapped in your mind, in the serpentine illusion, are you free?

You see here, I am the God of Freedom, the representative of the spiritual flame of freedom to the earth. My concern is to set people free. I am not saying there has not been a gradual process that has led to the current state of the modern democracies. I am not saying that this process has not brought a certain freedom at the physical level. Of course, you are more free in the modern democracies than you were in the feudal societies or in the Soviet Union, or in Rome, or in Ancient Egypt, or in Babylon or the far eastern civilizations.

Of course, you are more free, but you are only more free in an outer sense, and it is not only a matter of what you *can* do. Your real freedom depends on what you can *imagine* doing. What I am saying is that the elitist mindset has not only influenced the elite. It is true that in order to become members of the elite, you have to accept the elitist mindset and you have to not question it. What has happened is that the elite, in order to legitimize their existence and their agenda, they know, as we have said, that they have to get the consent of the governed. They have to get the people to go along with them and therefore the people have also been affected by the elitist mindset. They have been affected by the serpentine logic that has made so many things relative.

Members of the elite are not free

If you actually look at the power elite, you might think: "Well, they have the power to do anything they want. They have the money to do anything they want. They have the privileged position where they can do whatever they want." But the question is, what is it they want? What is it they can imagine doing, imagine wanting? You will see if you look at the minds of these people that they have no imagination. They are like automatons. Some are programmed to want more and more power and it is never enough. Some want more and more privilege and it is never enough. Some want more and more money and it is never enough. Some want more and more fame and it is never enough.

Are these people free? Certainly not according to a psychological definition of freedom. They are not free in their minds. They are more trapped in their minds than the average citizen. Of course, the average citizen is also trapped in the mindset of accepting that there must be an elite, that it is okay that 2% of the American population control 90% of the wealth, while more and more people are living under the poverty level and all of these illusions. There is an intellectual elite that knows best what is true and not true. There is a religious elite, who can tell them what to believe. There is a political elite. There is a media elite. There are all of these elites, who supposedly know better than the people. When the people accept this, they are limiting what they dare to imagine that they could do with the physical freedom they have.

How many people are really making use of the political freedom they have to live an entirely different lifestyle? Some are, but not many because most people have gone into another form of selling their soul to the devil. Just as I said the elite will go along with the elitist mindset in order to gain their privileged positions, you have many among the middle class in the modern democracies who still feel that even though they are not the elite, and even though they do not really have any power, and they do not really have great money, they still have a comfortable lifestyle. They have sold themselves to maintaining this comfortable lifestyle by fitting themselves into the system defined by the elite.

They become the worker bees that are actually producing the wealth that the elite is then siphoning off. But the elite has become smart enough that they are giving these people a more comfortable lifestyle and they are then settling for this. What are they doing with their political freedom?

Are they pursuing some great dream that they have? Or are they tying their lives down to the 30-year mortgage? And *that* becomes their goal in life: To pay off the mortgage so you own your house. To buy a bigger car than the Joneses. To go on some vacation or trip. This is all they can imagine doing. Are they free? Certainly not in my mind and certainly not in their own minds, although they may think they are.

In fact, you could say, if you look back throughout history, you could say that clearly the fallen beings created the Catholic church and the entire mindset that all people are sinners and that they should submit to the clergy and the kings. They created this and for some of them it was a great triumph that they were able to manipulate so many people into accepting this very, very limited position and accept that there was an elite that had such privileges beyond the general population.

The greatest triumph of the elite is America today

You can look at the Soviet Union and it was another triumph for the fallen beings that they made all of these people accept this very, very low material lifestyle that they were offered in a communist society. You can look at other societies where the fallen beings have managed to make people accept these limitations, becoming virtual slaves of the elite. But from a certain viewpoint and from the viewpoint of certain fallen beings, the greatest triumph for the fallen beings on this planet is actually America as it is today. Because here is an entire population who is so unfree that they are the virtual slaves of the power elite but Americans think they are free. They think they live in a free nation and some of them even think that they live in the greatest nation, the richest nation on earth. There are fallen beings who see this as their greatest accomplishment so far.

They have managed to enslave people, while making them believe that they are free. The people in the feudal societies, they knew they were enslaved. The people in the Soviet Union, they knew they were enslaved, they were oppressed. They had given up hope that they could free themselves so in a sense they were also very trapped, but at least they knew they were enslaved. Modern-day Americans, they believe they are free and they believe they live in the greatest country on earth and that their 30-year mortgage gives them a secure and privileged lifestyle with their house and their cars and their this and their that. They believe that this is all you can aspire to as a human being. They think they have it made. They think they have gone as high as they can as a human being on earth and they cannot envision that there is more. They cannot believe that there could be more and they cannot get themselves to even dare to demand it. They think this is all you can have.

My beloved, you look at America today, you look at the relative affluence compared to other nations. It is as nothing compared to what I envision for the Golden Age, not only for America, but for all nations on earth. It is such a poor substitute for my vision for the Golden Age that I sometimes look at this and it is almost unfathomable, even to an ascended master, how people can settle for so little when they could have so much just by asking for it. Just by standing up and demanding it. Just by demanding that their government does what a democratic government should do and prevents the formation of an elite that controls 90% of the wealth. And it is just 2% or less of the people who have that control.

How can this be a free society? How can anyone believe that this is a free society? How can anyone dispute the fact that such a small elite controls the majority of the wealth? You cannot deny this. Nobody can deny it, unless they are completely delusional. Of course, the fallen beings can deny anything and that is what they have always done whenever they felt they were threatened. But people who have common sense cannot deny the unequal distribution of wealth and they cannot deny that this is profoundly anti-democratic and anti-freedom.

This concludes my remarks for now. I will certainly return and give you other installments of what we have in store for this conference. Truly, if there was one thing that could make a difference, a huge difference in terms of elitism, it is that a critical mass of people could make that shift and see the elitist mindset that is behind the outer physical elite and they could see that this is where the real problem lies. This self-reinforcing effect where you think that current conditions could not be changed because they are based on some creation by God or creation by nature, therefore, we need to have an elite. You do not need an elite to rule you. You do not need it and you would do far better if you did not have an elite. This is of course a topic we will comment on in our coming dictations.

I thank you for your willingness to help me broadcast this message into the collective consciousness. You cannot see it, I know, but I see the effects. I see how the light carries, the rays of light carry these ideas into the collective consciousness and they find their way to those people who are open to receiving them. This is happening as we speak. It will continue to happen and it will be reinforced when you study these releases and give the invocations. Along with our teachings and tools on fanaticism and dictatorships, they will all have a tremendous impact in coming years and even decades. As people reinforce it, more and more people will be free from this illusion and suddenly see, as we have said so many times: "Oh, this is obvious. Why didn't we see it before?"

Well, it does not matter why you did not see it before. What matters is that you see it now, and that you accept it, and that you act on it to demand more. You will not get more until you demand it. Ask and ye shall receive. Ask with the knowledge that you will receive and you *shall* receive. Ask not and how can you receive? How can you receive that which you cannot envision and which you cannot accept that you are worthy to have? With this, my gratitude, my love and I seal you in that love for freedom that I AM.

12 | INVOKING THE EXPOSURE OF THE REAL CONSPIRACY (PART 1)

In the name of the I AM THAT I AM, Jesus Christ, I use the authority that I have as a being in embodiment on earth to call upon Saint Germain to reinforce my calls and use my chakras to project the statements in this invocation into the collective consciousness and awaken people to how the fallen beings are controlling the world without being seen. Awaken people to the reality that we are spiritual beings and that we can co-create a new future by working with the ascended masters. I especially call for …

[Make your own calls here.]

Part 1

1. Saint Germain, shatter the energetic matrix that prevents people from seeing that there are groups of people who think they belong to the elite. They think they have power and they attempt to meet both in secret and in public and create an agenda or policy for how they can influence the world.

O Saint Germain, you do inspire,
my vision raised forever higher,
with you I form a figure-eight,
your Golden Age I co-create.

**O Saint Germain, what love you bring,
it truly makes all matter sing,
your violet flame does all restore,
with you we are becoming more.**

2. Saint Germain, shatter the energetic matrix that prevents people from seeing the reality that there is no single group, no clearly defined group in the physical octave, that is running the world. There is no secret conspiracy in the physical octave that is running the world.

O Saint Germain, what Freedom Flame,
released when we recite your name,
acceleration is your gift,
our planet it will surely lift.

**O Saint Germain, what love you bring,
it truly makes all matter sing,
your violet flame does all restore,
with you we are becoming more.**

3. Saint Germain, shatter the energetic matrix that prevents people from seeing that there is an *unconscious* conspiracy. It is an *unaware* conspiracy where the people are not deliberately conspiring and plotting.

O Saint Germain, in love we claim,
our right to bring your violet flame,
from you Above, to us below,
it is an all-transforming flow.

**O Saint Germain, what love you bring,
it truly makes all matter sing,
your violet flame does all restore,
with you we are becoming more.**

4. Saint Germain, shatter the energetic matrix that prevents people from seeing that what is actually running the world is a mindset that is much more difficult to combat than an actual physical conspiracy, because we cannot single out individuals or groups and say: "They are the culprit, they are the ones who started it all"—at least not in the physical.

O Saint Germain, I love you so,
my aura filled with violet glow,
my chakras filled with violet fire,
I am your cosmic amplifier.

O Saint Germain, what love you bring,
it truly makes all matter sing,
your violet flame does all restore,
with you we are becoming more.

5. Saint Germain, shatter the energetic matrix that prevents people from seeing that for a very long time, the fallen beings in the higher realms, especially in the identity and mental realms, have introduced a number of subtle and persuasive ideas that have gradually become more and more accepted by a relatively small group of people.

O Saint Germain, I am now free,
your violet flame is therapy,
transform all hang-ups in my mind,
as inner peace I surely find.

O Saint Germain, what love you bring,
it truly makes all matter sing,
your violet flame does all restore,
with you we are becoming more.

6. Saint Germain, shatter the energetic matrix that prevents people from seeing that the people who accept these serpentine ideas are found in all nations and they believe in this elitist philosophy. This is the real conspiracy that is running the world.

O Saint Germain, my body pure,
your violet flame for all is cure,

consume the cause of all disease,
and therefore I am all at ease.

**O Saint Germain, what love you bring,
it truly makes all matter sing,
your violet flame does all restore,
with you we are becoming more.**

7. Saint Germain, shatter the energetic matrix that prevents people from seeing that there is a mindset, a set of beliefs, that has been developed over time. They all revolve around the division of humankind into at least two classes, the elite that has special abilities, powers and wisdom. This allows them to know better than the population how a country or the world should be run.

O Saint Germain, I'm karma-free,
the past no longer burdens me,
a brand new opportunity,
I am in Christic unity.

**O Saint Germain, what love you bring,
it truly makes all matter sing,
your violet flame does all restore,
with you we are becoming more.**

8. Saint Germain, shatter the energetic matrix that prevents people from seeing that this has been legitimized by religion, by Materialism, by political philosophies. The Soviet Union was based on an elitist philosophy because there are always the true revolutionaries, those in the party apparatus who know better than the people.

O Saint Germain, we are now one,
I am for you a violet sun,
as we transform this planet earth,
your Golden Age is given birth.

**O Saint Germain, what love you bring,
it truly makes all matter sing,**

your violet flame does all restore,
with you we are becoming more.

9. Saint Germain, shatter the energetic matrix that prevents people from seeing that the elite knows better, and that is why they must use violence to force their viewpoints upon the population. Or they must use more subtle kinds of force to get people to come into the fold and accept the paradigm that is currently being used to rule the earth.

O Saint Germain, the earth is free,
from burden of duality,
in oneness we bring what is best,
your Golden Age is manifest.

O Saint Germain, what love you bring,
it truly makes all matter sing,
your violet flame does all restore,
with you we are becoming more.

Part 2

1. Saint Germain, shatter the energetic matrix that prevents people from seeing that there is the outer justifications: religion, political philosophy, whether it is capitalism, whether it is communism, whether it is Materialism. There is an outer philosophical framework.

O Saint Germain, you do inspire,
my vision raised forever higher,
with you I form a figure-eight,
your Golden Age I co-create.

O Saint Germain, what love you bring,
it truly makes all matter sing,
your violet flame does all restore,
with you we are becoming more.

2. Saint Germain, shatter the energetic matrix that prevents people from seeing that behind this is a much more subtle mindset, and this mindset cannot be described as a clearly formulated philosophy. There is an elitist philosophy, but nobody has clearly defined it.

O Saint Germain, what Freedom Flame,
released when we recite your name,
acceleration is your gift,
our planet it will surely lift.

O Saint Germain, what love you bring,
it truly makes all matter sing,
your violet flame does all restore,
with you we are becoming more.

3. Saint Germain, shatter the energetic matrix that prevents people from seeing that members of the elite have come to believe in it, and the basis for this belief is the conviction that they are in a separate class of people that is superior to the general population.

O Saint Germain, in love we claim,
our right to bring your violet flame,
from you Above, to us below,
it is an all-transforming flow.

O Saint Germain, what love you bring,
it truly makes all matter sing,
your violet flame does all restore,
with you we are becoming more.

4. Saint Germain, shatter the energetic matrix that prevents people from seeing that besides the belief that there is an elite that is superior to the population, there is also the belief that there are different groupings in that elite.

O Saint Germain, I love you so,
my aura filled with violet glow,
my chakras filled with violet fire,
I am your cosmic amplifier.

O Saint Germain, what love you bring,
it truly makes all matter sing,
your violet flame does all restore,
with you we are becoming more.

5. Saint Germain, shatter the energetic matrix that prevents people from seeing that there is the belief that there are those who are opposing our group, those who have a different agenda and therefore are a threat to our power. Therefore, they must be destroyed by all means possible.

O Saint Germain, I am now free,
your violet flame is therapy,
transform all hang-ups in my mind,
as inner peace I surely find.

O Saint Germain, what love you bring,
it truly makes all matter sing,
your violet flame does all restore,
with you we are becoming more.

6. Saint Germain, shatter the energetic matrix that prevents people from seeing that the outer justifications of religion or political philosophy are used by one elite group as a justification to get the population to support their war against another elite group.

O Saint Germain, my body pure,
your violet flame for all is cure,
consume the cause of all disease,
and therefore I am all at ease.

O Saint Germain, what love you bring,
it truly makes all matter sing,
your violet flame does all restore,
with you we are becoming more.

7. Saint Germain, shatter the energetic matrix that prevents people from seeing that this mindset took over the world because many among the population, even many writers, philosophers, thinkers and media people came to believe in it.

O Saint Germain, I'm karma-free,
the past no longer burdens me,
a brand new opportunity,
I am in Christic unity.

O Saint Germain, what love you bring,
it truly makes all matter sing,
your violet flame does all restore,
with you we are becoming more.

8. Saint Germain, shatter the energetic matrix that prevents people from seeing that this mindset came to dominate because the fallen beings in a higher realm created a self-reinforcing effect. They defined a society where there was an elite that had special powers, special privileges and affluence beyond the general population.

O Saint Germain, we are now one,
I am for you a violet sun,
as we transform this planet earth,
your Golden Age is given birth.

O Saint Germain, what love you bring,
it truly makes all matter sing,
your violet flame does all restore,
with you we are becoming more.

9. Saint Germain, shatter the energetic matrix that prevents people from seeing that there was a certain amount of people who wanted to be part of this elite. These are not all fallen beings, even some among the people want to be part of the elite.

O Saint Germain, the earth is free,
from burden of duality,
in oneness we bring what is best,
your Golden Age is manifest.

O Saint Germain, what love you bring,
it truly makes all matter sing,

**your violet flame does all restore,
with you we are becoming more.**

Part 3

1. Saint Germain, shatter the energetic matrix that prevents people from seeing that some people have a desire to be special and to do something that is important. This can make such people want to be part of the elite.

O Saint Germain, you do inspire,
my vision raised forever higher,
with you I form a figure-eight,
your Golden Age I co-create.

**O Saint Germain, what love you bring,
it truly makes all matter sing,
your violet flame does all restore,
with you we are becoming more.**

2. Saint Germain, shatter the energetic matrix that prevents people from seeing that in order to become part of this elite, you cannot question the idea that there is such an elite, that it has some reality, that it was either created by God or created by nature.

O Saint Germain, what Freedom Flame,
released when we recite your name,
acceleration is your gift,
our planet it will surely lift.

**O Saint Germain, what love you bring,
it truly makes all matter sing,
your violet flame does all restore,
with you we are becoming more.**

3. Saint Germain, shatter the energetic matrix that prevents people from seeing that in order to be part of the elite, you must accept as valid that there is an elite, that the elite knows how to rule the world or society and

that the population does not. If you do not question these basic ideas, then you can become part of the elite.

> O Saint Germain, in love we claim,
> our right to bring your violet flame,
> from you Above, to us below,
> it is an all-transforming flow.

> **O Saint Germain, what love you bring,**
> **it truly makes all matter sing,**
> **your violet flame does all restore,**
> **with you we are becoming more.**

4. Saint Germain, shatter the energetic matrix that prevents people from seeing that once you are in the elite, you can fulfill the desire that makes you feel special, whether it is to have power, to have privileges, to enjoy a certain lifestyle or to have money.

> O Saint Germain, I love you so,
> my aura filled with violet glow,
> my chakras filled with violet fire,
> I am your cosmic amplifier.

> **O Saint Germain, what love you bring,**
> **it truly makes all matter sing,**
> **your violet flame does all restore,**
> **with you we are becoming more.**

5. Saint Germain, shatter the energetic matrix that prevents people from seeing that the condition for gaining membership in the elite is that you accept the elitist mindset and that you do not question it. If the elite is legitimizing themselves by some religion or philosophy, you cannot question that either.

> O Saint Germain, I am now free,
> your violet flame is therapy,
> transform all hang-ups in my mind,
> as inner peace I surely find.

O Saint Germain, what love you bring,
it truly makes all matter sing,
your violet flame does all restore,
with you we are becoming more.

6. Saint Germain, shatter the energetic matrix that prevents people from seeing that if there is a division in the elite, as there most often is, then you must choose one side or the other. It is difficult to be a member of the elite and be neutral. You must choose one grouping or the other.

O Saint Germain, my body pure,
your violet flame for all is cure,
consume the cause of all disease,
and therefore I am all at ease.

O Saint Germain, what love you bring,
it truly makes all matter sing,
your violet flame does all restore,
with you we are becoming more.

7. Saint Germain, shatter the energetic matrix that prevents people from seeing that people become pulled into fighting for whatever cause is defined, whatever epic struggle happens to be the one that is dominating the times.

O Saint Germain, I'm karma-free,
the past no longer burdens me,
a brand new opportunity,
I am in Christic unity.

O Saint Germain, what love you bring,
it truly makes all matter sing,
your violet flame does all restore,
with you we are becoming more.

8. Saint Germain, shatter the energetic matrix that prevents people from seeing that the elite has created this self-reinforcing effect. They have created this cloud that prevents people from seeing their own existence and the methods they use.

O Saint Germain, we are now one,
I am for you a violet sun,
as we transform this planet earth,
your Golden Age is given birth.

O Saint Germain, what love you bring,
it truly makes all matter sing,
your violet flame does all restore,
with you we are becoming more.

9. Saint Germain, shatter the energetic matrix that prevents people from seeing that the elite can create this cloud because they are dominating the institutions of society. The elite always attempt to dominate government, the media, the publication of ideas, education and business. The major institutions of society become dominated by the elite.

O Saint Germain, the earth is free,
from burden of duality,
in oneness we bring what is best,
your Golden Age is manifest.

O Saint Germain, what love you bring,
it truly makes all matter sing,
your violet flame does all restore,
with you we are becoming more.

Part 4

1. Saint Germain, shatter the energetic matrix that prevents people from seeing that members of the power elite, without consciously conspiring to do this, have managed to define the parameters for what is being debated in society. They are defining which issues need to be talked about, which issues are important. They are excluding anything that could threaten their dominance.

O Saint Germain, you do inspire,
my vision raised forever higher,

with you I form a figure-eight,
your Golden Age I co-create.

O Saint Germain, what love you bring,
it truly makes all matter sing,
your violet flame does all restore,
with you we are becoming more.

2. Saint Germain, shatter the energetic matrix that prevents people from seeing that they are not doing this as a result of some conscious conspiracy. They are doing this because the people who are part of the elite are willing to go along to get along.

O Saint Germain, what Freedom Flame,
released when we recite your name,
acceleration is your gift,
our planet it will surely lift.

O Saint Germain, what love you bring,
it truly makes all matter sing,
your violet flame does all restore,
with you we are becoming more.

3. Saint Germain, shatter the energetic matrix that prevents people from seeing that you have to go along with the basic mindset of the elite in order to become part of the elite. Once you are part of the elite, you have to continue to go along in order to remain in your position.

O Saint Germain, in love we claim,
our right to bring your violet flame,
from you Above, to us below,
it is an all-transforming flow.

O Saint Germain, what love you bring,
it truly makes all matter sing,
your violet flame does all restore,
with you we are becoming more.

4. Saint Germain, shatter the energetic matrix that prevents people from seeing that everyone who is part of the elite is willing to compromise basically anything. They are willing to compromise their own inner ability to know a higher truth, their intuitive sense of what is right from a higher perspective.

O Saint Germain, I love you so,
my aura filled with violet glow,
my chakras filled with violet fire,
I am your cosmic amplifier.

**O Saint Germain, what love you bring,
it truly makes all matter sing,
your violet flame does all restore,
with you we are becoming more.**

5. Saint Germain, shatter the energetic matrix that prevents people from seeing that it is not necessarily that they, with a malicious intent, accept a false belief or a false definition of good and evil. They are not consciously accepting the serpentine logic.

O Saint Germain, I am now free,
your violet flame is therapy,
transform all hang-ups in my mind,
as inner peace I surely find.

**O Saint Germain, what love you bring,
it truly makes all matter sing,
your violet flame does all restore,
with you we are becoming more.**

6. Saint Germain, shatter the energetic matrix that prevents people from seeing that people take on the serpentine logic because they want to be part of the elite, and they are willing to do whatever it takes to gain that power, privilege or money.

O Saint Germain, my body pure,
your violet flame for all is cure,

consume the cause of all disease,
and therefore I am all at ease.

O Saint Germain, what love you bring,
it truly makes all matter sing,
your violet flame does all restore,
with you we are becoming more.

7. Saint Germain, shatter the energetic matrix that prevents people from seeing that this is a characteristic that is not in human nature. People in the general population have often been manipulated into accepting this mind-set where they are willing to compromise their principles.

O Saint Germain, I'm karma-free,
the past no longer burdens me,
a brand new opportunity,
I am in Christic unity.

O Saint Germain, what love you bring,
it truly makes all matter sing,
your violet flame does all restore,
with you we are becoming more.

8. Saint Germain, shatter the energetic matrix that prevents people from seeing that we have been manipulated into going to war or going along with an elitist economy that we know is not serving our own interests.

O Saint Germain, we are now one,
I am for you a violet sun,
as we transform this planet earth,
your Golden Age is given birth.

O Saint Germain, what love you bring,
it truly makes all matter sing,
your violet flame does all restore,
with you we are becoming more.

9. Saint Germain, shatter the energetic matrix that prevents people from seeing that it is not actually in human nature to compromise. Human

beings, when we are not manipulated by the elite, have some sense of the basic humanity. This is a frame of reference that allows us to evaluate everything based on the rule: "Do unto others what you want them to do unto you."

O Saint Germain, the earth is free,
from burden of duality,
in oneness we bring what is best,
your Golden Age is manifest.

O Saint Germain, what love you bring,
it truly makes all matter sing,
your violet flame does all restore,
with you we are becoming more.

Part 5

1. Saint Germain, shatter the energetic matrix that prevents people from seeing that this is a universal principle that we are tuned in to when we are not manipulated by the serpentine mindset. We know it is in our own interest to treat other people fairly so that we will be treated fairly.

O Saint Germain, you do inspire,
my vision raised forever higher,
with you I form a figure-eight,
your Golden Age I co-create.

O Saint Germain, what love you bring,
it truly makes all matter sing,
your violet flame does all restore,
with you we are becoming more.

2. Saint Germain, shatter the energetic matrix that prevents people from seeing that the elite originally knew the Golden Rule, but they have given it up because they want their privilege, power or money so much that they are willing to set it aside in order to get these outer things.

O Saint Germain, what Freedom Flame,
released when we recite your name,
acceleration is your gift,
our planet it will surely lift.

O Saint Germain, what love you bring,
it truly makes all matter sing,
your violet flame does all restore,
with you we are becoming more.

3. Saint Germain, shatter the energetic matrix that prevents people from seeing that this is precisely why, if we let the people rule without being manipulated by the elite, the people will make far better decisions than the elite has been doing and is doing.

O Saint Germain, in love we claim,
our right to bring your violet flame,
from you Above, to us below,
it is an all-transforming flow.

O Saint Germain, what love you bring,
it truly makes all matter sing,
your violet flame does all restore,
with you we are becoming more.

4. Saint Germain, shatter the energetic matrix that prevents people from seeing that the primary feature of the duality consciousness is that it puts people in a state of illusion, and that state of illusion is self-reinforcing. There is no way to use the duality consciousness to escape the duality consciousness.

O Saint Germain, I love you so,
my aura filled with violet glow,
my chakras filled with violet fire,
I am your cosmic amplifier.

O Saint Germain, what love you bring,
it truly makes all matter sing,

your violet flame does all restore,
with you we are becoming more.

5. Saint Germain, shatter the energetic matrix that prevents people from seeing that once we have gone into the state of mind where we think we are gods, who can define good and evil based on our current level of consciousness, then our definition of good and evil will always be relative to our state of consciousness. There will be nothing objective, universal or absolute about it.

O Saint Germain, I am now free,
your violet flame is therapy,
transform all hang-ups in my mind,
as inner peace I surely find.

O Saint Germain, what love you bring,
it truly makes all matter sing,
your violet flame does all restore,
with you we are becoming more.

6. Saint Germain, shatter the energetic matrix that prevents people from seeing that only through the Christ consciousness can we gain a frame of reference from beyond duality. If we could free the population from the manipulation of the elite, they have that essential humanity, which is an element of the Christ consciousness.

O Saint Germain, my body pure,
your violet flame for all is cure,
consume the cause of all disease,
and therefore I am all at ease.

O Saint Germain, what love you bring,
it truly makes all matter sing,
your violet flame does all restore,
with you we are becoming more.

7. Saint Germain, shatter the energetic matrix that prevents people from seeing that once we step into the duality consciousness, we lose it because now everything is relative. There is no rock of Christ. We are basing our

lives, our minds, on the shifting sands of the serpentine mind, and in this mind everything is relative.

> O Saint Germain, I'm karma-free,
> the past no longer burdens me,
> a brand new opportunity,
> I am in Christic unity.

> **O Saint Germain, what love you bring,**
> **it truly makes all matter sing,**
> **your violet flame does all restore,**
> **with you we are becoming more.**

8. Saint Germain, shatter the energetic matrix that prevents people from seeing that Jesus gave a set of principles that were entirely nonviolent. The Catholic church managed to pervert Jesus' teachings to the point where they could be used to seemingly legitimize extremely violent actions.

> O Saint Germain, we are now one,
> I am for you a violet sun,
> as we transform this planet earth,
> your Golden Age is given birth.

> **O Saint Germain, what love you bring,**
> **it truly makes all matter sing,**
> **your violet flame does all restore,**
> **with you we are becoming more.**

9. Saint Germain, shatter the energetic matrix that prevents people from seeing that this is a clear example of how the serpentine logic makes everything relative. They made the teachings of Christ relative to their situation, their state of consciousness, their way of thinking and the outer political goals they had.

> O Saint Germain, the earth is free,
> from burden of duality,
> in oneness we bring what is best,
> your Golden Age is manifest.

**O Saint Germain, what love you bring,
it truly makes all matter sing,
your violet flame does all restore,
with you we are becoming more.**

Sealing

In the name of the I AM THAT I AM, I accept that Archangel Michael, Astrea and Shiva form an impenetrable shield around myself and all constructive people, sealing us from all fear-based energies in all four octaves. I accept that the Light of God is consuming and transforming all fear-based energies that make up the dark forces working against ending the era of elitism on earth!

13 | INVOKING THE EXPOSURE OF THE REAL CONSPIRACY (PART 2)

In the name of the I AM THAT I AM, Jesus Christ, I use the authority that I have as a being in embodiment on earth to call upon Saint Germain to reinforce my calls and use my chakras to project the statements in this invocation into the collective consciousness and awaken people to how the fallen beings are controlling the world without being seen. Awaken people to the reality that we are spiritual beings and that we can co-create a new future by working with the ascended masters. I especially call for …

[Make your own calls here.]

Part 1

1. Saint Germain, shatter the energetic matrix that prevents people from seeing that Jesus came to set people free, but the Catholic leaders used the teachings of Christ, a perverted version of them, to enslave people even more.

O Saint Germain, you do inspire,
my vision raised forever higher,
with you I form a figure-eight,
your Golden Age I co-create.

**O Saint Germain, what love you bring,
it truly makes all matter sing,
your violet flame does all restore,
with you we are becoming more.**

2. Saint Germain, shatter the energetic matrix that prevents people from seeing that the power elite is entirely enveloped in the serpentine consciousness that makes everything relative.

O Saint Germain, what Freedom Flame,
released when we recite your name,
acceleration is your gift,
our planet it will surely lift.

**O Saint Germain, what love you bring,
it truly makes all matter sing,
your violet flame does all restore,
with you we are becoming more.**

3. Saint Germain, shatter the energetic matrix that prevents people from seeing that when everything is relative, at any time, in any given society, in any given situation, there is always an elite who can use whatever philosophy is there to justify doing whatever they want to do. The elite can always justify what they want to do and they always have attempted to justify it.

O Saint Germain, in love we claim,
our right to bring your violet flame,
from you Above, to us below,
it is an all-transforming flow.

**O Saint Germain, what love you bring,
it truly makes all matter sing,
your violet flame does all restore,
with you we are becoming more.**

4. Saint Germain, shatter the energetic matrix that prevents people from seeing that elites have used the teachings of Christ, Muhammad and the Buddha. They have used the teachings of Marx, Adam Smith and Darwin to justify doing what they want to do, which is either to dominate and enslave the population or to defeat and destroy a competing power elite.

O Saint Germain, I love you so,
my aura filled with violet glow,
my chakras filled with violet fire,
I am your cosmic amplifier.

O Saint Germain, what love you bring,
it truly makes all matter sing,
your violet flame does all restore,
with you we are becoming more.

5. Saint Germain, shatter the energetic matrix that prevents people from seeing that sometimes an aspiring elite has used some teaching to justify dethroning the established power elite. Instead, they have set themselves up as the new elite, as we saw in the communist revolution and the French revolution.

O Saint Germain, I am now free,
your violet flame is therapy,
transform all hang-ups in my mind,
as inner peace I surely find.

O Saint Germain, what love you bring,
it truly makes all matter sing,
your violet flame does all restore,
with you we are becoming more.

6. Saint Germain, I call forth the judgment of Christ upon the fallen beings in the emotional realm and I call for the consuming of the demons, the entire structure in the emotional realm.

O Saint Germain, my body pure,
your violet flame for all is cure,

consume the cause of all disease,
and therefore I am all at ease.

O Saint Germain, what love you bring,
it truly makes all matter sing,
your violet flame does all restore,
with you we are becoming more.

7. Saint Germain, I call forth the judgment of Christ upon the fallen beings, those very deceptive beings in the mental realm.

O Saint Germain, I'm karma-free,
the past no longer burdens me,
a brand new opportunity,
I am in Christic unity.

O Saint Germain, what love you bring,
it truly makes all matter sing,
your violet flame does all restore,
with you we are becoming more.

8. Saint Germain, I call forth the judgment of Christ upon the higher ranking fallen beings in the identity realm, including the Dark Master.

O Saint Germain, we are now one,
I am for you a violet sun,
as we transform this planet earth,
your Golden Age is given birth.

O Saint Germain, what love you bring,
it truly makes all matter sing,
your violet flame does all restore,
with you we are becoming more.

9. Saint Germain, I call forth the judgment of Christ upon the groups of fallen beings in the mental realm who are polarized towards the two extremes of the duality consciousness, and are using the analytical mind, the dualistic state of mind, to argue against each other.

O Saint Germain, the earth is free,
from burden of duality,
in oneness we bring what is best,
your Golden Age is manifest.

O Saint Germain, what love you bring,
it truly makes all matter sing,
your violet flame does all restore,
with you we are becoming more.

Part 2

1. Saint Germain, I call forth the judgment of Christ upon the fallen beings in the identity realm who have submitted themselves to the rule of the Dark Master.

O Saint Germain, you do inspire,
my vision raised forever higher,
with you I form a figure-eight,
your Golden Age I co-create.

O Saint Germain, what love you bring,
it truly makes all matter sing,
your violet flame does all restore,
with you we are becoming more.

2. Saint Germain, I call forth the judgment of Christ upon the Dark Master and fallen beings in the identity realm who are more unified and have a more coherent strategy.

O Saint Germain, what Freedom Flame,
released when we recite your name,
acceleration is your gift,
our planet it will surely lift.

O Saint Germain, what love you bring,
it truly makes all matter sing,

**your violet flame does all restore,
with you we are becoming more.**

3. Saint Germain, I call forth the judgment of Christ upon the Dark Master and the fallen beings in the identity realm who are using the fallen beings in the mental realm, those in the emotional realm and those in physical embodiment, even those who are not fallen beings in physical embodiment, to further that agenda.

O Saint Germain, in love we claim,
our right to bring your violet flame,
from you Above, to us below,
it is an all-transforming flow.

**O Saint Germain, what love you bring,
it truly makes all matter sing,
your violet flame does all restore,
with you we are becoming more.**

4. Saint Germain, I call forth the judgment of Christ that authorizes the ascended masters to step in and consume this entire apparatus of the fallen beings. I call for people to be cut free from the lies promoted by these fallen beings.

O Saint Germain, I love you so,
my aura filled with violet glow,
my chakras filled with violet fire,
I am your cosmic amplifier.

**O Saint Germain, what love you bring,
it truly makes all matter sing,
your violet flame does all restore,
with you we are becoming more.**

5. Saint Germain, shatter the energetic matrix that prevents people from seeing that as long as a large number of people accept the serpentine lies and believe they are beneficial and believe in the elitist mindset, then it cannot be removed from the earth.

O Saint Germain, I am now free,
your violet flame is therapy,
transform all hang-ups in my mind,
as inner peace I surely find.

**O Saint Germain, what love you bring,
it truly makes all matter sing,
your violet flame does all restore,
with you we are becoming more.**

6. Saint Germain, shatter the energetic matrix that prevents people from seeing that if we will not awaken, we must learn from the School of Hard Knocks by seeing a more extreme outplaying of what the elitist mindset will do, namely that it will always create some kind of crisis, some kind of disaster.

O Saint Germain, my body pure,
your violet flame for all is cure,
consume the cause of all disease,
and therefore I am all at ease.

**O Saint Germain, what love you bring,
it truly makes all matter sing,
your violet flame does all restore,
with you we are becoming more.**

7. Saint Germain, shatter the energetic matrix that prevents people from seeing that the power elites of history have all repeated the same pattern. Whatever philosophy they had, whatever agenda they had, they could never stop in time. They always took it so far that it created some kind of crisis or conflict that led them to lose their position so that another elite would take over.

O Saint Germain, I'm karma-free,
the past no longer burdens me,
a brand new opportunity,
I am in Christic unity.

O Saint Germain, what love you bring,
it truly makes all matter sing,
your violet flame does all restore,
with you we are becoming more.

8. Saint Germain, shatter the energetic matrix that prevents people from seeing that historically, the elites have created one disaster, one crisis after another. The School of Hard Knocks works so that the elites will always take things too far.

O Saint Germain, we are now one,
I am for you a violet sun,
as we transform this planet earth,
your Golden Age is given birth.

O Saint Germain, what love you bring,
it truly makes all matter sing,
your violet flame does all restore,
with you we are becoming more.

9. Saint Germain, shatter the energetic matrix that prevents people from seeing that the elite cannot stop in time. That is what eventually will overturn their dominance, perhaps causing another elite to spring up, but also in the long run, causing more and more people to question elitism.

O Saint Germain, the earth is free,
from burden of duality,
in oneness we bring what is best,
your Golden Age is manifest.

O Saint Germain, what love you bring,
it truly makes all matter sing,
your violet flame does all restore,
with you we are becoming more.

Part 3

1. Saint Germain, shatter the energetic matrix that prevents people from seeing that we have democracies today because a certain number of people started to question elitism. They started to question elitism in the form we saw with the kings, the noblemen and the clergy of Europe.

O Saint Germain, you do inspire,
my vision raised forever higher,
with you I form a figure-eight,
your Golden Age I co-create.

**O Saint Germain, what love you bring,
it truly makes all matter sing,
your violet flame does all restore,
with you we are becoming more.**

2. Saint Germain, shatter the energetic matrix that prevents people from seeing that we need to question the elitist mindset itself and come to the awareness that there is a mindset behind the physical elite. It is this mindset that needs to be questioned in order for the modern democracies to become true democracies that are not dominated by an elite.

O Saint Germain, what Freedom Flame,
released when we recite your name,
acceleration is your gift,
our planet it will surely lift.

**O Saint Germain, what love you bring,
it truly makes all matter sing,
your violet flame does all restore,
with you we are becoming more.**

3. Saint Germain, shatter the energetic matrix that prevents people from seeing that we cannot have a true democracy if a power elite dominates the population. It is an antithesis to democracy. We can only then have a token democracy, a democracy by name, a democracy of pretending to be a free democratic society when it truly is not.

O Saint Germain, in love we claim,
our right to bring your violet flame,
from you Above, to us below,
it is an all-transforming flow.

O Saint Germain, what love you bring,
it truly makes all matter sing,
your violet flame does all restore,
with you we are becoming more.

4. Saint Germain, shatter the energetic matrix that prevents people from seeing that we do not actually have freedom if we have political freedom, but not psychological freedom. If we are still trapped in our minds, in the serpentine illusion, we are not truly free.

O Saint Germain, I love you so,
my aura filled with violet glow,
my chakras filled with violet fire,
I am your cosmic amplifier.

O Saint Germain, what love you bring,
it truly makes all matter sing,
your violet flame does all restore,
with you we are becoming more.

5. Saint Germain, shatter the energetic matrix that prevents people from seeing that a gradual process has led to the current state of the modern democracies. This process has brought a certain freedom at the physical level. We are more free in the modern democracies than people were in the feudal societies, in the Soviet Union or other civilizations.

O Saint Germain, I am now free,
your violet flame is therapy,
transform all hang-ups in my mind,
as inner peace I surely find.

O Saint Germain, what love you bring,
it truly makes all matter sing,

your violet flame does all restore,
with you we are becoming more.

6. Saint Germain, shatter the energetic matrix that prevents people from seeing that we are only more free in an outer sense, and it is not only a matter of what we *can* do. Our real freedom depends on what we can *imagine* doing.

O Saint Germain, my body pure,
your violet flame for all is cure,
consume the cause of all disease,
and therefore I am all at ease.

O Saint Germain, what love you bring,
it truly makes all matter sing,
your violet flame does all restore,
with you we are becoming more.

7. Saint Germain, shatter the energetic matrix that prevents people from seeing that the elitist mindset has not only influenced the elite. In order to become members of the elite, you have to accept the elitist mindset and you have to not question it.

O Saint Germain, I'm karma-free,
the past no longer burdens me,
a brand new opportunity,
I am in Christic unity.

O Saint Germain, what love you bring,
it truly makes all matter sing,
your violet flame does all restore,
with you we are becoming more.

8. Saint Germain, shatter the energetic matrix that prevents people from seeing that the elite, in order to legitimize their existence and their agenda, have to get the consent of the governed. They have to get the people to go along with them, and therefore the people have also been affected by the elitist mindset. We have been affected by the serpentine logic that has made so many things relative.

O Saint Germain, we are now one,
I am for you a violet sun,
as we transform this planet earth,
your Golden Age is given birth.

O Saint Germain, what love you bring,
it truly makes all matter sing,
your violet flame does all restore,
with you we are becoming more.

9. Saint Germain, shatter the energetic matrix that prevents people from seeing that members of the elite have the power, money and privilege to do anything they want, but what is it they want? What is it they can imagine doing?

O Saint Germain, the earth is free,
from burden of duality,
in oneness we bring what is best,
your Golden Age is manifest.

O Saint Germain, what love you bring,
it truly makes all matter sing,
your violet flame does all restore,
with you we are becoming more.

Part 4

1. Saint Germain, shatter the energetic matrix that prevents people from seeing that members of the power elite have no imagination. They are like automatons. Some are programmed to want more power and it is never enough. Some want more privilege and it is never enough. Some want more money and it is never enough. Some want more fame and it is never enough.

O Saint Germain, you do inspire,
my vision raised forever higher,

with you I form a figure-eight,
your Golden Age I co-create.

O Saint Germain, what love you bring,
it truly makes all matter sing,
your violet flame does all restore,
with you we are becoming more.

2. Saint Germain, shatter the energetic matrix that prevents people from seeing that members of the power elite are not free according to a psychological definition of freedom. They are not free in their minds. They are more trapped in their minds than the average citizen.

O Saint Germain, what Freedom Flame,
released when we recite your name,
acceleration is your gift,
our planet it will surely lift.

O Saint Germain, what love you bring,
it truly makes all matter sing,
your violet flame does all restore,
with you we are becoming more.

3. Saint Germain, shatter the energetic matrix that prevents people from seeing that the average citizen is also trapped in the mindset of accepting that there must be an elite, that it is okay that 2% of the population control 90% of the wealth, while more and more people are living under the poverty level.

O Saint Germain, in love we claim,
our right to bring your violet flame,
from you Above, to us below,
it is an all-transforming flow.

O Saint Germain, what love you bring,
it truly makes all matter sing,
your violet flame does all restore,
with you we are becoming more.

4. Saint Germain, shatter the energetic matrix that prevents people from seeing that we have been programmed to accept that there is an intellectual elite that knows best what is true and not true. There is a religious elite, who can tell us what to believe. There is a political elite and a media elite. All of these elites claim they know better than the people.

O Saint Germain, I love you so,
my aura filled with violet glow,
my chakras filled with violet fire,
I am your cosmic amplifier.

O Saint Germain, what love you bring,
it truly makes all matter sing,
your violet flame does all restore,
with you we are becoming more.

5. Saint Germain, shatter the energetic matrix that prevents people from seeing that when we accept that the elite knows best, we are limiting what we dare to imagine that we could do with the physical freedom we have.

O Saint Germain, I am now free,
your violet flame is therapy,
transform all hang-ups in my mind,
as inner peace I surely find.

O Saint Germain, what love you bring,
it truly makes all matter sing,
your violet flame does all restore,
with you we are becoming more.

6. Saint Germain, shatter the energetic matrix that prevents people from seeing that we are not really making use of the political freedom we have to live an entirely different lifestyle. Most people have gone into another form of selling their soul to the devil.

O Saint Germain, my body pure,
your violet flame for all is cure,
consume the cause of all disease,
and therefore I am all at ease.

O Saint Germain, what love you bring,
it truly makes all matter sing,
your violet flame does all restore,
with you we are becoming more.

7. Saint Germain, shatter the energetic matrix that prevents people from seeing that just as the elite will go along with the elitist mindset in order to gain their privileged positions, many among the middle class in the modern democracies feel that even though they are not the elite, they still have a comfortable lifestyle. They have sold themselves to maintaining this comfortable lifestyle by fitting themselves into the system defined by the elite.

O Saint Germain, I'm karma-free,
the past no longer burdens me,
a brand new opportunity,
I am in Christic unity.

O Saint Germain, what love you bring,
it truly makes all matter sing,
your violet flame does all restore,
with you we are becoming more.

8. Saint Germain, shatter the energetic matrix that prevents people from seeing that we become the worker bees that are producing the wealth that the elite is then siphoning off. The elite has become smart enough that they are giving people a more comfortable lifestyle and we are then settling for this.

O Saint Germain, we are now one,
I am for you a violet sun,
as we transform this planet earth,
your Golden Age is given birth.

O Saint Germain, what love you bring,
it truly makes all matter sing,
your violet flame does all restore,
with you we are becoming more.

9. Saint Germain, shatter the energetic matrix that prevents people from seeing that we are not using our political freedom to pursue some great dream that we have. We are tying our lives down to the 30-year mortgage, and it becomes our goal in life to pay off the mortgage so we own our houses and can buy a bigger car than the Joneses.

O Saint Germain, the earth is free,
from burden of duality,
in oneness we bring what is best,
your Golden Age is manifest.

O Saint Germain, what love you bring,
it truly makes all matter sing,
your violet flame does all restore,
with you we are becoming more.

Part 5

1. Saint Germain, shatter the energetic matrix that prevents people from seeing that the fallen beings created the Catholic church and the entire mindset that all people are sinners and that they should submit to the clergy and the kings.

O Saint Germain, you do inspire,
my vision raised forever higher,
with you I form a figure-eight,
your Golden Age I co-create.

O Saint Germain, what love you bring,
it truly makes all matter sing,
your violet flame does all restore,
with you we are becoming more.

2. Saint Germain, shatter the energetic matrix that prevents people from seeing that for some fallen beings it was a great triumph that they were able to manipulate so many people into accepting this limited position and

accept that there was an elite that had such privileges beyond the general population.

O Saint Germain, what Freedom Flame,
released when we recite your name,
acceleration is your gift,
our planet it will surely lift.

O Saint Germain, what love you bring,
it truly makes all matter sing,
your violet flame does all restore,
with you we are becoming more.

3. Saint Germain, shatter the energetic matrix that prevents people from seeing that the Soviet Union was another triumph for the fallen beings because they made so many people accept this low material lifestyle that they were offered in a communist society.

O Saint Germain, in love we claim,
our right to bring your violet flame,
from you Above, to us below,
it is an all-transforming flow.

O Saint Germain, what love you bring,
it truly makes all matter sing,
your violet flame does all restore,
with you we are becoming more.

4. Saint Germain, shatter the energetic matrix that prevents people from seeing that from the viewpoint of certain fallen beings, the greatest triumph for the fallen beings on this planet is actually the modern democracies, where the population is so unfree that they are the virtual slaves of the power elite but they think they are free.

O Saint Germain, I love you so,
my aura filled with violet glow,
my chakras filled with violet fire,
I am your cosmic amplifier.

O Saint Germain, what love you bring,
it truly makes all matter sing,
your violet flame does all restore,
with you we are becoming more.

5. Saint Germain, shatter the energetic matrix that prevents people from seeing that some fallen beings see it as their greatest accomplishment that they have managed to enslave people, while making them believe that they are free.

O Saint Germain, I am now free,
your violet flame is therapy,
transform all hang-ups in my mind,
as inner peace I surely find.

O Saint Germain, what love you bring,
it truly makes all matter sing,
your violet flame does all restore,
with you we are becoming more.

6. Saint Germain, shatter the energetic matrix that prevents people from seeing that people in the feudal societies knew they were enslaved. Yet many modern-day people believe they are free and they believe they live in the greatest society on earth.

O Saint Germain, my body pure,
your violet flame for all is cure,
consume the cause of all disease,
and therefore I am all at ease.

O Saint Germain, what love you bring,
it truly makes all matter sing,
your violet flame does all restore,
with you we are becoming more.

7. Saint Germain, shatter the energetic matrix that prevents people from seeing that many believe that their 30-year mortgage gives them a secure and privileged lifestyle, and that this is all one can aspire to as a human being.

O Saint Germain, I'm karma-free,
the past no longer burdens me,
a brand new opportunity,
I am in Christic unity.

O Saint Germain, what love you bring,
it truly makes all matter sing,
your violet flame does all restore,
with you we are becoming more.

8. Saint Germain, shatter the energetic matrix that prevents people from seeing that they think they have it made. They think they have gone as high as they can as a human being on earth and they cannot envision that there is more. They cannot believe that there could be more and they cannot get themselves to even dare to demand it. They think this is all you can have.

O Saint Germain, we are now one,
I am for you a violet sun,
as we transform this planet earth,
your Golden Age is given birth.

O Saint Germain, what love you bring,
it truly makes all matter sing,
your violet flame does all restore,
with you we are becoming more.

9. Saint Germain, shatter the energetic matrix that prevents people from seeing that the relative affluence many people have today compared to other nations is as nothing compared to what Saint Germain envisions for the Golden Age for all nations on earth.

O Saint Germain, the earth is free,
from burden of duality,
in oneness we bring what is best,
your Golden Age is manifest.

O Saint Germain, what love you bring,
it truly makes all matter sing,

your violet flame does all restore,
with you we are becoming more.

Part 6

1. Saint Germain, shatter the energetic matrix that prevents people from seeing that what we have today is such a poor substitute for Saint Germain's vision for the Golden Age that it is unfathomable how we can settle for so little when we could have so much just by asking for it.

O Saint Germain, you do inspire,
my vision raised forever higher,
with you I form a figure-eight,
your Golden Age I co-create.

O Saint Germain, what love you bring,
it truly makes all matter sing,
your violet flame does all restore,
with you we are becoming more.

2. Saint Germain, shatter the energetic matrix that prevents people from seeing that we could have so much more just by standing up and demanding that our government does what a democratic government should do, and prevents the formation of an elite that controls 90% of the wealth.

O Saint Germain, what Freedom Flame,
released when we recite your name,
acceleration is your gift,
our planet it will surely lift.

O Saint Germain, what love you bring,
it truly makes all matter sing,
your violet flame does all restore,
with you we are becoming more.

3. Saint Germain, shatter the energetic matrix that prevents people from seeing that no one can dispute the fact that a small elite controls the majority of the wealth. We cannot deny this unless we are completely delusional.

O Saint Germain, in love we claim,
our right to bring your violet flame,
from you Above, to us below,
it is an all-transforming flow.

O Saint Germain, what love you bring,
it truly makes all matter sing,
your violet flame does all restore,
with you we are becoming more.

4. Saint Germain, shatter the energetic matrix that prevents people from seeing that the fallen beings can deny anything and that is what they have always done whenever they felt threatened. People who have common sense cannot deny the unequal distribution of wealth and they cannot deny that this is profoundly anti-democratic and anti-freedom.

O Saint Germain, I love you so,
my aura filled with violet glow,
my chakras filled with violet fire,
I am your cosmic amplifier.

O Saint Germain, what love you bring,
it truly makes all matter sing,
your violet flame does all restore,
with you we are becoming more.

5. Saint Germain, shatter the energetic matrix that prevents people from seeing that it would make a huge difference in terms of elitism, if a critical mass of people could make the shift and see the elitist mindset that is behind the outer physical elite.

O Saint Germain, I am now free,
your violet flame is therapy,
transform all hang-ups in my mind,
as inner peace I surely find.

> **O Saint Germain, what love you bring,**
> **it truly makes all matter sing,**
> **your violet flame does all restore,**
> **with you we are becoming more.**

6. Saint Germain, shatter the energetic matrix that prevents people from seeing that the real problem is the self-reinforcing effect, where we think that current conditions could not be changed because they are based on some creation by God or creation by nature. Therefore, we need to have an elite to rule us.

> O Saint Germain, my body pure,
> your violet flame for all is cure,
> consume the cause of all disease,
> and therefore I am all at ease.

> **O Saint Germain, what love you bring,**
> **it truly makes all matter sing,**
> **your violet flame does all restore,**
> **with you we are becoming more.**

7. Saint Germain, shatter the energetic matrix that prevents people from seeing that we do not need an elite, and we would do far better if we did not have an elite.

> O Saint Germain, I'm karma-free,
> the past no longer burdens me,
> a brand new opportunity,
> I am in Christic unity.

> **O Saint Germain, what love you bring,**
> **it truly makes all matter sing,**
> **your violet flame does all restore,**
> **with you we are becoming more.**

8. Saint Germain, I hereby help broadcast your message into the collective consciousness. I call for your rays of light to carry these ideas into the collective consciousness and find their way to those people who are open to receiving them.

O Saint Germain, we are now one,
I am for you a violet sun,
as we transform this planet earth,
your Golden Age is given birth.

O Saint Germain, what love you bring,
it truly makes all matter sing,
your violet flame does all restore,
with you we are becoming more.

9. Saint Germain, shatter the energetic matrix that prevents people from seeing that we will not get more until we demand it. Ask and we shall receive. Ask with the knowledge that we will receive, and we *shall* receive. Ask not and how can we receive? How can we receive that which we cannot envision and which we cannot accept that we are worthy to have?

O Saint Germain, the earth is free,
from burden of duality,
in oneness we bring what is best,
your Golden Age is manifest.

O Saint Germain, what love you bring,
it truly makes all matter sing,
your violet flame does all restore,
with you we are becoming more.

Sealing

In the name of the I AM THAT I AM, I accept that Archangel Michael, Astrea and Shiva form an impenetrable shield around myself and all constructive people, sealing us from all fear-based energies in all four octaves. I accept that the Light of God is consuming and transforming all fear-based energies that make up the dark forces working against ending the era of elitism on earth!

14 | OVERCOMING THE FEAR BEHIND ELITISM

I AM the Ascended Master Jesus Christ. I want to continue my discourse on elitism as a divisive force. I said that elitism has created a fundamental division between the elite and the population, but of course the division does not stop there. First of all, there is not a unified elite. If there had been, they would have had much greater control on earth than they have had. There will never be a situation where the power elite on earth can all come together in a conscious, deliberate and organized effort to take control. There will always be rivaling factions that will want to destroy the competition and gain that control for themselves. By its very nature, the elite will be divided.

As Saint Germain said yesterday, there is the unconscious unity in the sense that all of them subscribe to the very mindset that allows an elite to exist. The other aspect of division created by the elite is that the people are divided into multiple factions. You can see throughout history how there has been this division of the people. There have been attempts to overcome this division by certain power elites seeking to force the people to come into some form of unity, as you saw in the Soviet Union, as you saw in the Roman Empire, as you saw in many of the past civilizations, even in Central America, South America, Egypt, the Middle East, the Far East and so on. In general, this of course has never worked on either a local or a global scale because there is always that very divisive nature of elitism that inevitably divides people into all of these rivaling factions.

The fallen beings are divided

What you actually have is an even greater division where you have a division between the fallen beings in embodiment and the fallen beings in the identity realm. The fallen beings in embodiment often have an agenda of wanting to have power and control and therefore wanting to create this one-world state, one-world government, whereas the fallen beings in the identity realm have an agenda of creating division, conflict and destruction, and so on. Look at how the people have been divided into all these different factions. There is nationality, there is religion, there is political belief, there is all of this. There is a certain underlying mindset where in so many civilizations, people have come to accept the existence of an elite, the inevitability of an elite, the beneficial aspect of an elite and they think that in many cases, they cannot live without it. One of the central lies spread by the power elite, for a very, very long time is that there needs to be a centralized leadership, an organized structure, kind of like a pyramid, where there is somebody on top. These are some of the things I want to examine here.

Jesus' intention for the Christian community

First, I want to go back and look at what kind of society, what kind of community, that I intended to create with my teachings and with my example. What was it that I had intended to create with my disciples, apostles and so forth? Very, very few people who call themselves Christians today understand this. Very few have even bothered to think about it and the reason for this is of course 1700 years of distortion by the Catholic church and then also by Protestant churches, who have distorted the central message that I came with.

What was the central message? Well, yesterday I said it was anti-elitist in nature but you can go a step further because you could also say it was anti-division. You can go a step even further and say it was not anti-anything, it was *for* something and it was for oneness, unity, unification. The Christ consciousness is the antidote to the consciousness of duality. Duality is by its nature divided, there will always be divisions, there will always be polarities, there will always be opposites. It cannot be any other way because that is the only way you can make things relative to what you want things to be. By its very nature, Christ is unified, the Christ consciousness will unify the people. Now, this statement needs to be balanced a little bit because there are stages of Christhood. There is a stage where you begin to have some Christ discernment and this allows you to see, for example, the lies of the fallen beings. It allows you to see that there is a power elite that is attempting to control the people. As you go into this stage, as you even saw me do in my life 2,000 years ago, you come to see yourself as somebody in opposition to this power elite.

If you look at my statements towards the scribes and Pharisees and the religious authorities, that could very well be construed as me seeing myself opposing these people and their reign over the people. In a sense, that is what I saw, that is how I saw it. But towards the end of my mission, I came to a higher vision and it is possible to go to higher visions than I actually manifested 2,000 years ago. Higher levels of Christhood where you become much more focused on the unity, the Oneness behind all of the outer divisions. So truly, if you want to understand the message of Christ, the true message of Christ, it is unity, it is oneness. It is that you overcome the divisions. In order to overcome the divisions, you need to go through a period where you are freeing yourself from the lies of the duality consciousness and those who are promoting those lies.

That is why you need to separate yourself out. You need to come apart and be a separate and chosen people, but this needs to be an interim stage. This is where so many of the Christian churches, but many other spiritual organizations in Pisces, have failed the initiation of Pisces. You do need to separate yourself out because you need to clear your mind from all of these lies, the dualistic illusions that are floating around in the mass consciousness. But when you go to the higher levels of Christhood, you stop separating yourself out. Because now you see that even though there is a power elite, you are not separated from all of the people.

You make a distinction between the power elite and the people and instead of seeing yourself as being apart from the people, you start seeing more and more oneness with the people. As you do this, the power elite becomes less and less of a factor in your mind. You are not seeing yourself in opposition to them. You are simply exposing their lies but you are not doing this to fight them or to destroy them. You are doing it to set the people free. You do not mind setting the power elite free, but that is not as likely to happen, but it is likely that you can set some of the people free.

Christianity has been a divisive force

Look back at Christianity and see how, even before the creation of the Catholic church, but certainly after the creation of the Catholic church, Christianity became not a unifying force, but a divisive force. Some will argue with that statement but you look at the Catholic church, and even when it had near absolute power, it was not a unifying force. It attempted of course to force everyone to come into the fold of becoming a Christian. But it created a clearly elitist society with an upper elite that could not be challenged by the population and the population were virtual slaves. It also was a very divisive force in itself because even though it had near total control, it still created these incredible divisions that you saw in the crusades, the witch hunts and the Inquisition.

You saw how the Catholic church after several centuries of its existence, was not even content to fight its external enemies. It turned upon its own members and started the Inquisition, which could be seen as a war against itself or at least its own members. You see, Christianity has fallen into the pattern that you see in so many other religions and spiritual movements, defining a boundary between those who are inside and those who are outside. I know that many Christian ministers would immediately argue: "But what about when Jesus said: 'Go ye into all the world and make all people my disciples.'" But did I say: "Go into all the world and make all people members of a Christian religion that is ready to kill anybody who opposes them?" Or for that matter, any Christian religion.

I said: "Make all people disciples of Christ." What does it mean to be a disciple of Christ? It means you are striving to put on the mind of Christ and attain that Christ discernment where you see beyond division and you see the unity behind all the divisions created by the duality consciousness and the fallen beings, the power elite, or whatever you want to call them, the prince of this world as I often used it, or Satan as another symbol or name for the divisive force. So that is what it truly means to be a disciple of Christ. Make all people disciples who are walking the path towards seeing unity behind division.

War and conflict could have been avoided

Now, just imagine if that had actually come to pass. Imagine that at least some Christian movements would have promoted that message for the past 2,000 years. These huge wars could have been avoided and many of the other divisions that you see. If you look at the past 2,000 years, you can see that there was a potential to have avoided all of the division, all of the fragmentation, all of the conflict. Would the Soviet Union have come into existence if there had been a critical mass of people walking the path of Christhood? It would not! There would not have been a Cold War. Capitalism would not have come into existence as a polarity to communism. All of these divisive forces could have been avoided. Why did they come into existence? Well, because when people will not walk the path of putting on the mind of Christ, there is only one other way they can learn and that is the School of Hard Knocks where they see that the divisive consciousness and the divisive forces become outplayed in more and more extreme ways.

This is truly what has happened over the past 2,000 years, and it is a result of the fact that so few people were able to understand the central message that it is possible (even in a world as divided as what it was 2,000 years ago and as divided as it is today, where it is even more divided) to find oneness and unity. It is possible to build that sense of unity among all people. We call it your essential or your basic humanity now. It could also be called your Christhood where you see the Christ in yourself, you see the Christ in all others because you are putting on that mind of Christ as Paul saw, but as Peter and most of the other disciples and apostles did not see. Realize here that so many things could have been different, but it is not a matter of lamenting what did not come to pass. Still, I wanted to give some vision of what kind of society you could have had, not to say that you *should* have had it but to say that you can have it very, very quickly.

The reality is that there has been a certain tension building, there has been a certain awareness building, over these past 2,000 years. Again, many people are ready to break through and come to see this higher vision. Even though it has not manifested yet, this kind of society can come to be manifest much more quickly within just a few decades. Many of the modern democracies can begin to manifest this kind of society, not through the Christian religion, which is forever lost for the cause of Christ, but through that general universal awareness, which truly is Christhood, the Christ mind.

One of the pivotal statements I made that points to unity is of course that "the kingdom of God is within you" and it is within *all* of you. This means that the kingdom of God is an inner condition. It is not so that I ever envisioned that the kingdom of God was some particular outer society that was supposed to manifest. The kingdom of God is an inner condition, which means what? It means that it is a state of consciousness—it is a state of consciousness where you rise above the dualistic divisions. Therefore, you see that deep inside of you there is something that is real, but it is beyond the outer personality. It is not something that could ever be divided. When you see it in yourself, it is only a short step to come to where you begin to see it in others and therefore you see it in all others. Therefore, you come to understand another pivotal statement I made, which is: "Inasmuch as ye have done it unto the least of these my little ones, ye have done it unto me."

The fabric that connects all people

When you see that oneness, you see that all people are part of the fabric of life. We are all connected. All people in embodiment are connected. We talk about a collective consciousness, a concept that would have been completely impossible to talk about 2,000 years ago because there was no way people could understand it. With the knowledge and awareness you have today, it is much easier for people to grasp this.

There is a fabric, a fabric of consciousness, of energy that connects all people. This means that when you have the Christ mind, you can see the complete illusion that is one of the primary illusions of the duality consciousness. This illusion is of course based on the sense of division. We have also called it the consciousness of separation. When you go into duality, you see yourself separated from most other people. You see yourself as belonging to a particular group that is distinctly different from all other people.

This gives rise to the illusion that what I do unto others does not affect me. It will not come back and hit me in the future. This is the central illusion of the fallen beings. They had it before they came here and they have spread it to the point where the vast majority of people on earth actually believe in this illusion, although we cannot necessarily say it is a conscious belief. It is not that they have actually chosen to believe this or they could even formulate it, but it has become so ingrained in the collective consciousness, so dominant in the collective consciousness, that most people believe this.

They actually believe that if they kill somebody, the fact that they will not immediately be struck by a bolt of lightning means they can get away with it. If they are not discovered by society and put in jail, they have gotten away with murder. There are many people who believe this. Now, many Christians would object to this and say that they actually believe that there will be a judgment after this lifetime. True. Many Christians do believe that, many people in East believe in karma and also believe that they will make karma for it. But certainly, they do not understand the Oneness behind it.

The Christ consciousness in its lower aspects can give people the sense that: "I will be punished by God or some other force for what I do." But the higher aspects of Christ consciousness seek to give you that sense of unity where you realize that what I do to others I am doing to myself because we are all connected. Christians do not see this. Most people in East who believe in karma do not see this. That is why I am saying the fallen beings have actually managed to spread this illusion of separation.

Christians think and project that if they kill somebody, God will judge them after this lifetime, God will punish them. But there is no God that punishes you. God has created an impersonal law and that law may return certain energy impulses to you. But first of all, it says that you will continue lifetime after lifetime to be in the same state of consciousness until you deliberately and consciously change your state of consciousness. That is why many people have this deeper sense that they are separated from other people, they are divided from other people. They see themselves as being, often, in opposition to other people.

The only real sin on earth

When you think about Christians, they may think that they will be punished by God or held accountable by God for certain actions they commit but there are other actions that they are constantly committing that they do not think they will be punished by God for, they instead think they will actually be rewarded. Christians, to this day, are one the primary forces on earth that are upholding the consciousness of division because they see themselves as being separated from all people who are not Christians. You even see within the Christian religion how for a thousand years or so the Catholic church managed to squash all other all divisions in Christianity but then, after the Reformation, you have seen this escalating division of the Christian religion into more and more different churches. You have, especially in the United States, these local churches with just a few hundred members who believe they are the only true Christians and that all others are believing in some false form of Christianity. Some even believe that their members will be saved when I come back and all the others will go to hell. Some Protestant churches believe that the Catholic church is a cult.

The reality here is that even though Christians may believe that there are certain sins they should not commit, the main sin they are committing, if you want to use their terminology, is that they are upholding and promoting the consciousness of division. They do not think they will be punished for this, but they *will* be punished for it because they will continue to carry that consciousness with them over into their next lifetimes until they consciously change it—and that consciousness is punishment in itself. If you could look at these Christians who think they are saved, who think they are the holy ones, who think that I will come back and elevate them to being my primary disciples on earth, you see that behind their outer facade of feeling saved or feeling superior, having spiritual pride, there is an enormous tension in their minds. They are incredibly tense because they are houses divided against themselves. They know within, deep within them, that they are not on the right track. They fear that they could not be saved but they have covered it over by all of these layers of the outer things: belonging to a certain church, doing all the right things and all of this. You see the same in other religions around the world. You see the same in political movements where the Marxists felt that they were the saved ones and you see many materialists today who believe that they will be favored by evolution in some way.

The unavoidable fear of separation

The reality here is that when you go into the consciousness of separation, there is a fear. You cannot avoid it. The only way to avoid fear is through oneness with the Christ consciousness. Once you step outside the Christ consciousness, there is an existential fear that enters your being. Because, the reality is that the being you were created as (we have called it the Conscious You and said it has no structure, therefore it cannot be divided) well, that being can never be destroyed. But the separate self that you create in order to step into separation and duality, that self *can* be destroyed, that self is mortal, that self can never ascend to heaven. As I said: "No man can ascend to heaven, save he that came down from heaven." The reality is that all people who have stepped into duality have an existential fear, they cannot escape it. You can try to cover it over, but you cannot escape it. The only way to escape it is to move towards oneness. But what does that mean? It means giving up the sense of self you have as a separate being. Of course, if you look at the Christians as an example (although there are many others), when you identify yourself as belonging to the only true church and therefore, being one of the few people who will be saved, how hard is it to give up that sense of self? It is very, very difficult.

You look at the scientific materialists who identify themselves as being intellectually superior to most other people. Once you step into that sense of being superior to the vast majority of the people on earth, it becomes very, very hard to give it up. It becomes very, very hard to let that self die. This is one of the primary dynamics that is upholding the elite because the elite have all been seduced by Satan, the consciousness of Satan, which is that some are superior and many are inferior. Once you step into that, it is very hard to give it up. You can only give it up when you truly realize what I said: "He who is willing to save his life shall lose it, but he who is willing to lose his life for my sake shall find it." You can see that even 2,000 years ago, I hinted at what we have now given you in a more detailed teaching about the separate selves that you just have to let die.

Each time you work on one of your separate selves and let it die, you are stepping closer to Christhood, to oneness with Christ. Do you see perhaps that what I really came to teach people is that you can attain oneness with the Christ mind? I offered of course, as an ascended master, that all people could come into oneness with me. This has been the offer that has been a standing offer for 2,000 years: I am with you always, even unto the end of the Piscean Age and beyond.

A society based on oneness

Those who are my disciples are walking a path of gradually coming closer and closer to oneness with the Ascended Master Jesus Christ. That is the essence of Christianity, or at least the message of Christ. Coming into oneness and thereby of course you come into oneness with all other people and you begin to see that oneness. When you create a society based on oneness instead of being based on division, that society will look very different from most of the societies you have seen throughout history.

One of you brought up the issue of poverty yesterday. Well, let us discuss that. The elite will say: "Oh, there are people that are poor because they are lazy or they are not willing to work hard. They are not willing to try to improve themselves. There's nothing you can do for them. Just let them be and we focus on living our lives." The reality is that poverty is created by the elite. It is created by an unequal distribution where a small elite is harvesting the fruits of the labor of the many.

If there was a more equal distribution of wealth, you would not have poverty. You may still have people who would find it very difficult to do what most people do: have a regular job, go to work every day, live in a house, doing all the practical things to make things work. Many of the people you see today, whether in other countries but even here in America, who are homeless, who are substance abusers, who are people walking around on the street talking to themselves with a crazy look in their eyes, many of these people would still be there if you had a more equal distribution of wealth, but they would not have to live in poverty.

In a society that was based on oneness, they would be taken care of physically. In a more enlightened society, they would also be taken care of psychologically because such a more aware society would recognize that there is a reason why these people are in the state they are in. It is not that they are lazy or stupid or unwilling to make an effort.

Once you realize reincarnation, you realize that these people that you see on the streets who cannot "get it together" as the American expression is, they were exposed to such trauma in past lives that their souls are so wounded, so scattered, so divided, that they cannot "keep it together" because their souls are scattered. It is not that they are lazy or stupid or unwilling to do anything. They were wounded very deeply in a past life.

Why where they wounded? Well, because they were exposed to some overwhelming trauma, many of them as a result of war. Who created the wars? The power elite. You see that the power elite has created the problem but instead of taking responsibility for it, they are blaming the people. The reality is that the power elite has created a problem and they do not want to take responsibility for it, they simply want it to go away.

This of course is the extreme outcome of the divisive consciousness, the duality consciousness. This is the very consciousness that I attempted to help people overcome by giving them an example, by giving them tools and teachings where they could come into oneness with each other. When you come into that greater oneness, then you see that in a society you are all linked together. You are all part of the fabric of life and instead of condemning someone for their lack of ability, you seek to help them. The reality is that there are societies in the modern world who have made tremendous progress towards that ideal of a more unified society. Primary among them, the Scandinavian countries where you have programs that, at least at the physical level, seek to alleviate poverty. Of course, they have not taken the step of also seeking to help people psychologically. The reality here is that there is a potential, there is a tension built in the collective consciousness, where many, many people can, with the help of your calls, make that switch and see that we need to have a more compassionate society.

America, of course is behind many of the other nations. You can see it in how they treat poverty—or do not treat poverty. You can see it in public health care where they basically say: "Well, if you get sick, it must be your own fault so you need to take care of it. It's not something society should take care of." As many of you know, the American nation is actually paying more for healthcare than many of the nations where they have what Americans would call socialized medicine.

You see here that despite the fact that America claims to be a Christian nation and many Americans see America as the primary Christian nation on earth, America has not even begun to really understand that deeper message of the oneness of Christ. The oneness of coming together, not because you feel forced to, not because you are trying to avoid hell, not because you are seeking a reward in heaven, but because you see the oneness of all life and therefore you see yourself one with others, and naturally you want for others what you want for yourself.

First of all, what do you want as a spiritual student for others? You want them to have the same healing that you have experienced. When you grow to the point of feeling at peace within, you want them to have that kind of peace. You want all people to have that kind of peace.

Overcoming the existential fear of duality

As you let those separate selves die and begin to come into oneness with Christ, you overcome that existential fear that is the eternal follower of the duality consciousness. We may call that fear Satan. I sometimes used the word Satan to denote this fear that is following all of these people, all people. You have the fear that you could go to hell, that you could die, that bad things could happen to you. But when you let go of the selves that have that fear, the fear disappears. Now, if you look at humankind, and look at the past 2,000 years, you see how individuals have attempted to overcome that fear by doing all kinds of things that made them feel secure. In a sense, you could say that the power elite are attempting to set themselves up in a position where they have power, they have privilege, they have money, all as an attempt to overcome their existential fear. You could also say that many of the people have gone along with some of the schemes of the power elite because they thought this would help them overcome their fears.

You see how many times people have gone into amazing extremes in order to alleviate their fear. They have gone to great lengths to try to solve the problem of this fear. You see in America today, why is America maintaining the largest military in the world? All in an attempt to alleviate the fear of the American people and of the power elite in America. Of course, there are fallen beings in the identity realm who have a different agenda but, in a sense, they also are driven by fear.

For all people in embodiment, this attempt to solve the problem of fear is a very, very important driving force. I knew this 2,000 years ago. I could not necessarily have put words on it as we can do today, because people know so much more, but I knew that people are in this state of fear. I knew, because I had experienced it, that the way out of this state of fear is the Christ consciousness: coming into unity by letting the separate selves die one by one.

It was my greatest desire to create a spiritual movement that would help people overcome that fear. What happened instead was of course, as you can all see, that the fallen beings managed to take the Christian teachings and turn it into a religion that was based on fear and that only made the fear worse by coming up with such concepts as original sin, and that all would go to hell who were not in the Christian religion and who were not good Christians.

The reality here is – and this is really the only way forward for the planet, for humanity – that you cannot overcome the fear by solving any problems. The fear is not a problem that can be solved. It does not matter what you do here on earth, you will never free yourself from that fear.

You may think that you are such a good Christian who belongs to the only true church of Christ but it will not solve the problem of your fear. You may think you are good Marxist, a good communist, who has historical necessity on your side and you are one of the leaders of the Soviet Union, which has the most powerful army. But it will not solve the problem of your fear. You may think you are a spiritual student and if you do enough decrees and violet flame, it will solve your problem. But you still will not overcome the fear.

You will overcome the fear only when you recognize that this fear is produced by a separate self, and instead of trying to solve the problem that the separate self projects at you, you separate yourself from the self and you let it die. You let it die for the sake of coming into oneness with Christ.

That is the only solution to the issue of elitism, the ultimate solution. There are of course other aspects that are very necessary because you cannot expect that the population will understand this message in the near future in its fullness. Therefore, there are interim steps of a growing awareness, as we have talked about before and will talk about for the remainder of this conference.

Nevertheless, I have given you the ultimate perspective from the perspective of the Christ mind and the mission that I started 2,000 years ago. It has been my joy and my privilege to give this to you, and to be able to use your chakras to broadcast this into the collective consciousness. Naturally, I do not in any way reject America or Americans, despite the fact that I am tough and direct, but all people have the potential to come into oneness with Christ.

None is rejected but of course you have to be willing. In order to come into oneness, you have to let that outer self die, there is no other way. I cannot do it for you, I never could. I never wanted to because I know, and I knew 2,000 years ago, the equation of free-will.

With this, I seal you in the love of my heart and I hope that some of you will have gained a new perspective and will come to that conscious realization: "I want oneness with Christ. I want oneness with Jesus." Certainly, if that is your decision, you can have it.

15 | INVOKING FREEDOM FROM THE FEAR BEHIND ELITISM (PART 1)

In the name of the I AM THAT I AM, Jesus Christ, I use the authority that I have as a being in embodiment on earth to call upon Jesus to reinforce my calls and use my chakras to project the statements in this invocation into the collective consciousness and awaken people from the fear that the elite uses to paralyze us. Awaken people to the reality that we are spiritual beings and that we can co-create a new future by working with the ascended masters. I especially call for …

[Make your own calls here.]

Part 1

1. Jesus, shatter the energetic matrix that prevents people from seeing that elitism is a divisive force. There is not a unified elite, or they would have had much greater control on earth.

O Jesus, blessed brother mine,
I walk the path that you outline,

a great example to us all,
I follow now your inner call.

**O Jesus, let the Fire of Joy,
consume the devil's subtle ploy,
transfigured is our planet earth,
the golden age is given birth.**

2. Jesus, shatter the energetic matrix that prevents people from seeing that there will never be a situation where the power elite can all come together in a conscious, deliberate and organized effort to take control.

O Jesus, open inner sight,
the ego wants to prove it's right,
but this I will no longer do,
I want to be all one with you.

**O Jesus, let the Fire of Joy,
consume the devil's subtle ploy,
transfigured is our planet earth,
the golden age is given birth.**

3. Jesus, shatter the energetic matrix that prevents people from seeing that there will always be rivaling factions that will want to destroy the competition and gain control for themselves. By its very nature, the elite will be divided.

O Jesus, I now clearly see,
the Key of Knowledge given me,
my Christ self I hereby embrace,
as you fill up my inner space.

**O Jesus, let the Fire of Joy,
consume the devil's subtle ploy,
transfigured is our planet earth,
the golden age is given birth.**

4. Jesus, shatter the energetic matrix that prevents people from seeing that there is an unconscious unity, in the sense that all of them subscribe to the very mindset that allows an elite to exist.

> O Jesus, show me serpent's lie,
> expose the beam in my own eye,
> as Christ discernment you me give,
> in oneness I forever live.

> **O Jesus, let the Fire of Joy,**
> **consume the devil's subtle ploy,**
> **transfigured is our planet earth,**
> **the golden age is given birth.**

5. Jesus, shatter the energetic matrix that prevents people from seeing that the other aspect of division created by the elite is that the people are divided into multiple factions. Throughout history we see this division of the people.

> O Jesus, I am truly meek,
> and thus I turn the other cheek,
> when the accuser attacks me,
> I go within and merge with thee.

> **O Jesus, let the Fire of Joy,**
> **consume the devil's subtle ploy,**
> **transfigured is our planet earth,**
> **the golden age is given birth.**

6. Jesus, shatter the energetic matrix that prevents people from seeing that there have been attempts to overcome this division by certain power elites, seeking to force the people to come into some form of unity, as we saw in the Soviet Union, the Roman Empire or many past civilizations.

> O Jesus, ego I let die,
> surrender ev'ry earthly tie,
> the dead can bury what is dead,
> I choose to walk with you instead.

O Jesus, let the Fire of Joy,
consume the devil's subtle ploy,
transfigured is our planet earth,
the golden age is given birth.

7. Jesus, shatter the energetic matrix that prevents people from seeing that in general, this has never worked on either a local or a global scale because there is always that very divisive nature of elitism that inevitably divides people into rivaling factions.

O Jesus, help me rise above,
the devil's test through higher love,
show me separate self unreal,
my formless self you do reveal.

O Jesus, let the Fire of Joy,
consume the devil's subtle ploy,
transfigured is our planet earth,
the golden age is given birth.

8. Jesus, shatter the energetic matrix that prevents people from seeing that there is a division between the fallen beings in embodiment and the fallen beings in the identity realm. The fallen beings in embodiment often have an agenda of wanting to have power and control and therefore wanting to create this one-world state, one-world government.

O Jesus, what is that to me,
I just let go and follow thee,
with this I do pass ev'ry test,
to find with you eternal rest.

O Jesus, let the Fire of Joy,
consume the devil's subtle ploy,
transfigured is our planet earth,
the golden age is given birth.

9. Jesus, shatter the energetic matrix that prevents people from seeing that the fallen beings in the identity realm have an agenda of creating division, conflict and destruction.

O Jesus, fiery master mine,
my heart now melting into thine,
I love with heart and mind and soul,
the God who is my highest goal.

**O Jesus, let the Fire of Joy,
consume the devil's subtle ploy,
transfigured is our planet earth,
the golden age is given birth.**

Part 2

1. Jesus, shatter the energetic matrix that prevents people from seeing that there is a certain underlying mindset where in many civilizations, people have come to accept the existence of an elite, the inevitability of an elite, the beneficial aspect of an elite. They think that they cannot live without the elite.

O Jesus, blessed brother mine,
I walk the path that you outline,
a great example to us all,
I follow now your inner call.

**O Jesus, let the Fire of Joy,
consume the devil's subtle ploy,
transfigured is our planet earth,
the golden age is given birth.**

2. Jesus, shatter the energetic matrix that prevents people from seeing that one of the central lies spread by the power elite for a very long time is that there needs to be a centralized leadership, an organized structure, like a pyramid where there is somebody on top.

O Jesus, open inner sight,
the ego wants to prove it's right,
but this I will no longer do,
I want to be all one with you.

**O Jesus, let the Fire of Joy,
consume the devil's subtle ploy,
transfigured is our planet earth,
the golden age is given birth.**

3. Jesus, shatter the energetic matrix that prevents people from seeing that after 1700 years of distortion by the Catholic church and Protestant churches, few understand that your central message was not only anti-elitist but also anti-division.

O Jesus, I now clearly see,
the Key of Knowledge given me,
my Christ self I hereby embrace,
as you fill up my inner space.

**O Jesus, let the Fire of Joy,
consume the devil's subtle ploy,
transfigured is our planet earth,
the golden age is given birth.**

4. Jesus, shatter the energetic matrix that prevents people from seeing that your message was not really anti-anything, it was *for* something and it was for oneness, unity, unification.

O Jesus, show me serpent's lie,
expose the beam in my own eye,
as Christ discernment you me give,
in oneness I forever live.

**O Jesus, let the Fire of Joy,
consume the devil's subtle ploy,
transfigured is our planet earth,
the golden age is given birth.**

5. Jesus, shatter the energetic matrix that prevents people from seeing that the Christ consciousness is the antidote to the consciousness of duality. Duality is by its nature divided, there will always be divisions, there will always be polarities, there will always be opposites. It cannot be any other

way because that is the only way we can make things relative to what we want things to be.

> O Jesus, I am truly meek,
> and thus I turn the other cheek,
> when the accuser attacks me,
> I go within and merge with thee.

> **O Jesus, let the Fire of Joy,**
> **consume the devil's subtle ploy,**
> **transfigured is our planet earth,**
> **the golden age is given birth.**

6. Jesus, shatter the energetic matrix that prevents people from seeing that by its very nature, Christ is unified, the Christ consciousness will unify the people.

> O Jesus, ego I let die,
> surrender ev'ry earthly tie,
> the dead can bury what is dead,
> I choose to walk with you instead.

> **O Jesus, let the Fire of Joy,**
> **consume the devil's subtle ploy,**
> **transfigured is our planet earth,**
> **the golden age is given birth.**

7. Jesus, shatter the energetic matrix that prevents people from seeing that there are stages of Christhood. There is a stage where we begin to have some Christ discernment and this allows us to see the lies of the fallen beings. It allows us to see that there is a power elite that is attempting to control the people.

> O Jesus, help me rise above,
> the devil's test through higher love,
> show me separate self unreal,
> my formless self you do reveal.

O Jesus, let the Fire of Joy,
consume the devil's subtle ploy,
transfigured is our planet earth,
the golden age is given birth.

8. Jesus, shatter the energetic matrix that prevents people from seeing that at this stage, we come to see ourselves as being in opposition to the power elite. At higher levels of Christhood we become much more focused on the unity, the Oneness behind all of the outer divisions.

O Jesus, what is that to me,
I just let go and follow thee,
with this I do pass ev'ry test,
to find with you eternal rest.

O Jesus, let the Fire of Joy,
consume the devil's subtle ploy,
transfigured is our planet earth,
the golden age is given birth.

9. Jesus, shatter the energetic matrix that prevents people from seeing that the true message of Christ is unity whereby we overcome the divisions. In order to overcome the divisions, we need to go through a period where we are freeing ourselves from the lies of the duality consciousness and those who are promoting those lies.

O Jesus, fiery master mine,
my heart now melting into thine,
I love with heart and mind and soul,
the God who is my highest goal.

O Jesus, let the Fire of Joy,
consume the devil's subtle ploy,
transfigured is our planet earth,
the golden age is given birth.

Part 3

1. Jesus, shatter the energetic matrix that prevents people from seeing that we need to separate ourselves, but this needs to be an interim stage. This is where many Christian churches and other spiritual organizations have failed the initiation of Pisces.

O Jesus, blessed brother mine,
I walk the path that you outline,
a great example to us all,
I follow now your inner call.

O Jesus, let the Fire of Joy,
consume the devil's subtle ploy,
transfigured is our planet earth,
the golden age is given birth.

2. Jesus, shatter the energetic matrix that prevents people from seeing that we do need to separate ourselves out, because we need to clear our minds from the dualistic illusions in the mass consciousness.

O Jesus, open inner sight,
the ego wants to prove it's right,
but this I will no longer do,
I want to be all one with you.

O Jesus, let the Fire of Joy,
consume the devil's subtle ploy,
transfigured is our planet earth,
the golden age is given birth.

3. Jesus, shatter the energetic matrix that prevents people from seeing that when we go to the higher levels of Christhood, we stop separating ourselves. Now we see that even though there is a power elite, we are not separated from all of the people.

O Jesus, I now clearly see,
the Key of Knowledge given me,

my Christ self I hereby embrace,
as you fill up my inner space.

**O Jesus, let the Fire of Joy,
consume the devil's subtle ploy,
transfigured is our planet earth,
the golden age is given birth.**

4. Jesus, shatter the energetic matrix that prevents people from seeing that we need to make a distinction between the power elite and the people. Instead of seeing ourselves as being apart from the people, we start seeing more and more oneness with the people.

O Jesus, show me serpent's lie,
expose the beam in my own eye,
as Christ discernment you me give,
in oneness I forever live.

**O Jesus, let the Fire of Joy,
consume the devil's subtle ploy,
transfigured is our planet earth,
the golden age is given birth.**

5. Jesus, shatter the energetic matrix that prevents people from seeing that as we do this, the power elite becomes less and less of a factor in our minds. We are not seeing ourselves in opposition to them.

O Jesus, I am truly meek,
and thus I turn the other cheek,
when the accuser attacks me,
I go within and merge with thee.

**O Jesus, let the Fire of Joy,
consume the devil's subtle ploy,
transfigured is our planet earth,
the golden age is given birth.**

6. Jesus, shatter the energetic matrix that prevents people from seeing that we are exposing their lies but we are not doing this to fight them or to destroy them. We are doing it to set the people free.

> O Jesus, ego I let die,
> surrender ev'ry earthly tie,
> the dead can bury what is dead,
> I choose to walk with you instead.

> **O Jesus, let the Fire of Joy,**
> **consume the devil's subtle ploy,**
> **transfigured is our planet earth,**
> **the golden age is given birth.**

7. Jesus, shatter the energetic matrix that prevents people from seeing that Christianity, especially after the creation of the Catholic church, became not a unifying force, but a divisive force.

> O Jesus, help me rise above,
> the devil's test through higher love,
> show me separate self unreal,
> my formless self you do reveal.

> **O Jesus, let the Fire of Joy,**
> **consume the devil's subtle ploy,**
> **transfigured is our planet earth,**
> **the golden age is given birth.**

8. Jesus, shatter the energetic matrix that prevents people from seeing that even when the Catholic church had near absolute power, it was not a unifying force. It attempted to force everyone to come into the fold of becoming a Christian, but it created an elitist society with an upper elite that could not be challenged.

> O Jesus, what is that to me,
> I just let go and follow thee,
> with this I do pass ev'ry test,
> to find with you eternal rest.

O Jesus, let the Fire of Joy,
consume the devil's subtle ploy,
transfigured is our planet earth,
the golden age is given birth.

9. Jesus, shatter the energetic matrix that prevents people from seeing that the Catholic church was a very divisive force in itself because even though it had near total control, it still created the divisions that we saw in the crusades, the witch hunts and the Inquisition.

O Jesus, fiery master mine,
my heart now melting into thine,
I love with heart and mind and soul,
the God who is my highest goal.

O Jesus, let the Fire of Joy,
consume the devil's subtle ploy,
transfigured is our planet earth,
the golden age is given birth.

Part 4

1. Jesus, shatter the energetic matrix that prevents people from seeing that the Catholic church was not content to fight its external enemies. It turned upon its own members and started the Inquisition, which could be seen as a war against itself or at least its own members.

O Jesus, blessed brother mine,
I walk the path that you outline,
a great example to us all,
I follow now your inner call.

O Jesus, let the Fire of Joy,
consume the devil's subtle ploy,
transfigured is our planet earth,
the golden age is given birth.

2. Jesus, shatter the energetic matrix that prevents people from seeing that Christianity has fallen into the pattern that we see in so many other religions and spiritual movements, namely defining a boundary between those who are inside and those who are outside.

O Jesus, open inner sight,
the ego wants to prove it's right,
but this I will no longer do,
I want to be all one with you.

O Jesus, let the Fire of Joy,
consume the devil's subtle ploy,
transfigured is our planet earth,
the golden age is given birth.

3. Jesus, shatter the energetic matrix that prevents people from seeing that when you said: "Go ye into all the world and make all people my disciples," you did not mean to make all people members of a Christian religion that is ready to kill anybody who opposes them.

O Jesus, I now clearly see,
the Key of Knowledge given me,
my Christ self I hereby embrace,
as you fill up my inner space.

O Jesus, let the Fire of Joy,
consume the devil's subtle ploy,
transfigured is our planet earth,
the golden age is given birth.

4. Jesus, shatter the energetic matrix that prevents people from seeing that you wanted all people to be disciples of Christ, which means we are striving to put on the mind of Christ and attain the Christ discernment, where we see the unity behind all the divisions created by the duality consciousness and the fallen beings, the power elite.

O Jesus, show me serpent's lie,
expose the beam in my own eye,

as Christ discernment you me give,
in oneness I forever live.

O Jesus, let the Fire of Joy,
consume the devil's subtle ploy,
transfigured is our planet earth,
the golden age is given birth.

5. Jesus, shatter the energetic matrix that prevents people from seeing that you wanted all people to be your disciples in the sense that we are walking the path towards seeing unity behind division.

O Jesus, I am truly meek,
and thus I turn the other cheek,
when the accuser attacks me,
I go within and merge with thee.

O Jesus, let the Fire of Joy,
consume the devil's subtle ploy,
transfigured is our planet earth,
the golden age is given birth.

6. Jesus, shatter the energetic matrix that prevents people from seeing that if at least some Christian movements had promoted that message for the past 2,000 years, these huge wars and many other divisions could have been avoided.

O Jesus, ego I let die,
surrender ev'ry earthly tie,
the dead can bury what is dead,
I choose to walk with you instead.

O Jesus, let the Fire of Joy,
consume the devil's subtle ploy,
transfigured is our planet earth,
the golden age is given birth.

7. Jesus, shatter the energetic matrix that prevents people from seeing that the Soviet Union would not have come into existence if there had been a critical mass of people walking the path of Christhood.

O Jesus, help me rise above,
the devil's test through higher love,
show me separate self unreal,
my formless self you do reveal.

**O Jesus, let the Fire of Joy,
consume the devil's subtle ploy,
transfigured is our planet earth,
the golden age is given birth.**

8. Jesus, shatter the energetic matrix that prevents people from seeing that there would not have been a Cold War. Capitalism would not have come into existence as a polarity to communism. All of these divisive forces could have been avoided.

O Jesus, what is that to me,
I just let go and follow thee,
with this I do pass ev'ry test,
to find with you eternal rest.

**O Jesus, let the Fire of Joy,
consume the devil's subtle ploy,
transfigured is our planet earth,
the golden age is given birth.**

9. Jesus, shatter the energetic matrix that prevents people from seeing that the divisive forces did come into existence because when people will not walk the path of putting on the mind of Christ, there is only one other way they can learn and that is the School of Hard Knocks, where they see that the divisive consciousness and the divisive forces become outplayed in more and more extreme ways.

O Jesus, fiery master mine,
my heart now melting into thine,

I love with heart and mind and soul,
the God who is my highest goal.

O Jesus, let the Fire of Joy,
consume the devil's subtle ploy,
transfigured is our planet earth,
the golden age is given birth.

Part 5

1. Jesus, shatter the energetic matrix that prevents people from seeing that even when the world is as divided as it is today, it is possible to build a sense of unity among all people through the essential humanity.

O Jesus, blessed brother mine,
I walk the path that you outline,
a great example to us all,
I follow now your inner call.

O Jesus, let the Fire of Joy,
consume the devil's subtle ploy,
transfigured is our planet earth,
the golden age is given birth.

2. Jesus, shatter the energetic matrix that prevents people from seeing that a more unified society can be manifest within just a few decades. Many of the modern democracies can begin to manifest this kind of society, not through the Christian religion, but through the universal awareness which truly is Christhood.

O Jesus, open inner sight,
the ego wants to prove it's right,
but this I will no longer do,
I want to be all one with you.

O Jesus, let the Fire of Joy,
consume the devil's subtle ploy,

**transfigured is our planet earth,
the golden age is given birth.**

3. Jesus, shatter the energetic matrix that prevents people from seeing that one of your pivotal statements is that the kingdom of God is within us, within *all* of us. The kingdom of God is an inner condition, a state of consciousness.

O Jesus, I now clearly see,
the Key of Knowledge given me,
my Christ self I hereby embrace,
as you fill up my inner space.

**O Jesus, let the Fire of Joy,
consume the devil's subtle ploy,
transfigured is our planet earth,
the golden age is given birth.**

4. Jesus, shatter the energetic matrix that prevents people from seeing that it is a state of consciousness where we rise above the dualistic divisions. Therefore, we see that deep inside of us there is something that is real, but it is beyond the outer personality. It is not something that could ever be divided.

O Jesus, show me serpent's lie,
expose the beam in my own eye,
as Christ discernment you me give,
in oneness I forever live.

**O Jesus, let the Fire of Joy,
consume the devil's subtle ploy,
transfigured is our planet earth,
the golden age is given birth.**

5. Jesus, shatter the energetic matrix that prevents people from seeing that when we see this in ourselves, it is only a short step to begin to see it in others. Therefore, we come to understand another pivotal statement: "Inasmuch as ye have done it unto the least of these my little ones, ye have done it unto me."

O Jesus, I am truly meek,
and thus I turn the other cheek,
when the accuser attacks me,
I go within and merge with thee.

O Jesus, let the Fire of Joy,
consume the devil's subtle ploy,
transfigured is our planet earth,
the golden age is given birth.

6. Jesus, shatter the energetic matrix that prevents people from seeing that when we see oneness, we know that all people are part of the fabric of life. We are all connected. All people in embodiment are connected.

O Jesus, ego I let die,
surrender ev'ry earthly tie,
the dead can bury what is dead,
I choose to walk with you instead.

O Jesus, let the Fire of Joy,
consume the devil's subtle ploy,
transfigured is our planet earth,
the golden age is given birth.

7. Jesus, shatter the energetic matrix that prevents people from seeing that there is a fabric of consciousness and energy that connects all people. When we have the Christ mind, we can see the complete illusion that is one of the primary illusions of the duality consciousness.

O Jesus, help me rise above,
the devil's test through higher love,
show me separate self unreal,
my formless self you do reveal.

O Jesus, let the Fire of Joy,
consume the devil's subtle ploy,
transfigured is our planet earth,
the golden age is given birth.

8. Jesus, shatter the energetic matrix that prevents people from seeing that when we go into duality, we see ourselves separated from most other people. We see ourselves as belonging to a particular group that is distinctly different from all other people.

O Jesus, what is that to me,
I just let go and follow thee,
with this I do pass ev'ry test,
to find with you eternal rest.

O Jesus, let the Fire of Joy,
consume the devil's subtle ploy,
transfigured is our planet earth,
the golden age is given birth.

9. Jesus, shatter the energetic matrix that prevents people from seeing that this gives rise to the illusion that what we do unto others does not affect ourselves. It will not come back and hit us in the future.

O Jesus, fiery master mine,
my heart now melting into thine,
I love with heart and mind and soul,
the God who is my highest goal.

O Jesus, let the Fire of Joy,
consume the devil's subtle ploy,
transfigured is our planet earth,
the golden age is given birth.

Sealing

In the name of the I AM THAT I AM, I accept that Archangel Michael, Astrea and Shiva form an impenetrable shield around myself and all constructive people, sealing us from all fear-based energies in all four octaves. I accept that the Light of God is consuming and transforming all fear-based energies that make up the dark forces working against ending the era of elitism on earth!

16 | INVOKING FREEDOM FROM THE FEAR BEHIND ELITISM (PART 2)

In the name of the I AM THAT I AM, Jesus Christ, I use the authority that I have as a being in embodiment on earth to call upon Jesus to reinforce my calls and use my chakras to project the statements in this invocation into the collective consciousness and awaken people from the fear that the elite uses to paralyze us. Awaken people to the reality that we are spiritual beings and that we can co-create a new future by working with the ascended masters. I especially call for …

[Make your own calls here.]

Part 1

1. Jesus, shatter the energetic matrix that prevents people from seeing that separation is the central illusion of the fallen beings. They had it before they came here and they have spread it to the point where the vast majority of people on earth believe in this illusion.

O Jesus, blessed brother mine,
I walk the path that you outline,
a great example to us all,
I follow now your inner call.

**O Jesus, let the Fire of Joy,
consume the devil's subtle ploy,
transfigured is our planet earth,
the golden age is given birth.**

2. Jesus, shatter the energetic matrix that prevents people from seeing that many people believe that if they kill somebody, the fact that they will not immediately be struck by a bolt of lightning means they can get away with it. If they are not discovered by society and put in jail, they have gotten away with murder.

O Jesus, open inner sight,
the ego wants to prove it's right,
but this I will no longer do,
I want to be all one with you.

**O Jesus, let the Fire of Joy,
consume the devil's subtle ploy,
transfigured is our planet earth,
the golden age is given birth.**

3. Jesus, shatter the energetic matrix that prevents people from seeing that the Christ consciousness in its lower aspects can give people the sense that: "I will be punished by God or some other force for what I do."

O Jesus, I now clearly see,
the Key of Knowledge given me,
my Christ self I hereby embrace,
as you fill up my inner space.

**O Jesus, let the Fire of Joy,
consume the devil's subtle ploy,
transfigured is our planet earth,
the golden age is given birth.**

4. Jesus, shatter the energetic matrix that prevents people from seeing that the higher aspects of Christ consciousness seek to give us the sense of unity, where we realize that what we do to others we are doing to ourselves because we are all connected.

O Jesus, show me serpent's lie,
expose the beam in my own eye,
as Christ discernment you me give,
in oneness I forever live.

O Jesus, let the Fire of Joy,
consume the devil's subtle ploy,
transfigured is our planet earth,
the golden age is given birth.

5. Jesus, shatter the energetic matrix that prevents people from seeing that Christians think that if they kill somebody, God will judge them after this lifetime. God will punish them. But there is no God that punishes us.

O Jesus, I am truly meek,
and thus I turn the other cheek,
when the accuser attacks me,
I go within and merge with thee.

O Jesus, let the Fire of Joy,
consume the devil's subtle ploy,
transfigured is our planet earth,
the golden age is given birth.

6. Jesus, shatter the energetic matrix that prevents people from seeing that God has created an impersonal law and that law may return certain energy impulses to us. But first of all, it says that we will continue lifetime after lifetime to be in the same state of consciousness until we deliberately and consciously change our state of consciousness.

O Jesus, ego I let die,
surrender ev'ry earthly tie,
the dead can bury what is dead,
I choose to walk with you instead.

O Jesus, let the Fire of Joy,
consume the devil's subtle ploy,
transfigured is our planet earth,
the golden age is given birth.

7. Jesus, shatter the energetic matrix that prevents people from seeing that Christians are one of the primary forces that is upholding the consciousness of division, because they see themselves as being separated from all people who are not Christians.

O Jesus, help me rise above,
the devil's test through higher love,
show me separate self unreal,
my formless self you do reveal.

O Jesus, let the Fire of Joy,
consume the devil's subtle ploy,
transfigured is our planet earth,
the golden age is given birth.

8. Jesus, shatter the energetic matrix that prevents people from seeing that since the Reformation, we have seen this escalating division of the Christian religion into more and more different churches. Some believe they are the only true Christians and that all others are believing in some false form of Christianity.

O Jesus, what is that to me,
I just let go and follow thee,
with this I do pass ev'ry test,
to find with you eternal rest.

O Jesus, let the Fire of Joy,
consume the devil's subtle ploy,
transfigured is our planet earth,
the golden age is given birth.

9. Jesus, shatter the energetic matrix that prevents people from seeing the reality that even though Christians may believe that there are certain sins

they should not commit, the main sin they are committing is that they are upholding and promoting the consciousness of division.

> O Jesus, fiery master mine,
> my heart now melting into thine,
> I love with heart and mind and soul,
> the God who is my highest goal.

> **O Jesus, let the Fire of Joy,**
> **consume the devil's subtle ploy,**
> **transfigured is our planet earth,**
> **the golden age is given birth.**

Part 2

1. Jesus, shatter the energetic matrix that prevents people from seeing that Christians will be punished for this in the sense that they will continue to carry that consciousness with them into their next lifetimes, until they consciously change it—and that consciousness is punishment in itself.

> O Jesus, blessed brother mine,
> I walk the path that you outline,
> a great example to us all,
> I follow now your inner call.

> **O Jesus, let the Fire of Joy,**
> **consume the devil's subtle ploy,**
> **transfigured is our planet earth,**
> **the golden age is given birth.**

2. Jesus, shatter the energetic matrix that prevents people from seeing that Christians who think they are saved, behind their outer facade of feeling saved or feeling superior, there is an enormous tension in their minds.

> O Jesus, open inner sight,
> the ego wants to prove it's right,

but this I will no longer do,
I want to be all one with you.

O Jesus, let the Fire of Joy,
consume the devil's subtle ploy,
transfigured is our planet earth,
the golden age is given birth.

3. Jesus, shatter the energetic matrix that prevents people from seeing that many Christians are incredibly tense because they are houses divided against themselves. They know within that they are not on the right track. They fear that they could not be saved but they have covered it over by these layers of doing outer things.

O Jesus, I now clearly see,
the Key of Knowledge given me,
my Christ self I hereby embrace,
as you fill up my inner space.

O Jesus, let the Fire of Joy,
consume the devil's subtle ploy,
transfigured is our planet earth,
the golden age is given birth.

4. Jesus, shatter the energetic matrix that prevents people from seeing that we see the same pattern in other religions, even in political movements and we see many materialists who believe that they will be favored by evolution in some way.

O Jesus, show me serpent's lie,
expose the beam in my own eye,
as Christ discernment you me give,
in oneness I forever live.

O Jesus, let the Fire of Joy,
consume the devil's subtle ploy,
transfigured is our planet earth,
the golden age is given birth.

5. Jesus, shatter the energetic matrix that prevents people from seeing that when we go into the consciousness of separation, there is fear. We cannot avoid it. The only way to avoid fear is through oneness with the Christ consciousness.

O Jesus, I am truly meek,
and thus I turn the other cheek,
when the accuser attacks me,
I go within and merge with thee.

**O Jesus, let the Fire of Joy,
consume the devil's subtle ploy,
transfigured is our planet earth,
the golden age is given birth.**

6. Jesus, shatter the energetic matrix that prevents people from seeing that once we step outside the Christ consciousness, there is an existential fear that enters our beings.

O Jesus, ego I let die,
surrender ev'ry earthly tie,
the dead can bury what is dead,
I choose to walk with you instead.

**O Jesus, let the Fire of Joy,
consume the devil's subtle ploy,
transfigured is our planet earth,
the golden age is given birth.**

7. Jesus, shatter the energetic matrix that prevents people from seeing that the being we were created as can never be destroyed. The separate self that we create in order to step into separation and duality, that self *can* be destroyed, that self is mortal, that self can never ascend to heaven.

O Jesus, help me rise above,
the devil's test through higher love,
show me separate self unreal,
my formless self you do reveal.

O Jesus, let the Fire of Joy,
consume the devil's subtle ploy,
transfigured is our planet earth,
the golden age is given birth.

8. Jesus, shatter the energetic matrix that prevents people from seeing that all people who have stepped into duality have an existential fear, they cannot escape it. We can try to cover it over, but we cannot escape it. The only way to escape it is to move towards oneness.

O Jesus, what is that to me,
I just let go and follow thee,
with this I do pass ev'ry test,
to find with you eternal rest.

O Jesus, let the Fire of Joy,
consume the devil's subtle ploy,
transfigured is our planet earth,
the golden age is given birth.

9. Jesus, shatter the energetic matrix that prevents people from seeing that this means giving up the sense of self we have as separate beings. When we identify ourselves as belonging to the only true belief system, it is hard to give up that sense of self.

O Jesus, fiery master mine,
my heart now melting into thine,
I love with heart and mind and soul,
the God who is my highest goal.

O Jesus, let the Fire of Joy,
consume the devil's subtle ploy,
transfigured is our planet earth,
the golden age is given birth.

Part 3

1. Jesus, shatter the energetic matrix that prevents people from seeing that once we step into that sense of being superior to the vast majority of people on earth, it becomes very hard to give it up. It becomes very hard to let that self die.

> O Jesus, blessed brother mine,
> I walk the path that you outline,
> a great example to us all,
> I follow now your inner call.

> **O Jesus, let the Fire of Joy,**
> **consume the devil's subtle ploy,**
> **transfigured is our planet earth,**
> **the golden age is given birth.**

2. Jesus, shatter the energetic matrix that prevents people from seeing that this is one of the primary dynamics that is upholding the elite because the elite have all been seduced by Satan, the consciousness of Satan, which is that some are superior and many are inferior.

> O Jesus, open inner sight,
> the ego wants to prove it's right,
> but this I will no longer do,
> I want to be all one with you.

> **O Jesus, let the Fire of Joy,**
> **consume the devil's subtle ploy,**
> **transfigured is our planet earth,**
> **the golden age is given birth.**

3. Jesus, shatter the energetic matrix that prevents people from seeing that once we step into that, it is very hard to give it up. We can only give it up when we truly realize: "He who is willing to save his life shall lose it, but he who is willing to lose his life for my sake, shall find it."

O Jesus, I now clearly see,
the Key of Knowledge given me,
my Christ self I hereby embrace,
as you fill up my inner space.

**O Jesus, let the Fire of Joy,
consume the devil's subtle ploy,
transfigured is our planet earth,
the golden age is given birth.**

4. Jesus, shatter the energetic matrix that prevents people from seeing that what you really came to teach us is that we can attain oneness with the Christ mind. As an ascended master, you offered that all of us can come into oneness with you. This offer has been standing for 2,000 years: I am with you always, even unto the end of the Piscean Age and beyond.

O Jesus, show me serpent's lie,
expose the beam in my own eye,
as Christ discernment you me give,
in oneness I forever live.

**O Jesus, let the Fire of Joy,
consume the devil's subtle ploy,
transfigured is our planet earth,
the golden age is given birth.**

5. Jesus, shatter the energetic matrix that prevents people from seeing that those who are your disciples are walking a path of gradually coming closer and closer to oneness with the Ascended Master Jesus Christ.

O Jesus, I am truly meek,
and thus I turn the other cheek,
when the accuser attacks me,
I go within and merge with thee.

**O Jesus, let the Fire of Joy,
consume the devil's subtle ploy,
transfigured is our planet earth,
the golden age is given birth.**

6. Jesus, shatter the energetic matrix that prevents people from seeing that the essence of the message of Christ is coming into oneness. Thereby, we come into oneness with all other people and we begin to see that oneness. When we create a society based on oneness instead of division, that society will look very different from most of the societies we have seen throughout history.

O Jesus, ego I let die,
surrender ev'ry earthly tie,
the dead can bury what is dead,
I choose to walk with you instead.

**O Jesus, let the Fire of Joy,
consume the devil's subtle ploy,
transfigured is our planet earth,
the golden age is given birth.**

7. Jesus, shatter the energetic matrix that prevents people from seeing that the elite says there are people that are poor because they are lazy or they are not willing to work hard. The reality is that poverty is created by the elite. It is created by an unequal distribution where a small elite is harvesting the fruits of the labor of the many.

O Jesus, help me rise above,
the devil's test through higher love,
show me separate self unreal,
my formless self you do reveal.

**O Jesus, let the Fire of Joy,
consume the devil's subtle ploy,
transfigured is our planet earth,
the golden age is given birth.**

8. Jesus, shatter the energetic matrix that prevents people from seeing that if there was a more equal distribution of wealth, we would not have poverty. We may still have people who would find it very difficult to have a regular job, but they would not have to live in poverty.

O Jesus, what is that to me,
I just let go and follow thee,
with this I do pass ev'ry test,
to find with you eternal rest.

**O Jesus, let the Fire of Joy,
consume the devil's subtle ploy,
transfigured is our planet earth,
the golden age is given birth.**

9. Jesus, shatter the energetic matrix that prevents people from seeing that in a society based on oneness, they would be taken care of physically. In a more enlightened society, they would also be taken care of psychologically because such a society would recognize that there is a reason why these people are in the state they are in.

O Jesus, fiery master mine,
my heart now melting into thine,
I love with heart and mind and soul,
the God who is my highest goal.

**O Jesus, let the Fire of Joy,
consume the devil's subtle ploy,
transfigured is our planet earth,
the golden age is given birth.**

Part 4

1. Jesus, shatter the energetic matrix that prevents people from seeing that once we accept reincarnation, we realize that these people were exposed to such trauma in past lives that their souls are so wounded, so scattered, so divided, that they cannot "keep it together." It is not that they are lazy or stupid or unwilling to do anything.

O Jesus, blessed brother mine,
I walk the path that you outline,

a great example to us all,
I follow now your inner call.

**O Jesus, let the Fire of Joy,
consume the devil's subtle ploy,
transfigured is our planet earth,
the golden age is given birth.**

2. Jesus, shatter the energetic matrix that prevents people from seeing that these people were wounded because they were exposed to some over-whelming trauma, many of them as a result of war. Who created the wars? The power elite.

O Jesus, open inner sight,
the ego wants to prove it's right,
but this I will no longer do,
I want to be all one with you.

**O Jesus, let the Fire of Joy,
consume the devil's subtle ploy,
transfigured is our planet earth,
the golden age is given birth.**

3. Jesus, shatter the energetic matrix that prevents people from seeing that the power elite has created the problem but instead of taking responsibility for it, they are blaming the people. The reality is that the power elite has created a problem and they do not want to take responsibility for it, they simply want it to go away.

O Jesus, I now clearly see,
the Key of Knowledge given me,
my Christ self I hereby embrace,
as you fill up my inner space.

**O Jesus, let the Fire of Joy,
consume the devil's subtle ploy,
transfigured is our planet earth,
the golden age is given birth.**

4. Jesus, shatter the energetic matrix that prevents people from seeing that this is the extreme outcome of the divisive consciousness. This is the very consciousness that you attempted to help people overcome by giving them an example, by giving them tools and teachings where they could come into oneness with each other.

O Jesus, show me serpent's lie,
expose the beam in my own eye,
as Christ discernment you me give,
in oneness I forever live.

O Jesus, let the Fire of Joy,
consume the devil's subtle ploy,
transfigured is our planet earth,
the golden age is given birth.

5. Jesus, shatter the energetic matrix that prevents people from seeing that when we come into that greater oneness, then we see that in a society we are all linked together. We are all part of the fabric of life and instead of condemning someone for their lack of ability, we seek to help them.

O Jesus, I am truly meek,
and thus I turn the other cheek,
when the accuser attacks me,
I go within and merge with thee.

O Jesus, let the Fire of Joy,
consume the devil's subtle ploy,
transfigured is our planet earth,
the golden age is given birth.

6. Jesus, shatter the energetic matrix that prevents people from seeing that there are societies in the modern world who have made tremendous progress towards that ideal of a more unified society. They have not yet taken the step of also seeking to help people psychologically.

O Jesus, ego I let die,
surrender ev'ry earthly tie,

the dead can bury what is dead,
I choose to walk with you instead.

**O Jesus, let the Fire of Joy,
consume the devil's subtle ploy,
transfigured is our planet earth,
the golden age is given birth.**

7. Jesus, shatter the energetic matrix that prevents people from seeing the need to have a more compassionate society. Help Americans see that America is behind many of the other nations in this respect.

O Jesus, help me rise above,
the devil's test through higher love,
show me separate self unreal,
my formless self you do reveal.

**O Jesus, let the Fire of Joy,
consume the devil's subtle ploy,
transfigured is our planet earth,
the golden age is given birth.**

8. Jesus, shatter the energetic matrix that prevents people from seeing that despite the fact that America claims to be a Christian nation, America has not even begun to understand the deeper message of the oneness of Christ.

O Jesus, what is that to me,
I just let go and follow thee,
with this I do pass ev'ry test,
to find with you eternal rest.

**O Jesus, let the Fire of Joy,
consume the devil's subtle ploy,
transfigured is our planet earth,
the golden age is given birth.**

9. Jesus, shatter the energetic matrix that prevents people from seeing that Americans do not see the oneness of coming together, not because we

feel forced to, but because we see the oneness of all life. Therefore, we see ourselves one with others, and naturally we want for others what we want for ourselves.

> O Jesus, fiery master mine,
> my heart now melting into thine,
> I love with heart and mind and soul,
> the God who is my highest goal.

> **O Jesus, let the Fire of Joy,**
> **consume the devil's subtle ploy,**
> **transfigured is our planet earth,**
> **the golden age is given birth.**

Part 5

1. Jesus, shatter the energetic matrix that prevents people from seeing that when we let the separate selves die and begin to come into oneness with Christ, we overcome the existential fear that is the eternal follower of the duality consciousness.

> O Jesus, blessed brother mine,
> I walk the path that you outline,
> a great example to us all,
> I follow now your inner call.

> **O Jesus, let the Fire of Joy,**
> **consume the devil's subtle ploy,**
> **transfigured is our planet earth,**
> **the golden age is given birth.**

2. Jesus, shatter the energetic matrix that prevents people from seeing that you sometimes used the word Satan to denote the fear that is following all people. We have the fear that we could go to hell, that we could die, that bad things could happen to us. But when we let go of the selves that have that fear, the fear disappears.

O Jesus, open inner sight,
the ego wants to prove it's right,
but this I will no longer do,
I want to be all one with you.

O Jesus, let the Fire of Joy,
consume the devil's subtle ploy,
transfigured is our planet earth,
the golden age is given birth.

3. Jesus, shatter the energetic matrix that prevents people from seeing that members of the power elite are attempting to set themselves up in a position where they have power, they have privilege, they have money, all as an attempt to overcome their existential fear. Many people have gone along with some of the schemes of the power elite because they thought this would help them overcome their fears.

O Jesus, I now clearly see,
the Key of Knowledge given me,
my Christ self I hereby embrace,
as you fill up my inner space.

O Jesus, let the Fire of Joy,
consume the devil's subtle ploy,
transfigured is our planet earth,
the golden age is given birth.

4. Jesus, shatter the energetic matrix that prevents people from seeing that many people have gone into amazing extremes in order to alleviate their fear. They have gone to great lengths to try to solve the problem of this fear.

O Jesus, show me serpent's lie,
expose the beam in my own eye,
as Christ discernment you me give,
in oneness I forever live.

O Jesus, let the Fire of Joy,
consume the devil's subtle ploy,

**transfigured is our planet earth,
the golden age is given birth.**

5. Jesus, shatter the energetic matrix that prevents people from seeing that for all people in embodiment, this attempt to solve the problem of fear is a very important driving force. The way out of this state of fear is the Christ consciousness: coming into unity by letting the separate selves die one by one.

O Jesus, I am truly meek,
and thus I turn the other cheek,
when the accuser attacks me,
I go within and merge with thee.

**O Jesus, let the Fire of Joy,
consume the devil's subtle ploy,
transfigured is our planet earth,
the golden age is given birth.**

6. Jesus, shatter the energetic matrix that prevents people from seeing that it was your greatest desire to create a spiritual movement that would help people overcome that fear. Instead, the fallen beings managed to turn Christianity into a religion that was based on fear and that only made the fear worse.

O Jesus, ego I let die,
surrender ev'ry earthly tie,
the dead can bury what is dead,
I choose to walk with you instead.

**O Jesus, let the Fire of Joy,
consume the devil's subtle ploy,
transfigured is our planet earth,
the golden age is given birth.**

7. Jesus, shatter the energetic matrix that prevents people from seeing that we cannot overcome the fear by solving any problems. The fear is not a problem that can be solved. It does not matter what we do here on earth, we will never free ourselves from that fear.

O Jesus, help me rise above,
the devil's test through higher love,
show me separate self unreal,
my formless self you do reveal.

**O Jesus, let the Fire of Joy,
consume the devil's subtle ploy,
transfigured is our planet earth,
the golden age is given birth.**

8. Jesus, shatter the energetic matrix that prevents people from seeing that we will overcome the fear only when we recognize that this fear is produced by a separate self, and instead of trying to solve the problem that the separate self projects at us, we separate ourselves from the self and let it die. We let it die for the sake of coming into oneness with Christ.

O Jesus, what is that to me,
I just let go and follow thee,
with this I do pass ev'ry test,
to find with you eternal rest.

**O Jesus, let the Fire of Joy,
consume the devil's subtle ploy,
transfigured is our planet earth,
the golden age is given birth.**

9. Jesus, shatter the energetic matrix that prevents people from seeing that this is the only solution to the issue of elitism. Oneness is the ultimate perspective from the Christ mind and the true goal of the mission that you started 2,000 years ago. We can all have oneness with Christ, oneness with Jesus. If we are willing, we can have it.

O Jesus, fiery master mine,
my heart now melting into thine,
I love with heart and mind and soul,
the God who is my highest goal.

**O Jesus, let the Fire of Joy,
consume the devil's subtle ploy,**

**transfigured is our planet earth,
the golden age is given birth.**

Sealing

In the name of the I AM THAT I AM, I accept that Archangel Michael, Astrea and Shiva form an impenetrable shield around myself and all constructive people, sealing us from all fear-based energies in all four octaves. I accept that the Light of God is consuming and transforming all fear-based energies that make up the dark forces working against ending the era of elitism on earth!

17 | THE ELITE RULES PEOPLE THROUGH OPINIONS

I AM the Ascended Master, Padmasambhava.

[Sound of a long outward breath.]

My peace I breathe onto you, the peace that cannot ever be disturbed by anything on earth. I am of course an ascended master and therefore cannot be disturbed by anything on earth. The gift I wish to give to you today is my peace, a flame of peace that I give to you, who are willing to take it and absorb it and nourish it, and call upon it and feel the presence of it and accept that presence in your being, in your four lower bodies. That peace cannot be disturbed by anything on earth. If you absorb that peace, then you can come to a point where you too, cannot be disturbed by anything on earth.

Why is it that the peace of Padmasambhava cannot be disturbed by anything on earth? It is because that peace springs from the awareness that anything and everything on earth is just an appearance. You may look at earth, you may look at various phenomena, and you may find it difficult to accept the concept that these are just appearances and have no substance, no reality, no continued existence. I understand this is difficult, therefore my gift of the flame of peace. Of course the flame of peace itself is not enough, you need to have some understanding to go with it. So, this I aim to give you.

Looking at the concept of elitism and the existence of various power elites on earth, as we have talked about, you can see throughout history what is behind it all. What is behind it? If you step back and look at the forest instead of looking at the trees, and then you step back from the forest and you keep stepping back, what do you see? Well, first of all, you see that the duality consciousness is what blinds people on earth. It is the duality consciousness that the power elite, or the forces behind them that we have called the fallen beings, is using to keep the population on earth trapped. In fact, the power elite in embodiment is also trapped in this duality consciousness, but how does the duality consciousness do this? How do the forces using the duality consciousness trap people so firmly in the duality consciousness that they might pursue a certain goal for lifetimes, thinking it is completely real, and not being open to the potential that it might just be an appearance. How do they do this?

How duality sets the stage for conflict

Many are the schemes they have come up with throughout the ages, but they all follow pretty much the same recipe. As we have said, the duality consciousness has the characteristic that there are always two polarities. You cannot create just one thing through the duality consciousness, you must create two—you must create what the Buddha called "the pairs." In order to create one thing, you at the same time create its opposite. You create good, you must create evil, for in the duality consciousness good must have an opposite. In the Christ consciousness good does not need an opposite, but in the duality consciousness it must have an opposite. By the very nature of the duality consciousness, any idea, any concept, any system that is created through that duality consciousness will have an opposition—there will be opposition to anything.

The result of this is that whatever you create in the duality consciousness sets the stage for conflict. What do the dark forces that want to trap humankind, and keep them trapped indefinitely, have to do? They just have to create these two polarities and then they have to get groups of people to somehow come to believe in or feel allegiance to one of the polarities. Then, by the fact that these two polarities are in conflict with each other, seem to threaten each other, seem to be mutually exclusive, you automatically have a conflict between the two groups of people who are believing in the reality of the polarities. You have the classical dualistic conflict between communism and capitalism, supposedly two economic systems that have the opposite approach—supposedly.

In communism, there is no private right to property or the means of production, it is all owned by the state. In capitalism there is no state ownership, there is no supposedly one entity that owns the means of production. As we have said of course the ultimate outcome of capitalism is that they merge as one corporation that can squash the competition from any other corporation. Thus, that corporation ends up owning all of the means of production, therefore also in reality owning the state, exactly as it is in the communist system. In a way, they are two ways to achieve the same end, namely that the population is under the control of a small elite: those who control the state or those who control the corporation. When you begin to become aware of this mechanism, you can take a more aware look at world history, at human conflict, at human behavior and thereby you can begin to see how many times throughout history people have become pulled into these kind of conflicts between two polarities.

What is real on earth?

Now, I know very well that there are many people who will say: "Well, are you saying that the conflict between capitalism and communism was not real?" And that is exactly what I am saying. Why am I saying this? Because I am an ascended master. How did I become an ascended master? By coming to the realization, which the Buddha called enlightenment, that everything on earth is just an appearance. So when they say that the struggle between capitalism and communism was real, the question really is: What is your definition of reality?

We have talked about how there is an elitist mindset behind the elite that makes it seem real that there is an elite, that there should be an elite, that the people cannot do without it, that the elite is a beneficial force and so on. We have said it is an illusion, why is it an illusion? Because anything you create in the duality consciousness will have an opposite. But, and here is the real insight that can liberate you: both polarities are unreal, both polarities are equally unreal.

Now again, what is your definition of reality? My definition of reality as an ascended master is that for something to be real, it must be created through the mind of an ascended being, a being who is not in duality. Why do I say this? Because only that which is created through the Christ mind is sustainable. If you create something through the Christ mind and take your attention away from it, it will endure over time. Not forever, but over time. If you create something through the duality consciousness and take your mind away from it, it will instantly start to break down and it can only be sustained over time if people are continually putting their attention on it and therefore feeding energy into upholding the matrix.

We have many times given the image of the movie projector where the images on the film strip have no substance in themselves. They can only exist as long as there is light flowing through the film strip in the projector. The moment you turn off that light, the images on the film strip disappear. Because of the density of the physical octave, it takes a little longer in the reality, or should we say *relativity,* of the physical octave. Nevertheless, the moment people do not feed energy into the matrix, it starts dissolving, self-destructing.

The illusion of the epic struggle

What is it that the fallen beings, the dark forces, have done in order to create something that can last over time in the physical octave? Well, they must get people to continually put their attention on it and feed their energy into that matrix. How do they do this? Well, they do it, as we have said before, through the epic mindset. The epic mindset says that here is a cause that is ultimately important, and therefore people must dedicate their lives to fighting for this cause and therefore, it is also justified that they kill other people in order to promote that cause. Again, with capitalism and communism, you can see how people in the Soviet Union believed that it was so epically important that communism took over the world that they were willing to risk being killed or to kill others in order to promote that cause. On the other side, people in America and the West were so convinced that it was epically important that communism would not take over the world, and therefore they were willing to kill or be killed in order to promote that cause.

What is the underlying mechanism behind this? It is that the fallen beings must make people believe that the dualistic polarities are real, they have some reality, they have some substance. If no one believed that the struggle was real, why would they give their lives to the struggle? How do they create this sense of reality? They do not. They *cannot*, but they do not have to. What they have managed to do a long time ago is to cause the majority of the people on earth to also go into the duality consciousness, and in the duality consciousness, there are certain things that seem real, absolutely real.

The easiest way to understand this is to look at your physical senses. You can open your eyes and see something. You can look at this building you are sitting in. From the vantage point of your eyes, this building seems very real, it seems solid. It seems to have the ability to sustain or to be sustained over time. Likewise, with your other senses. Over many lifetimes of embodying on earth, you have come to be convinced that the earth has some reality—it has some durability, some continuity. Now, this is not entirely an illusion in the sense that planet earth was originally created by the Elohim, seven ascended beings who created a matrix for the earth in the identity realm and gradually lowered it through the mental into the emotional and then into the physical. There is an enduring quality to the earth. Not that it will be sustainable forever, not that it is really self-sustainable, but as long as the Elohim continue to put their attention on this matrix and uphold it, the earth will endure. They do not have to put their attention on it constantly because it was originally created through the Christ consciousness, but they do need to put enough attention on it to uphold the matrix.

So is the earth real? Well, it is real in the sense that it is there. There is a physical planet that is a platform for life and for the experiences you have as self-aware beings on earth. It is not real in the sense that it will endure forever. Nor is it real in the sense that its form could not be changed. As we have told you, the Elohim originally created the earth in a much higher matrix than what you see today, and what actually happened is that after humankind fell into duality, the earth has become denser. Therefore, what you see today, what you experience with your senses today, is not what the Elohim created, is not the highest potential for earth and does not have the same longevity as that original matrix.

Is the earth real in its present state? Well, if you with "real" define something you can detect with your physical senses, then it has some reality to it. As I said, this current form of the earth in its current density is not sustainable. The reality is that it is possible to transform the earth into a lesser density where many of the problems you see today will fade away. What kind of problems would fade away if you raised the earth into a lesser density? Well, look at the density of your physical bodies. It is this density that causes your bodies to age in this incredibly short lifespan that you call a normal lifetime. There is nothing normal or natural about it. Your bodies could sustain themselves for much longer if the earth vibrated at a higher level. You would not have most of the diseases you have today, as they are the result of the density of the body. You also would not have, if the earth was raised enough, to earn a living by working at the sweat of your brow because the earth would provide what you needed to sustain yourself without this enormous struggle that you see today.

The limitations of the physical senses

These are of course ideas that most people find it difficult to accept but I am just giving you a sense that what you see on earth today is not ultimately real. When you begin to have glimpses that this could actually be a reality, when your intuition shows you that there is something to this, however incredible it might sound at first, then you can begin to realize that your senses, your physical senses, are calibrated to detect the dense vibrations that you currently have on earth.

Your senses cannot detect what is beyond the physical. What has happened over many lifetimes is that your minds have become so attached to the senses that your minds think that what your senses see is real. Or even that what your senses show you is the only way the earth could be. Now, you are all spiritual students and what do you do, when you become a spiritual student? You actually start to detach your mind from your physical body and your physical senses. You start to question, not necessarily in the beginning, the reality of what you see with the senses, but you start to question whether there is something beyond what the senses can detect.

You all started looking at some kind of phenomenon that was beyond the material world, beyond what the physical senses could detect. This opens you up to a process whereby you gradually disassociate your mind from the senses and the physical octave. You are no longer believing that the physical octave is completely real or that it is the only world there is. You become open to the potential that there is something beyond the physical world and that this something might be a spiritual world that is the source, the origin, of everything you see in the physical world. What you can do is that you can take this just a simple step further and realize that if there is a spiritual world beyond the physical and if this world, this spiritual world, is the real world in the sense that everything in the physical is made from the energies of the spiritual world that was lowered in vibration, then is the physical world as real as the spiritual world?

When you begin to intuitively sense that the physical world does not have the same reality, the same longevity, sustainability, as the spiritual world, then you can begin to make that switch where you realize why that is. Why is the physical world not as real as the spiritual world, as sustainable as the spiritual world? That is when you can begin to realize that the material world is like the images on a movie screen. The material world is a projection where the energy, what we have called the Mother light, or the Ma-ter light, that makes up the material world has taken on a certain form and it has done so because an image was projected onto the Ma-ter light and there was energy, attention, light flowing through that matrix, that image. The Ma-ter light has taken on that form because that is what the Ma-ter light is defined to do. This does not mean that this form is permanent. The Ma-ter light could as easily take on any other form as what you currently see.

When Jesus met the man with the withered arm, in his mind he did not look at the withered arm as most people looked at it, he did not see it as something real, something that could not be changed. He saw it as a projection and because he was so strong in his Christ consciousness, he projected a different matrix, and the Ma-ter light almost instantly took on that form. Now, I am not thereby trying to make you feel that you should be able to do the same, or that humankind could instantly project another image and many things in the world would change. In reality, this could happen, but it would require that all people would align their minds behind this vision. And that is of course not so likely to happen in the near future. What you can come to realize is that the current conditions that you see on earth, even the density of matter and the density of your physical bodies, was created by the collective consciousness of humankind where people came to accept the current conditions as real.

How the current density was created

The process of creating current conditions started a long time ago. As we have said, symbolic with the Genesis story of Adam and Eve being cast out of Paradise, as a symbol for them leaving the Christ consciousness (the consciousness of oneness), going into duality and separation. Gradually this has caused the density to increase to what you see today. Those who have been in embodiment for many lifetimes, have therefore come to believe that what you see currently on earth is natural. It was either created by God or created by nature, and it is the only way things could be.

This is the sense of reality that the fallen beings use where they on top of this sense of reality that you have based on your senses, they project out these dualistic ideas that create this sense of struggle. For example, going back in time, the Catholic church of the Middle Ages had projected out the image that God really is the way he was portrayed in the Old Testament, that God's only son really is Jesus. That there only is one way to go to heaven and avoid hell and that is through the Catholic church. Now, could the Catholic church exist on its own? Nay, because it was created out of the duality consciousness so it must have an opposite. And what became the opposite of the Catholic church in the Middle Ages was of course Islam. That is why the Catholic church was able to project the necessity of Christians engaging in this epic struggle with Muslims to eradicate this false religion that was only causing souls to be lost in hell. Of course, if you go to the other side, they had a very similar view that they had the only true religion and therefore any other religion had to be false. Therefore, there was an inevitable struggle between the two. You all saw how many people on both sides thought this struggle was absolutely real. They thought it was real that they should give their lives to this struggle and they should take the lives of other people in this struggle. They, on both sides, thought that they had the only true God and that they would be rewarded in heaven for killing the people on the other side.

You see here that what the fallen beings have done time and time again is that they have made use of your sense, your sensory-based sense of what is real, that there is something on earth that is real, and they have tied an idea into that. Or they have managed to project an idea and project that this idea is real, it is as real as what you are sensing with your senses. Now, in a sense they are right. The idea *is* as real as what you are sensing with your senses because what you are sensing with your senses is an appearance and so is the idea. Of course, people do not see this.

When you begin to see through this basic lie (and it is fairly simple, at a certain level of the spiritual path, to begin to see through it), then at first you have this period where your attention is directed outwards and you are focused on seeing how other people have been trapped in duality. We have given you many examples of this: capitalism-communism, Islam-the Catholic church, Nazism-Marxism, all of these ideologies that have been created that created the struggle. It is fairly easy to see that they were pulled into the dualistic struggle and this of course is perfectly acceptable. You need to go through that period where you are looking out and you are seeing how other people were trapped into taking these dualistic positions and therefore fighting against others. There is a more mature phase that most of you are ready to enter into and it is where you start looking at yourself, your own opinions, your own beliefs. You look at whether you perhaps have been caught in some version of this dualistic struggle.

The dualistic struggle in America

Let me focus on America, just to give you an example. What does the dualistic struggle always say, the epic struggle always say? There are two sides and one of them is good and the other one is bad. One of them is right and the other one is completely wrong. Does that remind you of anything in America? Does it remind you of anything in Washington, D.C.? Does it remind you of anything in this white building that is east of here that has this round dome at the top with a statue and there is a certain chamber in there. There are people in there who are elected representatives, but for reasons that are somewhat difficult to explain, there is a central aisle and the people are sitting on opposite sides of that aisle. The people on one side are saying: "Oh, the other ones are wrong." And the people on the other side are saying: "No, it's those over there that are wrong."

The American people, many of them, have allowed themselves to be aligned with this so they identify themselves as: "I'm a Republican." "I'm a Democrat." "The Democrats are completely wrong. They are going to take this country to hell." "No, it's the Republicans that are completely wrong. They are the ones who are destroying America." Can you not see, my beloved, that this is a classic dualistic struggle? Can you not see that as spiritual people who are aspiring to put on Christ discernment, you need to look beyond this? You cannot allow yourself to be pulled into this struggle and supporting this struggle. What is it that the struggle blinds people into doing? It blinds them into taking a particular position. Once you have said: "I'm a Christian," "I'm a Muslim," "I'm a Republican," "I'm a Democrat," what do you do? You suspend discernment because now you are saying: "No, the Democrats are always right," or "The Republicans are always right, and everything they say is right."

Some of your discussions here, my beloved, if you are willing to look at them, you will see that some of you are still caught up in this, thinking that the solution to America's problems is that your party takes over. What we have attempted to help you see (with all the dictations we gave last year and the ones we have given before), is that it is not that simple. It is not that one side is right and the other side is wrong. What is it that will take America forward? It is ideas, certain ideas that will shift the collective consciousness. It is not so that the Democrats have all the right ideas, or that the Republicans have all the right ideas and that the Democrats have no wrong ideas, or the Republicans have no wrong ideas. It is a mixed bag. There are some constructive ideas that are promoted by Democrats, but there are also some promoted by Republicans. Neither side has an absolute truth because they are too trapped in the dualistic mindset.

What is it you could envision if you want to envision a solution to America's problems? It will be that instead of focusing on the political parties, you use our teachings, our invocations to envision a shift, not only in Washington but in the American people, so that people see beyond this struggle between the two parties. They see that there emerges a new class of politicians who are dedicated to doing what is best for the people, not the elite and who are dedicated to bringing forth the ideas that are best for the people. My beloved, ask yourself this: How is the current gridlock, the current political situation, ever going to bring real solutions? You can look at the situation and you can say: "If the current situation could have brought forth the solution, it should already have done so, given how many decades this has been going on." Something new is needed. If you keep doing the same thing and expect different results, you know what Einstein said.

What could be different? Well, it could be that there was a change of mindset where people start looking at ideas instead of thinking: I have to align myself with a particular party and then once I have done this, I need to accept everything they say as good and everything the other party says as bad. This is the only thing that can really change the equation—that people become focused on the ideas and serving the people, rather than having two parties fighting for dominion. What can bring about this change? Where can it start? It is not likely to start in Congress—that is probably the last place it will manifest. It is not so likely to start among the American people. We have talked about the top 10% who have the highest level of Christ awareness so obviously that is where the change needs to start. If you are still trapped in this mindset of thinking that it is one party or the other that will provide the second coming of Christ, then how can you be the forerunners for that change?

Now, I have talked about the more extreme cases where you are so sucked into the dualistic struggle that you are ready to kill other people. Obviously, you are not in that category. Most Americans are not really in that category—among the people at least. There is a more subtle form of this struggle and it is where, as you grew up, as you engaged in whatever you have engaged in, you have come to accept some of these dualistic opinions. You do not see that they are dualistic. You think they represent some higher truth, some higher reality, they have some reality. Therefore, you are absolutely convinced that this is the way it is. It may be opinions about everything: the economy, the political system, religion, whatever you have.

Losing our strong opinions

Do you see that the subtle version of how the fallen beings have tricked people into the dualistic struggle is to make people accept a certain viewpoint, a certain opinion, and think it is the ultimate viewpoint. It is absolutely real. Therefore, you never need to examine it, you never need to question it, you never need to look beyond it.

We have seen over these many decades where we have sponsored ascended master organizations, how people have come in, time and time again, with very strong opinions. Even though they have studied our teachings, they have never actually questioned those opinions. They have actually, in many cases, found something in our teachings that they could use to validate those opinions. The sad reality is that people who are trapped in these opinions cannot be the forerunners for manifesting Saint Germain's Golden Age because Saint Germain's Golden Age can be manifest only through the Christ consciousness. If you have a very strong opinion that you are not willing to question, that is not the Christ consciousness. What did Jesus say earlier? "He who is willing to lose his life for my sake, shall find it." Lose the outer selves that have these strong one-sided dualistic opinions. Does that mean I am saying you should lose *all* of your opinions? That is exactly what I am saying.

For what is an opinion? It is precisely this: A very strong, simple statement that you believe represents some absolute truth, and that you are not willing to question. Many, many people over the decades have come into ascended master teachings and they have not understood what this messenger talked about. The ascended masters are in a fundamentally different state of consciousness than people in embodiment. The Christ consciousness is a fundamentally different state of consciousness than the duality consciousness. The whole purpose of being an ascended master student is to rise above the duality consciousness and put on the Christ consciousness. How can you do this, if you have a set of opinions that you think you never need to question? How can you learn from the ascended masters if you are so attached to these opinions that you are only looking for validation of them, instead of looking for a higher perspective from the Christ mind? How can you make use of ascended master teachings, if you are seeking to get the ascended masters to validate your dualistic opinions?

An opinion is something that is not based on the reality of the Christ mind. I know many of you are going to say: "But this particular thing that I believe I know, are you saying that isn't true?" What I am saying is: "How do you know it is true, if you have not been willing to give it up and see what comes to you from the Christ mind? If you have not been willing to let this self that has that opinion, that carries that opinion, die?"

How can you know what is real? You cannot know through that self. Until you have been willing to give up an opinion, give up a viewpoint, you cannot know what the Christ perspective on it is. I can guarantee you that when you do give it up and do get the Christ perspective, you see that there is so much more to the issue than that particular clearly defined opinion.

The Christ perspective versus human opinions

As I said, neither the Democrats, nor the Republicans are always right. They do each have some valid ideas, but they do not have ideas based on the mind of Christ for the most part. What do I mean with this? Well, there may be an idea that could be valid enough from a certain perspective. Take the economy. So many people will say: "The free market, isn't that a valid idea?" If you focus on the current definition and understanding of the free market, you will seek to manifest that. Instead of letting your current understanding die and seeking for a higher perspective from the Christ mind, whereby you will see that Saint Germain has a vision for the economy that goes way beyond what anyone has right now. There is so much more to know. Therefore, you could say, if you have a limited perspective that prevents you from seeing the greater context, your limited idea may have a certain validity. But if it prevents you from growing and seeing the bigger picture, then it actually becomes what we might call a false idea because it is preventing your growth. There is no idea you can find in the world today that is absolute, that is final. We have even said our own teachings are not final. As the collective consciousness is raised, people will begin to see ideas they cannot see today. Who is it that will be able to see these ideas? Those who are not attached to their existing ideas. We would like all of you, who are our direct students, to be among those people but that requires you to be willing to look at your opinions and just let them die.

When you are in the Christ mind, you do not have opinions. You just have understanding, observation but you are not judging them based on a scale of right and wrong, good or bad. You are not judging people. You are just looking at: "Here's an idea, what is the consequence because every idea has a consequence. Is that consequence going to limit people or liberate them?" This can change over time. As we said, when Plato formulated the idea of the philosopher king, it was a constructive idea, given the level of consciousness that was there back then. In today's world it is no longer valid because the need of this time is democracy where the people become engaged in governing their country. Can you then say that Plato's idea was false or wrong? It was valid, but if you insist on holding on to that idea today, it is limiting you.

The same with many of the opinions that you have, many of you. So, the question I put before you is: Where do you want to get your ideas from? From the power elite, the fallen beings, the duality consciousness or from the ascended masters? If you want it from us, then it is not enough to study our dictations and give invocations. You need to use the tools, look at yourself, look at your opinions, identify that certain of these strong opinions you have, that you are very sure are right, are dualistic ideas. They are anchored in a certain self in your being. It does not matter where they came from. They came from the fallen beings, but never mind. They are anchored in your being to a certain separate self. Instead of trying to solve the problem that your idea defines, or bring forth the solution that your idea defines, or destroy the opposition to your idea, you need to realize that you need to just let that self die. Then, go into that neutral state of mind and ask the Christ mind, a specific ascended master or your I AM Presence for the Christ perspective on the issue. What is the Christ perspective? As long as you are looking for the answer to that question through a separate self, you cannot see the Christ perspective. You will never see it. Therefore, you cannot be one of the forerunners for manifesting Saint Germain's Golden Age. At least not in a capacity of bringing forth these ideas and pulling up on the collective consciousness to come to see these ideas, accept them, implement them.

Truly, many of you are very, very close to breaking through to manifest a much higher level of consciousness, of Christ consciousness, than you are manifesting today. For many of you, there is one or a set of particular opinions that you have about life or about the spiritual path that you are very attached to and it is blocking your progress. It is preventing you from actually shedding this snakeskin of the human consciousness and being reborn into the Christ consciousness. If you were willing to take this dictation and use the tools we have given you to identify that these strong opinions come from one or several separate selves, and then use the tools from the books to let those selves die, you could make a major leap forward in a very short period of time.

The Christ consciousness is not polarized

You see my beloved, the fallen beings are precisely in this state of consciousness. They have certain views, certain opinions, certain ideas, a certain image of God and the universe and they are very, very sure that it is right, that it does not need to be questioned. This is not naked awareness. This is not pure awareness. It is polarized awareness. The Christ consciousness is not polarized. So many people think that the Christ consciousness will validate one of these outer opinions, ideas, ideologies or religions.

Look at how many Christians think that Jesus would approve of their particular church and their literal interpretation of the Bible. You know better than this as ascended master students. You could make tremendous progress if you were willing to look in the mirror, identify these strong opinions, see that they come from a separate self, see that instead of trying to solve the problem or bring forth the solution that your opinion defines, you could just let the self-die. Then, you would be free to see so much more than you can see today.

What eventually would happen is that you would have the peace of being willing to admit: "I don't really have opinions anymore. I just observe, I may share with others what I observe, but I don't have an opinion." What do I mean with an opinion? Well, of course various things, but there is one element, one characteristic, of opinions. It defines that something *should* happen. Other people should do this or they should agree with your opinion. It is because other people will not agree that the problem cannot be solved. As long as there is something that you think *should* happen, you are having opinions, human opinions, dualistic opinions.

Why do I say this? What did I come to give you initially? My gift of peace. How will you attain peace? Well, as we have said before, what happened after you came to earth as avatars, or even if you are the original inhabitants and encountered the fallen beings for the first time, you received a trauma. Ever since then, you have had a self that has attempted to compensate for this to prevent you from having it again.

What is that self based on? Well, it is based on an experience. It is an *understandable* experience. It is in a way an *inevitable* experience. What happened when you came to earth, when you encountered the fallen beings and you were exposed to this trauma? Your inner peace was disturbed. Outer conditions that were forced upon you in a very aggressive way disturbed your inner peace. You created various selves to deal with this and what do these selves believe, what belief are they based on? Outer conditions determine my state of peace. The selves are based on the belief that if you can just manifest, or get other people to manifest, specific outer conditions, then your peace will be restored.

What took away your peace? The separate selves. What will bring back your peace? That you let those separate selves die and stop trying to produce a state of inner peace by changing outer conditions. You will *never* be at peace as long as you think your peace depends on something outside yourself or that it depends on your selves and the opinions they have. There is no problem you could solve that will give you inner peace. You just need to let the self die.

What can help you make this switch? Ponder my statement that everything on earth is an appearance. When you begin to sense intuitively that everything is an appearance, *that* is when you can free yourself from the dualistic struggle. If the Catholic religion is just an appearance, how could it be of epic importance to kill all the Muslims that oppose the Catholic religion? How? I assume that none of you are ready to go fight the crusades all over again, but why are you then fighting other crusades that are defined in the modern age? Why are you fighting the crusade between Democrats and Republicans? Or many other of these epic causes defined in today's world. Just let it go, my beloved. If you want peace, just let it go. There is no other way to peace. I know it is difficult. That is why I offer you the flame of peace that can give you a frame of reference for what it can feel like to be in peace, in the vibration of peace. If you are just somewhat perceptive, you will have felt that peace during this dictation. If this dictation has agitated you, stirred up something in you, it is a separate self. If you will let that self die, then you can feel the state of peace.

Inner peace beyond opinions

The value of ascended masters giving you a gift like this, is that through the momentum of the flame that I offer you, you can have glimpses of a state of inner peace even though you still have these separate selves that prevent you from having the peace from within. This will not give you permanent peace but it can give you that frame of reference where you know what it is like to feel at peace. You know what it is like to be in a state of mind that is not constantly being pulled in different directions by all these separate selves, where you are not having the stress of feeling you have to do something to fight some epic battle.

Look at the earth, my beloved. Look at all these epic struggles that have taken place throughout history. See what incredible effort, what incredible sacrifices, what incredible suffering people have endured to fight for some cause. Look at the Christians throughout the centuries, what they have gone through of self-torture in order to supposedly win this epic battle for Jesus. Look at the Muslims, look at the communists, look at those in the so-called free world who fought the Nazis. Look how the fallen beings have enveloped people time and time again in these incredible struggles. Look at the amount of energy, the amount of attention that people have focused on this and the amount of physical suffering this has caused. It is all just appearances. *None of it is real.*

The elites who are promoting these physical struggles, these epic struggles, they believe it is real. Even the fallen beings in the higher realms, they believe it is real in the identity, mental and emotional bodies. At least they believe there is some struggle that is real, even if they know that they have manipulated people in embodiment into going into false struggles.

Will the elite be able to solve the problem of elitism? Nay. Is there a problem to solve? Nay. What then are we talking about that we want to see happen? It is that we shatter the illusion of elitism, the illusion that makes it seem real that God or nature has ordained the existence of an elite and that they are better equipped to rule than the people themselves.

Who can shatter that illusion? *The elite cannot.* Most of the people in the population cannot. Who can? Those who are dedicated to putting on the Christ consciousness. There must be someone who becomes the forerunners, who runs ahead and who cries out: "But the emperor has nothing on and here is why." If *you* cannot do this, who can?

Honestly my beloved, with the teachings you have on the duality consciousness, on the separate selves, on the power elite and the fallen beings if *you* cannot, who can? But you *can*—if you *will.* I am not going to ask you if you will. I am going to leave it up to you to answer that question. With this, you have my gratitude and I seal you in my flame of unconditional peace.

[Sound of long outward breath by Padmasambhava.]

18 | INVOKING FREEDOM FROM HUMAN OPINIONS (PART 1)

In the name of the I AM THAT I AM, Jesus Christ, I use the authority that I have as a being in embodiment on earth to call upon Padmasambhava to reinforce my calls and use my chakras to project the statements in this invocation into the collective consciousness and awaken people to the advantage of letting go of all human opinions. Awaken people to the reality that we are spiritual beings and that we can co-create a new future by working with the ascended masters. I especially call for …

[Make your own calls here.]

Part 1

1. Padmasambhava, I accept your flame of peace and I am willing to take it and absorb it and nourish it, and call upon it and feel the presence of it and accept that presence in my being, in my four lower bodies. I absorb the peace that cannot be disturbed by anything on earth so that I too cannot be disturbed by anything on earth.

I see how my senses can only deceive,
for nothing they tell me, I fully believe.
Behind all appearances is only light,
they only seem real to our limited sight.

**O Padmasambhava, in your Flame of Peace,
all human opinions I hereby release.
I see now the ultimate truth you reveal,
earth is an appearance, where nothing is real.**

2. Padmasambhava, shatter the energetic matrix that prevents people from seeing that your peace cannot be disturbed by anything on earth because that peace springs from the awareness that anything and everything on earth is just an appearance.

My mind and my senses are only a tool,
and I am determined to not be a fool.
My personal self, is no more who I am,
the earthly identity is but a scam.

O Padmasambhava, in your Flame of Peace,
all human opinions I hereby release.
I see now the ultimate truth you reveal,
earth is an appearance, where nothing is real.

3. Padmasambhava, shatter the energetic matrix that prevents people from seeing that all phenomena on earth are just appearances and have no substance, no reality, no continued existence.

From sense-based perception I want to be free,
clear my inner sight, so I truly can see.
My human opinions, they do make me blind,
with neutral awareness, new visions I find.

**O Padmasambhava, in your Flame of Peace,
all human opinions I hereby release.
I see now the ultimate truth you reveal,
earth is an appearance, where nothing is real.**

4. Padmasambhava, shatter the energetic matrix that prevents people from seeing that the duality consciousness is what blinds people on earth. It is the duality consciousness that the power elite, or the fallen beings behind them, are using to keep the population on earth trapped.

A self is what makes an opinion seem real,
it projects there's a problem, with which I must deal.
I will not be free, till I see through this life,
and say to the self: I am letting you die.

O Padmasambhava, in your Flame of Peace,
all human opinions I hereby release.
I see now the ultimate truth you reveal,
earth is an appearance, where nothing is real.

5. Padmasambhava, shatter the energetic matrix that prevents people from seeing that the power elite in embodiment is also trapped in this duality consciousness. Many people are so firmly trapped in the duality consciousness that they pursue a goal for lifetimes, thinking it is completely real and not being open to the potential that it might just be an appearance.

Through human opinions, I simply can't see,
the higher perspective—Christ reality,
When the self dualistic, I truly let die,
the Christ mind does open, up my inner eye.

O Padmasambhava, in your Flame of Peace,
all human opinions I hereby release.
I see now the ultimate truth you reveal,
earth is an appearance, where nothing is real.

6. Padmasambhava, shatter the energetic matrix that prevents people from seeing that the fallen beings have come up with many schemes throughout the ages, but they all follow the same recipe. In the duality consciousness there are always two polarities. You cannot create just one thing through the duality consciousness, you must create two.

O Padmasambhava, the world has gone mad,
as dualistic thinking, defines good and bad.

The judgment of Christ, upon forces so dark,
rekindle in people, our spiritual spark.

**O Padmasambhava, in your Flame of Peace,
all human opinions I hereby release.
I see now the ultimate truth you reveal,
earth is an appearance, where nothing is real.**

7. Padmasambhava, shatter the energetic matrix that prevents people from seeing that in order to create one thing, you at the same time create its opposite. You create good, you must create evil, for in the duality consciousness good must have an opposite.

O Padmasambhava, set all people free,
from mindset so epic, from duality.
Cut all people free from the serpentine lie,
so that to Christ Jesus, we all can draw nigh.

**O Padmasambhava, in your Flame of Peace,
all human opinions I hereby release.
I see now the ultimate truth you reveal,
earth is an appearance, where nothing is real.**

8. Padmasambhava, shatter the energetic matrix that prevents people from seeing that in the Christ consciousness good does not need an opposite, but in the duality consciousness it must have an opposite. By the very nature of the duality consciousness, any idea, any concept, any system that is created will have an opposition.

The serpentine lie, says that what we now see,
is all that our lives, on this planet can be.
Yet with the Christ mind, we can see there is more,
the earth will be brighter than ever before.

**O Padmasambhava, in your Flame of Peace,
all human opinions I hereby release.
I see now the ultimate truth you reveal,
earth is an appearance, where nothing is real.**

9. Padmasambhava, shatter the energetic matrix that prevents people from seeing that whatever we create in the duality consciousness sets the stage for conflict. The dark forces just have to create these two polarities and then they have to get groups of people to believe in or feel allegiance to the polarities.

> Saint Germain has the plans, for a bright Golden Age,
> to receive them, our minds must be free from the cage,
> O Padmasambhava, with your Flame of Peace,
> the vision of Oneness, to all you release.

> **O Padmasambhava, in your Flame of Peace,**
> **all human opinions I hereby release.**
> **I see now the ultimate truth you reveal,**
> **earth is an appearance, where nothing is real.**

Part 2

1. Padmasambhava, shatter the energetic matrix that prevents people from seeing that by the fact that the two polarities seem to be mutually exclusive, we automatically have a conflict between the two groups of people who are believing in the reality of the polarities.

> I see how my senses can only deceive,
> for nothing they tell me, I fully believe.
> Behind all appearances is only light,
> they only seem real to our limited sight.

> **O Padmasambhava, in your Flame of Peace,**
> **all human opinions I hereby release.**
> **I see now the ultimate truth you reveal,**
> **earth is an appearance, where nothing is real.**

2. Padmasambhava, shatter the energetic matrix that prevents people from seeing that we have the classical dualistic conflict between communism and capitalism, supposedly two economic systems that have the opposite approach.

My mind and my senses are only a tool,
and I am determined to not be a fool.
My personal self, is no more who I am,
the earthly identity is but a scam.

O Padmasambhava, in your Flame of Peace,
all human opinions I hereby release.
I see now the ultimate truth you reveal,
earth is an appearance, where nothing is real.

3. Padmasambhava, shatter the energetic matrix that prevents people from seeing that in communism, there is no private right to property or the means of production, it is all owned by the state. In capitalism there is no state ownership, but the ultimate outcome of capitalism is that one corporation ends up owning all of the means of production, therefore also owning the state.

From sense-based perception I want to be free,
clear my inner sight, so I truly can see.
My human opinions, they do make me blind,
with neutral awareness, new visions I find.

**O Padmasambhava, in your Flame of Peace,
all human opinions I hereby release.
I see now the ultimate truth you reveal,
earth is an appearance, where nothing is real.**

4. Padmasambhava, shatter the energetic matrix that prevents people from seeing that capitalism and communism are two ways to achieve the same end, namely that the population is under the control of a small elite: those who control the state or those who control the corporation.

A self is what makes an opinion seem real,
it projects there's a problem, with which I must deal.
I will not be free, till I see through this life,
and say to the self: I am letting you die.

**O Padmasambhava, in your Flame of Peace,
all human opinions I hereby release.**

I see now the ultimate truth you reveal,
earth is an appearance, where nothing is real.

5. Padmasambhava, shatter the energetic matrix that prevents people from seeing that we need to take a more aware look at world history, and see how many times people have become pulled into these kind of conflicts between two polarities.

Through human opinions, I simply can't see,
the higher perspective—Christ reality,
When the self dualistic, I truly let die,
the Christ mind does open, up my inner eye.

O Padmasambhava, in your Flame of Peace,
all human opinions I hereby release.
I see now the ultimate truth you reveal,
earth is an appearance, where nothing is real.

6. Padmasambhava, shatter the energetic matrix that prevents people from seeing that the conflict between capitalism and communism was not real. Everything on earth is just an appearance. So when people say the struggle between capitalism and communism was real, the question really is: What is our definition of reality?

O Padmasambhava, the world has gone mad,
as dualistic thinking, defines good and bad.
The judgment of Christ, upon forces so dark,
rekindle in people, our spiritual spark.

O Padmasambhava, in your Flame of Peace,
all human opinions I hereby release.
I see now the ultimate truth you reveal,
earth is an appearance, where nothing is real.

7. Padmasambhava, shatter the energetic matrix that prevents people from seeing that there is an elitist mindset behind the elite that makes it seem real that there is an elite, that there should be an elite, that the people cannot do without it, that the elite is a beneficial force.

O Padmasambhava, set all people free,
from mindset so epic, from duality.
Cut all people free from the serpentine lie,
so that to Christ Jesus, we all can draw nigh.

O Padmasambhava, in your Flame of Peace,
all human opinions I hereby release.
I see now the ultimate truth you reveal,
earth is an appearance, where nothing is real.

8. Padmasambhava, shatter the energetic matrix that prevents people from seeing that this is an illusion because anything we create in duality will have an opposite. Yet both polarities are unreal, both polarities are equally unreal.

The serpentine lie, says that what we now see,
is all that our lives, on this planet can be.
Yet with the Christ mind, we can see there is more,
the earth will be brighter than ever before.

O Padmasambhava, in your Flame of Peace,
all human opinions I hereby release.
I see now the ultimate truth you reveal,
earth is an appearance, where nothing is real.

9. Padmasambhava, shatter the energetic matrix that prevents people from seeing that for something to be real, it must be created through the mind of an ascended being, a being who is not in duality. Only that which is created through the Christ mind is sustainable.

Saint Germain has the plans, for a bright Golden Age,
to receive them, our minds must be free from the cage,
O Padmasambhava, with your Flame of Peace,
the vision of Oneness, to all you release.

O Padmasambhava, in your Flame of Peace,
all human opinions I hereby release.
I see now the ultimate truth you reveal,
earth is an appearance, where nothing is real.

Part 3

1. Padmasambhava, shatter the energetic matrix that prevents people from seeing that if we create something through the Christ mind and take our attention away from it, it will endure over time. If we create something through the duality consciousness and take our mind away from it, it will instantly start to break down.

> I see how my senses can only deceive,
> for nothing they tell me, I fully believe.
> Behind all appearances is only light,
> they only seem real to our limited sight.

> **O Padmasambhava, in your Flame of Peace,**
> **all human opinions I hereby release.**
> **I see now the ultimate truth you reveal,**
> **earth is an appearance, where nothing is real.**

2. Padmasambhava, shatter the energetic matrix that prevents people from seeing that what is created in duality can only be sustained over time if people are continually putting their attention on it and therefore feeding energy into upholding the matrix.

> My mind and my senses are only a tool,
> and I am determined to not be a fool.
> My personal self, is no more who I am,
> the earthly identity is but a scam.

> O Padmasambhava, in your Flame of Peace,
> all human opinions I hereby release.
> I see now the ultimate truth you reveal,
> earth is an appearance, where nothing is real.

3. Padmasambhava, shatter the energetic matrix that prevents people from seeing that in order to create something that can last over time in the physical octave, the dark forces must get people to continually put their attention on it and feed their energy into that matrix.

From sense-based perception I want to be free,
clear my inner sight, so I truly can see.
My human opinions, they do make me blind,
with neutral awareness, new visions I find.

O Padmasambhava, in your Flame of Peace,
all human opinions I hereby release.
I see now the ultimate truth you reveal,
earth is an appearance, where nothing is real.

4. Padmasambhava, shatter the energetic matrix that prevents people from seeing that the dark forces do this through the epic mindset. The epic mindset says that here is a cause that is ultimately important, and therefore people must dedicate their lives to fighting for this cause, and it is justified that they kill other people in order to promote that cause.

A self is what makes an opinion seem real,
it projects there's a problem, with which I must deal.
I will not be free, till I see through this life,
and say to the self: I am letting you die.

O Padmasambhava, in your Flame of Peace,
all human opinions I hereby release.
I see now the ultimate truth you reveal,
earth is an appearance, where nothing is real.

5. Padmasambhava, shatter the energetic matrix that prevents people from seeing that the underlying mechanism is that the fallen beings must make people believe that the dualistic polarities are real, they have some reality, they have some substance.

Through human opinions, I simply can't see,
the higher perspective—Christ reality,
When the self dualistic, I truly let die,
the Christ mind does open, up my inner eye.

O Padmasambhava, in your Flame of Peace,
all human opinions I hereby release.

**I see now the ultimate truth you reveal,
earth is an appearance, where nothing is real.**

6. Padmasambhava, shatter the energetic matrix that prevents people from seeing that if no one believed that the struggle was real, why would we give our lives to the struggle?

O Padmasambhava, the world has gone mad,
as dualistic thinking, defines good and bad.
The judgment of Christ, upon forces so dark,
rekindle in people, our spiritual spark.

**O Padmasambhava, in your Flame of Peace,
all human opinions I hereby release.
I see now the ultimate truth you reveal,
earth is an appearance, where nothing is real.**

7. Padmasambhava, shatter the energetic matrix that prevents people from seeing that the fallen beings cannot create this sense of reality, but they do not have to. A long time ago, they caused the majority of the people on earth to also go into the duality consciousness, and in the duality consciousness, there are certain things that seem absolutely real.

O Padmasambhava, set all people free,
from mindset so epic, from duality.
Cut all people free from the serpentine lie,
so that to Christ Jesus, we all can draw nigh.

**O Padmasambhava, in your Flame of Peace,
all human opinions I hereby release.
I see now the ultimate truth you reveal,
earth is an appearance, where nothing is real.**

8. Padmasambhava, shatter the energetic matrix that prevents people from seeing that our physical senses make matter seem very real and solid. Over many lifetimes of embodying on earth, we have come to be convinced that the earth has some reality—it has some durability, some continuity.

The serpentine lie, says that what we now see,
is all that our lives, on this planet can be.
Yet with the Christ mind, we can see there is more,
the earth will be brighter than ever before.

O Padmasambhava, in your Flame of Peace,
all human opinions I hereby release.
I see now the ultimate truth you reveal,
earth is an appearance, where nothing is real.

9. Padmasambhava, shatter the energetic matrix that prevents people from seeing that this is not entirely an illusion in the sense that planet earth was created by the Elohim, and as the Elohim continue to put their attention on this matrix, the earth will endure.

Saint Germain has the plans, for a bright Golden Age,
to receive them, our minds must be free from the cage,
O Padmasambhava, with your Flame of Peace,
the vision of Oneness, to all you release.

O Padmasambhava, in your Flame of Peace,
all human opinions I hereby release.
I see now the ultimate truth you reveal,
earth is an appearance, where nothing is real.

Part 4

1. Padmasambhava, shatter the energetic matrix that prevents people from seeing that the earth is real in the sense that it is there. There is a physical planet that is a platform for life and for the experiences we have as self-aware beings.

I see how my senses can only deceive,
for nothing they tell me, I fully believe.
Behind all appearances is only light,
they only seem real to our limited sight.

**O Padmasambhava, in your Flame of Peace,
all human opinions I hereby release.
I see now the ultimate truth you reveal,
earth is an appearance, where nothing is real.**

2. Padmasambhava, shatter the energetic matrix that prevents people from seeing that the earth is not real in the sense that it will endure forever. Nor is it real in the sense that its form could not be changed.

My mind and my senses are only a tool,
and I am determined to not be a fool.
My personal self, is no more who I am,
the earthly identity is but a scam.

O Padmasambhava, in your Flame of Peace,
all human opinions I hereby release.
I see now the ultimate truth you reveal,
earth is an appearance, where nothing is real.

3. Padmasambhava, shatter the energetic matrix that prevents people from seeing that the Elohim originally created the earth in a much higher matrix than what we see today, and after humankind fell into duality, the earth has become denser. What we see today is not what the Elohim created, it is not the highest potential for earth.

From sense-based perception I want to be free,
clear my inner sight, so I truly can see.
My human opinions, they do make me blind,
with neutral awareness, new visions I find.

**O Padmasambhava, in your Flame of Peace,
all human opinions I hereby release.
I see now the ultimate truth you reveal,
earth is an appearance, where nothing is real.**

4. Padmasambhava, shatter the energetic matrix that prevents people from seeing that if with "real" we define something we can detect with our physical senses, then the earth has some reality to it. Yet in its current form and density the earth is not sustainable.

A self is what makes an opinion seem real,
it projects there's a problem, with which I must deal.
I will not be free, till I see through this life,
and say to the self: I am letting you die.

O Padmasambhava, in your Flame of Peace,
all human opinions I hereby release.
I see now the ultimate truth you reveal,
earth is an appearance, where nothing is real.

5. Padmasambhava, shatter the energetic matrix that prevents people from seeing that it is possible to transform the earth into a lesser density where many of the problems we see today will fade away.

Through human opinions, I simply can't see,
the higher perspective—Christ reality,
When the self dualistic, I truly let die,
the Christ mind does open, up my inner eye.

O Padmasambhava, in your Flame of Peace,
all human opinions I hereby release.
I see now the ultimate truth you reveal,
earth is an appearance, where nothing is real.

6. Padmasambhava, shatter the energetic matrix that prevents people from seeing that if we raised the earth into a lesser density, our bodies could sustain themselves for much longer than what we call a normal lifespan because most diseases would disappear.

O Padmasambhava, the world has gone mad,
as dualistic thinking, defines good and bad.
The judgment of Christ, upon forces so dark,
rekindle in people, our spiritual spark.

O Padmasambhava, in your Flame of Peace,
all human opinions I hereby release.
I see now the ultimate truth you reveal,
earth is an appearance, where nothing is real.

7. Padmasambhava, shatter the energetic matrix that prevents people from seeing that if the earth was raised enough, we would not have to earn a living by working at the sweat of our brow, because the earth would provide what we needed to sustain ourselves without this enormous struggle that we see today.

O Padmasambhava, set all people free,
from mindset so epic, from duality.
Cut all people free from the serpentine lie,
so that to Christ Jesus, we all can draw nigh.

**O Padmasambhava, in your Flame of Peace,
all human opinions I hereby release.
I see now the ultimate truth you reveal,
earth is an appearance, where nothing is real.**

8. Padmasambhava, shatter the energetic matrix that prevents people from seeing that our physical senses are calibrated to detect the dense vibrations that we currently have on earth. Our senses cannot detect what is beyond the physical.

The serpentine lie, says that what we now see,
is all that our lives, on this planet can be.
Yet with the Christ mind, we can see there is more,
the earth will be brighter than ever before.

**O Padmasambhava, in your Flame of Peace,
all human opinions I hereby release.
I see now the ultimate truth you reveal,
earth is an appearance, where nothing is real.**

9. Padmasambhava, shatter the energetic matrix that prevents people from seeing that over many lifetimes, our minds have become so attached to the senses that our minds think that what our senses see is real, even that what our senses show us is the only way the earth could be.

Saint Germain has the plans, for a bright Golden Age,
to receive them, our minds must be free from the cage,

O Padmasambhava, with your Flame of Peace,
the vision of Oneness, to all you release.

**O Padmasambhava, in your Flame of Peace,
all human opinions I hereby release.
I see now the ultimate truth you reveal,
earth is an appearance, where nothing is real.**

Sealing

In the name of the I AM THAT I AM, I accept that Archangel Michael, Astrea and Shiva form an impenetrable shield around myself and all constructive people, sealing us from all fear-based energies in all four octaves. I accept that the Light of God is consuming and transforming all fear-based energies that make up the dark forces working against ending the era of elitism on earth!

19 | INVOKING FREEDOM FROM HUMAN OPINIONS (PART 2)

In the name of the I AM THAT I AM, Jesus Christ, I use the authority that I have as a being in embodiment on earth to call upon Padmasambhava to reinforce my calls and use my chakras to project the statements in this invocation into the collective consciousness and awaken people to the advantage of letting go of all human opinions. Awaken people to the reality that we are spiritual beings and that we can co-create a new future by working with the ascended masters. I especially call for ...

[Make your own calls here.]

Part 1

1. Padmasambhava, shatter the energetic matrix that prevents people from seeing that when we become spiritual students, we start to detach our minds from our physical bodies and physical senses. We start to question whether there is something beyond what the senses can detect.

I see how my senses can only deceive,
for nothing they tell me, I fully believe.
Behind all appearances is only light,
they only seem real to our limited sight.

O Padmasambhava, in your Flame of Peace,
all human opinions I hereby release.
I see now the ultimate truth you reveal,
earth is an appearance, where nothing is real.

2. Padmasambhava, shatter the energetic matrix that prevents people from seeing that we gradually disassociate our minds from the senses and the physical octave. We are no longer believing that the physical octave is completely real or that it is the only world there is.

My mind and my senses are only a tool,
and I am determined to not be a fool.
My personal self, is no more who I am,
the earthly identity is but a scam.

O Padmasambhava, in your Flame of Peace,
all human opinions I hereby release.
I see now the ultimate truth you reveal,
earth is an appearance, where nothing is real.

3. Padmasambhava, shatter the energetic matrix that prevents people from seeing that we become open to the potential that there is something beyond the physical world, and that this something might be a spiritual world that is the source of everything we see in the physical world.

From sense-based perception I want to be free,
clear my inner sight, so I truly can see.
My human opinions, they do make me blind,
with neutral awareness, new visions I find.

O Padmasambhava, in your Flame of Peace,
all human opinions I hereby release.
I see now the ultimate truth you reveal,
earth is an appearance, where nothing is real.

4. Padmasambhava, shatter the energetic matrix that prevents people from seeing that we can take this a step further and realize that if there is a spiritual world beyond the physical, and if everything in the physical is made from the energy of the spiritual world that was lowered in vibration, then the physical world is not as real as the spiritual world.

A self is what makes an opinion seem real,
it projects there's a problem, with which I must deal.
I will not be free, till I see through this life,
and say to the self: I am letting you die.

**O Padmasambhava, in your Flame of Peace,
all human opinions I hereby release.
I see now the ultimate truth you reveal,
earth is an appearance, where nothing is real.**

5. Padmasambhava, shatter the energetic matrix that prevents people from making the switch where we realize that he material world is a projection, where the energy that makes up the material world has taken on a certain form, and it has done so because an image was projected onto the light and there was energy and attention flowing through that matrix.

Through human opinions, I simply can't see,
the higher perspective—Christ reality,
When the self dualistic, I truly let die,
the Christ mind does open, up my inner eye.

**O Padmasambhava, in your Flame of Peace,
all human opinions I hereby release.
I see now the ultimate truth you reveal,
earth is an appearance, where nothing is real.**

6. Padmasambhava, shatter the energetic matrix that prevents people from seeing that the light has taken on that form because that is what the light is defined to do. This does not mean that this form is permanent. The light could as easily take on any other form as what we currently see.

O Padmasambhava, the world has gone mad,
as dualistic thinking, defines good and bad.

The judgment of Christ, upon forces so dark,
rekindle in people, our spiritual spark.

O Padmasambhava, in your Flame of Peace,
all human opinions I hereby release.
I see now the ultimate truth you reveal,
earth is an appearance, where nothing is real.

7. Padmasambhava, shatter the energetic matrix that prevents people from seeing that the current conditions we see on earth, even the density of matter and the density of our physical bodies, was created by the collective consciousness of humankind, where people came to accept the current conditions as real.

O Padmasambhava, set all people free,
from mindset so epic, from duality.
Cut all people free from the serpentine lie,
so that to Christ Jesus, we all can draw nigh.

O Padmasambhava, in your Flame of Peace,
all human opinions I hereby release.
I see now the ultimate truth you reveal,
earth is an appearance, where nothing is real.

8. Padmasambhava, shatter the energetic matrix that prevents people from seeing that the process of creating the current conditions started a long time ago. Gradually, this has caused the density to increase to what we see today.

The serpentine lie, says that what we now see,
is all that our lives, on this planet can be.
Yet with the Christ mind, we can see there is more,
the earth will be brighter than ever before.

O Padmasambhava, in your Flame of Peace,
all human opinions I hereby release.
I see now the ultimate truth you reveal,
earth is an appearance, where nothing is real.

9. Padmasambhava, shatter the energetic matrix that prevents people from seeing that over many lifetimes, we come to believe that what we see currently on earth is natural. It was either created by God or created by nature, and it is the only way things could be.

> Saint Germain has the plans, for a bright Golden Age,
> to receive them, our minds must be free from the cage,
> O Padmasambhava, with your Flame of Peace,
> the vision of Oneness, to all you release.

> **O Padmasambhava, in your Flame of Peace,**
> **all human opinions I hereby release.**
> **I see now the ultimate truth you reveal,**
> **earth is an appearance, where nothing is real.**

Part 2

1. Padmasambhava, shatter the energetic matrix that prevents people from seeing that this is the sense of reality that the fallen beings use. On top of the sense of reality based on our senses, they project these dualistic ideas that create the sense of struggle.

> I see how my senses can only deceive,
> for nothing they tell me, I fully believe.
> Behind all appearances is only light,
> they only seem real to our limited sight.

> **O Padmasambhava, in your Flame of Peace,**
> **all human opinions I hereby release.**
> **I see now the ultimate truth you reveal,**
> **earth is an appearance, where nothing is real.**

2. Padmasambhava, shatter the energetic matrix that prevents people from seeing that the Catholic church of the Middle Ages was dualistic, and its opposite became Islam.

My mind and my senses are only a tool,
and I am determined to not be a fool.
My personal self, is no more who I am,
the earthly identity is but a scam.

O Padmasambhava, in your Flame of Peace,
all human opinions I hereby release.
I see now the ultimate truth you reveal,
earth is an appearance, where nothing is real.

3. Padmasambhava, shatter the energetic matrix that prevents people from seeing that this is why the Catholic church was able to project the necessity of Christians engaging in this epic struggle with Muslims to eradicate this false religion that was only causing souls to be lost in hell.

From sense-based perception I want to be free,
clear my inner sight, so I truly can see.
My human opinions, they do make me blind,
with neutral awareness, new visions I find.

**O Padmasambhava, in your Flame of Peace,
all human opinions I hereby release.
I see now the ultimate truth you reveal,
earth is an appearance, where nothing is real.**

4. Padmasambhava, shatter the energetic matrix that prevents people from seeing that the other side had a similar view that they had the only true religion and therefore any other religion had to be false. Therefore, there was an inevitable struggle between the two.

A self is what makes an opinion seem real,
it projects there's a problem, with which I must deal.
I will not be free, till I see through this life,
and say to the self: I am letting you die.

**O Padmasambhava, in your Flame of Peace,
all human opinions I hereby release.
I see now the ultimate truth you reveal,
earth is an appearance, where nothing is real.**

5. Padmasambhava, shatter the energetic matrix that prevents people from seeing that people on both sides thought this struggle was absolutely real. They thought it was real that they should give their lives to this struggle and they should take the lives of other people in this struggle. On both sides, they thought that they had the only true God and that they would be rewarded in heaven for killing the people on the other side.

Through human opinions, I simply can't see,
the higher perspective—Christ reality,
When the self dualistic, I truly let die,
the Christ mind does open, up my inner eye.

**O Padmasambhava, in your Flame of Peace,
all human opinions I hereby release.
I see now the ultimate truth you reveal,
earth is an appearance, where nothing is real.**

6. Padmasambhava, shatter the energetic matrix that prevents people from seeing that what the fallen beings have done time and time again is that they have made use of our sensory-based sense of what is real, and they have tied an idea into that.

O Padmasambhava, the world has gone mad,
as dualistic thinking, defines good and bad.
The judgment of Christ, upon forces so dark,
rekindle in people, our spiritual spark.

**O Padmasambhava, in your Flame of Peace,
all human opinions I hereby release.
I see now the ultimate truth you reveal,
earth is an appearance, where nothing is real.**

7. Padmasambhava, shatter the energetic matrix that prevents people from seeing that they have managed to project an idea and project that this idea is real, it is as real as what we are sensing with our senses. In a sense they are right. The idea *is* as real as what we are sensing with our senses because what we are sensing with our senses is an appearance and so is the idea.

O Padmasambhava, set all people free,
from mindset so epic, from duality.
Cut all people free from the serpentine lie,
so that to Christ Jesus, we all can draw nigh.

O Padmasambhava, in your Flame of Peace,
all human opinions I hereby release.
I see now the ultimate truth you reveal,
earth is an appearance, where nothing is real.

8. Padmasambhava, shatter the energetic matrix that prevents people from seeing that when we begin to expose this basic lie, we need to go through a period where we are looking out and we are seeing how other people were trapped into taking these dualistic positions and therefore fighting against others.

The serpentine lie, says that what we now see,
is all that our lives, on this planet can be.
Yet with the Christ mind, we can see there is more,
the earth will be brighter than ever before.

O Padmasambhava, in your Flame of Peace,
all human opinions I hereby release.
I see now the ultimate truth you reveal,
earth is an appearance, where nothing is real.

9. Padmasambhava, shatter the energetic matrix that prevents people from seeing that there is a more mature phase, where we start looking at ourselves, our own opinions, our own beliefs. We look at whether we have been caught in some version of this dualistic struggle.

Saint Germain has the plans, for a bright Golden Age,
to receive them, our minds must be free from the cage,
O Padmasambhava, with your Flame of Peace,
the vision of Oneness, to all you release.

O Padmasambhava, in your Flame of Peace,
all human opinions I hereby release.

**I see now the ultimate truth you reveal,
earth is an appearance, where nothing is real.**

Part 3

1. Padmasambhava, shatter the energetic matrix that prevents people from seeing that the dualistic struggle, the epic struggle, always says there are two sides and one of them is good and the other one is bad. One of them is right and the other is completely wrong.

I see how my senses can only deceive,
for nothing they tell me, I fully believe.
Behind all appearances is only light,
they only seem real to our limited sight.

**O Padmasambhava, in your Flame of Peace,
all human opinions I hereby release.
I see now the ultimate truth you reveal,
earth is an appearance, where nothing is real.**

2. Padmasambhava, shatter the energetic matrix that prevents people from seeing that many people have allowed themselves to think that one political party is right and the other is wrong.

My mind and my senses are only a tool,
and I am determined to not be a fool.
My personal self, is no more who I am,
the earthly identity is but a scam.

O Padmasambhava, in your Flame of Peace,
all human opinions I hereby release.
I see now the ultimate truth you reveal,
earth is an appearance, where nothing is real.

3. Padmasambhava, shatter the energetic matrix that prevents people from seeing that as spiritual people who are aspiring to put on Christ

discernment, we need to look beyond this. We cannot allow ourselves to be pulled into supporting this struggle.

> From sense-based perception I want to be free,
> clear my inner sight, so I truly can see.
> My human opinions, they do make me blind,
> with neutral awareness, new visions I find.

> **O Padmasambhava, in your Flame of Peace,**
> **all human opinions I hereby release.**
> **I see now the ultimate truth you reveal,**
> **earth is an appearance, where nothing is real.**

4. Padmasambhava, shatter the energetic matrix that prevents people from seeing that the struggle blinds us into taking a particular position. Once we have taken a position, we suspend discernment because now we are saying one side is right and the other side is wrong.

> A self is what makes an opinion seem real,
> it projects there's a problem, with which I must deal.
> I will not be free, till I see through this life,
> and say to the self: I am letting you die.

> **O Padmasambhava, in your Flame of Peace,**
> **all human opinions I hereby release.**
> **I see now the ultimate truth you reveal,**
> **earth is an appearance, where nothing is real.**

5. Padmasambhava, shatter the energetic matrix that prevents people from seeing that it is not that one side is right and the other side is wrong. What will take society forward is certain ideas that will shift the collective consciousness.

> Through human opinions, I simply can't see,
> the higher perspective—Christ reality,
> When the self dualistic, I truly let die,
> the Christ mind does open, up my inner eye.

**O Padmasambhava, in your Flame of Peace,
all human opinions I hereby release.
I see now the ultimate truth you reveal,
earth is an appearance, where nothing is real.**

6. Padmasambhava, shatter the energetic matrix that prevents people from seeing that it is not so that one side is always right and has no wrong ideas. It is a mixed bag. There are some constructive ideas that are promoted by one side, but there are also some promoted by the other side. Neither side has an absolute truth because they are too trapped in the dualistic mindset.

O Padmasambhava, the world has gone mad,
as dualistic thinking, defines good and bad.
The judgment of Christ, upon forces so dark,
rekindle in people, our spiritual spark.

**O Padmasambhava, in your Flame of Peace,
all human opinions I hereby release.
I see now the ultimate truth you reveal,
earth is an appearance, where nothing is real.**

7. Padmasambhava, shatter the energetic matrix that prevents people from seeing beyond this struggle between two parties. We look for a new class of politicians who are dedicated to doing what is best for the people, not the elite. They are dedicated to bringing forth the ideas that are best for the people.

O Padmasambhava, set all people free,
from mindset so epic, from duality.
Cut all people free from the serpentine lie,
so that to Christ Jesus, we all can draw nigh.

**O Padmasambhava, in your Flame of Peace,
all human opinions I hereby release.
I see now the ultimate truth you reveal,
earth is an appearance, where nothing is real.**

8. Padmasambhava, shatter the energetic matrix that prevents people from seeing that the current political situation cannot bring real solutions. If the

current situation could have brought forth the solution, it should already have done so, given how many decades this has been going on.

> The serpentine lie, says that what we now see,
> is all that our lives, on this planet can be.
> Yet with the Christ mind, we can see there is more,
> the earth will be brighter than ever before.

> **O Padmasambhava, in your Flame of Peace,**
> **all human opinions I hereby release.**
> **I see now the ultimate truth you reveal,**
> **earth is an appearance, where nothing is real.**

9. Padmasambhava, shatter the energetic matrix that prevents people from seeing that something new is needed. If we keep doing the same thing and expect different results, we are insane.

> Saint Germain has the plans, for a bright Golden Age,
> to receive them, our minds must be free from the cage,
> O Padmasambhava, with your Flame of Peace,
> the vision of Oneness, to all you release.

> **O Padmasambhava, in your Flame of Peace,**
> **all human opinions I hereby release.**
> **I see now the ultimate truth you reveal,**
> **earth is an appearance, where nothing is real.**

Part 4

1. Padmasambhava, shatter the energetic matrix that prevents people from seeing that we cannot simply align ourselves with a particular party and then once we have done this, we need to accept everything they say as good and everything the other party says as bad.

> I see how my senses can only deceive,
> for nothing they tell me, I fully believe.

Behind all appearances is only light,
they only seem real to our limited sight.

O Padmasambhava, in your Flame of Peace,
all human opinions I hereby release.
I see now the ultimate truth you reveal,
earth is an appearance, where nothing is real.

2. Padmasambhava, shatter the energetic matrix that prevents people from seeing that we need to become focused on the ideas and serving the people, rather than having two parties fighting for dominion.

My mind and my senses are only a tool,
and I am determined to not be a fool.
My personal self, is no more who I am,
the earthly identity is but a scam.

O Padmasambhava, in your Flame of Peace,
all human opinions I hereby release.
I see now the ultimate truth you reveal,
earth is an appearance, where nothing is real.

3. Padmasambhava, shatter the energetic matrix that prevents people from seeing that this change can only start among the most spiritual people, the top 10% who have the highest level of Christ awareness. If we think one party or the other will provide the only truth, we cannot be the forerunners for that change.

From sense-based perception I want to be free,
clear my inner sight, so I truly can see.
My human opinions, they do make me blind,
with neutral awareness, new visions I find.

O Padmasambhava, in your Flame of Peace,
all human opinions I hereby release.
I see now the ultimate truth you reveal,
earth is an appearance, where nothing is real.

4. Padmasambhava, shatter the energetic matrix that prevents people from seeing that there is a more subtle form of the dualistic struggle where we have grown up accepting certain dualistic opinions, and we do not see that they are dualistic.

> A self is what makes an opinion seem real,
> it projects there's a problem, with which I must deal.
> I will not be free, till I see through this life,
> and say to the self: I am letting you die.

> **O Padmasambhava, in your Flame of Peace,**
> **all human opinions I hereby release.**
> **I see now the ultimate truth you reveal,**
> **earth is an appearance, where nothing is real.**

5. Padmasambhava, shatter the energetic matrix that prevents people from seeing that we may think these ideas represent some higher truth, and we are absolutely convinced that this is the way it is.

> Through human opinions, I simply can't see,
> the higher perspective—Christ reality,
> When the self dualistic, I truly let die,
> the Christ mind does open, up my inner eye.

> **O Padmasambhava, in your Flame of Peace,**
> **all human opinions I hereby release.**
> **I see now the ultimate truth you reveal,**
> **earth is an appearance, where nothing is real.**

6. Padmasambhava, shatter the energetic matrix that prevents people from seeing that the subtle version of how the fallen beings have tricked people into the dualistic struggle is to make people accept a certain viewpoint, a certain opinion, and think it is the ultimate viewpoint. Therefore, we never need to examine it, we never need to question it, we never need to look beyond it.

> O Padmasambhava, the world has gone mad,
> as dualistic thinking, defines good and bad.

The judgment of Christ, upon forces so dark,
rekindle in people, our spiritual spark.

O Padmasambhava, in your Flame of Peace,
all human opinions I hereby release.
I see now the ultimate truth you reveal,
earth is an appearance, where nothing is real.

7. Padmasambhava, shatter the energetic matrix that prevents people from seeing that many people have come into ascended master organizations with strong opinions, and they have found something in the teachings that they could use to validate their opinions.

O Padmasambhava, set all people free,
from mindset so epic, from duality.
Cut all people free from the serpentine lie,
so that to Christ Jesus, we all can draw nigh.

O Padmasambhava, in your Flame of Peace,
all human opinions I hereby release.
I see now the ultimate truth you reveal,
earth is an appearance, where nothing is real.

8. Padmasambhava, shatter the energetic matrix that prevents people from seeing that people who are trapped in these opinions cannot be the fore-runners for manifesting Saint Germain's Golden Age, because Saint Germain's Golden Age can be manifest only through the Christ consciousness.

The serpentine lie, says that what we now see,
is all that our lives, on this planet can be.
Yet with the Christ mind, we can see there is more,
the earth will be brighter than ever before.

O Padmasambhava, in your Flame of Peace,
all human opinions I hereby release.
I see now the ultimate truth you reveal,
earth is an appearance, where nothing is real.

9. Padmasambhava, shatter the energetic matrix that prevents people from seeing that if we have very strong opinions that we are not willing to question, that is not the Christ consciousness. We need to be willing to lose the outer selves that have these strong, one-sided, dualistic opinions.

> Saint Germain has the plans, for a bright Golden Age,
> to receive them, our minds must be free from the cage,
> O Padmasambhava, with your Flame of Peace,
> the vision of Oneness, to all you release.

> **O Padmasambhava, in your Flame of Peace,**
> **all human opinions I hereby release.**
> **I see now the ultimate truth you reveal,**
> **earth is an appearance, where nothing is real.**

Sealing

In the name of the I AM THAT I AM, I accept that Archangel Michael, Astrea and Shiva form an impenetrable shield around myself and all constructive people, sealing us from all fear-based energies in all four octaves. I accept that the Light of God is consuming and transforming all fear-based energies that make up the dark forces working against ending the era of elitism on earth!

20 | INVOKING FREEDOM FROM HUMAN OPINIONS (PART 3)

In the name of the I AM THAT I AM, Jesus Christ, I use the authority that I have as a being in embodiment on earth to call upon Padmasambhava to reinforce my calls and use my chakras to project the statements in this invocation into the collective consciousness and awaken people to the advantage of letting go of all human opinions. Awaken people to the reality that we are spiritual beings and that we can co-create a new future by working with the ascended masters. I especially call for …

[Make your own calls here.]

Part 1

1. Padmasambhava, shatter the energetic matrix that prevents people from seeing that in order to become the Christ, we must be willing to lose *all* of our opinions.

> I see how my senses can only deceive,
> for nothing they tell me, I fully believe.

Behind all appearances is only light,
they only seem real to our limited sight.

O Padmasambhava, in your Flame of Peace,
all human opinions I hereby release.
I see now the ultimate truth you reveal,
earth is an appearance, where nothing is real.

2. Padmasambhava, shatter the energetic matrix that prevents people from seeing that an opinion is a very strong, simple statement that we believe represents some absolute truth, and that we are not willing to question.

My mind and my senses are only a tool,
and I am determined to not be a fool.
My personal self, is no more who I am,
the earthly identity is but a scam.

O Padmasambhava, in your Flame of Peace,
all human opinions I hereby release.
I see now the ultimate truth you reveal,
earth is an appearance, where nothing is real.

3. Padmasambhava, shatter the energetic matrix that prevents people from seeing that the ascended masters are in a fundamentally different state of consciousness than people in embodiment. The Christ consciousness is a fundamentally different state of consciousness than the duality consciousness.

From sense-based perception I want to be free,
clear my inner sight, so I truly can see.
My human opinions, they do make me blind,
with neutral awareness, new visions I find.

O Padmasambhava, in your Flame of Peace,
all human opinions I hereby release.
I see now the ultimate truth you reveal,
earth is an appearance, where nothing is real.

4. Padmasambhava, shatter the energetic matrix that prevents people from seeing that the whole purpose of being a spiritual student is to rise above the duality consciousness and put on the Christ consciousness. How can we do this, if we have a set of opinions that we think we never need to question?

A self is what makes an opinion seem real,
it projects there's a problem, with which I must deal.
I will not be free, till I see through this life,
and say to the self: I am letting you die.

O Padmasambhava, in your Flame of Peace,
all human opinions I hereby release.
I see now the ultimate truth you reveal,
earth is an appearance, where nothing is real.

5. Padmasambhava, shatter the energetic matrix that prevents people from seeing that we cannot learn from the ascended masters if we are so attached to these opinions that we are only looking for validation of them, instead of looking for a higher perspective from the Christ mind.

Through human opinions, I simply can't see,
the higher perspective—Christ reality,
When the self dualistic, I truly let die,
the Christ mind does open, up my inner eye.

O Padmasambhava, in your Flame of Peace,
all human opinions I hereby release.
I see now the ultimate truth you reveal,
earth is an appearance, where nothing is real.

6. Padmasambhava, shatter the energetic matrix that prevents people from seeing that we cannot make use of ascended master teachings if we are seeking to get the ascended masters to validate our dualistic opinions.

O Padmasambhava, the world has gone mad,
as dualistic thinking, defines good and bad.
The judgment of Christ, upon forces so dark,
rekindle in people, our spiritual spark.

**O Padmasambhava, in your Flame of Peace,
all human opinions I hereby release.
I see now the ultimate truth you reveal,
earth is an appearance, where nothing is real.**

7. Padmasambhava, shatter the energetic matrix that prevents people from seeing that an opinion is something that is not based on the reality of the Christ mind. We cannot know if something is true if we have not been willing to give it up and see what comes to us from the Christ mind.

O Padmasambhava, set all people free,
from mindset so epic, from duality.
Cut all people free from the serpentine lie,
so that to Christ Jesus, we all can draw nigh.

**O Padmasambhava, in your Flame of Peace,
all human opinions I hereby release.
I see now the ultimate truth you reveal,
earth is an appearance, where nothing is real.**

8. Padmasambhava, shatter the energetic matrix that prevents people from seeing that we cannot know what is real unless we are willing to let the self that carries a strong opinion die.

The serpentine lie, says that what we now see,
is all that our lives, on this planet can be.
Yet with the Christ mind, we can see there is more,
the earth will be brighter than ever before.

**O Padmasambhava, in your Flame of Peace,
all human opinions I hereby release.
I see now the ultimate truth you reveal,
earth is an appearance, where nothing is real.**

9. Padmasambhava, shatter the energetic matrix that prevents people from seeing that until we have been willing to give up an opinion, we cannot know what the Christ perspective on it is. When we do give it up and get the Christ perspective, we see that there is so much more to the issue than that particular opinion.

Saint Germain has the plans, for a bright Golden Age,
to receive them, our minds must be free from the cage,
O Padmasambhava, with your Flame of Peace,
the vision of Oneness, to all you release.

O Padmasambhava, in your Flame of Peace,
all human opinions I hereby release.
I see now the ultimate truth you reveal,
earth is an appearance, where nothing is real.

Part 2

1. Padmasambhava, shatter the energetic matrix that prevents people from seeing that if we think our current definition and understanding of an issue is real, we will seek to manifest that. Instead, we need to let our current understanding die and seek a higher perspective from the Christ mind.

I see how my senses can only deceive,
for nothing they tell me, I fully believe.
Behind all appearances is only light,
they only seem real to our limited sight.

O Padmasambhava, in your Flame of Peace,
all human opinions I hereby release.
I see now the ultimate truth you reveal,
earth is an appearance, where nothing is real.

2. Padmasambhava, shatter the energetic matrix that prevents people from seeing that Saint Germain has a vision for any issue that goes far beyond what anyone on earth has right now. There is so much more to know.

My mind and my senses are only a tool,
and I am determined to not be a fool.
My personal self, is no more who I am,
the earthly identity is but a scam.

O Padmasambhava, in your Flame of Peace,
all human opinions I hereby release.
I see now the ultimate truth you reveal,
earth is an appearance, where nothing is real.

3. Padmasambhava, shatter the energetic matrix that prevents people from seeing that from a limited perspective an idea may seem to have a certain validity. But if it prevents us from growing and seeing the bigger picture, then it becomes a false idea because it is preventing our growth.

From sense-based perception I want to be free,
clear my inner sight, so I truly can see.
My human opinions, they do make me blind,
with neutral awareness, new visions I find.

**O Padmasambhava, in your Flame of Peace,
all human opinions I hereby release.
I see now the ultimate truth you reveal,
earth is an appearance, where nothing is real.**

4. Padmasambhava, shatter the energetic matrix that prevents people from seeing that there is no idea in the world today that is absolute, that is final. As the collective consciousness is raised, we will begin to see ideas we cannot see today.

A self is what makes an opinion seem real,
it projects there's a problem, with which I must deal.
I will not be free, till I see through this life,
and say to the self: I am letting you die.

**O Padmasambhava, in your Flame of Peace,
all human opinions I hereby release.
I see now the ultimate truth you reveal,
earth is an appearance, where nothing is real.**

5. Padmasambhava, shatter the energetic matrix that prevents people from seeing that those who will be able to see these ideas are those who are not attached to their existing ideas. In order to receive new ideas, we must be willing to look at our opinions and just let them die.

Through human opinions, I simply can't see,
the higher perspective—Christ reality,
When the self dualistic, I truly let die,
the Christ mind does open, up my inner eye.

O Padmasambhava, in your Flame of Peace,
all human opinions I hereby release.
I see now the ultimate truth you reveal,
earth is an appearance, where nothing is real.

6. Padmasambhava, shatter the energetic matrix that prevents people from seeing that when we are in the Christ mind, we do not have opinions. We just have understanding and observations, but we are not judging them based on a scale of right and wrong, good or bad.

O Padmasambhava, the world has gone mad,
as dualistic thinking, defines good and bad.
The judgment of Christ, upon forces so dark,
rekindle in people, our spiritual spark.

O Padmasambhava, in your Flame of Peace,
all human opinions I hereby release.
I see now the ultimate truth you reveal,
earth is an appearance, where nothing is real.

7. Padmasambhava, shatter the energetic matrix that prevents people from seeing that in the Christ mind we are not judging people. We are looking at the consequences of ideas. Is the consequences going to limit people or liberate them?

O Padmasambhava, set all people free,
from mindset so epic, from duality.
Cut all people free from the serpentine lie,
so that to Christ Jesus, we all can draw nigh.

O Padmasambhava, in your Flame of Peace,
all human opinions I hereby release.
I see now the ultimate truth you reveal,
earth is an appearance, where nothing is real.

8. Padmasambhava, shatter the energetic matrix that prevents people from seeing that we need to consider where we want to get our ideas from. From the power elite, the fallen beings, the duality consciousness or from the ascended masters?

> The serpentine lie, says that what we now see,
> is all that our lives, on this planet can be.
> Yet with the Christ mind, we can see there is more,
> the earth will be brighter than ever before.

> **O Padmasambhava, in your Flame of Peace,**
> **all human opinions I hereby release.**
> **I see now the ultimate truth you reveal,**
> **earth is an appearance, where nothing is real.**

9. Padmasambhava, shatter the energetic matrix that prevents people from seeing that we need to identify that certain of these strong opinions we have, that we are very sure are right, are dualistic ideas. They are anchored in a certain self in our beings.

> Saint Germain has the plans, for a bright Golden Age,
> to receive them, our minds must be free from the cage,
> O Padmasambhava, with your Flame of Peace,
> the vision of Oneness, to all you release.

> **O Padmasambhava, in your Flame of Peace,**
> **all human opinions I hereby release.**
> **I see now the ultimate truth you reveal,**
> **earth is an appearance, where nothing is real.**

Part 3

1. Padmasambhava, shatter the energetic matrix that prevents people from seeing that instead of trying to solve the problem that our ideas define, bring forth the solution, or destroy the opposition, we need to just let that self die. Then, we go into a neutral state of mind and ask for the Christ perspective on the issue.

I see how my senses can only deceive,
for nothing they tell me, I fully believe.
Behind all appearances is only light,
they only seem real to our limited sight.

O Padmasambhava, in your Flame of Peace,
all human opinions I hereby release.
I see now the ultimate truth you reveal,
earth is an appearance, where nothing is real.

2. Padmasambhava, shatter the energetic matrix that prevents people from seeing that as long as we are looking for answers through a separate self, we cannot see the Christ perspective. Therefore, we cannot be one of the forerunners for manifesting Saint Germain's Golden Age.

My mind and my senses are only a tool,
and I am determined to not be a fool.
My personal self, is no more who I am,
the earthly identity is but a scam.

O Padmasambhava, in your Flame of Peace,
all human opinions I hereby release.
I see now the ultimate truth you reveal,
earth is an appearance, where nothing is real.

3. Padmasambhava, shatter the energetic matrix that prevents people from breaking through and manifesting a much higher level of Christ consciousness than we are manifesting today.

From sense-based perception I want to be free,
clear my inner sight, so I truly can see.
My human opinions, they do make me blind,
with neutral awareness, new visions I find.

O Padmasambhava, in your Flame of Peace,
all human opinions I hereby release.
I see now the ultimate truth you reveal,
earth is an appearance, where nothing is real.

4. Padmasambhava, shatter the energetic matrix that prevents people from seeing that there is one or a set of particular opinions that we have about life or about the spiritual path that we are very attached to, and it is blocking our progress. It is preventing us from shedding the snakeskin of the human consciousness and being reborn into the Christ consciousness.

A self is what makes an opinion seem real,
it projects there's a problem, with which I must deal.
I will not be free, till I see through this life,
and say to the self: I am letting you die.

**O Padmasambhava, in your Flame of Peace,
all human opinions I hereby release.
I see now the ultimate truth you reveal,
earth is an appearance, where nothing is real.**

5. Padmasambhava, shatter the energetic matrix that prevents people from identifying that these strong opinions come from one or several separate selves. Help us let those selves die so we can make a major leap forward in a very short period of time.

Through human opinions, I simply can't see,
the higher perspective—Christ reality,
When the self dualistic, I truly let die,
the Christ mind does open, up my inner eye.

**O Padmasambhava, in your Flame of Peace,
all human opinions I hereby release.
I see now the ultimate truth you reveal,
earth is an appearance, where nothing is real.**

6. Padmasambhava, shatter the energetic matrix that prevents people from seeing that the fallen beings have certain opinions, a certain image of God and the universe and they are very sure that it is right, that it does not need to be questioned.

O Padmasambhava, the world has gone mad,
as dualistic thinking, defines good and bad.

The judgment of Christ, upon forces so dark,
rekindle in people, our spiritual spark.

**O Padmasambhava, in your Flame of Peace,
all human opinions I hereby release.
I see now the ultimate truth you reveal,
earth is an appearance, where nothing is real.**

7. Padmasambhava, shatter the energetic matrix that prevents people from seeing that this is not naked awareness. This is not pure awareness. It is polarized awareness. The Christ consciousness is not polarized.

O Padmasambhava, set all people free,
from mindset so epic, from duality.
Cut all people free from the serpentine lie,
so that to Christ Jesus, we all can draw nigh.

**O Padmasambhava, in your Flame of Peace,
all human opinions I hereby release.
I see now the ultimate truth you reveal,
earth is an appearance, where nothing is real.**

8. Padmasambhava, shatter the energetic matrix that prevents people from seeing that so many people think that the Christ consciousness will validate one of these outer opinions, ideas, ideologies or religions. Many Christians think that Jesus would approve of their particular church and their literal interpretation of the Bible.

The serpentine lie, says that what we now see,
is all that our lives, on this planet can be.
Yet with the Christ mind, we can see there is more,
the earth will be brighter than ever before.

**O Padmasambhava, in your Flame of Peace,
all human opinions I hereby release.
I see now the ultimate truth you reveal,
earth is an appearance, where nothing is real.**

9. Padmasambhava, shatter the energetic matrix that prevents people from seeing that we could make tremendous progress if we were willing to look in the mirror, identify these strong opinions, see that they come from a separate self, see that instead of trying to solve the problem, we could just let the self-die and be free to see much more than we can see today.

> Saint Germain has the plans, for a bright Golden Age,
> to receive them, our minds must be free from the cage,
> O Padmasambhava, with your Flame of Peace,
> the vision of Oneness, to all you release.

> **O Padmasambhava, in your Flame of Peace,**
> **all human opinions I hereby release.**
> **I see now the ultimate truth you reveal,**
> **earth is an appearance, where nothing is real.**

Part 4

1. Padmasambhava, shatter the energetic matrix that prevents people from seeing how to have the peace of being willing to admit that we don't have opinions anymore. We just observe, we may share with others what we observe, but we don't have opinions.

> I see how my senses can only deceive,
> for nothing they tell me, I fully believe.
> Behind all appearances is only light,
> they only seem real to our limited sight.

> **O Padmasambhava, in your Flame of Peace,**
> **all human opinions I hereby release.**
> **I see now the ultimate truth you reveal,**
> **earth is an appearance, where nothing is real.**

2. Padmasambhava, shatter the energetic matrix that prevents people from seeing that one characteristic of opinions is that they define that something *should* happen. Other people should do this or they should agree with our

opinion. It is because other people will not agree that the problem cannot be solved.

My mind and my senses are only a tool,
and I am determined to not be a fool.
My personal self, is no more who I am,
the earthly identity is but a scam.

O Padmasambhava, in your Flame of Peace,
all human opinions I hereby release.
I see now the ultimate truth you reveal,
earth is an appearance, where nothing is real.

3. Padmasambhava, shatter the energetic matrix that prevents people from seeing that as long as there is something that we think *should* happen, we are having opinions, human opinions, dualistic opinions.

From sense-based perception I want to be free,
clear my inner sight, so I truly can see.
My human opinions, they do make me blind,
with neutral awareness, new visions I find.

O Padmasambhava, in your Flame of Peace,
all human opinions I hereby release.
I see now the ultimate truth you reveal,
earth is an appearance, where nothing is real.

4. Padmasambhava, shatter the energetic matrix that prevents people from seeing that ever since we encountered the fallen beings, we have had a self that has attempted to compensate for the trauma in order to prevent us from having it again.

A self is what makes an opinion seem real,
it projects there's a problem, with which I must deal.
I will not be free, till I see through this life,
and say to the self: I am letting you die.

O Padmasambhava, in your Flame of Peace,
all human opinions I hereby release.

I see now the ultimate truth you reveal,
earth is an appearance, where nothing is real.

5. Padmasambhava, shatter the energetic matrix that prevents people from seeing that this self is based on an experience. It is an *understandable* experience. It is in a way an *inevitable* experience.

Through human opinions, I simply can't see,
the higher perspective—Christ reality,
When the self dualistic, I truly let die,
the Christ mind does open, up my inner eye.

O Padmasambhava, in your Flame of Peace,
all human opinions I hereby release.
I see now the ultimate truth you reveal,
earth is an appearance, where nothing is real.

6. Padmasambhava, shatter the energetic matrix that prevents people from seeing that what happened when we encountered the fallen beings and we were exposed to this trauma was that our inner peace was disturbed. Outer conditions, that were forced upon us in a very aggressive way, disturbed our inner peace.

O Padmasambhava, the world has gone mad,
as dualistic thinking, defines good and bad.
The judgment of Christ, upon forces so dark,
rekindle in people, our spiritual spark.

O Padmasambhava, in your Flame of Peace,
all human opinions I hereby release.
I see now the ultimate truth you reveal,
earth is an appearance, where nothing is real.

7. Padmasambhava, shatter the energetic matrix that prevents people from seeing that we have created various selves to deal with this, and these selves believe that outer conditions determine our state of peace. The selves are based on the belief that if we can just manifest, or get other people to manifest, specific outer conditions, then our peace will be restored.

O Padmasambhava, set all people free,
from mindset so epic, from duality.
Cut all people free from the serpentine lie,
so that to Christ Jesus, we all can draw nigh.

**O Padmasambhava, in your Flame of Peace,
all human opinions I hereby release.
I see now the ultimate truth you reveal,
earth is an appearance, where nothing is real.**

8. Padmasambhava, shatter the energetic matrix that prevents people from seeing that what took away our peace was the separate selves. What will bring back our peace is that we let those separate selves die and stop trying to produce a state of inner peace by changing outer conditions.

The serpentine lie, says that what we now see,
is all that our lives, on this planet can be.
Yet with the Christ mind, we can see there is more,
the earth will be brighter than ever before.

**O Padmasambhava, in your Flame of Peace,
all human opinions I hereby release.
I see now the ultimate truth you reveal,
earth is an appearance, where nothing is real.**

9. Padmasambhava, shatter the energetic matrix that prevents people from seeing that we will *never* be at peace as long as we think our peace depends on something outside ourselves, or that it depends on our selves and the opinions they have. There is no problem we could solve that will give us inner peace. We just need to let the self die.

Saint Germain has the plans, for a bright Golden Age,
to receive them, our minds must be free from the cage,
O Padmasambhava, with your Flame of Peace,
the vision of Oneness, to all you release.

**O Padmasambhava, in your Flame of Peace,
all human opinions I hereby release.**

I see now the ultimate truth you reveal,
earth is an appearance, where nothing is real.

Part 5

1. Padmasambhava, shatter the energetic matrix that prevents people from seeing that everything on earth is an appearance. When we sense intuitively that everything is an appearance, we can free ourselves from the dualistic struggle. If we want peace, we must let go of the epic causes defined in today's world. There is no other way to peace than to let go.

I see how my senses can only deceive,
for nothing they tell me, I fully believe.
Behind all appearances is only light,
they only seem real to our limited sight.

O Padmasambhava, in your Flame of Peace,
all human opinions I hereby release.
I see now the ultimate truth you reveal,
earth is an appearance, where nothing is real.

2. Padmasambhava, shatter the energetic matrix that prevents people from accepting your flame of peace that can give us a frame of reference for what it feels like to be in the vibration of peace. Help us glimpse a state of inner peace even though we still have these separate selves that prevent us from having the peace from within.

My mind and my senses are only a tool,
and I am determined to not be a fool.
My personal self, is no more who I am,
the earthly identity is but a scam.

O Padmasambhava, in your Flame of Peace,
all human opinions I hereby release.
I see now the ultimate truth you reveal,
earth is an appearance, where nothing is real.

3. Padmasambhava, shatter the energetic matrix that prevents people from having a frame of reference where we know what it is like to feel at peace. We know what it is like to be in a state of mind that is not constantly being pulled in different directions by all these separate selves, where we are not having the stress of feeling we have to do something to fight some epic battle.

From sense-based perception I want to be free,
clear my inner sight, so I truly can see.
My human opinions, they do make me blind,
with neutral awareness, new visions I find.

O Padmasambhava, in your Flame of Peace,
all human opinions I hereby release.
I see now the ultimate truth you reveal,
earth is an appearance, where nothing is real.

4. Padmasambhava, shatter the energetic matrix that prevents people from seeing how the fallen beings have enveloped people time and time again in these incredible struggles, seeing the amount of energy, the amount of attention, that people have focused on this and the amount of physical suffering this has caused.

A self is what makes an opinion seem real,
it projects there's a problem, with which I must deal.
I will not be free, till I see through this life,
and say to the self: I am letting you die.

O Padmasambhava, in your Flame of Peace,
all human opinions I hereby release.
I see now the ultimate truth you reveal,
earth is an appearance, where nothing is real.

5. Padmasambhava, shatter the energetic matrix that prevents people from seeing that it is all just appearances. *None of it is real.*

Through human opinions, I simply can't see,
the higher perspective—Christ reality,

When the self dualistic, I truly let die,
the Christ mind does open, up my inner eye.

**O Padmasambhava, in your Flame of Peace,
all human opinions I hereby release.
I see now the ultimate truth you reveal,
earth is an appearance, where nothing is real.**

6. Padmasambhava, shatter the energetic matrix that prevents people from seeing that the elites who are promoting these epic struggles, they believe it is real. Even the fallen beings in the higher realms believe it is real.

O Padmasambhava, the world has gone mad,
as dualistic thinking, defines good and bad.
The judgment of Christ, upon forces so dark,
rekindle in people, our spiritual spark.

**O Padmasambhava, in your Flame of Peace,
all human opinions I hereby release.
I see now the ultimate truth you reveal,
earth is an appearance, where nothing is real.**

7. Padmasambhava, shatter the energetic matrix that prevents people from seeing that the elite will not be able to solve the problem of elitism. In reality, there is no problem to solve.

O Padmasambhava, set all people free,
from mindset so epic, from duality.
Cut all people free from the serpentine lie,
so that to Christ Jesus, we all can draw nigh.

**O Padmasambhava, in your Flame of Peace,
all human opinions I hereby release.
I see now the ultimate truth you reveal,
earth is an appearance, where nothing is real.**

8. Padmasambhava, shatter the energetic matrix that prevents people from shattering the illusion of elitism, the illusion that makes it seem real that

God or nature has ordained the existence of an elite and that they are better equipped to rule than the people themselves.

> The serpentine lie, says that what we now see,
> is all that our lives, on this planet can be.
> Yet with the Christ mind, we can see there is more,
> the earth will be brighter than ever before.

> **O Padmasambhava, in your Flame of Peace,**
> **all human opinions I hereby release.**
> **I see now the ultimate truth you reveal,**
> **earth is an appearance, where nothing is real.**

9. Padmasambhava, shatter the energetic matrix that prevents spiritual people from seeing that the elite cannot shatter that illusion. Most of the people in the population cannot. Only those who are dedicated to putting on the Christ consciousness can do so. Help us become the forerunners who cry out: "But the emperor has nothing on and here is why."

> Saint Germain has the plans, for a bright Golden Age,
> to receive them, our minds must be free from the cage,
> O Padmasambhava, with your Flame of Peace,
> the vision of Oneness, to all you release.

> **O Padmasambhava, in your Flame of Peace,**
> **all human opinions I hereby release.**
> **I see now the ultimate truth you reveal,**
> **earth is an appearance, where nothing is real.**

Sealing

In the name of the I AM THAT I AM, I accept that Archangel Michael, Astrea and Shiva form an impenetrable shield around myself and all constructive people, sealing us from all fear-based energies in all four octaves. I accept that the Light of God is consuming and transforming all fear-based energies that make up the dark forces working against ending the era of elitism on earth!

21 | THE ELITE RULES BY CREATING LABELS

I AM the Ascended Master Saint Germain. I wish to give you the perspective here on how the Seventh Ray of Freedom relates to the topic of elitism.

Clearly, you can all see that the essence of what the power elite has been attempting to do from the very beginning is to restrict the freedom of the people. Why do they do this? Well, from a certain outer perspective, they do it in order to gain power, in order to gain privilege or in order to gain money. They must take something from the people in order to concentrate it in the hands of the power elite that is in embodiment.

That of course is not why the fallen beings in the identity realm are seeking to restrict the freedom of the people. They do it for two reasons: Number one, they hate the people, number two, they hate freedom. Why do they hate freedom? Because they do not have it and they can never have it. Now, you might say, if you look at some of the dictators you have seen in physical embodiment, like Hitler, Stalin, Mao, did they not have freedom to do whatever they wanted? Did they not have the freedom that they could say: "This needs to be done" and people would do it? But was that freedom? Is it freedom that you can do whatever you want? Freedom is not an *outer* condition. It is not even a *physical* condition. It is an emotional, mental and identity level condition. It is a condition of the mind.

If you are not free in your mind, you can never be free, no matter what conditions you have in the physical octave. The fallen beings are not free in their minds. They have not been free since they fell because a fallen being can never have freedom of the mind. Why not? Because the very essence, the very mechanism of falling, means that you fall into a separate self, a separate identity that you have created. Thereby, you disconnect yourself from your I AM Presence, and the Conscious You disconnects itself from the ability to experience pure awareness and traps itself in this outer self that it has created. By the very fact of doing this, you are not free because what is freedom?

Well, it has two aspects. There is the alpha aspect that as the Conscious You, you can connect to the I AM presence and thereby you can receive energy, ideas, insights from the I AM Presence or from ascended masters. This is one aspect of freedom. The other aspect of freedom is that the Conscious You can return to pure awareness can step outside of any outer self it has created in the identity, mental and emotional realms. Therefore, you know that you are not your own creation, you are *more* than your own creation and you can actually escape your own creation and return to oneness with the I AM Presence. Now, *that* is freedom. The fallen beings of course, as long as they are in the fallen state of consciousness, cannot have that freedom, they cannot connect to the I AM presence and they cannot step outside of the separate self they have created.

What must they do? They must seek to take away the freedom of the population as they have taken away their own freedom because when people are free, it is a threat to the fallen beings. Just the fact that the fallen beings saw that Jesus was free of these outer personalities that they were so entrapped in, was a threat to them because they now saw that there was an alternative to their state of consciousness.

The elite feels inherently inferior

What is it they are more afraid of than almost anything else? It is of being reminded that there is that alternative, there is more than their present state of consciousness, there is more than the fallen state of consciousness, there is more than duality and separation, more than the epic mindset. They are afraid of being reminded of this, why? Because when they encounter a being who has a certain level of Christ consciousness, they are reminded of their own existential inferiority. They are existentially inferior to those like Jesus. When he reached a certain level of Christhood, when he started his public mission, he radiated such a light that it was almost impossible to meet him physically without sensing it. Therefore, those in the Jewish leadership that he met, they sensed the light in him, and it reminded them that they did not have it and they felt inferior.

You will say of course that one characteristic of the power elite is the sense of superiority, but that sense of superiority is based on something they have created here on earth. Regardless of the amazing structures they have built to prove their superiority, all these mighty empires and kingdoms and this and that, when they meet a person who has the Christ consciousness, they see that all of these outer things are as nothing compared to the Christ light. This reminds them of the inferiority that they felt after they first fell. They covered it over very, very quickly but they felt it and they knew they had lost something. They do not want to be reminded that they have lost something so they attempt to set themselves up in these positions that seem to be unassailable. They seek to prevent anyone among the people from attaining the level of Christhood that they cannot ignore.

The human mind is afraid of freedom

How do they do this? How do they seek to control people? Well, they do it through the duality consciousness of course, the epic mindset and so forth. I want to give you one more view of this, one more facet. The fallen beings have realized that the human mind has a certain tendency. The human mind is actually afraid of freedom. It is afraid of freedom of thought, freedom of ideas. This is partly a quality that comes from being in duality. It is also a quality engineered by the fallen beings where they have, for such a long time, set themselves up as those who had the only truth. They have pushed the people down as those who cannot know truth on their own so people are afraid to know on their own, to evaluate on their own, what is true, what is not true, what is right, what is not right. The human mind, when it goes into this state, has a tendency that it wants to submit to what it feels is right, true, good.

What the fallen beings have realized is that if they create a label and project it with enough force, they can get people to submit to this without actually thinking about what they are submitting to. In other words, in order to escape this freedom of having to evaluate ideas, many people just want to accept a certain idea that is projected at them with enough authority and then they do not want to think about the idea. They do not want to evaluate: "Is it logical? Is it true? Does it make sense? Is it consistent?"

And all of these things. People have a tendency to submit to something that is projected with enough force and authority.

The fallen beings have this strategy of creating these labels, everything has to be labeled. Of course, once you have labeled something, it fits into the overall system that the fallen beings have created based on that main characteristic of the duality consciousness, the value judgment. Is it good or evil, right or wrong? They have created the scale and then they have created these labels and once that label is projected, then it is projected to be on a certain position of the scale between good and evil, right and wrong. People will then submit to this without thinking about it and without thinking about: "Is there an alternative? Is there a higher understanding than this label?"

How fallen beings use the concept of God

Let us start at the top and look at one of the primary labels created by the fallen beings—the word "God." Over a very, very long time, the fallen beings have used the word "God" (in whatever variation it had in different languages) and they have created a certain mindset that underpins the word itself. There is the word and there is the structure underneath the word and this becomes the label. When people hear the word "God," they have been conditioned to think that this is the supreme authority of the universe and therefore, they cannot really know what God is like.

Whether the description of God presented by a particular religion is true or not true, they just need to submit because you cannot gainsay God, you cannot go against God. This is dangerous, it is blasphemy. You will be put down, you will be persecuted. More than that, you will be punished by God by burning forever in hell.

You see how the word God has been, from a very, very long time ago, misused by the fallen beings to create this label and it has been projected with such force that many, many people have submitted to it. Now, you will, if you look at yourselves, many of you will have been presented with this label in childhood. "God," often through the Christian religion, where God is the angry judge in the sky. Therefore, those who supposedly represent God on earth now have that authority that you cannot say anything against.

There is hardly another word, in fact there is no other word currently, that has been misused more than the word "God." A close second is the word "Christ." You can see this in your own lives. This messenger when he was younger, despite the fact that he was not brought up in a particular religion because his parents were not religious, still felt that cultural pressure where he felt that he could not say anything against God, he could not go against God, he could not rebel against God, and therefore he could not really question God and that label of "God." It took him many years on the spiritual path to come to a point where he was willing to question the image of God projected by the Christian religion, and start to question whether God really was an angry judge in the sky, or whether there was another way to look at God.

It took him a long time to realize that God is entirely different, God is not the angry judge, God has unconditional love for all of his sons and daughters. Therefore, he could make that distinction between the actual Creator, the real God, and the false god created and projected by the fallen beings. This then led him to have an experience he has described of experiencing God's being from a neutral state of mind and feeling the Presence of God as something that he first could only describe as unconditional love, but which is not really even love or unconditional, it just *is*, and there is no way to describe it with words. There is no way to put a label on the Creator's Being. You either experience it or you do not and if you experience it, it changes you. If you have not experienced it, God remains just that: a label. Of course, that is how the fallen beings want God to remain so that people are trapped in this label where they look at God the way the fallen beings want them to look at God. Therefore, they do not even dare to think that they could have a direct experience of God's Presence that would set them free from the label of "God."

This applies equally to the label "Christ," which has been projected out there, especially since the formation of the Catholic church. They have created an entirely false image of Christ and the only antidote to that false image is of course to experience the presence of the Ascended Master Jesus. Once you experience that, you are freed from the label but the Catch-22 is that as long as you are trapped in the label, you cannot experience the Presence.

Questioning the label

What can you then do? Well, you can start to question the label. You can open your mind to looking beyond the label and you can open your mind to having the direct experience because when you are still trapped in the label, you do not want the experience. Look at most of the Christians in this world. They may feel they revere Jesus, perhaps even that they love Jesus, but where do they see Jesus? Up there in the sky far, far away from them. The last thing they would want is to experience the Presence of Jesus. Why? Because then they could not maintain their image and they are happy with the image.

They do not want Christ to come down and disturb them, as you saw many people when Jesus walked the earth, who did not want him to disturb them. This was not just the leaders of the Jewish religion, but also many among the people who did not want to be disturbed by the living Christ in embodiment. Even some of his disciples, most notably Peter, did not want to be disturbed beyond a certain limit where he still felt he had some control over the universe.

What is it that the fallen beings gain by creating these labels? They gain a sense of being in control, even in control of God (when they can get all people to believe in their image of God) or in control of the universe and how the universe works. That is what can help them cover over their sense of inferiority, their sense of loss, where they feel they do not have it because they have all of these outer powers.

Consider, as spiritual students, the importance of starting a process where you consciously look at some of these labels that you have taken on as you grew up. Consider the need to gently look at them, one at a time, to consider them, to see whether they are contradictory, whether they make sense, to see beyond them. We have given you so many teachings that go beyond these labels. We know that you already have a greater understanding than most of the labels you were brought up with.

Most of you have not yet come to the point where you have taken that conscious look at the label, seen it for what it is (that it *is* just a label), and then let it go. In order to do this, you will in some cases have to recognize that the label actually created such a reaction in you in the past that you created a separate self that is now defending the label and therefore, you need to come to see this and you need to let that self die.

The label of what it means to be a human being

There are many of these labels. I said that the greatest abuse of this is the word "God" and the word "Christ," But number three on the list is "human being." The fallen beings have created such a structure underpinning the word human being. It is a structure that has the effect of limiting what human beings think they can and cannot do.

First of all, they cannot stand up to the fallen beings, they cannot challenge the authority figures of the power elite, they cannot question them, and they cannot withdraw from them either. If you accept this label, of what it means to be a human being according to the fallen beings, there is no way out other than remaining as a slave. Look again at the many Christians who sit in their churches every Sunday and they worship this false image of Christ. They also worship, without realizing it, that image of what it means to be a human being, a sinner who needs deliverance. Ultimately, the deliverance comes from Christ, but it does not come directly, it comes through the agency of the church and its hierarchy.

They sit there and cannot question, they *dare* not question, the church and the priests. Even when those priests sexually abuse their own children, do they sometimes not dare to question the priest. Because a human being just cannot do this, in their minds.

What would be the greatest factor that could start liberating the people on earth from the power elite and the fallen beings? It would be that they dare to question the definition of what it means to be a human being. What was it that Jesus and the Buddha attempted to accomplish by walking the earth with the level of consciousness they had? It was, among other things, to challenge the concept people had of what it means to be a human being.

According to the definition of the fallen beings, a human being is inherently and by nature, limited. Most religions, certainly the Christian religion, define very strict limitations of what it means to be a human being—what you can and cannot do. The religion of Marxism/communism, also defined very tight boundaries for what a human being could and could not do. You certainly could not stand up to the state, or those people who are in charge of the state. The religion of Scientific Materialism also defines very strict limits to what a human being can do. Because, after all, a human being is just a genetic accident and a slight step up from the animals.

You can see how the fallen beings, for a very long time, have attempted to create these labels and put labels on people, what they can and cannot do. Once people accept the label, they set aside their critical thinking, their intuitive promptings, their Christ discernment. They surrender it, they stop it. They submit themselves to the fallen beings and that label, and they accept that the label is an absolute truth. There is no need to even question it because it is the "truth." *That* is just the way it is. This is the ultimate state of non-freedom that you can be in. You are trapped in these labels that are completely unreal, but you think they are real, and they are real boundaries that you cannot break free from. This is the ultimate state of non-freedom for human beings. The fallen beings are in another state of non-freedom because of the dynamics of their consciousness. I am not here concerned about liberating the fallen beings, I am concerned about liberating as many people among the population as possible.

This was also the driving vision behind the creation of the United States: to give people freedom. How did the founding fathers see it at the time? Well, they saw it as freedom from the British king and the Catholic church, the tyranny of religion, the tyranny of the king. There is of course much more to it. It was really an attempt to give people freedom from the fallen beings and their false philosophy. Of course, this could only be done to a certain degree, given the times. Today, we can take this to an entirely different level and we can truly start helping people attain that freedom from these labels. There is the label of God, which we have given many teachings to help you free yourselves from and also help others be free from it. There is the label of Christ, which Jesus has done tremendous work to free people from. We have all contributed to challenging the label of what it means to be a human being.

Freedom from opinions

I wish to tie into what Padmasambhava said about freeing yourself from opinions. What does it mean to have an opinion? What is an opinion based on? Well, quite frankly, a human opinion is a label. Not always created by the fallen beings, sometimes created by human beings, but it is a label. Instead of actually thinking, evaluating, intuiting about a topic, you have accepted the label. Now, you shut down your mind for a higher understanding. You do not think you need a higher understanding, you have the label and that is the way it is.

You can see that, how have the fallen beings created conflict after conflict? Because they have created labels that define different groups of human beings. Once people have accepted the labels, they have accepted that: "We are Christians, we are doing God's work, those Muslims, they are opposing God's work." The Muslims of course have accepted the label that they are the ones doing God's work, and the Christians are opposing it. Same thing: capitalism-communism, but look how this goes throughout society. So many of these labels. Nationality: "Oh, he's a German. Gosh, they were the ones who created the Holocaust." "He's a Frenchman, you know what the Frenchmen are like." "He's a stuck-up Brit," and so forth. There are many of these labels, but even more: "He's a man." "She's a woman." "He's gay." All of these labels. "He's a Republican" "He's a Democrat." Look how the labels have been used to create division, layers of division, almost an infinitude of divisions.

I have said that one of the most insidious labels is that of a human being. Within that label of human being, there are so many other labels that define different groups and categories of human beings, and often define conflict between them. Yet they are all within the parameters of the overall label of what it means to be a human being, because they are all limited. They all limit what you can do and cannot do as a human being. We could say that the very label "human being" defines certain boundaries, and then all of the secondary labels simply tighten those boundaries, put more restrictions on what it means to be a human being.

One of the most insidious labels is of course, "women." Made especially insidious by the Christian religion, making women responsible for the fall. Once you accept that label, there are certain things that women cannot do. If the Catholic church had not created this label that women were responsible for the fall, then women would have been given the right to vote in 1776. The witch hunts would not have happened. All of the discrimination against women would not have happened if it had not been for that label. Of course, there are other societies that are not Christian that still have discriminated against women. This all comes from the fallen beings who have a hatred of women. They also have a hatred of men, but the hatred of women is actually stronger in the fallen beings.

What does this mean? Well, it means that when people identify themselves based on a certain label, they very often also identify themselves as being in an inherent, irresolvable, irreconcilable conflict with another group of human beings. There you have the essence of most human conflicts.

It all starts with that label where nobody thinks about it. What is it all these labels do about what it means to be a human being? Well, it prevents people from connecting to that essential humanity. When you have labeled yourself, you are not intuitively connected to your humanity, you identify with the label. Therefore, when you cannot see the humanity in yourself, how can you see it in someone else. It cannot happen, and right there is the seed of conflict. You see how the labels have been used at the physical level to create physical conflict. You see how they have been used to control people's actions. "You should do this, you should not do that." In certain situations, you *must* do this. Go to the Middle East and see how they have a label that says that if someone attacks you and spills the blood of your family, it must be erased by spilling the blood of theirs, and this has been going on for thousands of years.

Feelings and thoughts are labels

Then, you go to the emotional level, and you see how many labels have been created there. Does anger actually exist? Does it have an objective existence? Is there any enduring reality to anger? Is there really a feeling of anger? Or did it start as a label created by the fallen beings that has now become so powerful in the collective consciousness that people think that in certain situations, the only reaction is anger?

One could say there is only one real emotion, fear, and that all other emotions are just labels that build upon that fear. The fear is something that you experience. The fallen beings experienced fear when they fell. Many people have experienced fear upon encountering the fallen beings. In a sense, all other emotions are just labels created within that framework, set by fear. Who says that you have to react with anger? Did not Jesus say: "turn the other cheek?" If you affirm in your mind that you will turn the other cheek, what is the need for anger? It is not so that a human being *must* respond with anger in certain situations.

Now go to the mental level where the fallen beings have created so many ideas, ideologies, religions, thought systems, theories, axioms, and they have projected them out as these labels. They always come with that value judgment that this is true, this is not true.

Materialism has nothing to do with science. Materialism is a label, used by the fallen beings to stop the potential that science has from liberating human thought. What is the essence of the scientific process? It is that you do not accept the labels; you investigate. You do not accept the label that the earth is the center of the universe and the sun and all the stars revolve around the earth. You investigate, you make observations, you use critical thinking, you might use intuition. Do the actual movements of the stars in the heaven conform to the label of an earth-centric universe? Aha! They do not! What do we then need to do? Go beyond the label and look at how the universe actually works instead of how somebody created a label that says how it *should* work.

This is the promise of the scientific process that I sponsored. Both while I was in embodiment as Roger Bacon and Francis Bacon, and after I took my ascension. Many other masters were involved with this also and why did we do it this way? Because there came a point where the Catholic church had for so long destroyed people's intuitive faculties that we evaluated that the only way to liberate them was to give them that process of science, which always is the omega to the alpha of the mystical path, the spiritual path of raising your consciousness.

True spirituality is also given. It also is a method for helping people escape the labels. How? Because you do not accept the label for God created by the fallen beings. You go within, you go through a process of purifying yourself until you can have a direct, inner mystical experience that is beyond the labels, even beyond words. Therefore, it gives you a sense of reality that is beyond the sense of reality you get from the labels.

Of course, many people think the labels are real, but when you have a mystical experience, you are directly experiencing something that is more real than the label. Why? Because the label must exist in your four lower bodies, primarily the three higher bodies, but a mystical experience takes you beyond your four lower bodies to experience different realms than the physical, or the pure awareness of the Conscious You. This is more real than what you experience through the senses and the outer mind.

Two ways to be free from labels

There are two ways to free human beings from the labels: the true inner mystical path and the path of scientific discovery. They go hand in hand, they are the alpha and the omega. It is not that one cannot exist without the other, they are not a dualistic polarity. You can walk the mystical path and attain great growth without knowing anything about science. You can be a true scientist who is investigating openly and with a neutral state of mind and make tremendous progress that way also. These are the two ways to free society from the tyranny, the prison, of these labels created by the fallen beings.

Now, when it comes to going up to the identity level, then science is not quite as suited because science mainly investigates the physical world. Science could be developed to also be combined with the mystical path so that you could use the scientific method to investigate mystical experiences and this could be used to develop a more effective path. Of course, the mystical path has always been there and it is a viable path for questioning the labels you have in your identity body.

Are you more than your beliefs, more than your opinions, more than this sense of identity (that you are of a certain nationality, of a certain sex, of a certain ethnic group) more than the sense that you are a human being? This you can question and this is one of the primary purposes of our teachings: To help you question that label that you are just a human being.

You are not just a *human* being. You are a *spiritual* being, and you are no more limited by the label of a human being than you decide you are willing to be. We have given you the knowledge, we have given you the tools to free yourself from that label. When you do so, you will, even without doing anything else, help free humankind from that label. When people stop seeing themselves as human beings, they will no longer see any need to submit to the power elite, whether the embodied power elite or the disembodied power elite of fallen beings.

Truly, there cannot be a Golden Age of Saint Germain unless people become free of these labels. Why not? Because the Golden Age that I envision is so far beyond current conditions that as long as you think current conditions have reality, or are the ultimate or the only way things can be, you cannot open yourself to the ideas of the Golden Age.

Labels limit the quest for knowledge

More than that, what is the effect of labels? It is to shut down the growth in knowledge. You may look at the development (say, over the past 2,000 years, from when Jesus walked the earth) and you may see the incredible technological progress in society and you may say: "What is it based on?" It is based on an increase of knowledge and understanding of how the universe works. Humankind knows a lot more today than they knew 2,000 years ago.

You may think, as many civilizations in the past have thought, that this civilization has very near the ultimate understanding of the universe. The fallen beings will, in any era, project that label that this is the ultimate knowledge. The fallen beings are against the expansion of knowledge and understanding, they try to prevent it as much as they possibly can. When they cannot prevent it, they try to make use of it.

One of the ways they seek to make use of it is of course to control people. You often see an old and established power elite that cling to the old knowledge, for example, cling to the Catholic church. They cannot even really fathom the new knowledge of science. Then, you see the emergence of an aspiring power elite who will make use of the new knowledge (science or something else) and use that to put themselves in positions of power. Now, they are the ones who are defining for the people what is real, what is true.

Look how during the Middle Ages, the Catholic church, defined for people what was real, defined what questions they were allowed to ask, and look how it limited them. Has science freed people from this tyranny of the mind? Only for a certain time, only within certain parameters, because even though there is still an expansion of knowledge due to the scientific process itself, Materialism has formed an overlay that has restricted the growth of scientific knowledge in many, many ways.

What did the fallen beings do? They said: "The scientific knowledge we have now is the ultimate scientific knowledge." This they said about Isaac Newton and his laws. "We now know how the universe works, there is no further knowledge." Then, comes Einstein who opened his mind to an intuitive inspiration that opens up new areas of scientific exploration. Now, they want to say that this is somehow the ultimate, and even beyond that, what are they saying? They are saying: "Science has proven that there is nothing beyond the material universe and that we can explain everything by looking only at the material universe."

In other words, the ultimate label for scientific inquiry is "Materialism." Just as you could not question the priests of the Catholic religion, you cannot today question the priests of the materialist religion. You will not be burned at the stake but you will be excluded from the inner circle of the intellectual elite. How are they better than the Catholic tyrants that they claim to have freed humanity from? They have just become another form of tyrant.

Let me give you a slight perspective. There is a tremendous difference between what people knew 2,000 years ago and what they know today. How much more knowledge is there to be discovered? Is this progress we have seen—has it brought humanity near the limits of knowledge?

Well, my beloved, the knowledge people had 2,000 years ago could be represented by a teaspoon. The knowledge people have today, with all the sophisticated scientific knowledge, could be represented by a tablespoon. The knowledge that is left to discover and that could be discovered in the next 2,000 years of the Golden Age could be compared to the ocean. Here are the people of 2,000 years ago standing with their teaspoon, saying:

"We have the ultimate knowledge of the universe!" Here are the popes of science standing today with their tablespoon: "We have the ultimate knowledge of the universe!" But none of them can see the ocean. That is how much is left to be discovered when humankind frees their minds from the labels that have only one purpose: to limit the freedom of thought, the freedom of knowledge, the freedom of experience.

Look at yourselves. Look at the knowledge about spirituality that you were brought up with. Look at the knowledge we have given you in these teachings and others. Is there more to give? Surely. Your knowledge may not be a teaspoon, it may be a good-sized bucket. But I am right now walking on the waters of the ocean of knowledge, I see that knowledge. I cannot give it to you all at once, you could not possibly handle it. There is no point in giving it to you at once because it will be my joy for the next 2,000 years to gradually reveal this knowledge to humankind.

Always looking for more knowledge

You have the opportunity to not be satisfied with a bucket and to still look for more. Ask for more and you shall receive more, as you have already received more. How will you receive it? By getting rid of the labels that are closing your mind to the higher knowledge, to the higher experience. *That,* my beloved, is freedom. Freedom from the fallen beings, freedom from the power elite.

What set people free from the feudal societies of the middle ages? It was knowledge. Not just factual knowledge, but an expansion of awareness, a different perspective. They suddenly became able to accept this idea that perhaps there was an alternative to having a small elite rule a country, perhaps the people could actually vote for their leaders, they could choose their leaders. What a revolutionary thought it was, from the perspective of these feudal lords who thought they had humanity locked up for the indefinite future.

There is so much more that could be given to set people free, and this of course is what we all in the ascended realm desire to give to people. What you can do is open your minds to it yourself, and you can make the calls to cut other people free to accept that there is so much knowledge beyond all of these labels and that the labels only limit you.

What do you need the labels for? Only because your outer self wants the security that it thinks it gets by belonging to those right groups of people that will be saved when Jesus comes back, or that are intellectually superior because they have this scientific knowledge and therefore have the incredible privilege of knowing that life is meaningless and has no purpose.

My beloved, make the calls that more and more people will begin to see it. Why are we asking you to make the calls for this? Because it is a very real potential. Many, many people are ready at inner levels to have that shift where they see this with their outer awareness. They suddenly wake up and realize: "The labels have nothing on, I AM more than the label. Knowledge, understanding is more than the labels."

Knowledge cannot be reduced to all of these labels, all of these ideologies, all of these -isms. Knowledge is the infinite sea that moves constantly back and forth, it ebbs and flows, it has waves, and it never stands still. Only the human mind can stand still when it is trapped by the labels. But you have the potential to break free at any time and reconnect to the ocean itself.

That, my beloved, is my desire for you and for mankind as a whole. I am grateful for your willingness to hear this message and to allow me to broadcast it to the collective consciousness through your chakras. For this, you have my gratitude and therefore I seal you in that Flame of Freedom, that despite the labels they have attempted to create about freedom, cannot be limited by any label. For it is always more than any label that could ever be created.

22 | INVOKING FREEDOM FROM LABELS (PART 1)

In the name of the I AM THAT I AM, Jesus Christ, I use the authority that I have as a being in embodiment on earth to call upon Saint Germain to reinforce my calls and use my chakras to project the statements in this invocation into the collective consciousness and awaken people to how the fallen beings are controlling the world by creating labels. Awaken people to the reality that we are spiritual beings and that we can co-create a new future by working with the ascended masters. I especially call for …

[Make your own calls here.]

Part 1

1. Saint Germain, shatter the energetic matrix that prevents people from seeing that the essence of what the power elite has been attempting to do from the very beginning is to restrict the freedom of the people.

O Saint Germain, you do inspire,
my vision raised forever higher,
with you I form a figure-eight,
your Golden Age I co-create.

O Saint Germain, what love you bring,
it truly makes all matter sing,
your violet flame does all restore,
with you we are becoming more.

2. Saint Germain, shatter the energetic matrix that prevents people from seeing that from an outer perspective, they do it in order to gain power, in order to gain privilege or in order to gain money. They must take something from the people in order to concentrate it in the hands of the power elite that is in embodiment.

O Saint Germain, what Freedom Flame,
released when we recite your name,
acceleration is your gift,
our planet it will surely lift.

O Saint Germain, what love you bring,
it truly makes all matter sing,
your violet flame does all restore,
with you we are becoming more.

3. Saint Germain, shatter the energetic matrix that prevents people from seeing that this is not why the fallen beings in the identity realm are seeking to restrict the freedom of the people. They do it because they hate the people and they hate freedom.

O Saint Germain, in love we claim,
our right to bring your violet flame,
from you Above, to us below,
it is an all-transforming flow.

O Saint Germain, what love you bring,
it truly makes all matter sing,
your violet flame does all restore,
with you we are becoming more.

4. Saint Germain, shatter the energetic matrix that prevents people from seeing that the fallen beings hate freedom because they do not have it and they can never have it.

O Saint Germain, I love you so,
my aura filled with violet glow,
my chakras filled with violet fire,
I am your cosmic amplifier.

**O Saint Germain, what love you bring,
it truly makes all matter sing,
your violet flame does all restore,
with you we are becoming more.**

5. Saint Germain, shatter the energetic matrix that prevents people from seeing that it is not freedom that we can do whatever we want. Freedom is not an *outer* condition, it is not a *physical* condition. It is an emotional, mental and identity level condition. It is a condition of the mind.

O Saint Germain, I am now free,
your violet flame is therapy,
transform all hang-ups in my mind,
as inner peace I surely find.

**O Saint Germain, what love you bring,
it truly makes all matter sing,
your violet flame does all restore,
with you we are becoming more.**

6. Saint Germain, shatter the energetic matrix that prevents people from seeing that if we are not free in our minds, we can never be free, no matter what conditions we have in the physical octave.

O Saint Germain, my body pure,
your violet flame for all is cure,
consume the cause of all disease,
and therefore I am all at ease.

**O Saint Germain, what love you bring,
it truly makes all matter sing,
your violet flame does all restore,
with you we are becoming more.**

7. Saint Germain, shatter the energetic matrix that prevents people from seeing that the fallen beings are not free in their minds. They have not been free since they fell because a fallen being can never have freedom of the mind.

> O Saint Germain, I'm karma-free,
> the past no longer burdens me,
> a brand new opportunity,
> I am in Christic unity.

> **O Saint Germain, what love you bring,**
> **it truly makes all matter sing,**
> **your violet flame does all restore,**
> **with you we are becoming more.**

8. Saint Germain, shatter the energetic matrix that prevents people from seeing that the mechanism of falling means that you fall into a separate self, a separate identity that you have created.

> O Saint Germain, we are now one,
> I am for you a violet sun,
> as we transform this planet earth,
> your Golden Age is given birth.

> **O Saint Germain, what love you bring,**
> **it truly makes all matter sing,**
> **your violet flame does all restore,**
> **with you we are becoming more.**

9. Saint Germain, shatter the energetic matrix that prevents people from seeing that when beings fall, they disconnect themselves from their I AM Presence, and the Conscious You disconnects itself from the ability to experience pure awareness and traps itself in this outer self that it has created. By the very fact of doing this, you are not free.

> O Saint Germain, the earth is free,
> from burden of duality,
> in oneness we bring what is best,
> your Golden Age is manifest.

**O Saint Germain, what love you bring,
it truly makes all matter sing,
your violet flame does all restore,
with you we are becoming more.**

Part 2

1. Saint Germain, shatter the energetic matrix that prevents people from seeing that freedom has two aspects. There is the alpha aspect that as the Conscious You, you can connect to the I AM presence and thereby you can receive energy, ideas, insights from the I AM Presence or from ascended masters.

O Saint Germain, you do inspire,
my vision raised forever higher,
with you I form a figure-eight,
your Golden Age I co-create.

**O Saint Germain, what love you bring,
it truly makes all matter sing,
your violet flame does all restore,
with you we are becoming more.**

2. Saint Germain, shatter the energetic matrix that prevents people from seeing that the other aspect of freedom is that the Conscious You can return to pure awareness, can step outside of any outer self it has created in the identity, mental and emotional realms.

O Saint Germain, what Freedom Flame,
released when we recite your name,
acceleration is your gift,
our planet it will surely lift.

**O Saint Germain, what love you bring,
it truly makes all matter sing,
your violet flame does all restore,
with you we are becoming more.**

3. Saint Germain, shatter the energetic matrix that prevents people from seeing that we can know that we are not our own creation, we are more than our own creation and we can escape our own creation and return to oneness with the I AM Presence. This is freedom.

O Saint Germain, in love we claim,
our right to bring your violet flame,
from you Above, to us below,
it is an all-transforming flow.

**O Saint Germain, what love you bring,
it truly makes all matter sing,
your violet flame does all restore,
with you we are becoming more.**

4. Saint Germain, shatter the energetic matrix that prevents people from seeing that the fallen beings, as long as they are in the fallen state of consciousness, cannot have that freedom, they cannot connect to the I AM presence and they cannot step outside of the separate self they have created.

O Saint Germain, I love you so,
my aura filled with violet glow,
my chakras filled with violet fire,
I am your cosmic amplifier.

**O Saint Germain, what love you bring,
it truly makes all matter sing,
your violet flame does all restore,
with you we are becoming more.**

5. Saint Germain, shatter the energetic matrix that prevents people from seeing that the fallen beings must seek to take away the freedom of the population, as they have taken away their own freedom, because when people are free, it is a threat to the fallen beings.

O Saint Germain, I am now free,
your violet flame is therapy,
transform all hang-ups in my mind,
as inner peace I surely find.

**O Saint Germain, what love you bring,
it truly makes all matter sing,
your violet flame does all restore,
with you we are becoming more.**

6. Saint Germain, shatter the energetic matrix that prevents people from seeing that when the fallen beings saw that Jesus was free of these outer personalities that they were so trapped in, it was a threat to them because they now saw that there was an alternative to their state of consciousness.

O Saint Germain, my body pure,
your violet flame for all is cure,
consume the cause of all disease,
and therefore I am all at ease.

**O Saint Germain, what love you bring,
it truly makes all matter sing,
your violet flame does all restore,
with you we are becoming more.**

7. Saint Germain, shatter the energetic matrix that prevents people from seeing that the fallen beings are afraid of being reminded that there is an alternative, there is more than their present state of consciousness, there is more than the fallen state of consciousness, there is more than duality and separation, more than the epic mindset.

O Saint Germain, I'm karma-free,
the past no longer burdens me,
a brand new opportunity,
I am in Christic unity.

**O Saint Germain, what love you bring,
it truly makes all matter sing,
your violet flame does all restore,
with you we are becoming more.**

8. Saint Germain, shatter the energetic matrix that prevents people from seeing that they are afraid of being reminded of this because when they encounter a being who has a certain level of Christ consciousness, they are

reminded of their own existential inferiority. They are existentially inferior to those like Jesus.

> O Saint Germain, we are now one,
> I am for you a violet sun,
> as we transform this planet earth,
> your Golden Age is given birth.

> **O Saint Germain, what love you bring,**
> **it truly makes all matter sing,**
> **your violet flame does all restore,**
> **with you we are becoming more.**

9. Saint Germain, shatter the energetic matrix that prevents people from seeing that when Jesus reached a certain level of Christhood, when he started his public mission, he radiated such a light that it was almost impossible to meet him physically without sensing it. The fallen beings sensed the light in him, and it reminded them that they did not have it and they felt inferior.

> O Saint Germain, the earth is free,
> from burden of duality,
> in oneness we bring what is best,
> your Golden Age is manifest.

> **O Saint Germain, what love you bring,**
> **it truly makes all matter sing,**
> **your violet flame does all restore,**
> **with you we are becoming more.**

Part 3

1. Saint Germain, shatter the energetic matrix that prevents people from seeing that one characteristic of the power elite is the sense of superiority, but that sense of superiority is based on something they have created here on earth.

O Saint Germain, you do inspire,
my vision raised forever higher,
with you I form a figure-eight,
your Golden Age I co-create.

O Saint Germain, what love you bring,
it truly makes all matter sing,
your violet flame does all restore,
with you we are becoming more.

2. Saint Germain, shatter the energetic matrix that prevents people from seeing that regardless of the amazing structures they have built to prove their superiority, all these mighty empires and kingdoms, when they meet a person who has the Christ consciousness, they see that all of these outer things are as nothing compared to the Christ light.

O Saint Germain, what Freedom Flame,
released when we recite your name,
acceleration is your gift,
our planet it will surely lift.

O Saint Germain, what love you bring,
it truly makes all matter sing,
your violet flame does all restore,
with you we are becoming more.

3. Saint Germain, shatter the energetic matrix that prevents people from seeing that this reminds them of the inferiority that they felt after they first fell. They covered it over, but they felt it and they knew they had lost something.

O Saint Germain, in love we claim,
our right to bring your violet flame,
from you Above, to us below,
it is an all-transforming flow.

O Saint Germain, what love you bring,
it truly makes all matter sing,

**your violet flame does all restore,
with you we are becoming more.**

4. Saint Germain, shatter the energetic matrix that prevents people from seeing that they do not want to be reminded that they have lost something, so they attempt to set themselves up in positions that seem to be unassailable. They seek to prevent anyone among the people from attaining the level of Christhood that they cannot ignore.

O Saint Germain, I love you so,
my aura filled with violet glow,
my chakras filled with violet fire,
I am your cosmic amplifier.

**O Saint Germain, what love you bring,
it truly makes all matter sing,
your violet flame does all restore,
with you we are becoming more.**

5. Saint Germain, shatter the energetic matrix that prevents people from seeing that the fallen beings seek to control people through the duality consciousness, the epic mindset. They have also realized that the human mind has a certain tendency.

O Saint Germain, I am now free,
your violet flame is therapy,
transform all hang-ups in my mind,
as inner peace I surely find.

**O Saint Germain, what love you bring,
it truly makes all matter sing,
your violet flame does all restore,
with you we are becoming more.**

6. Saint Germain, shatter the energetic matrix that prevents people from seeing that the human mind is actually afraid of freedom. It is afraid of freedom of thought, freedom of ideas.

O Saint Germain, my body pure,
your violet flame for all is cure,
consume the cause of all disease,
and therefore I am all at ease.

O Saint Germain, what love you bring,
it truly makes all matter sing,
your violet flame does all restore,
with you we are becoming more.

7. Saint Germain, shatter the energetic matrix that prevents people from seeing that this is partly a quality that comes from being in duality. It is also a quality engineered by the fallen beings, where they have set themselves up as those who have the only truth.

O Saint Germain, I'm karma-free,
the past no longer burdens me,
a brand new opportunity,
I am in Christic unity.

O Saint Germain, what love you bring,
it truly makes all matter sing,
your violet flame does all restore,
with you we are becoming more.

8. Saint Germain, shatter the energetic matrix that prevents people from seeing that the fallen beings have pushed the people down as those who cannot know truth on their own, so people are afraid to evaluate on their own what is true and untrue. The human mind in this state has a tendency to submit to what it feels is right, true or good.

O Saint Germain, we are now one,
I am for you a violet sun,
as we transform this planet earth,
your Golden Age is given birth.

O Saint Germain, what love you bring,
it truly makes all matter sing,

**your violet flame does all restore,
with you we are becoming more.**

9. Saint Germain, shatter the energetic matrix that prevents people from seeing that the fallen beings have realized that if they create a label and project it with enough force, they can get people to submit to this without thinking about what they are submitting to.

O Saint Germain, the earth is free,
from burden of duality,
in oneness we bring what is best,
your Golden Age is manifest.

**O Saint Germain, what love you bring,
it truly makes all matter sing,
your violet flame does all restore,
with you we are becoming more.**

Part 4

1. Saint Germain, shatter the energetic matrix that prevents people from seeing that in order to escape the freedom of having to evaluate ideas, many people want to accept a certain idea that is projected at them with enough authority, and then they do not want to think about the idea.

O Saint Germain, you do inspire,
my vision raised forever higher,
with you I form a figure-eight,
your Golden Age I co-create.

**O Saint Germain, what love you bring,
it truly makes all matter sing,
your violet flame does all restore,
with you we are becoming more.**

2. Saint Germain, shatter the energetic matrix that prevents people from seeing that many of us do not want to evaluate: "Is it logical? Is it true?

Does it make sense? Is it consistent?" People have a tendency to submit to something that is projected with enough force and authority.

> O Saint Germain, what Freedom Flame,
> released when we recite your name,
> acceleration is your gift,
> our planet it will surely lift.

> **O Saint Germain, what love you bring,**
> **it truly makes all matter sing,**
> **your violet flame does all restore,**
> **with you we are becoming more.**

3. Saint Germain, shatter the energetic matrix that prevents people from seeing that the fallen beings have this strategy of creating labels, everything has to be labeled. Once they have labeled something, it fits into the overall system that the fallen beings have created based on that main characteristic of the duality consciousness: the value judgment.

> O Saint Germain, in love we claim,
> our right to bring your violet flame,
> from you Above, to us below,
> it is an all-transforming flow.

> **O Saint Germain, what love you bring,**
> **it truly makes all matter sing,**
> **your violet flame does all restore,**
> **with you we are becoming more.**

4. Saint Germain, shatter the energetic matrix that prevents people from seeing that the fallen beings have created the scale and they have created these labels. Once a label is projected, then it is projected to be on a certain position of the scale between good and evil, right and wrong.

> O Saint Germain, I love you so,
> my aura filled with violet glow,
> my chakras filled with violet fire,
> I am your cosmic amplifier.

**O Saint Germain, what love you bring,
it truly makes all matter sing,
your violet flame does all restore,
with you we are becoming more.**

5. Saint Germain, shatter the energetic matrix that prevents people from seeing that we will often submit to this without thinking about it and without thinking: "Is there an alternative? Is there a higher understanding than this label?"

O Saint Germain, I am now free,
your violet flame is therapy,
transform all hang-ups in my mind,
as inner peace I surely find.

**O Saint Germain, what love you bring,
it truly makes all matter sing,
your violet flame does all restore,
with you we are becoming more.**

6. Saint Germain, shatter the energetic matrix that prevents people from seeing that one of the primary labels created by the fallen beings is the word "God." Over a very long time, the fallen beings have used the word "God," and they have created a certain mindset that underpins the word itself.

O Saint Germain, my body pure,
your violet flame for all is cure,
consume the cause of all disease,
and therefore I am all at ease.

**O Saint Germain, what love you bring,
it truly makes all matter sing,
your violet flame does all restore,
with you we are becoming more.**

7. Saint Germain, shatter the energetic matrix that prevents people from seeing that there is the word and there is the structure underneath the word and this becomes the label. When we hear the word "God," we have

been conditioned to think that this is the supreme authority of the universe and therefore, we cannot really know what God is like.

> O Saint Germain, I'm karma-free,
> the past no longer burdens me,
> a brand new opportunity,
> I am in Christic unity.

> **O Saint Germain, what love you bring,**
> **it truly makes all matter sing,**
> **your violet flame does all restore,**
> **with you we are becoming more.**

8. Saint Germain, shatter the energetic matrix that prevents people from seeing that whether the description of God presented by a particular religion is true or not true, we just need to submit because we cannot gainsay God, we cannot go against God. This is dangerous, it is blasphemy. We will be put down, we will be persecuted. More than that, we will be punished by God by burning forever in hell.

> O Saint Germain, we are now one,
> I am for you a violet sun,
> as we transform this planet earth,
> your Golden Age is given birth.

> **O Saint Germain, what love you bring,**
> **it truly makes all matter sing,**
> **your violet flame does all restore,**
> **with you we are becoming more.**

9. Saint Germain, shatter the energetic matrix that prevents people from seeing that the word God has been misused by the fallen beings to create this label, and it has been projected with such force that many people have submitted to it.

> O Saint Germain, the earth is free,
> from burden of duality,
> in oneness we bring what is best,
> your Golden Age is manifest.

**O Saint Germain, what love you bring,
it truly makes all matter sing,
your violet flame does all restore,
with you we are becoming more.**

Sealing

In the name of the I AM THAT I AM, I accept that Archangel Michael, Astrea and Shiva form an impenetrable shield around myself and all constructive people, sealing us from all fear-based energies in all four octaves. I accept that the Light of God is consuming and transforming all fear-based energies that make up the dark forces working against ending the era of elitism on earth!

23 | INVOKING FREEDOM FROM LABELS (PART 2)

In the name of the I AM THAT I AM, Jesus Christ, I use the authority that I have as a being in embodiment on earth to call upon Saint Germain to reinforce my calls and use my chakras to project the statements in this invocation into the collective consciousness and awaken people to how the fallen beings are controlling the world by creating labels. Awaken people to the reality that we are spiritual beings and that we can co-create a new future by working with the ascended masters. I especially call for …

[Make your own calls here.]

Part 1

1. Saint Germain, shatter the energetic matrix that prevents people from seeing that the Christian religion has projected that God is the angry judge in the sky. Therefore, those who supposedly represent God on earth now have an authority that we cannot say anything against.

O Saint Germain, you do inspire,
my vision raised forever higher,

with you I form a figure-eight,
your Golden Age I co-create.

**O Saint Germain, what love you bring,
it truly makes all matter sing,
your violet flame does all restore,
with you we are becoming more.**

2. Saint Germain, shatter the energetic matrix that prevents people from seeing that there is no other word that has been misused more than the word "God." A close second is the word "Christ."

O Saint Germain, what Freedom Flame,
released when we recite your name,
acceleration is your gift,
our planet it will surely lift.

**O Saint Germain, what love you bring,
it truly makes all matter sing,
your violet flame does all restore,
with you we are becoming more.**

3. Saint Germain, shatter the energetic matrix that prevents people from seeing that we need to go beyond our upbringing and question whether God really is an angry judge in the sky, or whether there is another way to look at God.

O Saint Germain, in love we claim,
our right to bring your violet flame,
from you Above, to us below,
it is an all-transforming flow.

**O Saint Germain, what love you bring,
it truly makes all matter sing,
your violet flame does all restore,
with you we are becoming more.**

4. Saint Germain, shatter the energetic matrix that prevents people from seeing that God is entirely different, God is not the angry judge, God has unconditional love for all of his sons and daughters.

O Saint Germain, I love you so,
my aura filled with violet glow,
my chakras filled with violet fire,
I am your cosmic amplifier.

**O Saint Germain, what love you bring,
it truly makes all matter sing,
your violet flame does all restore,
with you we are becoming more.**

5. Saint Germain, shatter the energetic matrix that prevents people from seeing that we can make a distinction between the actual Creator, the real God, and the false god created and projected by the fallen beings.

O Saint Germain, I am now free,
your violet flame is therapy,
transform all hang-ups in my mind,
as inner peace I surely find.

**O Saint Germain, what love you bring,
it truly makes all matter sing,
your violet flame does all restore,
with you we are becoming more.**

6. Saint Germain, shatter the energetic matrix that prevents people from seeing that this can open our minds to experiencing God's being from a neutral state of mind and feeling the Presence of God as something that is unconditional love, even something beyond words.

O Saint Germain, my body pure,
your violet flame for all is cure,
consume the cause of all disease,
and therefore I am all at ease.

O Saint Germain, what love you bring,
it truly makes all matter sing,
your violet flame does all restore,
with you we are becoming more.

7. Saint Germain, shatter the energetic matrix that prevents people from seeing that there is no way to put a label on the Creator's Being. We either experience it or we do not, and if we experience it, it changes us.

O Saint Germain, I'm karma-free,
the past no longer burdens me,
a brand new opportunity,
I am in Christic unity.

O Saint Germain, what love you bring,
it truly makes all matter sing,
your violet flame does all restore,
with you we are becoming more.

8. Saint Germain, shatter the energetic matrix that prevents people from seeing that if we have not experienced it, God remains just that: a label. That is how the fallen beings want God to remain so that we are trapped in this label, where we look at God the way the fallen beings want us to look at God.

O Saint Germain, we are now one,
I am for you a violet sun,
as we transform this planet earth,
your Golden Age is given birth.

O Saint Germain, what love you bring,
it truly makes all matter sing,
your violet flame does all restore,
with you we are becoming more.

9. Saint Germain, shatter the energetic matrix that prevents people from seeing that this applies equally to the label "Christ," which has been projected since the formation of the Catholic church.

O Saint Germain, the earth is free,
from burden of duality,
in oneness we bring what is best,
your Golden Age is manifest.

O Saint Germain, what love you bring,
it truly makes all matter sing,
your violet flame does all restore,
with you we are becoming more.

Part 2

1. Saint Germain, shatter the energetic matrix that prevents people from seeing that the fallen beings have created a false image of Christ and the only antidote is to experience the presence of the Ascended Master Jesus. Once we experience that, we are freed from the label, but as long as we are trapped in the label, we cannot experience the Presence.

O Saint Germain, you do inspire,
my vision raised forever higher,
with you I form a figure-eight,
your Golden Age I co-create.

O Saint Germain, what love you bring,
it truly makes all matter sing,
your violet flame does all restore,
with you we are becoming more.

2. Saint Germain, shatter the energetic matrix that prevents people from seeing that we can start to question the label. We can open our minds to looking beyond the label and we can open our minds to having the direct experience.

O Saint Germain, what Freedom Flame,
released when we recite your name,
acceleration is your gift,
our planet it will surely lift.

**O Saint Germain, what love you bring,
it truly makes all matter sing,
your violet flame does all restore,
with you we are becoming more.**

3. Saint Germain, shatter the energetic matrix that prevents people from seeing that most Christians may feel they revere Jesus, but they see Jesus up there in the sky, far away from them. The last thing they want is to experience the presence of Jesus because then they could not maintain their image and they are happy with the image.

O Saint Germain, in love we claim,
our right to bring your violet flame,
from you Above, to us below,
it is an all-transforming flow.

**O Saint Germain, what love you bring,
it truly makes all matter sing,
your violet flame does all restore,
with you we are becoming more.**

4. Saint Germain, shatter the energetic matrix that prevents people from seeing that most Christians do not want Christ to disturb them, as we saw many people when Jesus walked the earth, who did not want him to disturb them.

O Saint Germain, I love you so,
my aura filled with violet glow,
my chakras filled with violet fire,
I am your cosmic amplifier.

**O Saint Germain, what love you bring,
it truly makes all matter sing,
your violet flame does all restore,
with you we are becoming more.**

5. Saint Germain, shatter the energetic matrix that prevents people from seeing that by creating these labels, the fallen beings gain a sense of being

in control, even in control of God—when they can get all people to believe in their image of God.

> O Saint Germain, I am now free,
> your violet flame is therapy,
> transform all hang-ups in my mind,
> as inner peace I surely find.

> **O Saint Germain, what love you bring,**
> **it truly makes all matter sing,**
> **your violet flame does all restore,**
> **with you we are becoming more.**

6. Saint Germain, shatter the energetic matrix that prevents people from seeing that this can help them cover over their sense of inferiority, their sense of loss. They feel they are not inferior because they have all of these outer powers.

> O Saint Germain, my body pure,
> your violet flame for all is cure,
> consume the cause of all disease,
> and therefore I am all at ease.

> **O Saint Germain, what love you bring,**
> **it truly makes all matter sing,**
> **your violet flame does all restore,**
> **with you we are becoming more.**

7. Saint Germain, shatter the energetic matrix that prevents people from seeing that we need to consciously look at some of the labels that we have taken on as we grew up. We need to consider whether they are contradictory, whether they make sense.

> O Saint Germain, I'm karma-free,
> the past no longer burdens me,
> a brand new opportunity,
> I am in Christic unity.

**O Saint Germain, what love you bring,
it truly makes all matter sing,
your violet flame does all restore,
with you we are becoming more.**

8. Saint Germain, shatter the energetic matrix that prevents people from seeing that a label may have created such a reaction in us in the past that we created a separate self. The self is now defending the label and we need to come to see this, and we need to let the self die.

O Saint Germain, we are now one,
I am for you a violet sun,
as we transform this planet earth,
your Golden Age is given birth.

**O Saint Germain, what love you bring,
it truly makes all matter sing,
your violet flame does all restore,
with you we are becoming more.**

9. Saint Germain, shatter the energetic matrix that prevents people from seeing that another label created by the fallen beings is "human being." The fallen beings have created such a structure underpinning the word human being, and it has the effect of limiting what we think we can and cannot do.

O Saint Germain, the earth is free,
from burden of duality,
in oneness we bring what is best,
your Golden Age is manifest.

**O Saint Germain, what love you bring,
it truly makes all matter sing,
your violet flame does all restore,
with you we are becoming more.**

Part 3

1. Saint Germain, shatter the energetic matrix that prevents people from seeing that most people think we cannot challenge the authority figures of the power elite, we cannot question them, and we cannot withdraw from them either.

O Saint Germain, you do inspire,
my vision raised forever higher,
with you I form a figure-eight,
your Golden Age I co-create.

O Saint Germain, what love you bring,
it truly makes all matter sing,
your violet flame does all restore,
with you we are becoming more.

2. Saint Germain, shatter the energetic matrix that prevents people from seeing that if we accept this label, of what it means to be a human being according to the fallen beings, there is no way out other than remaining as a slave.

O Saint Germain, what Freedom Flame,
released when we recite your name,
acceleration is your gift,
our planet it will surely lift.

O Saint Germain, what love you bring,
it truly makes all matter sing,
your violet flame does all restore,
with you we are becoming more.

3. Saint Germain, shatter the energetic matrix that prevents people from seeing that most Christians worship a false image of Christ and of what it means to be a human being, a sinner who needs deliverance. They think their deliverance comes through the agency of the church and its hierarchy.

O Saint Germain, in love we claim,
our right to bring your violet flame,
from you Above, to us below,
it is an all-transforming flow.

O Saint Germain, what love you bring,
it truly makes all matter sing,
your violet flame does all restore,
with you we are becoming more.

4. Saint Germain, shatter the energetic matrix that prevents people from seeing that Christians cannot question, *dare* not question, the church and the priests. Even when those priests sexually abuse their own children, they sometimes do not dare to question the priest because a human being cannot do this, in their minds.

O Saint Germain, I love you so,
my aura filled with violet glow,
my chakras filled with violet fire,
I am your cosmic amplifier.

O Saint Germain, what love you bring,
it truly makes all matter sing,
your violet flame does all restore,
with you we are becoming more.

5. Saint Germain, shatter the energetic matrix that prevents people from seeing that the greatest factor that could start liberating people from the power elite and the fallen beings would be that we dare to question the definition of what it means to be a human being.

O Saint Germain, I am now free,
your violet flame is therapy,
transform all hang-ups in my mind,
as inner peace I surely find.

O Saint Germain, what love you bring,
it truly makes all matter sing,

**your violet flame does all restore,
with you we are becoming more.**

6. Saint Germain, shatter the energetic matrix that prevents people from seeing that Jesus and the Buddha attempted to challenge the concept people had of what it means to be a human being.

O Saint Germain, my body pure,
your violet flame for all is cure,
consume the cause of all disease,
and therefore I am all at ease.

**O Saint Germain, what love you bring,
it truly makes all matter sing,
your violet flame does all restore,
with you we are becoming more.**

7. Saint Germain, shatter the energetic matrix that prevents people from seeing that according to the definition of the fallen beings, a human being is inherently and by nature limited. Most religions, certainly the Christian religion, define strict limitations for what it means to be a human being.

O Saint Germain, I'm karma-free,
the past no longer burdens me,
a brand new opportunity,
I am in Christic unity.

**O Saint Germain, what love you bring,
it truly makes all matter sing,
your violet flame does all restore,
with you we are becoming more.**

8. Saint Germain, shatter the energetic matrix that prevents people from seeing that the religion of Marxism/communism also defined very tight boundaries for what a human being could and could not do. You could not stand up to the state, or those people who are in charge of the state.

O Saint Germain, we are now one,
I am for you a violet sun,

as we transform this planet earth,
your Golden Age is given birth.

O Saint Germain, what love you bring,
it truly makes all matter sing,
your violet flame does all restore,
with you we are becoming more.

9. Saint Germain, shatter the energetic matrix that prevents people from seeing that the religion of Scientific Materialism also defines very strict limits to what a human being can do. After all, a human being is just a genetic accident and a slight step up from the animals.

O Saint Germain, the earth is free,
from burden of duality,
in oneness we bring what is best,
your Golden Age is manifest.

O Saint Germain, what love you bring,
it truly makes all matter sing,
your violet flame does all restore,
with you we are becoming more.

Part 4

1. Saint Germain, shatter the energetic matrix that prevents people from seeing that the fallen beings have attempted to put labels on us. Once we accept the label, we set aside our critical thinking, our intuitive promptings, our Christ discernment.

O Saint Germain, you do inspire,
my vision raised forever higher,
with you I form a figure-eight,
your Golden Age I co-create.

O Saint Germain, what love you bring,
it truly makes all matter sing,

**your violet flame does all restore,
with you we are becoming more.**

2. Saint Germain, shatter the energetic matrix that prevents people from seeing that when we accept the label, we submit ourselves to the fallen beings and that label. There is no need to even question it because it is the "truth." *That* is just the way it is.

O Saint Germain, what Freedom Flame,
released when we recite your name,
acceleration is your gift,
our planet it will surely lift.

**O Saint Germain, what love you bring,
it truly makes all matter sing,
your violet flame does all restore,
with you we are becoming more.**

3. Saint Germain, shatter the energetic matrix that prevents people from seeing that this is the ultimate state of non-freedom that we can be in. We are trapped in these labels that are completely unreal, but we think they are real, and they are real boundaries that we cannot break free from.

O Saint Germain, in love we claim,
our right to bring your violet flame,
from you Above, to us below,
it is an all-transforming flow.

**O Saint Germain, what love you bring,
it truly makes all matter sing,
your violet flame does all restore,
with you we are becoming more.**

4. Saint Germain, shatter the energetic matrix that prevents people from seeing that this is the ultimate state of non-freedom for human beings. The fallen beings are in another state of non-freedom because of the dynamics of their consciousness.

O Saint Germain, I love you so,
my aura filled with violet glow,
my chakras filled with violet fire,
I am your cosmic amplifier.

O Saint Germain, what love you bring,
it truly makes all matter sing,
your violet flame does all restore,
with you we are becoming more.

5. Saint Germain, shatter the energetic matrix that prevents people from seeing that the driving vision behind the creation of the United States was to give people freedom. It was really an attempt to give people freedom from the fallen beings and their false philosophy.

O Saint Germain, I am now free,
your violet flame is therapy,
transform all hang-ups in my mind,
as inner peace I surely find.

O Saint Germain, what love you bring,
it truly makes all matter sing,
your violet flame does all restore,
with you we are becoming more.

6. Saint Germain, shatter the energetic matrix that prevents people from seeing that today, we can take this to an entirely different level and we can truly start attaining freedom from the labels. We can all contribute to challenging the label of what it means to be a human being.

O Saint Germain, my body pure,
your violet flame for all is cure,
consume the cause of all disease,
and therefore I am all at ease.

O Saint Germain, what love you bring,
it truly makes all matter sing,
your violet flame does all restore,
with you we are becoming more.

7. Saint Germain, shatter the energetic matrix that prevents people from seeing that a human opinion is a label. It is not always created by the fallen beings, sometimes it is created by human beings, but it is a label.

O Saint Germain, I'm karma-free,
the past no longer burdens me,
a brand new opportunity,
I am in Christic unity.

O Saint Germain, what love you bring,
it truly makes all matter sing,
your violet flame does all restore,
with you we are becoming more.

8. Saint Germain, shatter the energetic matrix that prevents people from seeing that instead of actually thinking, evaluating, intuiting about a topic, we have accepted the label. Now, we shut down our minds for a higher understanding. We do not think we need a higher understanding, we have the label and that is the way it is.

O Saint Germain, we are now one,
I am for you a violet sun,
as we transform this planet earth,
your Golden Age is given birth.

O Saint Germain, what love you bring,
it truly makes all matter sing,
your violet flame does all restore,
with you we are becoming more.

9. Saint Germain, shatter the energetic matrix that prevents people from seeing that the fallen beings have created conflict after conflict because they have created labels that define different groups of human beings. Once people have accepted the labels, we have accepted that we are in opposition to another group.

O Saint Germain, the earth is free,
from burden of duality,

in oneness we bring what is best,
your Golden Age is manifest.

**O Saint Germain, what love you bring,
it truly makes all matter sing,
your violet flame does all restore,
with you we are becoming more.**

Sealing

In the name of the I AM THAT I AM, I accept that Archangel Michael, Astrea and Shiva form an impenetrable shield around myself and all constructive people, sealing us from all fear-based energies in all four octaves. I accept that the Light of God is consuming and transforming all fear-based energies that make up the dark forces working against ending the era of elitism on earth!

24 | INVOKING FREEDOM FROM LABELS (PART 3)

In the name of the I AM THAT I AM, Jesus Christ, I use the authority that I have as a being in embodiment on earth to call upon Saint Germain to reinforce my calls and use my chakras to project the statements in this invocation into the collective consciousness and awaken people to how the fallen beings are controlling the world by creating labels. Awaken people to the reality that we are spiritual beings and that we can co-create a new future by working with the ascended masters. I especially call for …

[Make your own calls here.]

Part 1

1. Saint Germain, shatter the energetic matrix that prevents people from seeing that labels have been used to create division, layers of division, almost an infinitude of divisions.

> O Saint Germain, you do inspire,
> my vision raised forever higher,
> with you I form a figure-eight,
> your Golden Age I co-create.

O Saint Germain, what love you bring,
it truly makes all matter sing,
your violet flame does all restore,
with you we are becoming more.

2. Saint Germain, shatter the energetic matrix that prevents people from seeing that one of the most insidious labels is that of a human being, but within that label are many other labels that define different groups and categories of human beings, and often define conflict between them.

O Saint Germain, what Freedom Flame,
released when we recite your name,
acceleration is your gift,
our planet it will surely lift.

O Saint Germain, what love you bring,
it truly makes all matter sing,
your violet flame does all restore,
with you we are becoming more.

3. Saint Germain, shatter the energetic matrix that prevents people from seeing that they are all within the parameters of the overall label of what it means to be a human being, because they are all limited. They all limit what we can do and cannot do as a human being.

O Saint Germain, in love we claim,
our right to bring your violet flame,
from you Above, to us below,
it is an all-transforming flow.

O Saint Germain, what love you bring,
it truly makes all matter sing,
your violet flame does all restore,
with you we are becoming more.

4. Saint Germain, shatter the energetic matrix that prevents people from seeing that the very label "human being" defines certain boundaries, and then all of the secondary labels tighten those boundaries, put more restrictions on what it means to be a human being.

O Saint Germain, I love you so,
my aura filled with violet glow,
my chakras filled with violet fire,
I am your cosmic amplifier.

O Saint Germain, what love you bring,
it truly makes all matter sing,
your violet flame does all restore,
with you we are becoming more.

5. Saint Germain, shatter the energetic matrix that prevents people from seeing that one of the most insidious labels is: "women." It was made especially insidious by the Christian religion, making women responsible for the fall. Once we accept that label, there are certain things that women cannot do.

O Saint Germain, I am now free,
your violet flame is therapy,
transform all hang-ups in my mind,
as inner peace I surely find.

O Saint Germain, what love you bring,
it truly makes all matter sing,
your violet flame does all restore,
with you we are becoming more.

6. Saint Germain, shatter the energetic matrix that prevents people from seeing that if the Catholic church had not created the label that women were responsible for the fall, then women would have been given the right to vote in 1776. The witch hunts would not have happened. All of the discrimination against women would not have happened.

O Saint Germain, my body pure,
your violet flame for all is cure,
consume the cause of all disease,
and therefore I am all at ease.

O Saint Germain, what love you bring,
it truly makes all matter sing,

your violet flame does all restore,
with you we are becoming more.

7. Saint Germain, shatter the energetic matrix that prevents people from seeing that there are other societies that are not Christian that still have discriminated against women. This all comes from the fallen beings who have a hatred of women. They also have a hatred of men, but the hatred of women is stronger in the fallen beings.

O Saint Germain, I'm karma-free,
the past no longer burdens me,
a brand new opportunity,
I am in Christic unity.

O Saint Germain, what love you bring,
it truly makes all matter sing,
your violet flame does all restore,
with you we are becoming more.

8. Saint Germain, shatter the energetic matrix that prevents people from seeing that when we identify ourselves based on a certain label, we often also identify ourselves as being in an inherent, irresolvable, irreconcilable conflict with another group of human beings. This is the essence of most human conflicts.

O Saint Germain, we are now one,
I am for you a violet sun,
as we transform this planet earth,
your Golden Age is given birth.

O Saint Germain, what love you bring,
it truly makes all matter sing,
your violet flame does all restore,
with you we are becoming more.

9. Saint Germain, shatter the energetic matrix that prevents people from seeing that it all starts with that label where nobody thinks about it. What the labels do is to prevent us from connecting to our essential humanity.

O Saint Germain, the earth is free,
from burden of duality,
in oneness we bring what is best,
your Golden Age is manifest.

**O Saint Germain, what love you bring,
it truly makes all matter sing,
your violet flame does all restore,
with you we are becoming more.**

Part 2

1. Saint Germain, shatter the energetic matrix that prevents people from seeing that when we have labeled ourselves, we are not intuitively connected to our humanity, we identify with the label. When we cannot see the humanity in ourselves, how can we see it in someone else, and this is the seed of conflict.

O Saint Germain, you do inspire,
my vision raised forever higher,
with you I form a figure-eight,
your Golden Age I co-create.

**O Saint Germain, what love you bring,
it truly makes all matter sing,
your violet flame does all restore,
with you we are becoming more.**

2. Saint Germain, shatter the energetic matrix that prevents people from seeing that the labels have been used at the physical level to create physical conflict. They have been used to control people's actions. You *should* do this, or you *must* do this.

O Saint Germain, what Freedom Flame,
released when we recite your name,
acceleration is your gift,
our planet it will surely lift.

**O Saint Germain, what love you bring,
it truly makes all matter sing,
your violet flame does all restore,
with you we are becoming more.**

3. Saint Germain, shatter the energetic matrix that prevents people from seeing that in the Middle East they have a label that says that if someone attacks you and spills the blood of your family, it must be erased by spilling the blood of theirs, and this has been going on for thousands of years.

O Saint Germain, in love we claim,
our right to bring your violet flame,
from you Above, to us below,
it is an all-transforming flow.

**O Saint Germain, what love you bring,
it truly makes all matter sing,
your violet flame does all restore,
with you we are becoming more.**

4. Saint Germain, shatter the energetic matrix that prevents people from seeing that many labels have been created at the emotional level. Anger does not actually exist, it has no objective existence. It started as a label created by the fallen beings. It has now become so powerful in the collective consciousness that people think that in certain situations, the only reaction is anger.

O Saint Germain, I love you so,
my aura filled with violet glow,
my chakras filled with violet fire,
I am your cosmic amplifier.

**O Saint Germain, what love you bring,
it truly makes all matter sing,
your violet flame does all restore,
with you we are becoming more.**

5. Saint Germain, shatter the energetic matrix that prevents people from seeing that the only real emotion is fear, and all other emotions are just labels that build upon that fear.

O Saint Germain, I am now free,
your violet flame is therapy,
transform all hang-ups in my mind,
as inner peace I surely find.

O Saint Germain, what love you bring,
it truly makes all matter sing,
your violet flame does all restore,
with you we are becoming more.

6. Saint Germain, shatter the energetic matrix that prevents people from seeing that fear is something we experience. The fallen beings experienced fear when they fell. Many people have experienced fear upon encountering the fallen beings.

O Saint Germain, my body pure,
your violet flame for all is cure,
consume the cause of all disease,
and therefore I am all at ease.

O Saint Germain, what love you bring,
it truly makes all matter sing,
your violet flame does all restore,
with you we are becoming more.

7. Saint Germain, shatter the energetic matrix that prevents people from seeing that all other emotions are just labels created within the framework set by fear. If we affirm in our minds that we will turn the other cheek, there is no need for anger. We do not have to respond with anger in certain situations.

O Saint Germain, I'm karma-free,
the past no longer burdens me,
a brand new opportunity,
I am in Christic unity.

O Saint Germain, what love you bring,
it truly makes all matter sing,
your violet flame does all restore,
with you we are becoming more.

8. Saint Germain, shatter the energetic matrix that prevents people from seeing that at the mental level the fallen beings have created so many ideas, ideologies, religions, thought systems, theories, axioms, and they have projected them out as labels. They always come with that value judgment that this is true, this is not true.

O Saint Germain, we are now one,
I am for you a violet sun,
as we transform this planet earth,
your Golden Age is given birth.

O Saint Germain, what love you bring,
it truly makes all matter sing,
your violet flame does all restore,
with you we are becoming more.

9. Saint Germain, shatter the energetic matrix that prevents people from seeing that Materialism has nothing to do with science. Materialism is a label, used by the fallen beings to stop the potential of science for liberating human thought.

O Saint Germain, the earth is free,
from burden of duality,
in oneness we bring what is best,
your Golden Age is manifest.

O Saint Germain, what love you bring,
it truly makes all matter sing,
your violet flame does all restore,
with you we are becoming more.

Part 3

1. Saint Germain, shatter the energetic matrix that prevents people from seeing that the essence of the scientific process is that we do not accept the labels, we investigate, we make observations, we use critical thinking, we use intuition.

O Saint Germain, you do inspire,
my vision raised forever higher,
with you I form a figure-eight,
your Golden Age I co-create.

O Saint Germain, what love you bring,
it truly makes all matter sing,
your violet flame does all restore,
with you we are becoming more.

2. Saint Germain, shatter the energetic matrix that prevents people from seeing that we need to go beyond all labels and look at how the universe actually works, instead of how somebody created a label that says how it *should* work.

O Saint Germain, what Freedom Flame,
released when we recite your name,
acceleration is your gift,
our planet it will surely lift.

O Saint Germain, what love you bring,
it truly makes all matter sing,
your violet flame does all restore,
with you we are becoming more.

3. Saint Germain, shatter the energetic matrix that prevents people from seeing that the Catholic church had for so long destroyed people's intuitive faculties that the only way to liberate us was through the process of science, which is the omega to the alpha of the mystical path.

O Saint Germain, in love we claim,
our right to bring your violet flame,
from you Above, to us below,
it is an all-transforming flow.

**O Saint Germain, what love you bring,
it truly makes all matter sing,
your violet flame does all restore,
with you we are becoming more.**

4. Saint Germain, shatter the energetic matrix that prevents people from seeing that true spirituality is also a method for helping people escape the labels. We do not accept the label for God created by the fallen beings, we go within and seek a direct mystical experience that is beyond the labels.

O Saint Germain, I love you so,
my aura filled with violet glow,
my chakras filled with violet fire,
I am your cosmic amplifier.

**O Saint Germain, what love you bring,
it truly makes all matter sing,
your violet flame does all restore,
with you we are becoming more.**

5. Saint Germain, shatter the energetic matrix that prevents people from seeing that when we have a mystical experience, we are directly experiencing something that is more real than the label.

O Saint Germain, I am now free,
your violet flame is therapy,
transform all hang-ups in my mind,
as inner peace I surely find.

**O Saint Germain, what love you bring,
it truly makes all matter sing,
your violet flame does all restore,
with you we are becoming more.**

6. Saint Germain, shatter the energetic matrix that prevents people from seeing that the label must exist in our four lower bodies, but a mystical experience takes us beyond our four lower bodies to experience different realms or the pure awareness of the Conscious You. This is more real than what we experience through the senses and the outer mind.

O Saint Germain, my body pure,
your violet flame for all is cure,
consume the cause of all disease,
and therefore I am all at ease.

O Saint Germain, what love you bring,
it truly makes all matter sing,
your violet flame does all restore,
with you we are becoming more.

7. Saint Germain, shatter the energetic matrix that prevents people from seeing that there are two ways to free ourselves from the labels: the true inner mystical path and the path of scientific discovery. They go hand in hand, they are the alpha and the omega.

O Saint Germain, I'm karma-free,
the past no longer burdens me,
a brand new opportunity,
I am in Christic unity.

O Saint Germain, what love you bring,
it truly makes all matter sing,
your violet flame does all restore,
with you we are becoming more.

8. Saint Germain, shatter the energetic matrix that prevents people from seeing that we can walk the mystical path and attain great growth without knowing anything about science. We can be true scientists who investigate openly and with a neutral state of mind and make tremendous progress that way also.

O Saint Germain, we are now one,
I am for you a violet sun,

as we transform this planet earth,
your Golden Age is given birth.

O Saint Germain, what love you bring,
it truly makes all matter sing,
your violet flame does all restore,
with you we are becoming more.

9. Saint Germain, shatter the energetic matrix that prevents people from seeing that at the identity level, we are more than our beliefs, more than our opinions, more than the sense of identity of being a certain nationality, sex or ethnic group. We are more than the sense that we are human beings.

O Saint Germain, the earth is free,
from burden of duality,
in oneness we bring what is best,
your Golden Age is manifest.

O Saint Germain, what love you bring,
it truly makes all matter sing,
your violet flame does all restore,
with you we are becoming more.

Part 4

1. Saint Germain, shatter the energetic matrix that prevents people from seeing that we must question the label that we are just human beings. We are not just *human* beings; we are *spiritual* beings.

O Saint Germain, you do inspire,
my vision raised forever higher,
with you I form a figure-eight,
your Golden Age I co-create.

O Saint Germain, what love you bring,
it truly makes all matter sing,

**your violet flame does all restore,
with you we are becoming more.**

2. Saint Germain, shatter the energetic matrix that prevents people from seeing that we are no more limited by the label of a human being than we decide we are willing to be. The ascended masters have given us the knowledge and tools to free ourselves from that label.

O Saint Germain, what Freedom Flame,
released when we recite your name,
acceleration is your gift,
our planet it will surely lift.

**O Saint Germain, what love you bring,
it truly makes all matter sing,
your violet flame does all restore,
with you we are becoming more.**

3. Saint Germain, shatter the energetic matrix that prevents people from seeing that when we free ourselves, we will help free humankind from that label. When we stop seeing ourselves as human beings, we will no longer submit to the power elite, whether the embodied power elite or the disembodied power elite of fallen beings.

O Saint Germain, in love we claim,
our right to bring your violet flame,
from you Above, to us below,
it is an all-transforming flow.

**O Saint Germain, what love you bring,
it truly makes all matter sing,
your violet flame does all restore,
with you we are becoming more.**

4. Saint Germain, shatter the energetic matrix that prevents people from seeing that there cannot be a Golden Age of Saint Germain unless we become free of these labels.

O Saint Germain, I love you so,
my aura filled with violet glow,
my chakras filled with violet fire,
I am your cosmic amplifier.

**O Saint Germain, what love you bring,
it truly makes all matter sing,
your violet flame does all restore,
with you we are becoming more.**

5. Saint Germain, shatter the energetic matrix that prevents people from seeing that the Golden Age of Saint Germain is so far beyond current conditions that as long as we think current conditions have reality, or are the ultimate or the only way things can be, we cannot open ourselves to the ideas of the Golden Age.

O Saint Germain, I am now free,
your violet flame is therapy,
transform all hang-ups in my mind,
as inner peace I surely find.

**O Saint Germain, what love you bring,
it truly makes all matter sing,
your violet flame does all restore,
with you we are becoming more.**

6. Saint Germain, shatter the energetic matrix that prevents people from seeing that the effect of labels is to shut down the growth in knowledge. The technological progress in society is based on an increase of knowledge and understanding of how the universe works.

O Saint Germain, my body pure,
your violet flame for all is cure,
consume the cause of all disease,
and therefore I am all at ease.

**O Saint Germain, what love you bring,
it truly makes all matter sing,**

your violet flame does all restore,
with you we are becoming more.

7. Saint Germain, shatter the energetic matrix that prevents people from seeing that the fallen beings will project the label that any society has the ultimate knowledge. The fallen beings are against the expansion of knowledge and understanding, they try to prevent it as much as they possibly can.

O Saint Germain, I'm karma-free,
the past no longer burdens me,
a brand new opportunity,
I am in Christic unity.

O Saint Germain, what love you bring,
it truly makes all matter sing,
your violet flame does all restore,
with you we are becoming more.

8. Saint Germain, shatter the energetic matrix that prevents people from seeing that if the fallen beings cannot prevent the growth of knowledge, they try to make use of it to control people.

O Saint Germain, we are now one,
I am for you a violet sun,
as we transform this planet earth,
your Golden Age is given birth.

O Saint Germain, what love you bring,
it truly makes all matter sing,
your violet flame does all restore,
with you we are becoming more.

9. Saint Germain, shatter the energetic matrix that prevents people from seeing that there is often an old and established power elite that clings to the old knowledge, such as the Catholic church. Then, there is an aspiring power elite who will make use of the new knowledge to put themselves in positions of power. Now, they are the ones who are defining for the people what is real, what is true.

O Saint Germain, the earth is free,
from burden of duality,
in oneness we bring what is best,
your Golden Age is manifest.

O Saint Germain, what love you bring,
it truly makes all matter sing,
your violet flame does all restore,
with you we are becoming more.

Part 5

1. Saint Germain, shatter the energetic matrix that prevents people from seeing that during the Middle Ages, the Catholic church defined for people what was real, defined what questions they were allowed to ask. Science freed people from this tyranny of the mind, but only for a time.

O Saint Germain, you do inspire,
my vision raised forever higher,
with you I form a figure-eight,
your Golden Age I co-create.

O Saint Germain, what love you bring,
it truly makes all matter sing,
your violet flame does all restore,
with you we are becoming more.

2. Saint Germain, shatter the energetic matrix that prevents people from seeing that even though there is still an expansion of knowledge due to the scientific process itself, Materialism has formed an overlay that has restricted the growth of scientific knowledge in many ways.

O Saint Germain, what Freedom Flame,
released when we recite your name,
acceleration is your gift,
our planet it will surely lift.

**O Saint Germain, what love you bring,
it truly makes all matter sing,
your violet flame does all restore,
with you we are becoming more.**

3. Saint Germain, shatter the energetic matrix that prevents people from seeing that the fallen beings said that the scientific knowledge we have now is the ultimate scientific knowledge. Science has proven that there is nothing beyond the material universe and that we can explain everything by looking only at the material universe.

O Saint Germain, in love we claim,
our right to bring your violet flame,
from you Above, to us below,
it is an all-transforming flow.

**O Saint Germain, what love you bring,
it truly makes all matter sing,
your violet flame does all restore,
with you we are becoming more.**

4. Saint Germain, shatter the energetic matrix that prevents people from seeing that the ultimate label for scientific inquiry is "Materialism." Just as we could not question the priests of the Catholic religion, today we cannot question the priests of the materialist religion.

O Saint Germain, I love you so,
my aura filled with violet glow,
my chakras filled with violet fire,
I am your cosmic amplifier.

**O Saint Germain, what love you bring,
it truly makes all matter sing,
your violet flame does all restore,
with you we are becoming more.**

5. Saint Germain, shatter the energetic matrix that prevents people from seeing that the knowledge people have today, with all the sophisticated scientific knowledge, could be represented by a tablespoon. The knowledge

that is left to discover and that could be discovered in the next 2,000 years of the Golden Age could be compared to the ocean.

O Saint Germain, I am now free,
your violet flame is therapy,
transform all hang-ups in my mind,
as inner peace I surely find.

**O Saint Germain, what love you bring,
it truly makes all matter sing,
your violet flame does all restore,
with you we are becoming more.**

6. Saint Germain, shatter the energetic matrix that prevents people from seeing that there is so much left to be discovered when we free our minds from the labels that have only one purpose: to limit the freedom of thought, the freedom of knowledge, the freedom of experience.

O Saint Germain, my body pure,
your violet flame for all is cure,
consume the cause of all disease,
and therefore I am all at ease.

**O Saint Germain, what love you bring,
it truly makes all matter sing,
your violet flame does all restore,
with you we are becoming more.**

7. Saint Germain, shatter the energetic matrix that prevents people from seeing that we will only receive more knowledge by getting rid of the labels that are closing our minds to the higher knowledge, to the higher experience. *That,* is freedom. Freedom from the fallen beings, freedom from the power elite.

O Saint Germain, I'm karma-free,
the past no longer burdens me,
a brand new opportunity,
I am in Christic unity.

**O Saint Germain, what love you bring,
it truly makes all matter sing,
your violet flame does all restore,
with you we are becoming more.**

8. Saint Germain, shatter the energetic matrix that prevents people from seeing that what set people free from the feudal societies of the middle ages was knowledge. They suddenly became able to accept the idea that there was an alternative to having a small elite rule a country.

O Saint Germain, we are now one,
I am for you a violet sun,
as we transform this planet earth,
your Golden Age is given birth.

**O Saint Germain, what love you bring,
it truly makes all matter sing,
your violet flame does all restore,
with you we are becoming more.**

9. Saint Germain, cut people free to accept that there is so much knowledge beyond all of these labels and that the labels only limit us. I call for you to cut free the people who are ready at inner levels to have that shift where they see this with their outer awareness: "The labels have nothing on, I AM more than the label. Knowledge, understanding is more than the labels."

O Saint Germain, the earth is free,
from burden of duality,
in oneness we bring what is best,
your Golden Age is manifest.

**O Saint Germain, what love you bring,
it truly makes all matter sing,
your violet flame does all restore,
with you we are becoming more.**

Sealing

In the name of the I AM THAT I AM, I accept that Archangel Michael, Astrea and Shiva form an impenetrable shield around myself and all constructive people, sealing us from all fear-based energies in all four octaves. I accept that the Light of God is consuming and transforming all fear-based energies that make up the dark forces working against ending the era of elitism on earth!

25 | HOW THE ELITE CAN HIDE FROM THE PEOPLE

I AM the Ascended Master Sanat Kumara. Most of you are familiar with the story of how I came to earth with 144,000 lifestreams from Venus, vowing to hold the spiritual balance for the earth during a dark period of its history. I have in a previous dictation, compared myself to the cosmic garbage collector, who has gone to a number of these planets who have been in the process of self-destruction and helped to pull them out of there. Therefore, you might say that I have seen everything there is to see about the fallen beings, and what they do and how their minds work. There is not much that could surprise me at this point.

What I wish to share with you is some thoughts about the mindset of these fallen beings who either form the elite in embodiment or who are behind the elite in higher realms. When some of these beings fell, they went into a state of denial and the reason they did this was, as we have told you, there was a previous sphere where there were certain civilizations where certain beings had set themselves up as an elite. They were in power and they had all of the people in a civilization or even on an entire planet who were blindly following them. There came that point where the sphere was ready to ascend and then these beings were confronted with the ascended masters.

The beings, who were not fallen at the time, thought they had mastered their sphere and that they had complete power in their sphere. Then, they are confronted by the ascended masters and they realized they did not have absolute power, in fact, they had hardly any power compared to an ascended being. This was not Archangel Michael that you know, but the Archangel Michael that you do not know. There is no power in the four levels of the material universe that can go against or stand against the power of Archangel Michael. This was a shock to these fallen beings, in a way comparable to what we have called the birth trauma of an avatar coming to earth or an original inhabitant encountering the fallen beings and their intent to destroy you.

Now, of course the ascended masters did not have an intent to destroy these beings, prideful beings we might call them, they had the intent to awaken them. Since some of these beings decided they did not want to be awakened, they had to go into this state of denial and what they denied was the power of the ascended masters, and even the power of God, to stand against them. In their denial, they actually believe that there is no power in the universe that can go against them, there is no power that they cannot somehow either conquer, manipulate or corrupt.

The denial of ascended masters

This is one of the reasons they have created, as we talked about, this false image of God. They have attempted to create an image of God that upholds this illusion that God does not have the power to override their power. God is the remote being in the sky. God does not interfere with human beings. God cannot go against certain things that are happening on earth. There is a devil that opposes God and that has as much power as God, and many of these other subtle ideas of course going all the way up to the materialistic idea that there is no God.

The other aspect of this is of course that it was not actually God, the Creator, who did anything to the prideful beings in the fourth sphere or the fifth or the sixth, it was the ascended masters. What the fallen beings associated with earth have attempted to do is to eradicate all awareness of the ascended masters. They do this because they know that it is not God, the Creator, who comes down and says: "Thus far no farther." It is the ascended masters. They want to exclude all knowledge of ascended masters on earth. Why? Because, as we have said many times, the ascended masters do not have the authority to interfere with earth. Those in embodiment, have the authority. We have the power to remove the fallen beings, like that, but we do not have the authority to do so, only human beings in embodiment can give us that authority. That is of course why the fallen beings do not want human beings to know that we exist, the power we have and what we could do if we were given the authority.

You will see how they have created these religions that deny any existence of ascended masters. You have Scientific Materialism, Marxism, other materialistic philosophies, that deny the existence of spiritual beings. Now, part of the reason they do this is of course that they do not want to be challenged, they want to continue doing what they are doing. That is, so to speak, the alpha aspect of it, but there is an omega aspect as well and that is that they do not want to be held accountable for what they do. They do not want to be held accountable by a higher power, such as the ascended masters, but also they do not want to be held accountable by the population, by the people that they are suppressing and manipulating. When you look at the power elites of history, you can see this clear pattern. You look at the clergy of the Catholic church during the Middle Ages, and how nobody could speak out against the Pope, or the cardinals or the priests. Even today, many Catholics believe they cannot speak out against their priest. Even if their local priest is abusing their own children, they should not say anything, so as not to damage the reputation of the church.

Exercising power without accountability

You saw that the clergy could do whatever they wanted: crusades, Inquisition, witch hunts, and so forth and nobody could speak out against them. Of course, if you are burned at the stake for speaking out, it is difficult to speak out, but you see the pattern. They had set themselves up in a position where they could exercise power over other people without any accountability. The same for the feudal lords of the Middle Ages, the same for the kings or the Middle Ages, many of the emperors you have seen, the Russian tsars, and then look at the communist leaders, Lenin and Stalin, where was their accountability? If you ever bother to read a biography of Stalin, you will know that he pretty much killed everybody who was close to him, everybody who had supported him. They only survived for a certain time and then he got paranoid, thinking they might try to take away his power, and then he had them killed. There was no accountability, nobody could hold him accountable. The great Chairman Mao, no accountability.

You see the same thing in capitalism. When you are the sole owner of a Standard Oil Company that has a near monopoly, who is going to hold you accountable? When you control large banks, who is going to hold you accountable? What did you see in the 2008 financial crisis? The leaders of these large investment banks had created this entire spiral of the mortgage problem and then, when it became so severe that it threatened their own existence, they refused to be held accountable and wanted the government to bail them out in order to escape accountability. You see in the educational institutions of the world how you have this elite of intellectuals, who sit there in their fortresses of these universities and nobody can hold them accountable. You see in the media how you have these media conglomerates, owned by just a few people, that give a completely biased and skewed version of the news, but who can hold them accountable? If you own all the newspapers, who is going to write about the flaws and expose it to the people?

There is of course the Internet and that is the first thing, really, that has given the possibility that these hidden power elites can be held accountable and can be exposed to the people. In a sense, what the fallen beings have created is a situation where they have attempted to set themselves up as Gods on earth. Because obviously, most people think that God is not accountable for anything. God is the almighty being in the sky, and nobody here on earth can say: "Hey God, I think you made a mistake." That is actually a completely false image of the real Creator, who is the ultimately accountable being in the universe. Why? Because every self-aware being in the entire world of form is created out of the Creator's Being. So the Creator experiences whatever is going on in its creation. It cannot run away from anything, it cannot deny anything, not that it wants to, but therefore it is ultimately accountable.

What the fallen beings want is to become false gods who can exercise power without ever being held accountable for the consequences that this has for people. They want to do whatever they want to do, no matter what the consequences are for the people, but they never want the people to hold them accountable. This is something that you need to make the calls on so that people become aware of this, because it is one of the factors that can help people start becoming more aware of the elite and making the determination that we will not allow this elite to run our societies. Why should we allow an elite to do whatever they want and exploit us without being ever held accountable for what they do? Why should we allow a small elite to create suffering for the entire population and never be held accountable for this? This makes no sense and many people can already see it, many more are ready to see it and they are ready to take this and apply it to specific elites, for example, the financial elite.

Why do we allow an elite to run the economy?

Why are we allowing a small elite of people in the financial system to create crisis after crisis, and then taxpayer money is being used to bail them out when their system is in danger of collapse? This can lead to an awareness that the financial system you have today is created for this entire purpose: That a small elite can concentrate money in their own hands by doing whatever they want, creating whatever schemes they want, but they are not held accountable when the schemes fail.

It can even lead to an awareness that in a capitalist economy, by the very nature of capitalism, there will always be an elite and they will be driven by greed, the desire for profit. It is never going to be enough. You do not have an elite that can say: "We are happy owning a factory that produces automobiles. We make those automobiles in a fair quality, we sell them at a fair price, we make a certain profit and therefore we gradually build our savings through that profit." The power elite cannot say this. It is not enough for them to produce a product or provide a service and get paid reasonably for that. They want more and they want it faster and therefore they create these schemes that they think can give them this faster return.

Now, they do know that there is a certain risk involved, but they tend to deny it and look for the rosy picture, the short-term profit. The fact of the matter is that there are certain basic principles for how the economy works. It is not a matter of capitalism or communism because it does not matter what theoretical overlay you put on the economy. There are certain basic principles and it is very simple. If you provide a product or a service, then you can have a sustainable economy that gives you a sustainable profit, but when you start making money off of money, creating these investment schemes, you are creating an unbalanced economy and in an unbalanced economy, there will be risk.

The more people are blinded by greed, the bigger of a risk they are willing to take in order to get that short-term profit or that extraordinary profit and therefore they will inevitably create a crisis. It is only a matter of time. When people begin to see this, they can clearly say: "Why should we allow this elite to run the financial system and then time and time again escape accountability?" We either do as they say and let the market take care of itself and let them fail, or we have to find another approach to the economy where we do not allow these high risk investments that lead from crisis to crisis. This is something that many, many people are ready to come to see. It is again this, where the people have been blinded by a cloud of energy and they cannot see the obvious, but when you make the calls for this, the equation can shift and they begin to see it, as many people already have. This leads me to the next topic I want to cover, which is the cloud of energy that burdens people.

Making the astral plane visible

It is a plan of Saint Germain to gradually release more and more scientific technology that allows people to detect what cannot be detected by the senses. We have talked about ultimately releasing the technology to read the Akashic Records, which of course is the ultimate way to hold people accountable, because then you can never escape accountability, but that is a little more into the future. What has already to some degree been released (and which will be refined and other technology will be released within the relatively near future), is the technology to make energy visible that is not visible to the senses or normal instruments. You have the first example of this with x-rays, but you have other examples already and there is more technology that will be released. There will come a point where it will be possible to detect these energies, and just as you can take an image or a scan of the human aura and see which energies a person has in his or her individual energy field, there will come a point where you can use satellites to take an image of the energy field of the earth.

It is one of the plans of Saint Germain to use technology because technology is difficult to argue against. You could say that you could potentially argue against you having bones inside your body, but when you see an x-ray, the argumentation is over. Of course, you could also wait till you died or you could see another dead person and see the bones being exposed. My point is this, once you see something, it is difficult to argue against it. You can of course argue about what it means, but nevertheless, once people begin to see that an individual human being has an energy field around its physical body, and you can detect certain patterns of energies in that field that are linked to a specific organ, and you can see that when the energy reaches a certain intensity, that organ starts becoming ill and not functioning properly, then it becomes relatively difficult to argue against the fact that there is a realm of invisible energy and it is linked to the physical realm and it has an influence on the physical realm.

Now, I said I was the garbage collector of the universe because I have gone to these dark planets, and I can assure you that when you look at the earth, it is a very, very dark picture that emerges when you look at the astral plane, the emotional body. You have different visions of hell that have been around for a long time. You have some medieval painters who painted some very grotesque images of hell. You have even in the modern age people who have had near-death experiences, out of body experiences and so forth. You even have some modern movies that have depicted various levels of hell, and it is even more ugly than what has been depicted so far. If people could see the astral plane, they would be absolutely shocked, absolutely shocked at how ugly it is, how aggressive it is and how there are these beings in the astral plane that we normally call demons who have a completely aggressive intent to steal energy from human beings. They are trying to do anything they can to overpower anybody they can overpower. What would shock people the most, aside from the ugliness of these beings, is that you cannot reason with them. There is absolutely no way to reason with these beings.

Now, I know that when the technology becomes available that will allow people to get at least some glimpse of the energies in the astral plane, it will give rise to some fear, but unfortunately that is necessary. It is a necessary phase to go through because people have been lulled into such a state of denial by materialistic science, or Materialism primarily. There will be a need for this rude awakening where people begin to actually see that there are these fear-based energies that are seeking to influence people. You will be able to see on this satellite scan that there are certain parts of the world where there is a stronger concentration of these fear-based energies. Then, it will not be so difficult to see that one of these areas is the Middle East and maybe that is why there is such conflict there and has been such conflict for so many centuries. You can also see how there is a concentration of darker energies over the larger cities and maybe that is why there is such stress from living in these cities, there are people who cannot handle it and go crazy from dealing with the energy. This can be a rude awakening and when there comes that awareness that there are these beings in the astral plane, it is not just material energy, so to speak. It is not just neutral energy.

There are actually beings who have an intent. That will be an extra shock and a big shock will be: "But these beings cannot be reasoned with." They have no self-awareness. You cannot actually make them feel any empathy or compassion for human beings. They are in a sense exactly like a lion in the jungle. The lion is starving, the lion is hungry, you happen to walk by. For you, your life has an entire history, you have an entire lifetime of experiences that you feel have value and should be allowed to endure, but for the lion, you are just lunch. It has absolutely no humanity, no concern whatsoever. The same with a shark in the ocean, it will eat you with no concern for your awareness and history as a human being. When people begin to see that there are such beings, it will be a shock but it will also lead some people to say: "But, what can we then do about this? What can we do? We now see that these beings are there, they have been talked about for centuries, some clairvoyants have talked about it, what can we do? How can we defend ourselves from this?" That is then when people can become open to the existence of ascended masters.

Ascended masters are the anti-dote to darkness

We are the natural God-ordained antidote to these dark beings and dark forces. We have the power, we have the high-frequency energy that can counteract these beings. If you invoke spiritual protection around your personal energy field, then your energy field cannot be invaded by these beings. At least, if you do not have some belief that invites them in. This can open up that at least many people, many *more* people, will begin to accept this phenomenon and see that they have to do something about it.

You already have of course ascended masters students and other spiritual people who are accepting this, but you have many, many people in the New Age, spiritual movement who are still trapped in the "It's all good" philosophy and refuse to look at anything dark or evil. You see that you have this concept that you should not put your attention on darkness because you give it power. Well, does that mean that when people suspected there was something called bacteria, they should not have put their attention on it because it will give the bacteria power? Or should they study the phenomenon, come to understand it so you can see what you can do to protect yourself? Once people realize that there are these beings, there really is no technology that can protect you from them. You cannot reason with them. So you need to do something else. You may say: "How can you protect yourself from a lion?" Well, you can carry a gun that can kill the lion. How can you protect yourself from a demon in the astral plane? Well, you need the spiritual, the energetic equivalent of a gun, and that is to make calls to the ascended masters and this can open up a new understanding.

Energetic signatures of people

Then, the next step can be that people can begin to actually create energetic signatures of human beings. You can take people that outpicture some extreme form of psychology, such as a narcissist. You can scan their aura and you can create an energetic blueprint for such a person, you can see what kind of energies exist in that person's energy field. You can even come to the point where you can see the link between the individual's energy field and the astral plane, for example, and see how a certain person might be overpowered or possessed by demons in the astral plane.

The real value of this is that people can begin to see that, as there are these beings in the astral plane that you cannot reason with, there are also certain human beings that you cannot reason with. They have no humanity, they have no empathy. People are already beginning to become aware of this with narcissists, but it can reach that higher level of awareness where they actually see the energetic signature of a narcissist's energy field. You begin to connect this and you see that most of the people that have been leaders throughout history and are leaders today, have that same signature in their auras. Therefore, you realize that up until this point, most of the leaders of humankind have been narcissists and have been the kind of people who have no empathy for the population and you cannot reason with them. It does not matter what suffering they create because it does not even touch them that they are creating suffering for millions of people. Chairman Mao had no human empathetic reaction to millions of people starving to death. If he had had this reaction, he could not have carried through the cultural revolution and this is what people need to see.

Then, people can begin to ask themselves: "Are these the kind of leaders we want? Do we really want to continue to have these kind of leaders?" Once you ask yourself this question, or people ask themselves this question, many, many avenues can open up. People can become open to many ideas that the masters want to release, many of the New Age ideas of Saint Germain for a new kind of leadership, a new kind of economy.

Suddenly, there will be an understanding that will begin to dawn on the more aware, the more creative, people. Now, you take the messenger mentioning this article: Is it possible to create an economy that is not driven by profit, but is sustainable and is actually aimed at serving the interests of all the people, giving everybody a good life? The article says that it is possible but not right now. Well, but why is it not possible right now? You can look at democracy and say: "Here is, in theory, a political system that gives freedom and rights to the people. So why is it that democracy still has an elite of narcissistic leaders? Why is it that a country as rich as the United States has not been able to eradicate poverty?" Well, it is because wealth is concentrated in the hands of a small elite. But why is that? Why is that being allowed? There can come this awareness, which can be one of these tremendous awakenings. It is an awareness where people begin to realize that you already have the foundation for a free democratic society, you already have the foundation for a sustainable economy. So, why is it not working?

The elite sabotages society

The principles are there, the knowledge is there. Most people have the good intentions, but why is it not working? There can come this realization that it is not working because there is a small class of people in embodiment, and some beings outside of embodiment, who are doing everything they can to sabotage the system, to sabotage the economy, to sabotage democracy, to take away people's freedoms, to undermine them, to manipulate people.

This ties in with what we have said before: Evil, committing evil is not in human nature. The problem is not that we need to change human nature in order to get society to work, or we need to find some other system. No, we need to recognize that there are beings who have no empathy, no humanity, who are deliberately, aggressively and maliciously attempting to sabotage every good initiative that we have seen on this planet. We need to become aware that these beings exist and therefore not allow them to run our societies, not allow them to sabotage every new initiative that comes up.

This is an awakening that is possible, not tomorrow, not next week, not next year, but within a matter of decades. It is entirely possible and your calls can have an impact on shortening the time before it begins to break through. We are not giving you a utopian fantasy here, we are giving you a realistic goal and again, we are not asking you to feel burdened. We are not asking you to feel this burden of responsibility. We are asking you to feel empowered and to do what you *can* do, because whatever you do is better than doing nothing.

The elite wants to stay hidden

Another important awakening that can happen is that people come to realize that there is an elite and what they have done throughout history is trying to stay hidden from the people so that people did not know. It is comparable to when people did not know about bacteria and they had no defense when their bodies were infected. Well, the power elite, the fallen beings, the dark forces in the astral realm, the deceptive forces in the mental realm, the fallen beings in the identity realm, they are like a virus or bacteria. They can infect the energy bodies, the minds, of human beings, they can infect entire societies and they have done so time and time again. They do it partly, as we have described, by the false ideas, the labels, all of these things, but they also do it simply through energy and this is what will be an important shift when people become able to see this.

You will become able to see, for example, that an important element of mental illness is that people are overpowered by energy that comes from outside their personal energy fields, comes in and overburdens their chakras and that is why they become mentally ill. It will also be possible to see that an entire area, such as the Middle East, can be overpowered by a certain dark energy and that is why people go into this conflict. This will actually enable people to see that when you look at the energetic signature of a person who is mentally ill and then look at the energetic signature of the Middle East, you can see that people in the Middle East, the culture of the Middle East, is mentally ill.

The whole area, the energy field of the whole area, has the same signature as a mentally ill person. That is why there is so much conflict. That is why there can be no resolution because you cannot reason with this, when people are overpowered by this energy. You are not dealing with a normal human being that you can talk to, you have a person who is blinded, overpowered by this energy. Now, they also have false beliefs of course, but as long as they are overpowered by the energy, there is no way they can look at their beliefs.

Look at these fanatical Muslims, look at their eyes when they make these videos on the internet. You can see, you cannot connect to that person. There is nothing to reason with, and when people begin to recognize this, that opens up so that at least some people will be open to saying: "Well, what can we do about these energies?" That is again when they can become open to ascended masters, the tools we have given or other tools that are not given directly by us, but indirectly. People can do something about these energies and they can become aware that throughout history, many of these spiritual tools that have been available, chanting, for example, even singing, have the effect of transforming energy.

This messenger lived in Estonia for some time and they have a tradition there of having these singing festivals were up to 100,000 people come together and sing. This was even an aspect of what helped the Baltic nations free themselves from the communist yoke. They did not protest, they sang but thereby they transformed some of the black energy hanging over their nation, which prevented them from seeing that they could just walk away from the Soviet Union and say: "This is enough."

This is what people can come to realize so that people, even many people who do not need to know about ascended masters, but they can realize the value of using such things as singing or music or dancing or coming together, chanting, whatever, to transform energy. You can suddenly see that instead of sending the US Army to bring freedom and democracy to the Middle East, if a critical mass of people made the calls to transform the energy, the cloud of energy that is hanging over the Middle East, then suddenly people would be awakened. They would come to their senses, so to speak. They would stop having that fanatical shine in their eyes and they would wake up, shake their heads and say: "So, where do we go from here? What do we do now?" Because they realize they no longer have to repeat the old patterns.

The lion lying down with the lamb

Really, you have this concept in the Bible that there will come a point where the lion will lie down with the lamb and everything will be peaceful and quiet. Our vision is not that the lion will lie down with the lamb. If we could just get the Jew to lie down with the Arab, we would be more than happy. You see here that you yourselves have come into this awareness or you would not be here. You would not be studying ascended master teachings and what is the motto of the ascended masters: "What one has done, all can do." I know that many times you feel overwhelmed. You feel like: How could I possibly communicate this to people? You look at the distance you have come yourself between where you started, as you were brought up in life, and where you are now, and you see this tremendous difference and all of these shifts you have gone through.

As we have said, you make the calls, that is the alpha and then you just share your own process with people. You do not need to have this burden of conversion, having to convert people. You just share your insights and your ideas and you will be surprised at how many people either have already reached the same conclusion or can hear something you say, read something you say and say: "Oh, but that is obvious, now I see it" and this is how you can make a contribution to making this shift happen.

We are not asking you to feel burdened at all. We are not asking you to feel overwhelmed, but as the messenger said, pick an certain area of society that is close to your heart, study it so you know, make the calls for it, perhaps speak out about it and then be content that this is your contribution. You can do this along with living a normal active life, fulfilling whatever obligations you have in life.

You understand, I hope, that when we have a conference like this, we have an agenda, a purpose that reaches out on the planetary level. We have an agenda to use the opening we have to broadcast something that can have an impact on the collective consciousness. When you are here, a relatively small number of you, it is clear that you are in the focal point of our release from above and the mass consciousness out there and the resistance of the mass consciousness. You might feel this as a burden for yourself or you might feel the intensity of the energy and be overwhelmed by it. The way to balance this is to realize that you do not have to personally act upon or be concerned about everything that was said at a conference. You just pick that one topic and then you go with that, you focus on that. You do not have to personally solve every problem on earth. You do not have to make calls about every problem on earth. If each of you picks an area and each of the people who study the teachings and will read the book, if you pick one area and focus on that, then there will come a point where between all of you, you have covered all of the areas.

We have in previous ascended master organizations seen this deficit attitude to the path where you feel overwhelmed by everything the masters are telling you. You feel you have to decree for so many hours a day, make calls for this and that and the next thing. You saw, for example, in a previous dispensation where they had these call sheets that could be 10 pages long, with just about every possible problem in a certain area that you could come up with and people would make these calls very, very fast and go through all of these topics without really putting their attention on any of them. They were just letting their mouth run on autopilot and it had a relatively little effect. It has more of an effect if you focus on one particular area, put your attention on it, give the calls from the heart and if you also have knowledge of that area so you can make more specific calls and do more specific visualizations.

Shift to a joyful approach to the spiritual path

What we are asking you to do is try to make this deliberate shift where you shift into a positive, upward momentum on the path where it becomes a joy for you to do what you are doing. You are not burdened by it, you are not beating yourself up. You are not making this decision: I have to decree for three hours a day from now on. And then after some weeks, you can no longer maintain it and then you beat yourself up because you could not keep the goal and then you will feel bad. After this has gone on for some time, you have created such a strain that you just have to abandon the ascended master teachings because you cannot deal with it anymore. That is not what we are asking you to do. We are asking you to be balanced and to set a goal for yourself that is realistic and then you can eventually build on it, but do not let it become a strain in your life.

This is not the Via Dolorosa. We are asking you to walk a joyful path. What do *you* need to do individually to keep it joyful? Then, you do *that*, my beloved. Look back to what we have said during this conference. Take Padmasambahva's concept of the labels. What have ascended master students done to themselves in the past? They created a label. This is what it means to be an ascended master student: "I got to get up at five o'clock in the morning, decree for two and a half hours, then I go to work, when I come home, I have to decree again for two and a half hours before I fall asleep exhausted and then I can barely wake up the next morning."

This is not the joyful path, this is not the spiritual path that we are asking you to engage in. Do not put that label on yourself of how you *should* be as an ascended master student. Allow yourself to walk a joyful path. Now, I grant you that many of you cannot do this because, as we have said, now over and over again, you have some separate self that you have not resolved and the separate self is compelling you to do something in order to compensate. There is one self that projects that you are not good enough, there is another self that projects that you have to then do all of this to prove that you are good enough or to compensate for your flaws and your sins from the past. These are just selves, and you can come to see them, let them die and have that peace of mind where you are walking the path, not from a state of *having* to do something, but *wanting* to do something, doing it with love. *That* will have a far greater effect than any of those frantic efforts that we have seen so many students engage in.

My beloved, as the cosmic garbage collector I had to make a decision at a very early stage. In fact, when I dealt with my very first planet that was in a downward spiral, I had to make the same decision that I just described. Would I focus on the deficit and so much more that needed to be done or would I make a shift and see that I had taken on this job voluntarily and that I could decide to be joyful and at peace about carrying it out? That is why I have been able to do this several times.

Now you, my beloved, why are you on earth? Why are you on a planet that is full of garbage, if you are not one of the cosmic garbage collectors? Can you not make that same shift, instead of focusing on the garbage, focus on the joyful aspects of the path and of life. Allow yourself to enjoy whatever aspects of life on earth you enjoy and find that balance that gives you inner peace. If your inner peace is disturbed, then expose those selves that take it away from you, let them die, and then you will have inner peace. Even on a planet like earth, it is possible to have inner peace. It is more difficult than on a natural planet because there are so many outer conditions that give your separate selves an excuse for pulling you into these frantic obsessive-compulsive patterns. So it takes more work to dismiss those selves, but it can be done and what one has done, all can do.

With this, I seal you in the love of my heart, and I want to convey to you that there are many, many beings on the planet Venus who have great love and great respect for the work you are doing and the courage you have to be in embodiment on earth and to stay in embodiment on earth. Naturally, some of you were among the 144,000, others of you are avatars that came before, some of you are the original inhabitants. Regardless, we from Venus have great love for you and we want you to know that if you tune in to us, we will send you that love and you will be able to feel it.

26 | INVOKING THE TOTAL EXPOSURE OF THE ELITE (PART 1)

In the name of the I AM THAT I AM, Jesus Christ, I use the authority that I have as a being in embodiment on earth to call upon Sanat Kumara to reinforce my calls and use my chakras to project the statements in this invocation into the collective consciousness and bring about a total exposure of the elite so they can no longer hide from the people. Awaken people to the reality that we are spiritual beings and that we can co-create a new future by working with the ascended masters. I especially call for …

[Make your own calls here.]

Part 1

1. Sanat Kumara, shatter the energetic matrix that prevents people from seeing that in the distant past, some beings were confronted by the ascended masters with the need to self-transcend.

Sanat Kumara, Ruby Fire,
I seek my place in love's own choir,

with open hearts we sing your praise,
together we the earth do raise.

Sanat Kumara, Ruby Ray,
bring to earth a higher way,
light this planet with your fire,
clothe her in a new attire.

2. Sanat Kumara, shatter the energetic matrix that prevents people from seeing that some beings refused to be awakened, and they instead went into a state of denying the power of the ascended masters, and even the power of God, to stand against them.

Sanat Kumara, Ruby Fire,
initiations I desire,
I am for you an electrode,
Shamballa is my true abode.

Sanat Kumara, Ruby Ray,
bring to earth a higher way,
light this planet with your fire,
clothe her in a new attire.

3. Sanat Kumara, shatter the energetic matrix that prevents people from seeing that in their denial, the fallen beings believe that there is no power in the universe that can go against them, there is no power that they cannot either conquer, manipulate or corrupt.

Sanat Kumara, Ruby Fire,
I follow path that you require,
initiate me with your love,
the open door for Holy Dove.

Sanat Kumara, Ruby Ray,
bring to earth a higher way,
light this planet with your fire,
clothe her in a new attire.

4. Sanat Kumara, shatter the energetic matrix that prevents people from seeing that this is one of the reasons they have created a false image of God. They have attempted to create an image of God that upholds this illusion that God does not have the power to override their power.

Sanat Kumara, Ruby Fire,
your great example all inspire,
with non-attachment and great mirth,
we give the earth a true rebirth.

Sanat Kumara, Ruby Ray,
bring to earth a higher way,
light this planet with your fire,
clothe her in a new attire.

5. Sanat Kumara, shatter the energetic matrix that prevents people from seeing that the false image says God is the remote being in the sky. God does not interfere with human beings. God cannot go against certain things that are happening on earth. There is a devil that opposes God and that has as much power as God. There is also the materialistic idea that there is no God.

Sanat Kumara, Ruby Fire,
you are this planet's purifier,
consume on earth all spirits dark,
reveal the inner Spirit Spark.

Sanat Kumara, Ruby Ray,
bring to earth a higher way,
light this planet with your fire,
clothe her in a new attire.

6. Sanat Kumara, shatter the energetic matrix that prevents people from seeing that it was not God, the Creator, who stopped the prideful beings, it was the ascended masters. The fallen beings associated with earth have attempted to eradicate all awareness of the ascended masters.

Sanat Kumara, Ruby Fire,
you are a cosmic amplifier,

the lower forces can't withstand,
vibrations from Venusian band.

**Sanat Kumara, Ruby Ray,
bring to earth a higher way,
light this planet with your fire,
clothe her in a new attire.**

7. Sanat Kumara, shatter the energetic matrix that prevents people from seeing that the fallen beings do this because they know it is not God, the Creator, who comes down and says: "Thus far no farther." It is the ascended masters.

Sanat Kumara, Ruby Fire,
I am on earth your magnifier,
the flow of love I do restore,
my chakras are your open door.

**Sanat Kumara, Ruby Ray,
bring to earth a higher way,
light this planet with your fire,
clothe her in a new attire.**

8. Sanat Kumara, shatter the energetic matrix that prevents people from seeing that the fallen beings want to exclude all knowledge of ascended masters on earth, because the masters do not have the authority to interfere with earth, only those in embodiment have the authority.

Sanat Kumara, Ruby Fire,
Venusian song the multiplier,
as we your love reverberate,
the densest minds we penetrate.

**Sanat Kumara, Ruby Ray,
bring to earth a higher way,
light this planet with your fire,
clothe her in a new attire.**

9. Sanat Kumara, shatter the energetic matrix that prevents people from seeing that the ascended masters have the power to remove the fallen beings, but they do not have the authority to do so, only human beings in embodiment can give them that authority. That is why the fallen beings do not want human beings to know that the masters exist, the power they have and what they could do if they were given the authority.

Sanat Kumara, Ruby Fire,
you are for all the sanctifier,
the earth is now a holy place,
purified by cosmic grace.

**Sanat Kumara, Ruby Ray,
bring to earth a higher way,
light this planet with your fire,
clothe her in a new attire.**

Part 2

1. Sanat Kumara, shatter the energetic matrix that prevents people from seeing that the fallen beings have created these religions that deny any existence of ascended masters. Scientific Materialism, Marxism and other materialistic philosophies also deny the existence of spiritual beings.

Sanat Kumara, Ruby Fire,
I seek my place in love's own choir,
with open hearts we sing your praise,
together we the earth do raise.

**Sanat Kumara, Ruby Ray,
bring to earth a higher way,
light this planet with your fire,
clothe her in a new attire.**

2. Sanat Kumara, shatter the energetic matrix that prevents people from seeing that part of the reason the fallen beings do this is that they do not

want to be challenged, but they also do not want to be held accountable for what they do.

> Sanat Kumara, Ruby Fire,
> initiations I desire,
> I am for you an electrode,
> Shamballa is my true abode.

> **Sanat Kumara, Ruby Ray,**
> **bring to earth a higher way,**
> **light this planet with your fire,**
> **clothe her in a new attire.**

3. Sanat Kumara, shatter the energetic matrix that prevents people from seeing that the fallen beings do not want to be held accountable by a higher power, such as the ascended masters, but also they do not want to be held accountable by the population, by the people that they are suppressing and manipulating.

> Sanat Kumara, Ruby Fire,
> I follow path that you require,
> initiate me with your love,
> the open door for Holy Dove.

> **Sanat Kumara, Ruby Ray,**
> **bring to earth a higher way,**
> **light this planet with your fire,**
> **clothe her in a new attire.**

4. Sanat Kumara, shatter the energetic matrix that prevents people from seeing that the power elites of history have this clear pattern of setting themselves up as an elite, who could do whatever they wanted and nobody could speak out against them.

> Sanat Kumara, Ruby Fire,
> your great example all inspire,
> with non-attachment and great mirth,
> we give the earth a true rebirth.

Sanat Kumara, Ruby Ray,
bring to earth a higher way,
light this planet with your fire,
clothe her in a new attire.

5. Sanat Kumara, shatter the energetic matrix that prevents people from seeing that the fallen beings set themselves up in a position where they can exercise power over other people, without any accountability.

Sanat Kumara, Ruby Fire,
you are this planet's purifier,
consume on earth all spirits dark,
reveal the inner Spirit Spark.

Sanat Kumara, Ruby Ray,
bring to earth a higher way,
light this planet with your fire,
clothe her in a new attire.

6. Sanat Kumara, shatter the energetic matrix that prevents people from seeing that the tendency to exercise power without accountability can be seen in the Catholic clergy, the feudal lords of the Middle Ages, the kings or emperors, the Russian tsars, communist leaders, and the large capitalists.

Sanat Kumara, Ruby Fire,
you are a cosmic amplifier,
the lower forces can't withstand,
vibrations from Venusian band.

Sanat Kumara, Ruby Ray,
bring to earth a higher way,
light this planet with your fire,
clothe her in a new attire.

7. Sanat Kumara, shatter the energetic matrix that prevents people from seeing that the leaders of large investment banks had created the mortgage problem and when it became so severe that it threatened their own existence, they refused to be held accountable and wanted the government to bail them out in order to escape accountability.

Sanat Kumara, Ruby Fire,
I am on earth your magnifier,
the flow of love I do restore,
my chakras are your open door.

**Sanat Kumara, Ruby Ray,
bring to earth a higher way,
light this planet with your fire,
clothe her in a new attire.**

8. Sanat Kumara, shatter the energetic matrix that prevents people from seeing that in the educational institutions of the world there is this elite of intellectuals, who sit there in the fortresses of these universities and nobody can hold them accountable.

Sanat Kumara, Ruby Fire,
Venusian song the multiplier,
as we your love reverberate,
the densest minds we penetrate.

**Sanat Kumara, Ruby Ray,
bring to earth a higher way,
light this planet with your fire,
clothe her in a new attire.**

9. Sanat Kumara, shatter the energetic matrix that prevents people from seeing that in the media there are these media conglomerates, owned by just a few people, that give a completely biased and skewed version of the news, but who can hold them accountable? If you own all the newspapers, who is going to write about the flaws and expose it to the people?

Sanat Kumara, Ruby Fire,
you are for all the sanctifier,
the earth is now a holy place,
purified by cosmic grace.

**Sanat Kumara, Ruby Ray,
bring to earth a higher way,**

**light this planet with your fire,
clothe her in a new attire.**

Part 3

1. Sanat Kumara, shatter the energetic matrix that prevents people from seeing that the Internet is the first thing that has given the possibility that these hidden power elites can be held accountable and can be exposed to the people.

Sanat Kumara, Ruby Fire,
I seek my place in love's own choir,
with open hearts we sing your praise,
together we the earth do raise.

**Sanat Kumara, Ruby Ray,
bring to earth a higher way,
light this planet with your fire,
clothe her in a new attire.**

2. Sanat Kumara, shatter the energetic matrix that prevents people from seeing that the fallen beings have created a situation where they have attempted to set themselves up as Gods on earth. Most people think that God is not accountable for anything and nobody can say he made a mistake.

Sanat Kumara, Ruby Fire,
initiations I desire,
I am for you an electrode,
Shamballa is my true abode.

**Sanat Kumara, Ruby Ray,
bring to earth a higher way,
light this planet with your fire,
clothe her in a new attire.**

3. Sanat Kumara, shatter the energetic matrix that prevents people from seeing that this is a completely false image of the real Creator, who is the ultimately accountable being in the universe. Every self-aware being in the entire world of form is created out of the Creator's Being.

Sanat Kumara, Ruby Fire,
I follow path that you require,
initiate me with your love,
the open door for Holy Dove.

Sanat Kumara, Ruby Ray,
bring to earth a higher way,
light this planet with your fire,
clothe her in a new attire.

4. Sanat Kumara, shatter the energetic matrix that prevents people from seeing that the Creator experiences whatever is going on in its creation. It cannot run away from anything, it cannot deny anything and therefore it is ultimately accountable.

Sanat Kumara, Ruby Fire,
your great example all inspire,
with non-attachment and great mirth,
we give the earth a true rebirth.

Sanat Kumara, Ruby Ray,
bring to earth a higher way,
light this planet with your fire,
clothe her in a new attire.

5. Sanat Kumara, shatter the energetic matrix that prevents people from seeing that the fallen beings want to become false gods who can exercise power without being held accountable for the consequences this has for people. They want to do whatever they want to do, no matter what the consequences are for the people, but they never want the people to hold them accountable.

Sanat Kumara, Ruby Fire,
you are this planet's purifier,

consume on earth all spirits dark,
reveal the inner Spirit Spark.

**Sanat Kumara, Ruby Ray,
bring to earth a higher way,
light this planet with your fire,
clothe her in a new attire.**

6. Sanat Kumara, shatter the energetic matrix that prevents people from becoming aware of the elite and making the determination that we will not allow this elite to run our societies. Why should we allow an elite to do whatever they want and exploit us without being held accountable for what they do? Why should we allow a small elite to create suffering for the entire population and never be held accountable for this?

Sanat Kumara, Ruby Fire,
you are a cosmic amplifier,
the lower forces can't withstand,
vibrations from Venusian band.

**Sanat Kumara, Ruby Ray,
bring to earth a higher way,
light this planet with your fire,
clothe her in a new attire.**

7. Sanat Kumara, shatter the energetic matrix that prevents people from awakening and saying: Why are we allowing a small elite of people in the financial system to create crisis after crisis, and then taxpayer money is being used to bail them out when their system is in danger of collapse?

Sanat Kumara, Ruby Fire,
I am on earth your magnifier,
the flow of love I do restore,
my chakras are your open door.

**Sanat Kumara, Ruby Ray,
bring to earth a higher way,
light this planet with your fire,
clothe her in a new attire.**

8. Sanat Kumara, shatter the energetic matrix that prevents people from seeing that the financial system we have today is created for one purpose: That a small elite can concentrate money in their own hands by doing whatever they want, creating whatever schemes they want, but they are not held accountable when the schemes fail.

Sanat Kumara, Ruby Fire,
Venusian song the multiplier,
as we your love reverberate,
the densest minds we penetrate.

Sanat Kumara, Ruby Ray,
bring to earth a higher way,
light this planet with your fire,
clothe her in a new attire.

9. Sanat Kumara, shatter the energetic matrix that prevents people from seeing that in a capitalist economy, by the very nature of capitalism, there will always be an elite and they will be driven by greed, the desire for profit. It is never going to be enough.

Sanat Kumara, Ruby Fire,
you are for all the sanctifier,
the earth is now a holy place,
purified by cosmic grace.

Sanat Kumara, Ruby Ray,
bring to earth a higher way,
light this planet with your fire,
clothe her in a new attire.

Part 4

1. Sanat Kumara, shatter the energetic matrix that prevents people from seeing that to the power elite, it is not enough to produce a product or provide a service and get paid reasonably for that. They want more and

they want it faster, and therefore they create these schemes that they think can give them a faster return.

Sanat Kumara, Ruby Fire,
I seek my place in love's own choir,
with open hearts we sing your praise,
together we the earth do raise.

**Sanat Kumara, Ruby Ray,
bring to earth a higher way,
light this planet with your fire,
clothe her in a new attire.**

2. Sanat Kumara, shatter the energetic matrix that prevents people from seeing that members of the elite know there is a certain risk involved, but they tend to deny it and look for the short-term profit.

Sanat Kumara, Ruby Fire,
initiations I desire,
I am for you an electrode,
Shamballa is my true abode.

**Sanat Kumara, Ruby Ray,
bring to earth a higher way,
light this planet with your fire,
clothe her in a new attire.**

3. Sanat Kumara, shatter the energetic matrix that prevents people from seeing that there are certain basic principles for how the economy works. It is not a matter of capitalism or communism because it does not matter what theoretical overlay we put on the economy. There are certain basic principles that are very simple.

Sanat Kumara, Ruby Fire,
I follow path that you require,
initiate me with your love,
the open door for Holy Dove.

Sanat Kumara, Ruby Ray,
bring to earth a higher way,
light this planet with your fire,
clothe her in a new attire.

4. Sanat Kumara, shatter the energetic matrix that prevents people from seeing that if we provide a product or a service, then we can have a sustainable economy that gives us a sustainable profit, but when we start making money off of money, creating these investment schemes, we are creating an unbalanced economy and in an unbalanced economy, there will be risk.

Sanat Kumara, Ruby Fire,
your great example all inspire,
with non-attachment and great mirth,
we give the earth a true rebirth.

Sanat Kumara, Ruby Ray,
bring to earth a higher way,
light this planet with your fire,
clothe her in a new attire.

5. Sanat Kumara, shatter the energetic matrix that prevents people from seeing that the more people are blinded by greed, the bigger of a risk they are willing to take in order to get that short-term profit or that extraordinary profit, and therefore they will inevitably create a crisis. It is only a matter of time.

Sanat Kumara, Ruby Fire,
you are this planet's purifier,
consume on earth all spirits dark,
reveal the inner Spirit Spark.

Sanat Kumara, Ruby Ray,
bring to earth a higher way,
light this planet with your fire,
clothe her in a new attire.

6. Sanat Kumara, shatter the energetic matrix that prevents people from waking up and saying: "Why should we allow this elite to run the financial

system and then time and time again escape accountability?" We either do as they say and let the market take care of itself and let them fail, or we have to find another approach to the economy where we do not allow these high risk investments that lead from crisis to crisis.

Sanat Kumara, Ruby Fire,
you are a cosmic amplifier,
the lower forces can't withstand,
vibrations from Venusian band.

Sanat Kumara, Ruby Ray,
bring to earth a higher way,
light this planet with your fire,
clothe her in a new attire.

7. Sanat Kumara, I call forth Saint Germain's scientific technology for detecting what cannot be detected by the senses. I call forth technology to read the Akashic Records, which is the ultimate way to hold people accountable.

Sanat Kumara, Ruby Fire,
I am on earth your magnifier,
the flow of love I do restore,
my chakras are your open door.

Sanat Kumara, Ruby Ray,
bring to earth a higher way,
light this planet with your fire,
clothe her in a new attire.

8. Sanat Kumara, I call forth the technology to make energy visible that is not visible to the senses or normal instruments. I call forth technology to take an image or scan of the human aura, and an image of the energy field of the earth.

Sanat Kumara, Ruby Fire,
Venusian song the multiplier,
as we your love reverberate,
the densest minds we penetrate.

Sanat Kumara, Ruby Ray,
bring to earth a higher way,
light this planet with your fire,
clothe her in a new attire.

9. Sanat Kumara, shatter the energetic matrix that prevents people from seeing that an individual human being has an energy field around its physical body, and we can detect certain patterns of energies in that field that are linked to a specific organ. We can see that when the energy reaches a certain intensity, that organ starts becoming ill and not functioning properly.

Sanat Kumara, Ruby Fire,
you are for all the sanctifier,
the earth is now a holy place,
purified by cosmic grace.

Sanat Kumara, Ruby Ray,
bring to earth a higher way,
light this planet with your fire,
clothe her in a new attire.

Sealing

In the name of the I AM THAT I AM, I accept that Archangel Michael, Astrea and Shiva form an impenetrable shield around myself and all constructive people, sealing us from all fear-based energies in all four octaves. I accept that the Light of God is consuming and transforming all fear-based energies that make up the dark forces working against ending the era of elitism on earth!

27 | INVOKING THE TOTAL EXPOSURE OF THE ELITE (PART 2)

In the name of the I AM THAT I AM, Jesus Christ, I use the authority that I have as a being in embodiment on earth to call upon Sanat Kumara to reinforce my calls and use my chakras to project the statements in this invocation into the collective consciousness and bring about a total exposure of the elite so they can no longer hide from the people. Awaken people to the reality that we are spiritual beings and that we can co-create a new future by working with the ascended masters. I especially call for ...

[Make your own calls here.]

Part 1

1. Sanat Kumara, shatter the energetic matrix that prevents people from seeing that there is a realm of invisible energy, and it is linked to the physical realm and it has an influence on the physical realm.

Sanat Kumara, Ruby Fire,
I seek my place in love's own choir,

with open hearts we sing your praise,
together we the earth do raise.

Sanat Kumara, Ruby Ray,
bring to earth a higher way,
light this planet with your fire,
clothe her in a new attire.

2. Sanat Kumara, shatter the energetic matrix that prevents people from seeing that the emotional realm around earth is so dark that if we could see the astral plane, we would be absolutely shocked at how ugly it is, how aggressive it is and how there are demons in the astral plane that have a completely aggressive intent to steal energy from us.

Sanat Kumara, Ruby Fire,
initiations I desire,
I am for you an electrode,
Shamballa is my true abode.

Sanat Kumara, Ruby Ray,
bring to earth a higher way,
light this planet with your fire,
clothe her in a new attire.

3. Sanat Kumara, shatter the energetic matrix that prevents people from seeing that the demons are trying to do anything they can to overpower anybody they can overpower. We cannot reason with them. There is absolutely no way to reason with these beings.

Sanat Kumara, Ruby Fire,
I follow path that you require,
initiate me with your love,
the open door for Holy Dove.

Sanat Kumara, Ruby Ray,
bring to earth a higher way,
light this planet with your fire,
clothe her in a new attire.

4. Sanat Kumara, I call forth the technology that will allow us to get a glimpse of the energies in the astral plane, even though this will give rise to some fear. I accept that the fear is a necessary phase because people have been lulled into such a state of denial by Materialism.

Sanat Kumara, Ruby Fire,
your great example all inspire,
with non-attachment and great mirth,
we give the earth a true rebirth.

Sanat Kumara, Ruby Ray,
bring to earth a higher way,
light this planet with your fire,
clothe her in a new attire.

5. Sanat Kumara, I call forth a rude awakening where people begin to see that there are these fear-based energies that are seeking to influence us. There are these beings in the astral plane, it is not just material energy or neutral energy.

Sanat Kumara, Ruby Fire,
you are this planet's purifier,
consume on earth all spirits dark,
reveal the inner Spirit Spark.

Sanat Kumara, Ruby Ray,
bring to earth a higher way,
light this planet with your fire,
clothe her in a new attire.

6. Sanat Kumara, shatter the energetic matrix that prevents people from seeing that there are certain parts of the world where there is a stronger concentration of these fear-based energies. One of these areas is the Middle East and that is why there is such conflict there.

Sanat Kumara, Ruby Fire,
you are a cosmic amplifier,
the lower forces can't withstand,
vibrations from Venusian band.

Sanat Kumara, Ruby Ray,
bring to earth a higher way,
light this planet with your fire,
clothe her in a new attire.

7. Sanat Kumara, shatter the energetic matrix that prevents people from seeing that there is a concentration of darker energies over the larger cities and that is why there is such stress from living in these cities, there are people who cannot handle it and go crazy from dealing with the energy.

Sanat Kumara, Ruby Fire,
I am on earth your magnifier,
the flow of love I do restore,
my chakras are your open door.

Sanat Kumara, Ruby Ray,
bring to earth a higher way,
light this planet with your fire,
clothe her in a new attire.

8. Sanat Kumara, shatter the energetic matrix that prevents people from seeing that there are beings in the astral plane who have an intent. These beings cannot be reasoned with because they have no self-awareness. We cannot actually make them feel any empathy or compassion for human beings.

Sanat Kumara, Ruby Fire,
Venusian song the multiplier,
as we your love reverberate,
the densest minds we penetrate.

Sanat Kumara, Ruby Ray,
bring to earth a higher way,
light this planet with your fire,
clothe her in a new attire.

9. Sanat Kumara, shatter the energetic matrix that prevents people from seeing that when we acknowledge that these dark beings exist, we can

begin to consider what we can do to protect ourselves from them, and that is when we need to consider the existence of ascended masters.

Sanat Kumara, Ruby Fire,
you are for all the sanctifier,
the earth is now a holy place,
purified by cosmic grace.

**Sanat Kumara, Ruby Ray,
bring to earth a higher way,
light this planet with your fire,
clothe her in a new attire.**

Part 2

1. Sanat Kumara, shatter the energetic matrix that prevents people from seeing that the ascended masters are the natural God-ordained antidote to the dark beings and dark forces. The masters have the power, they have the high-frequency energy that can counteract these beings.

Sanat Kumara, Ruby Fire,
I seek my place in love's own choir,
with open hearts we sing your praise,
together we the earth do raise.

**Sanat Kumara, Ruby Ray,
bring to earth a higher way,
light this planet with your fire,
clothe her in a new attire.**

2. Sanat Kumara, shatter the energetic matrix that prevents people from seeing that if we invoke spiritual protection around our personal energy field, then our energy field cannot be invaded by the dark beings—if we do not invite them in.

Sanat Kumara, Ruby Fire,
initiations I desire,

I am for you an electrode,
Shamballa is my true abode.

Sanat Kumara, Ruby Ray,
bring to earth a higher way,
light this planet with your fire,
clothe her in a new attire.

3. Sanat Kumara, shatter the energetic matrix that prevents people from seeing that many people in the New Age, spiritual movement are still trapped in the "It's all good" philosophy and refuse to look at anything dark or evil.

Sanat Kumara, Ruby Fire,
I follow path that you require,
initiate me with your love,
the open door for Holy Dove.

Sanat Kumara, Ruby Ray,
bring to earth a higher way,
light this planet with your fire,
clothe her in a new attire.

4. Sanat Kumara, shatter the energetic matrix that prevents people from seeing beyond the concept that we should not put our attention on darkness because we give it power. Instead, we need to study the phenomenon, come to understand it so we can see what we can do to protect ourselves.

Sanat Kumara, Ruby Fire,
your great example all inspire,
with non-attachment and great mirth,
we give the earth a true rebirth.

Sanat Kumara, Ruby Ray,
bring to earth a higher way,
light this planet with your fire,
clothe her in a new attire.

5. Sanat Kumara, shatter the energetic matrix that prevents people from seeing that there are these dark beings, there is no technology that can protect us from them and we cannot reason with them, so we need to do something else.

Sanat Kumara, Ruby Fire,
you are this planet's purifier,
consume on earth all spirits dark,
reveal the inner Spirit Spark.

**Sanat Kumara, Ruby Ray,
bring to earth a higher way,
light this planet with your fire,
clothe her in a new attire.**

6. Sanat Kumara, shatter the energetic matrix that prevents people from seeing that we can protect ourselves from a demon in the astral plane by making calls to the ascended masters.

Sanat Kumara, Ruby Fire,
you are a cosmic amplifier,
the lower forces can't withstand,
vibrations from Venusian band.

**Sanat Kumara, Ruby Ray,
bring to earth a higher way,
light this planet with your fire,
clothe her in a new attire.**

7. Sanat Kumara, I call forth the technology whereby we can create energetic signatures of human beings. We can create an energetic blueprint for a person, and we can see what kind of energies exist in that person's energy field.

Sanat Kumara, Ruby Fire,
I am on earth your magnifier,
the flow of love I do restore,
my chakras are your open door.

Sanat Kumara, Ruby Ray,
bring to earth a higher way,
light this planet with your fire,
clothe her in a new attire.

8. Sanat Kumara, shatter the energetic matrix that prevents people from seeing that we can see the link between the individual's energy field and the astral plane, and see how a certain person might be overpowered or possessed by demons in the astral plane.

Sanat Kumara, Ruby Fire,
Venusian song the multiplier,
as we your love reverberate,
the densest minds we penetrate.

Sanat Kumara, Ruby Ray,
bring to earth a higher way,
light this planet with your fire,
clothe her in a new attire.

9. Sanat Kumara, shatter the energetic matrix that prevents people from seeing that there are these beings in the astral plane that we cannot reason with, there are also certain human beings that we cannot reason with. They have no humanity, they have no empathy.

Sanat Kumara, Ruby Fire,
you are for all the sanctifier,
the earth is now a holy place,
purified by cosmic grace.

Sanat Kumara, Ruby Ray,
bring to earth a higher way,
light this planet with your fire,
clothe her in a new attire.

Part 3

1. Sanat Kumara, shatter the energetic matrix that prevents people from seeing that we can create an energetic signature of a narcissist's energy field. We can see that most of the people who have been leaders throughout history and are leaders today, have that same signature in their auras.

Sanat Kumara, Ruby Fire,
I seek my place in love's own choir,
with open hearts we sing your praise,
together we the earth do raise.

Sanat Kumara, Ruby Ray,
bring to earth a higher way,
light this planet with your fire,
clothe her in a new attire.

2. Sanat Kumara, shatter the energetic matrix that prevents people from seeing that up until this point, most of the leaders of humankind have been narcissists and have been the kind of people who have no empathy for the population, and that is why we cannot reason with them.

Sanat Kumara, Ruby Fire,
initiations I desire,
I am for you an electrode,
Shamballa is my true abode.

Sanat Kumara, Ruby Ray,
bring to earth a higher way,
light this planet with your fire,
clothe her in a new attire.

3. Sanat Kumara, shatter the energetic matrix that prevents people from seeing that it does not matter what suffering they create because it does not even touch them that they are creating suffering for millions of people. Chairman Mao had no human empathetic reaction to millions of people starving to death.

Sanat Kumara, Ruby Fire,
I follow path that you require,
initiate me with your love,
the open door for Holy Dove.

Sanat Kumara, Ruby Ray,
bring to earth a higher way,
light this planet with your fire,
clothe her in a new attire.

4. Sanat Kumara, shatter the energetic matrix that prevents people from seeing that we can then begin to ask ourselves: "Are these the kind of leaders we want? Do we really want to continue to have these kind of leaders?"

Sanat Kumara, Ruby Fire,
your great example all inspire,
with non-attachment and great mirth,
we give the earth a true rebirth.

Sanat Kumara, Ruby Ray,
bring to earth a higher way,
light this planet with your fire,
clothe her in a new attire.

5. Sanat Kumara, shatter the energetic matrix that prevents people from becoming open to many ideas that Saint Germain wants to release for a new kind of leadership, a new kind of economy.

Sanat Kumara, Ruby Fire,
you are this planet's purifier,
consume on earth all spirits dark,
reveal the inner Spirit Spark.

Sanat Kumara, Ruby Ray,
bring to earth a higher way,
light this planet with your fire,
clothe her in a new attire.

6. Sanat Kumara, shatter the energetic matrix that prevents people from seeing that democracy is a political system that gives freedom and rights to the people. So why is it that democracy still has an elite of narcissistic leaders? Why is it that a country as rich as the United States has not been able to eradicate poverty?

Sanat Kumara, Ruby Fire,
you are a cosmic amplifier,
the lower forces can't withstand,
vibrations from Venusian band.

Sanat Kumara, Ruby Ray,
bring to earth a higher way,
light this planet with your fire,
clothe her in a new attire.

7. Sanat Kumara, shatter the energetic matrix that prevents people from seeing that this is because wealth is concentrated in the hands of a small elite. We already have the foundation for a free democratic society, we already have the foundation for a sustainable economy. So, why is it not working?

Sanat Kumara, Ruby Fire,
I am on earth your magnifier,
the flow of love I do restore,
my chakras are your open door.

Sanat Kumara, Ruby Ray,
bring to earth a higher way,
light this planet with your fire,
clothe her in a new attire.

8. Sanat Kumara, shatter the energetic matrix that prevents people from seeing that the principles are there, the knowledge is there. Most people have the good intentions, but why is it not working?

Sanat Kumara, Ruby Fire,
Venusian song the multiplier,

as we your love reverberate,
the densest minds we penetrate.

**Sanat Kumara, Ruby Ray,
bring to earth a higher way,
light this planet with your fire,
clothe her in a new attire.**

9. Sanat Kumara, shatter the energetic matrix that prevents people from seeing that it is not working because there is a small class of people in embodiment, and some beings outside of embodiment, who are doing everything they can to sabotage the system, to sabotage the economy, to sabotage democracy, to take away people's freedoms, to undermine them, to manipulate people.

Sanat Kumara, Ruby Fire,
you are for all the sanctifier,
the earth is now a holy place,
purified by cosmic grace.

**Sanat Kumara, Ruby Ray,
bring to earth a higher way,
light this planet with your fire,
clothe her in a new attire.**

Part 4

1. Sanat Kumara, shatter the energetic matrix that prevents people from seeing that committing evil is not in human nature. The problem is not that we need to change human nature in order to get society to work, or we need to find some other system.

Sanat Kumara, Ruby Fire,
I seek my place in love's own choir,
with open hearts we sing your praise,
together we the earth do raise.

**Sanat Kumara, Ruby Ray,
bring to earth a higher way,
light this planet with your fire,
clothe her in a new attire.**

2. Sanat Kumara, shatter the energetic matrix that prevents people from seeing that we need to recognize that there are beings who have no empathy, no humanity, who are deliberately, aggressively and maliciously attempting to sabotage every good initiative that we have seen on this planet. We need to become aware that these beings exist and therefore not allow them to run our societies, not allow them to sabotage every new initiative that comes up.

Sanat Kumara, Ruby Fire,
initiations I desire,
I am for you an electrode,
Shamballa is my true abode.

**Sanat Kumara, Ruby Ray,
bring to earth a higher way,
light this planet with your fire,
clothe her in a new attire.**

3. Sanat Kumara, shatter the energetic matrix so we can shorten the time before this awakening begins to break through. Help people feel empowered and realize that we can actually do something about elitism.

Sanat Kumara, Ruby Fire,
I follow path that you require,
initiate me with your love,
the open door for Holy Dove.

**Sanat Kumara, Ruby Ray,
bring to earth a higher way,
light this planet with your fire,
clothe her in a new attire.**

4. Sanat Kumara, shatter the energetic matrix that prevents people from seeing that there is an elite, and what they have done throughout history is

trying to stay hidden from the people so that we did not know. It is comparable to when we did not know about bacteria and we had no defense when our bodies were infected.

Sanat Kumara, Ruby Fire,
your great example all inspire,
with non-attachment and great mirth,
we give the earth a true rebirth.

**Sanat Kumara, Ruby Ray,
bring to earth a higher way,
light this planet with your fire,
clothe her in a new attire.**

5. Sanat Kumara, shatter the energetic matrix that prevents people from seeing that the power elite, the fallen beings, the dark forces in the astral realm, the deceptive forces in the mental realm, the fallen beings in the identity realm, they are like a virus or bacteria.

Sanat Kumara, Ruby Fire,
you are this planet's purifier,
consume on earth all spirits dark,
reveal the inner Spirit Spark.

**Sanat Kumara, Ruby Ray,
bring to earth a higher way,
light this planet with your fire,
clothe her in a new attire.**

6. Sanat Kumara, shatter the energetic matrix that prevents people from seeing that the dark beings can infect the energy bodies, the minds, of human beings, they can infect entire societies and they have done so time and time again. They do it partly by the false ideas, the labels, but they also do it through energy.

Sanat Kumara, Ruby Fire,
you are a cosmic amplifier,
the lower forces can't withstand,
vibrations from Venusian band.

**Sanat Kumara, Ruby Ray,
bring to earth a higher way,
light this planet with your fire,
clothe her in a new attire.**

7. Sanat Kumara, shatter the energetic matrix that prevents people from seeing that an important element of mental illness is that people are overpowered by energy that comes from outside their personal energy fields. It comes in and overburdens their chakras and that is why they become mentally ill.

Sanat Kumara, Ruby Fire,
I am on earth your magnifier,
the flow of love I do restore,
my chakras are your open door.

**Sanat Kumara, Ruby Ray,
bring to earth a higher way,
light this planet with your fire,
clothe her in a new attire.**

8. Sanat Kumara, shatter the energetic matrix that prevents people from seeing that an entire area, such as the Middle East, can be overpowered by a certain dark energy and that is why people go into this conflict. When we look at the energetic signature of a person who is mentally ill and then look at the energetic signature of the Middle East, we can see that people in the Middle East, the culture of the Middle East, is mentally ill.

Sanat Kumara, Ruby Fire,
Venusian song the multiplier,
as we your love reverberate,
the densest minds we penetrate.

**Sanat Kumara, Ruby Ray,
bring to earth a higher way,
light this planet with your fire,
clothe her in a new attire.**

9. Sanat Kumara, shatter the energetic matrix that prevents people from seeing that the energy field of the whole area has the same signature as a mentally ill person. That is why there is so much conflict.

Sanat Kumara, Ruby Fire,
you are for all the sanctifier,
the earth is now a holy place,
purified by cosmic grace.

**Sanat Kumara, Ruby Ray,
bring to earth a higher way,
light this planet with your fire,
clothe her in a new attire.**

Part 5

1. Sanat Kumara, shatter the energetic matrix that prevents people from seeing that we cannot reason with people who are overpowered by dark energy. We are not dealing with normal human beings that we can talk to, we have people who are blinded, overpowered by this energy.

Sanat Kumara, Ruby Fire,
I seek my place in love's own choir,
with open hearts we sing your praise,
together we the earth do raise.

**Sanat Kumara, Ruby Ray,
bring to earth a higher way,
light this planet with your fire,
clothe her in a new attire.**

2. Sanat Kumara, shatter the energetic matrix that prevents people from seeing that people also have false beliefs, but as long as they are overpowered by the energy, there is no way they can look at their beliefs.

Sanat Kumara, Ruby Fire,
initiations I desire,

I am for you an electrode,
Shamballa is my true abode.

Sanat Kumara, Ruby Ray,
bring to earth a higher way,
light this planet with your fire,
clothe her in a new attire.

3. Sanat Kumara, shatter the energetic matrix that prevents people from seeing that when it comes to fanatical persons, we cannot connect to them. There is nothing to reason with, and that means we need to find a different way to deal with these energies.

Sanat Kumara, Ruby Fire,
I follow path that you require,
initiate me with your love,
the open door for Holy Dove.

Sanat Kumara, Ruby Ray,
bring to earth a higher way,
light this planet with your fire,
clothe her in a new attire.

4. Sanat Kumara, shatter the energetic matrix that prevents people from seeing that we can do something about dark energies when we make use of the tools that the ascended masters have released throughout the ages.

Sanat Kumara, Ruby Fire,
your great example all inspire,
with non-attachment and great mirth,
we give the earth a true rebirth.

Sanat Kumara, Ruby Ray,
bring to earth a higher way,
light this planet with your fire,
clothe her in a new attire.

5. Sanat Kumara, shatter the energetic matrix that prevents people from seeing that all people do not need to know about ascended masters, but

they can still use tools to transform energy. If a critical mass of people made the calls to transform the cloud of energy that is hanging over the Middle East, then suddenly people would be awakened and come to their senses.

> Sanat Kumara, Ruby Fire,
> you are this planet's purifier,
> consume on earth all spirits dark,
> reveal the inner Spirit Spark.

> **Sanat Kumara, Ruby Ray,**
> **bring to earth a higher way,**
> **light this planet with your fire,**
> **clothe her in a new attire.**

6. Sanat Kumara, shatter the energetic matrix that prevents people from overcoming the fanatical mindset and saying: "So, where do we go from here? What do we do now?" Because we realize we no longer have to repeat the old patterns.

> Sanat Kumara, Ruby Fire,
> you are a cosmic amplifier,
> the lower forces can't withstand,
> vibrations from Venusian band.

> **Sanat Kumara, Ruby Ray,**
> **bring to earth a higher way,**
> **light this planet with your fire,**
> **clothe her in a new attire.**

7. Sanat Kumara, shatter the energetic matrix that prevents people from seeing that we can all help raise the energy level of earth by picking an area of society that is close to our hearts, studying it and making the calls for it, perhaps speaking out about it and then being content that this is our contribution.

> Sanat Kumara, Ruby Fire,
> I am on earth your magnifier,

the flow of love I do restore,
my chakras are your open door.

Sanat Kumara, Ruby Ray,
bring to earth a higher way,
light this planet with your fire,
clothe her in a new attire.

8. Sanat Kumara, shatter the energetic matrix that prevents spiritual people from making this deliberate shift where we shift into a positive, upward momentum on the path, where it becomes a joy for us to do what we are doing. We are not burdened by it because we take a balanced approach to the spiritual path.

Sanat Kumara, Ruby Fire,
Venusian song the multiplier,
as we your love reverberate,
the densest minds we penetrate.

Sanat Kumara, Ruby Ray,
bring to earth a higher way,
light this planet with your fire,
clothe her in a new attire.

9. Sanat Kumara, shatter the energetic matrix that prevents spiritual people from making the shift so that instead of focusing on the garbage, we focus on the joyful aspects of the path and of life. We allow ourselves to enjoy whatever aspects of life on earth we enjoy and find the balance that gives us inner peace.

Sanat Kumara, Ruby Fire,
you are for all the sanctifier,
the earth is now a holy place,
purified by cosmic grace.

Sanat Kumara, Ruby Ray,
bring to earth a higher way,
light this planet with your fire,
clothe her in a new attire.

Sealing

In the name of the I AM THAT I AM, I accept that Archangel Michael, Astrea and Shiva form an impenetrable shield around myself and all constructive people, sealing us from all fear-based energies in all four octaves. I accept that the Light of God is consuming and transforming all fear-based energies that make up the dark forces working against ending the era of elitism on earth!

28 | A SECOND FEMINIST REVOLUTION

I AM the Ascended Master the Goddess of Liberty. I wish to give you some thoughts about an observable fact, when you look at history, that should give rise to a question: If there is a power elite, which of course there is, why is it that most of them are men? How many who study politics, sociology, psychology have asked that question? The reality is, when you look at it, that the vast majority of people who have been part of the power elite, historically have been men. Even today, there have been relatively few women in what you could call the power elite or the leadership of society.

You will of course, when you look at history, see that there have been certain queens or empresses who have been as aggressive or as deceptive and scheming as the "best" among the men. Thereby, you can reason that they have, in most cases, been fallen beings. In general, you must say that women have not been part of the power elite. It is important to consider why. It has something to do with the fact that women are mothers, or at least many women are mothers. When people have given birth to children, you have a deeper personal relationship to your children. In that deeper relationship you recognize the essential humanity of your children. That makes it easier for women to recognize the essential humanity of all people, or at least in many other people than themselves and their children.

This is part of the reason why men have traditionally been warriors. It is easier for a man to fall in love with an idea and forget about the basic humanity so he becomes willing to kill other people for the sake of the idea. This is what the fallen beings knew when they came to earth and saw the dynamic, the psychological dynamic, of men and women. They instantly saw how to take advantage of this by turning men into warriors. Then, they started this very long history of putting women down.

Now, we have talked about how the fallen beings are always seeking to divide the population into various groups and set them up against each other. The basic of these dualistic divisions that you see is the division between men and women. Here you have divided the human population into two parts that are almost the same size. You have set them in what some would call an existential conflict against each other. Now, I know some of course will immediately say: "But isn't there a difference between men and women?" I would say: "Is there?" Yes, there is a physical difference of course. But is there, does there have to be, a psychological difference? Does there have to be the psychological difference that there is today?

The roles of men and women

If there had not been this millennia-old effort by the fallen beings to manipulate people, would men have stepped into the roles that you have seen throughout history and see today? Would women have stepped into the roles for women that have been defined through history? In other words, going back to what we have said before, is it human nature that men behave a certain way and women behave a certain way? Of course, from the ascended perspective, we know it is not. It is not inevitable that men must act *this* way and women must act *this* way.

The reality here is that, as we have said before, the fallen beings attempt to take a certain physical condition, we have talked about the density of matter but the density of matter leads to the density of the physical bodies. This means that instead of materializing a body, you have to bring it forth through this "natural process" of childbearing. This is what the fallen beings have looked at. They have then created an ideological overlay, projecting it upon this and saying: "Men are like this because that is the nature of men, and women are like this because that is the nature of women."

The thing is, you can look at current conditions on earth and you can say: "But any psychologist will tell you that there are certain characteristics of male psychology and certain characteristics of female psychology." All

I am saying here is, this is not something ordained by nature or created by God, or mandated by some physical difference between male and female brains. This is a created condition, a manipulated condition, where the fallen beings have attempted to create a label for what it means to be a man and a label for what it means to be a woman. They have done this in such a way that the two sexes are in many ways in opposition to each other. This is a completely artificial condition.

This is important to realize because when you realize this, you know you have the potential to free yourself from these artificially inserted conditions for how you should be as a man and how you should be as a woman. When you free yourself from this, you will be able to have an entirely different relationship to the opposite sex or even to your own sex, to your own role in whatever type of body you are in. We have said before that there are no people that always embody in male bodies or in female bodies. There will be some switching around. There may be some people who have for several lifetimes been in the same type of body, but all have experienced both sexes.

As we have said, the reality is, you start out as the Conscious You, which has a point-like sense of identity. In a point, where is the room for division? Where is the room for two sides, one male and one female? The Conscious You is neither male nor female, it is neutral. It takes on a physical body. It can over time build certain structures in the identity, mental and emotional body relating to both sexes. For example, when it is in a female body, it then ties into these structures that have been built in past lifetimes and you think you have to behave a certain way as a woman.

Women's Liberation Movement

This of course is the real importance, the underlying spiritual significance, of the Women's Liberation Movement. It is not so much a matter of challenging the outer things, the physical discrimination, although that is also necessary. The real underlying element of women's liberation is to help women see that they are not women. You are a spiritual being inhabiting a female body this time around.

Therefore, you can see that all of this historical, cultural overlay, ideological overlay, that has been put upon women is just artificial. You can choose to consciously, systematically separate yourself from it, until you reach a state where you can be at peace with being in embodiment on earth and with being in a female body, or for that matter in a male body. What you see here is that these cultural roles, historical roles, for men and women have been created by the fallen beings. They have defined that men are the outgoing aggressive sex, and this is why most of the fallen beings who take embodiment, they always try to manipulate themselves into a male body so they can more easily attain a position of power. Also for the general population, the male role has become so strong that most people think that when they are men, they have to live up to a certain image. They have to be the more aggressive, outgoing. They have to be leading the woman in the ballroom dance, as was said, and they have to take on this particular role. The effect of this for men has been that men are more susceptible to being manipulated by the power elite. Men are more susceptible to being manipulated into going to war and killing other men.

In other words, there has been created an incredibly dense cloud hanging over the planet, over the collective consciousness, that overpowers many men to think this is what you have to do as a man. For example, if your country is attacked, you have to be a soldier, you have to defend your country, give your life for your country. This is just a cultural overlay.

Can men free society from a power elite?

What does that mean in practical terms? It means that if we consider, how can humanity become free from the power elite, we have said the power elite cannot do it. We must ask the question: "Can the men do it?" Obviously, some men *can*, but men in general are not as likely to do it as women.

In other words, the biggest potential for liberating humanity from the fallen beings, or the power elite, is women who connect to that essential humanity they see in their children and they say: "Do I want my children to grow up in a society dominated and manipulated by this elite of narcissists who have no concern for my children whatsoever, for whom my children are just numbers, they are cannon fodder? They have no respect for them whatsoever. Why would I want these kind of people to lead my society?" This could lead to a second feminist revolution that was at a higher level, had a higher awareness of what is really at stake.

You might say that the feminist revolution that you have seen was based on the level of the collective consciousness, and the collective consciousness was so trapped in the black-and-white dualistic thinking that, as in many revolutions you have seen throughout history, there had to be an enemy. There had to be an opponent you were fighting and for women it became men. We might say that the collective consciousness is still at a level where many people need an opponent, they need someone to blame, to say that is where the problem is. For the second feminist revolution this could be, instead of men in general, it could be the men in the power elite.

Not that of course women would go out and fight them with physical means, but they would fight them with knowledge, with awareness, with demands for change. This is not the highest possible, because obviously what we are calling you to do is to not see the power elite as an enemy, not see the fallen beings as an enemy, but just make the calls and let us deal with it.

A second feminist revolution

This is not what the majority of women can do at this point, so therefore the potential is there for an awakening to a second feminist revolution that would identify that the real problem in society is the power elite. They are the ones who are manipulating society, who are upholding these traditional roles for men and women, causing the men to go to war and the women to be confined to the roles they are confined to as mothers and housewives and all of the abuse that has been attached to that throughout the centuries.

This is a potential that you can envision, that you can make calls on. Some of you may feel more strongly about this and you can then study the Women's Liberation Movement. You can compare it to spiritual teachings. You may be able to receive the ideas from us on how this could be taken to a higher level and become not necessarily more spiritual in an open way, but become more aware, more based on the basic humanity. You understand here that of course we do not ideally want people to label the fallen beings as enemies. When you connect to the basic humanity, it is necessary for people to say: "But there are people who do not have that basic humanity. They are the leaders that abuse us, that manipulate us because they have no humanity. They don't care about us and we can't allow them to lead. We don't need to go out and kill them. We need to simply create a society where there is an awareness that these are not the leaders we want."

Therefore, you could say that women's liberation could really be expanded to women liberating society from the dominance of this male elite, male elitism. After all, when you look at society realistically, it is not all men that are suppressing women deliberately and aggressively. It is the leaders in the power elite that have created and are upholding the roles that are causing the suppression of women. Of course, as part of this revolution it is necessary to demand that more women come into leadership positions, because when they have that sense of humanity, they will not do some of the aggressive things that the male leaders are doing.

A new form of leadership

This goes far, far beyond setting quotas for how many women should be on the board of corporations and what some nations have attempted to do. It actually goes beyond to the point where women can create a new awareness of what true leadership means, what servant leadership in the Aquarian Age means. It is that you serve *all* of the people and not the elite. Therefore, women can present themselves as a more humane alternative to male leaders. In other words, you can transcend the situation you have now where many of the female leaders in politics or business have had to deny their femininity in order to get up in the system. They have to almost become as men. This is something that a new awareness can change and say: "This is passé, this is outdated, this is the dark Middle Ages. We demand a different form of society where there is room for compassion, there is room for humanity."

With this, my beloved, I have given you the impetus I wanted to release into the collective consciousness because there are people out there who are ready to receive it, and who simply need a jolt to get over that hump where they see: "Here is the next goal. Here is what we have been looking for. We could not see it, but here it is."

By some of you making the calls for this, they will be awakened, they will be empowered and there will be a shift towards not creating a power elite of women, but dethroning the power elite that has been there for far too long on this planet.

29 | INVOKING A SECOND FEMINIST REVOLUTION

In the name of the I AM THAT I AM, Jesus Christ, I use the authority that I have as a being in embodiment on earth to call upon the Goddess of Liberty to reinforce my calls and use my chakras to project the statements in this invocation into the collective consciousness and awaken people to the fact that we need a second feminist revolution to free society from the power elite. Awaken people to the reality that we are spiritual beings and that we can co-create a new future by working with the ascended masters. I especially call for …

[Make your own calls here.]

Part 1

1. Goddess of Liberty, shatter the energetic matrix that prevents people from seeing that historically the vast majority of people who have been part of the power elite have been men. Even today, there are relatively few women in the power elite or the leadership of society.

O Liberty now set me free
from devil's curse of poverty.

I blame not Mother for my lack,
O Blessed Mother, take me back.

**O Cosmic Mother Liberty,
conduct Abundance Symphony.
My highest service I now see,
abundance is now real for me.**

2. Goddess of Liberty, shatter the energetic matrix that prevents people from seeing that in general, women have not been part of the power elite, and it is important to consider why.

O Liberty, from distant shore,
I come with longing to be More.
I see abundance is a flow,
abundance consciousness I grow.

**O Cosmic Mother Liberty,
conduct Abundance Symphony.
My highest service I now see,
abundance is now real for me.**

3. Goddess of Liberty, shatter the energetic matrix that prevents people from seeing that this has something to do with the fact that many women are mothers. When people have given birth to children, we have a deeper personal relationship to our children.

O Liberty, expose the lie,
that limitations can me tie.
The Ma-ter light is not my foe,
true opulence it does bestow.

**O Cosmic Mother Liberty,
conduct Abundance Symphony.
My highest service I now see,
abundance is now real for me.**

4. Goddess of Liberty, shatter the energetic matrix that prevents people from seeing that it is easier for women to recognize the essential humanity

of their children. This makes it easier for women to recognize the essential humanity of all people.

> O Liberty, expose the plot,
> projected by the fallen lot.
> O Cosmic Mother, I now see,
> that Mother's not my enemy.

> **O Cosmic Mother Liberty,**
> **conduct Abundance Symphony.**
> **My highest service I now see,**
> **abundance is now real for me.**

5. Goddess of Liberty, shatter the energetic matrix that prevents people from seeing that this is part of the reason why men have traditionally been warriors. It is easier for a man to fall in love with an idea and forget about the basic humanity, so he becomes willing to kill other people for the sake of the idea.

> O Liberty, with opened eyes,
> I now reject the devil's lies.
> I now embrace the Mother realm,
> for I see Father at the helm.

> **O Cosmic Mother Liberty,**
> **conduct Abundance Symphony.**
> **My highest service I now see,**
> **abundance is now real for me.**

6. Goddess of Liberty, shatter the energetic matrix that prevents people from seeing that this is what the fallen beings knew when they came to earth and saw the psychological dynamic of men and women.

> O Liberty, a chalice pure,
> my lower bodies are for sure.
> Release through me your symphony,
> your gift of Cosmic Liberty.

O Cosmic Mother Liberty,
conduct Abundance Symphony.
My highest service I now see,
abundance is now real for me.

7. Goddess of Liberty, shatter the energetic matrix that prevents people from seeing that the fallen beings instantly saw how to take advantage of this by turning men into warriors. Then, they started the long process of putting women down.

O Liberty, the open door,
I am for Symphony of More.
In chakras mine light you release,
the flow of love shall never cease.

O Cosmic Mother Liberty,
conduct Abundance Symphony.
My highest service I now see,
abundance is now real for me.

8. Goddess of Liberty, shatter the energetic matrix that prevents people from seeing that the fallen beings are always seeking to divide the population into various groups and set them up against each other. The basic of these dualistic divisions is the division between men and women.

O Liberty, release the flow,
of opulence that you bestow.
For I am willing to receive,
the Golden Fleece that you now weave.

O Cosmic Mother Liberty,
conduct Abundance Symphony.
My highest service I now see,
abundance is now real for me.

9. Goddess of Liberty, shatter the energetic matrix that prevents people from seeing that the fallen being have divided the human population into two parts that are almost the same size. They have set them in an existential conflict against each other.

O Liberty, release the cure,
to free the tired and the poor.
The huddled masses are set free,
by loving Song of Liberty.

O Cosmic Mother Liberty,
conduct Abundance Symphony.
My highest service I now see,
abundance is now real for me.

Part 2

1. Goddess of Liberty, shatter the energetic matrix that prevents people from asking whether there has to be a psychological difference between men and women? Does there have to be the psychological difference that there is today?

O Liberty now set me free
from devil's curse of poverty.
I blame not Mother for my lack,
O Blessed Mother, take me back.

O Cosmic Mother Liberty,
conduct Abundance Symphony.
My highest service I now see,
abundance is now real for me.

2. Goddess of Liberty, shatter the energetic matrix that prevents people from seeing that there is a millennia-old effort by the fallen beings to manipulate people.

O Liberty, from distant shore,
I come with longing to be More.
I see abundance is a flow,
abundance consciousness I grow.

O Cosmic Mother Liberty,
conduct Abundance Symphony.
My highest service I now see,
abundance is now real for me.

3. Goddess of Liberty, shatter the energetic matrix that prevents people from seeing that without the manipulation of the fallen beings, men would not have stepped into the roles that we have seen throughout history and see today. Women would not have stepped into the roles for women that have been defined throughout history.

O Liberty, expose the lie,
that limitations can me tie.
The Ma-ter light is not my foe,
true opulence it does bestow.

O Cosmic Mother Liberty,
conduct Abundance Symphony.
My highest service I now see,
abundance is now real for me.

4. Goddess of Liberty, shatter the energetic matrix that prevents people from seeing that it is not human nature that men behave a certain way and women behave a certain way. It is not inevitable that men must act *this* way and women must act *that* way.

O Liberty, expose the plot,
projected by the fallen lot.
O Cosmic Mother, I now see,
that Mother's not my enemy.

O Cosmic Mother Liberty,
conduct Abundance Symphony.
My highest service I now see,
abundance is now real for me.

5. Goddess of Liberty, shatter the energetic matrix that prevents people from seeing that the fallen beings have used the physical condition of childbearing, and they have created an ideological overlay, projecting it

upon this and saying: "Men are like this because that is the nature of men, and women are like this because that is the nature of women."

O Liberty, with opened eyes,
I now reject the devil's lies.
I now embrace the Mother realm,
for I see Father at the helm.

**O Cosmic Mother Liberty,
conduct Abundance Symphony.
My highest service I now see,
abundance is now real for me.**

6. Goddess of Liberty, shatter the energetic matrix that prevents people from seeing that although psychologist will say that there are certain characteristics of male psychology and certain characteristics of female psychology, this is not something ordained by nature, created by God or mandated by some physical difference between male and female brains.

O Liberty, a chalice pure,
my lower bodies are for sure.
Release through me your symphony,
your gift of Cosmic Liberty.

**O Cosmic Mother Liberty,
conduct Abundance Symphony.
My highest service I now see,
abundance is now real for me.**

7. Goddess of Liberty, shatter the energetic matrix that prevents people from seeing that this is a created condition, a manipulated condition. The fallen beings have attempted to create a label for what it means to be a man and a label for what it means to be a woman. They have done this in such a way that the two sexes are in many ways in opposition to each other. This is a completely artificial condition.

O Liberty, the open door,
I am for Symphony of More.

In chakras mine light you release,
the flow of love shall never cease.

**O Cosmic Mother Liberty,
conduct Abundance Symphony.
My highest service I now see,
abundance is now real for me.**

8. Goddess of Liberty, shatter the energetic matrix that prevents people from seeing that we have the potential to free ourselves from these artificially inserted conditions for how we should be as a man and how we should be as a woman.

O Liberty, release the flow,
of opulence that you bestow.
For I am willing to receive,
the Golden Fleece that you now weave.

**O Cosmic Mother Liberty,
conduct Abundance Symphony.
My highest service I now see,
abundance is now real for me.**

9. Goddess of Liberty, shatter the energetic matrix that prevents people from seeing that when we free ourselves from this, we will be able to have an entirely different relationship to the opposite sex or even to our own sex, to our own role in whatever type of body we are in.

O Liberty, release the cure,
to free the tired and the poor.
The huddled masses are set free,
by loving Song of Liberty.

**O Cosmic Mother Liberty,
conduct Abundance Symphony.
My highest service I now see,
abundance is now real for me.**

Part 3

1. Goddess of Liberty, shatter the energetic matrix that prevents people from seeing that there are no people that always embody in male bodies or in female bodies. There will be some switching around. There may be some people who have for several lifetimes been in the same type of body, but all have experienced both sexes.

> O Liberty now set me free
> from devil's curse of poverty.
> I blame not Mother for my lack,
> O Blessed Mother, take me back.

> **O Cosmic Mother Liberty,**
> **conduct Abundance Symphony.**
> **My highest service I now see,**
> **abundance is now real for me.**

2. Goddess of Liberty, shatter the energetic matrix that prevents people from seeing that we start out as the Conscious You, which has a point-like sense of identity. In a point, there is no room for division, there is no room for two sides, one male and one female.

> O Liberty, from distant shore,
> I come with longing to be More.
> I see abundance is a flow,
> abundance consciousness I grow.

> **O Cosmic Mother Liberty,**
> **conduct Abundance Symphony.**
> **My highest service I now see,**
> **abundance is now real for me.**

3. Goddess of Liberty, shatter the energetic matrix that prevents people from seeing that the Conscious You is neither male nor female, it is neutral when it takes on a physical body.

O Liberty, expose the lie,
that limitations can me tie.
The Ma-ter light is not my foe,
true opulence it does bestow.

**O Cosmic Mother Liberty,
conduct Abundance Symphony.
My highest service I now see,
abundance is now real for me.**

4. Goddess of Liberty, shatter the energetic matrix that prevents people from seeing that the Conscious You can over time build certain structures in the identity, mental and emotional body relating to both sexes. When it is in a female body, it ties in to the structures that have been built in past lifetimes and we think we have to behave a certain way as a woman.

O Liberty, expose the plot,
projected by the fallen lot.
O Cosmic Mother, I now see,
that Mother's not my enemy.

**O Cosmic Mother Liberty,
conduct Abundance Symphony.
My highest service I now see,
abundance is now real for me.**

5. Goddess of Liberty, shatter the energetic matrix that prevents people from seeing that the underlying spiritual significance of the Women's Liberation Movement is not so much a matter of challenging the outer things, the physical discrimination, although that is also necessary.

O Liberty, with opened eyes,
I now reject the devil's lies.
I now embrace the Mother realm,
for I see Father at the helm.

**O Cosmic Mother Liberty,
conduct Abundance Symphony.**

**My highest service I now see,
abundance is now real for me.**

6. Goddess of Liberty, shatter the energetic matrix that prevents people from seeing that the real underlying significance of women's liberation is to help women see that they are not women. We are a spiritual beings inhabiting female bodies this time around.

O Liberty, a chalice pure,
my lower bodies are for sure.
Release through me your symphony,
your gift of Cosmic Liberty.

**O Cosmic Mother Liberty,
conduct Abundance Symphony.
My highest service I now see,
abundance is now real for me.**

7. Goddess of Liberty, shatter the energetic matrix that prevents people from seeing that all of this historical, cultural, ideological overlay that has been put upon women is artificial.

O Liberty, the open door,
I am for Symphony of More.
In chakras mine light you release,
the flow of love shall never cease.

**O Cosmic Mother Liberty,
conduct Abundance Symphony.
My highest service I now see,
abundance is now real for me.**

8. Goddess of Liberty, shatter the energetic matrix that prevents people from seeing that we can choose to consciously, systematically separate ourselves from it, until we reach a state where we can be at peace with being in embodiment on earth and with being in a female body, or in a male body.

O Liberty, release the flow,
of opulence that you bestow.

For I am willing to receive,
the Golden Fleece that you now weave.

**O Cosmic Mother Liberty,
conduct Abundance Symphony.
My highest service I now see,
abundance is now real for me.**

9. Goddess of Liberty, shatter the energetic matrix that prevents people from seeing that these cultural roles, historical roles, for men and women have been created by the fallen beings. They have defined that men are the outgoing aggressive sex.

O Liberty, release the cure,
to free the tired and the poor.
The huddled masses are set free,
by loving Song of Liberty.

**O Cosmic Mother Liberty,
conduct Abundance Symphony.
My highest service I now see,
abundance is now real for me.**

Part 4

1. Goddess of Liberty, shatter the energetic matrix that prevents people from seeing that most of the fallen beings who take embodiment always try to manipulate themselves into a male body so they can more easily attain a position of power.

O Liberty now set me free
from devil's curse of poverty.
I blame not Mother for my lack,
O Blessed Mother, take me back.

**O Cosmic Mother Liberty,
conduct Abundance Symphony.**

My highest service I now see,
abundance is now real for me.

2. Goddess of Liberty, shatter the energetic matrix that prevents people from seeing that for the general population, the male role has become so strong that most people think that when they are men, they have to live up to a certain image.

O Liberty, from distant shore,
I come with longing to be More.
I see abundance is a flow,
abundance consciousness I grow.

O Cosmic Mother Liberty,
conduct Abundance Symphony.
My highest service I now see,
abundance is now real for me.

3. Goddess of Liberty, shatter the energetic matrix that prevents people from seeing that we are programmed to think men have to be more aggressive. Men have to take on this particular role.

O Liberty, expose the lie,
that limitations can me tie.
The Ma-ter light is not my foe,
true opulence it does bestow.

O Cosmic Mother Liberty,
conduct Abundance Symphony.
My highest service I now see,
abundance is now real for me.

4. Goddess of Liberty, shatter the energetic matrix that prevents people from seeing that the effect of this has been that men are more susceptible to being manipulated by the power elite. Men are more susceptible to being manipulated into going to war and killing other men.

O Liberty, expose the plot,
projected by the fallen lot.

O Cosmic Mother, I now see,
that Mother's not my enemy.

**O Cosmic Mother Liberty,
conduct Abundance Symphony.
My highest service I now see,
abundance is now real for me.**

5. Goddess of Liberty, shatter the energetic matrix that prevents people from seeing that the fallen beings have created an incredibly dense cloud hanging over the planet, over the collective consciousness, that overpowers many men to think this is what you have to do as a man. If your country is attacked, you have to be a soldier, you have to defend your country, give your life for your country.

O Liberty, with opened eyes,
I now reject the devil's lies.
I now embrace the Mother realm,
for I see Father at the helm.

**O Cosmic Mother Liberty,
conduct Abundance Symphony.
My highest service I now see,
abundance is now real for me.**

6. Goddess of Liberty, shatter the energetic matrix that prevents people from seeing that for humanity to become free from the power elite, the power elite cannot do it. And although men *can* do it, men in general are not as likely to do it as women.

O Liberty, a chalice pure,
my lower bodies are for sure.
Release through me your symphony,
your gift of Cosmic Liberty.

**O Cosmic Mother Liberty,
conduct Abundance Symphony.
My highest service I now see,
abundance is now real for me.**

7. Goddess of Liberty, shatter the energetic matrix that prevents people from seeing that the biggest potential for liberating humanity from the fallen beings, or the power elite, is women who connect to the essential humanity they see in their children.

O Liberty, the open door,
I am for Symphony of More.
In chakras mine light you release,
the flow of love shall never cease.

O Cosmic Mother Liberty,
conduct Abundance Symphony.
My highest service I now see,
abundance is now real for me.

8. Goddess of Liberty, shatter the energetic matrix that prevents people from seeing that women need to say: "Do I want my children to grow up in a society dominated and manipulated by this elite of narcissists who have no concern for my children whatsoever, for whom my children are just numbers, they are cannon fodder? They have no respect for them whatsoever. Why would I want these kind of people to lead my society?"

O Liberty, release the flow,
of opulence that you bestow.
For I am willing to receive,
the Golden Fleece that you now weave.

O Cosmic Mother Liberty,
conduct Abundance Symphony.
My highest service I now see,
abundance is now real for me.

9. Goddess of Liberty, shatter the energetic matrix that prevents people from seeing that we need a second feminist revolution that is at a higher level, has a higher awareness of what is really at stake.

O Liberty, release the cure,
to free the tired and the poor.

The huddled masses are set free,
by loving Song of Liberty.

O Cosmic Mother Liberty,
conduct Abundance Symphony.
My highest service I now see,
abundance is now real for me.

Part 5

1. Goddess of Liberty, shatter the energetic matrix that prevents people from seeing that the first feminist revolution was based on the level of the collective consciousness. The collective consciousness was so trapped in the black-and-white dualistic thinking that, as in many revolutions, there had to be an enemy.

O Liberty now set me free
from devil's curse of poverty.
I blame not Mother for my lack,
O Blessed Mother, take me back.

O Cosmic Mother Liberty,
conduct Abundance Symphony.
My highest service I now see,
abundance is now real for me.

2. Goddess of Liberty, shatter the energetic matrix that prevents people from seeing that there had to be an opponent women were fighting and it became men.

O Liberty, from distant shore,
I come with longing to be More.
I see abundance is a flow,
abundance consciousness I grow.

O Cosmic Mother Liberty,
conduct Abundance Symphony.

**My highest service I now see,
abundance is now real for me.**

3. Goddess of Liberty, shatter the energetic matrix that prevents people from seeing that the collective consciousness is still at a level where many people need an opponent, they need someone to blame for creating the problem. For the second feminist revolution, instead of men in general, this could be the men in the power elite.

O Liberty, expose the lie,
that limitations can me tie.
The Ma-ter light is not my foe,
true opulence it does bestow.

**O Cosmic Mother Liberty,
conduct Abundance Symphony.
My highest service I now see,
abundance is now real for me.**

4. Goddess of Liberty, shatter the energetic matrix that prevents people from seeing that we do not need women to go out and fight them with physical means, but we would fight them with knowledge, with awareness, with demands for change.

O Liberty, expose the plot,
projected by the fallen lot.
O Cosmic Mother, I now see,
that Mother's not my enemy.

**O Cosmic Mother Liberty,
conduct Abundance Symphony.
My highest service I now see,
abundance is now real for me.**

5. Goddess of Liberty, shatter the energetic matrix that prevents people from seeing that the highest possible reaction is to not see the power elite as an enemy. Yet this is not what the majority of women can do at this point.

O Liberty, with opened eyes,
I now reject the devil's lies.
I now embrace the Mother realm,
for I see Father at the helm.

**O Cosmic Mother Liberty,
conduct Abundance Symphony.
My highest service I now see,
abundance is now real for me.**

6. Goddess of Liberty, shatter the energetic matrix that prevents people from seeing the potential for an awakening to a second feminist revolution that would identify that the real problem in society is the power elite.

O Liberty, a chalice pure,
my lower bodies are for sure.
Release through me your symphony,
your gift of Cosmic Liberty.

**O Cosmic Mother Liberty,
conduct Abundance Symphony.
My highest service I now see,
abundance is now real for me.**

7. Goddess of Liberty, shatter the energetic matrix that prevents people from seeing that members of the elite are the ones who are manipulating society, who are upholding these traditional roles for men and women, causing the men to go to war.

O Liberty, the open door,
I am for Symphony of More.
In chakras mine light you release,
the flow of love shall never cease.

**O Cosmic Mother Liberty,
conduct Abundance Symphony.
My highest service I now see,
abundance is now real for me.**

8. Goddess of Liberty, shatter the energetic matrix that prevents people from seeing that the power elite is causing women to be confined to the roles they are confined to as mothers and housewives and all of the abuse that has been attached to that throughout the centuries.

O Liberty, release the flow,
of opulence that you bestow.
For I am willing to receive,
the Golden Fleece that you now weave.

O Cosmic Mother Liberty,
conduct Abundance Symphony.
My highest service I now see,
abundance is now real for me.

9. Goddess of Liberty, shatter the energetic matrix that prevents people from receiving ideas from the ascended masters on how this revolution could be taken to a higher level and become more aware, more based on the basic humanity.

O Liberty, release the cure,
to free the tired and the poor.
The huddled masses are set free,
by loving Song of Liberty.

O Cosmic Mother Liberty,
conduct Abundance Symphony.
My highest service I now see,
abundance is now real for me.

Part 6

1. Goddess of Liberty, shatter the energetic matrix that prevents people from seeing that it is not ideal to label the fallen beings as enemies. When we connect to the basic humanity, it is necessary to say: "But there are people who do not have that basic humanity."

O Liberty now set me free
from devil's curse of poverty.
I blame not Mother for my lack,
O Blessed Mother, take me back.

**O Cosmic Mother Liberty,
conduct Abundance Symphony.
My highest service I now see,
abundance is now real for me.**

2. Goddess of Liberty, shatter the energetic matrix that prevents people from saying: "The elite are the leaders that abuse us, that manipulate us because they have no humanity. They don't care about us and we can't allow them to lead. We don't need to go out and kill them. We need to create a society where there is an awareness that these are not the leaders we want."

O Liberty, from distant shore,
I come with longing to be More.
I see abundance is a flow,
abundance consciousness I grow.

**O Cosmic Mother Liberty,
conduct Abundance Symphony.
My highest service I now see,
abundance is now real for me.**

3. Goddess of Liberty, shatter the energetic matrix that prevents people from seeing that women's liberation could be expanded to women liberating society from the dominance of this male elite, male elitism.

O Liberty, expose the lie,
that limitations can me tie.
The Ma-ter light is not my foe,
true opulence it does bestow.

**O Cosmic Mother Liberty,
conduct Abundance Symphony.**

**My highest service I now see,
abundance is now real for me.**

4. Goddess of Liberty, shatter the energetic matrix that prevents people from seeing that when we look at society realistically, it is not all men that are suppressing women deliberately and aggressively. It is the leaders in the power elite that have created and are upholding the roles that are causing the suppression of women.

O Liberty, expose the plot,
projected by the fallen lot.
O Cosmic Mother, I now see,
that Mother's not my enemy.

**O Cosmic Mother Liberty,
conduct Abundance Symphony.
My highest service I now see,
abundance is now real for me.**

5. Goddess of Liberty, shatter the energetic matrix that prevents people from seeing that as part of the revolution it is necessary to demand that more women come into leadership positions, because when they have that sense of humanity, they will not do some of the aggressive things that the male leaders are doing.

O Liberty, with opened eyes,
I now reject the devil's lies.
I now embrace the Mother realm,
for I see Father at the helm.

**O Cosmic Mother Liberty,
conduct Abundance Symphony.
My highest service I now see,
abundance is now real for me.**

6. Goddess of Liberty, shatter the energetic matrix that prevents people from seeing that this goes far beyond setting quotas for how many women should be on the board of corporations. Women can create a new

awareness of what true leadership means, what servant leadership in the Aquarian Age means. It is that we serve *all* of the people and not the elite.

> O Liberty, a chalice pure,
> my lower bodies are for sure.
> Release through me your symphony,
> your gift of Cosmic Liberty.

> **O Cosmic Mother Liberty,**
> **conduct Abundance Symphony.**
> **My highest service I now see,**
> **abundance is now real for me.**

7. Goddess of Liberty, shatter the energetic matrix that prevents people from seeing that women can present themselves as a more humane alternative to male leaders. We can transcend the situation where many of the female leaders in politics or business have had to deny their femininity in order to get up in the system. They have to almost become as men.

> O Liberty, the open door,
> I am for Symphony of More.
> In chakras mine light you release,
> the flow of love shall never cease.

> **O Cosmic Mother Liberty,**
> **conduct Abundance Symphony.**
> **My highest service I now see,**
> **abundance is now real for me.**

8. Goddess of Liberty, shatter the energetic matrix that prevents people from seeing that we can change this and say: "This is passé, this is outdated, this is the dark Middle Ages. We demand a different form of society where there is room for compassion, there is room for humanity."

> O Liberty, release the flow,
> of opulence that you bestow.
> For I am willing to receive,
> the Golden Fleece that you now weave.

**O Cosmic Mother Liberty,
conduct Abundance Symphony.
My highest service I now see,
abundance is now real for me.**

9. Goddess of Liberty, shatter the energetic matrix that prevents people from getting over that hump where they see: "Here is the next goal. Here is what we have been looking for. We could not see it, but here it is."

O Liberty, release the cure,
to free the tired and the poor.
The huddled masses are set free,
by loving Song of Liberty.

**O Cosmic Mother Liberty,
conduct Abundance Symphony.
My highest service I now see,
abundance is now real for me.**

Sealing

In the name of the I AM THAT I AM, I accept that Archangel Michael, Astrea and Shiva form an impenetrable shield around myself and all constructive people, sealing us from all fear-based energies in all four octaves. I accept that the Light of God is consuming and transforming all fear-based energies that make up the dark forces working against ending the era of elitism on earth!

30 | HOW THE ELITE LIMITS IMAGINATION

I AM the Ascended Master Gautama Buddha. It is my joy, it is my privilege, to give the sealing dictation for this conference.

I wish to give you some thoughts based on what other masters have told you. I wish to reach back to Padmasambhava and his concept that the fallen beings have managed to deceive and control people by creating all of these labels. What would be the response of the fallen beings, if they read that dictation? They would say: "But are you not labeling us by calling us fallen beings? Are you not labeling us by calling us a power elite? Are you not doing the exact same thing that you are accusing us of doing?" Such is the serpentine mind, the serpentine logic. Whatever you try to say about the power elite in order to expose them, they will attempt to turn it around and use it against you. Whatever source, and you can see this in history so many times, where whenever an individual or group came up with an exposure of the lies and the manipulation of the power elite, they would seek to attack that person in return, seek to discredit them, and thereby supposedly counteract what was said.

Now, you have a concept that has been going around in the collective consciousness for a very, very long time, the concept of "truth." There is this idea that many people subscribe to, that certain ideas or certain expressions can be the truth, can be true. You will see so many Christians, who of course believe that the Bible is the literal word of God and therefore is true. You will see Buddhists who believe the same about at least some of the Buddhist scriptures, not necessarily that they are the word of God, but they represent some ultimate truth. You see in Islam the same thing about the Koran. You see even scientific materialists who essentially believe the same about not only the discoveries of science, but a materialistic interpretation of those discoveries.

Many, many people, including many ascended master students, have looked at the situation in the New Testament where Jesus is facing the Roman authorities, and Pontius Pilate makes the statement: "What is truth?" Many have looked down upon this and said he obviously did not recognize Jesus, but actually, from a certain perspective, that was a very wise statement or question.

The limitations of words

Many, many people in the world could make tremendous progress if they would ask themselves the question: "What is truth?" Or perhaps a little more nuanced question: "What is my concept of truth, my current concept of truth?" Many would therefore realize that their current concept of truth is just a label. In many cases it is a label created by the power elite specifically to deceive people. As we said, you create the label, you create a superstructure that supports that label, such as the word "God," you create a structure about how you define God, and then you project with enough force and authority that this is the absolute truth about God. This causes people to not question that expression, that label. If they would be willing to question it, they could make tremendous progress. As Padmasambhava said, this labeling everything is the primary tool used by the fallen beings to deceive people, to trap them in some false belief that they cannot get out of because they will not question the label. They think it is the truth.

As we have said before, the more mature view is to realize that you live on a planet that is dense. It has a high density of matter, it has a high density of the collective consciousness. This affects everything on earth, it affects your physical bodies, causes a lowering of the lifespan, causes many diseases. It causes many other limitations that you experience. Why would it be so difficult to realize that the density of the planet also causes limitations to what you can do with words? Everything else on earth is limited so why would words not also be limited? In other words, the concept that you could formulate a worded statement that was an absolute truth or the word of God, is a rather limited understanding of the reality of life on this planet. God would never even attempt to give people a worded statement about itself, because it is clear for any ascended being, how much words have been misused throughout history, how much words are open to interpretation.

Now, of course you can say: "But there are certain words that refer to specific things. There is apples and oranges." When you say the word apple, pretty much everyone knows what you are talking about, and this is precisely the point. Words on a dense planet like earth are a means for communicating practical things. You have a need to communicate about practical everyday matters, and you have the need to have a certain precision. When you are talking about apples, people know what you mean with the word apple. They know it is not an orange, is not a pear, is not a banana and so forth. So this is the practical aspect of words. There is little room for interpretation. You know very well that words have some limitations when it comes to describing more complex aspects. For example, most people still say today: "The sun rises in the east, moves across the sky and sets in the west." But you have known for several centuries that the sun does not rise and set. It is the earth that is spinning on its axis. The sun does not do anything. It is what you see from your vantage point on earth that changes. You see that even here, even though you have a physical event, words cannot describe that event accurately, at least not the way most people use words.

What then happens when we come to more complex ideas? Is it not obvious that there is a limitation to what can be expressed in words? Take a very commonly used word, at least by many religious or spiritual people: "soul." If you were to look at the many different philosophies or religions out there that use the word soul, you will find quite a big range of how they define it. You will find many, many people who use the word without clearly defining it, not really knowing what they are talking about. They just assume, many people assume that when they say the word soul, everybody who hears it will have the same interpretation of it as they do. When you begin to ponder these things, you realize that words should be, as the saying goes, taken with a grain of salt. You should not actually assume that words can precisely express ideas.

Why then is it so that you have an entire culture, both in the West and elsewhere, that is based on using words to describe ideas? Well, it is because the fallen beings have created these labels, and they use the labels to stop people from thinking more deeply. The label is always a word, such as the word "God." It is underpinned by some structure of what, over the course of a long time, has been defined as God, and then it is projected with this energy that causes many people to simply be overwhelmed by the energy. They feel it as an authority, and therefore they shut down their minds and accept that this is what it means, this is what God is like. The purpose of using words in this way is to get people to accept the word at face value and not use the faculties that people have to investigate deeper, to look behind the word, behind the label, and see what is really there.

Looking behind words

What faculties do you have for looking behind the words? Well, you have critical thinking. Even the analytical mind can be used to some degree here, to think logically, to look for inconsistencies, to compare this to something else, and to therefore see: "Is there a consistent definition of a particular word." Does it actually make sense what the words say, how they describe a certain idea, what does the idea actually mean? You can ask clarifying questions.

Many people who are overpowered by these authoritative labels, they go into a state of mental paralysis where they do not ask those kinds of questions. This particularly happens when you have an institution or system, such as a particular religion or the scientific establishment. How many of those who grew up Catholic have asked a question, only to hear from the priest: "It's a mystery, my child," thereby discouraging you from continuing to ask these questions? How many of you in school have asked a question, and the teacher could not answer it, either because he did not know, he was not a scientist, or because Materialism has no answer for it? Again, you were discouraged from asking the questions that the authority figures, from parents to teachers, to the leaders of society, could not answer. This is one faculty, using critical thinking to evaluate and ask further questions. You are going beyond the label, you are going beyond the word, and asking: "What does the word actually mean? What do those words actually say? What kind of an idea are they actually expressing?" You are going beyond the words, going beyond the label.

The other faculty you have is the one that we call intuition. It is actually a faculty that can help you gain understanding and insight, but it is really a faculty that gives you an experience. What do I mean with an experience, are there not many types of experiences? Well, certainly. As an example, just consider this: How would you use words to describe the taste of an apple? A very common experience, in fact so common that you would never need to describe the taste of an apple because everybody has had the experience. Just ponder how you could possibly describe the taste of an apple to someone who had never had the experience. It is virtually impossible to use words to convey that experience. Even as common of a thing as the taste of an apple is an experience that is beyond words.

What the fallen beings do not want people to realize is that when it comes to absolutely any aspect of life, whether it is a practical thing, a physical thing or an abstract idea, it is possible to have an intuitive or mystical experience where you directly experience the essence of the phenomenon beyond the words used to name it, label it or describe it. If you go back to Plato and his idea that there, beyond the material world, was a higher realm of ideal forms, this is what we have called the emotional, mental and identity realms. Let us go with Plato's description: There is a higher realm in which there exists certain ideal forms, and these forms are what become manifest as the things you see in the physical world. In other words, you have a physical thing called an apple, but the apple is a manifestation of, an expression of, this ideal form that exists in a higher realm. It contains the essence of an apple. It is actually possible to have an intuitive experience where you experience that ideal form, the essence of an apple. The same with any complex abstract idea, you can have an intuitive experience whereby you experience the essence of the idea, the matrix of the idea. This means you can actually then experience: Where does the idea come from? Where did it originate? When you sharpen your intuition in this way, you can come to the point where you can read an idea in a book, and you can sense intuitively: Oh that idea came from the emotional realm, from the astral plane. Or that idea comes from the mental realm, or that idea comes from the lower identity realm, or that idea comes from the higher identity realm or the spiritual realm. You can sense this by intuitively feeling the vibration, the vibrational matrix of the idea. Therefore, you can know whether it is a valid idea, whether it came from a higher source or a lower source. You may not be able to explain this in words, but you can know it.

They are many spiritual people who have had their intuitive faculties open from childhood. There are many more who had them open during childhood, and then closed them during the teenage years due to the influence from the outside, whether from a religion or from Materialism that discouraged them from using these faculties. There are many spiritual people who can pick a book from a bookshelf and sense whether it comes from a higher or lower source, sense the purity of the ideas in that book. You can also cultivate the ability to read a book and sense that, this idea expressed here has a lower vibration, but that idea expressed in the next paragraph has a higher vibration. This then, is an ability that allows you (that allows all people, because all people have it if they are willing to use it) to go beyond these labels that are created by using words and projecting that they have a specific interpretation.

Words cannot describe God

If you cannot, my beloved, know the taste of an apple through words, how could you possibly know the nature of God through words? Would you not say that the Creator is more complex than an apple? I certainly would think so. Is it not non-constructive to think that any description of the Creator given by words on this dense planet, could be accurate or adequate? You realize here a very simple truth: What the fallen beings have done is to create these labels, "God," and then there is the overlay of what God is. There is the intense energy momentum that has been built up over thousands of years that overpowers people so they dare not question what God is. They dare not gainsay God, they dare not challenge. They are not challenging God, you are challenging a worded expression, an interpretation.

What this does is, it prevents people from ever going beyond that label, and the understanding of the concept embedded in the label. They simply do not think about it. When you accept this matrix, this process, these labels, you are trapped by those who have defined the labels. You cannot go beyond the minds of the people or beings who define the label, you are stuck in the label. That is why societies, for centuries, can be stuck at a certain level, as Europe was stuck in the Catholic mindset for over a thousand years. It could not break out of that stalemate of the kings, the noble class and the Catholic clergy holding the majority of the population as slaves, virtual slaves, even in a physical sense, as slaves. You see the same thing many times throughout history. You see the same thing today where science is stuck in Materialism, where the economy is stuck in capitalism, thinking you have a free market when you do not.

The realization you can come to is that, if you really want to know, if you really want to know anything, or know about anything, you need to go beyond the word, you need to go beyond the label. You need to have that inner experience where you experience the essence of the idea. This is mental freedom. This is the only way to mental freedom: To use critical thinking and intuition to free yourself from these interpretations that are so powerful in the collective consciousness.

What are the interpretations based on? Many times, they are based on assumptions. Go back to when people believed the earth was the center of the universe. This was a very, very strong belief. You can scarcely imagine how strong of a momentum there was in the collective consciousness behind this belief. What was it based on? An assumption. Not on actual investigation, not on a higher experience, because you can intuitively experience that the earth is not the center of the universe because it revolves around the sun. You can intuitively experience that the sun is not the center of the universe. You can intuitively experience that the universe does not have a center because the universe is in a process of unfolding and therefore has no geographical center. Despite the concept of the Big Bang, where everything started from a singularity, and supposedly that singularity is the geographical center of the universe, and all of the galaxies revolve around it, this is not an accurate observation. You can intuitively realize that the universe is not expanding from one point, from a singularity.

The universe was manifested simultaneously as a spherical shape that is constantly evolving and pulsating. It had myriad origins, multiple origins, there was not one point from which all exploded. There were many points from which the matrix of the universe was lowered in vibration through the four levels of the material world, and therefore came into the physical octave as a whole, not as the whole it is today, because it has been in the process of evolving ever since. It did not come into manifestation as a singularity. This is what we in Buddhism call the interdependent originations where everything is connected.

Once you begin to have these kinds of intuitive experiences, which many of you have had, then you can see beyond these labels and you can realize that words are not the ultimate expression of truth. This means that you can also see that if the fallen beings say: "Well, the ascended masters are just using labels. They are trying to do the same that we are doing, they are just projecting out these labels: 'fallen beings,' 'ascension,' 'higher spheres,' this and that." Where in the teachings of this dispensation have we said that our words represent an absolute truth, a final statement? Where have we said that you should blindly believe in the words and never strive to have a direct experience beyond the words? Nowhere. So the difference here is that when we give a worded teaching, we have to use words, as words can be used, given the density of earth. That is our only option. Whereas the fallen beings never want you to go beyond the words and the labels they have defined, we have again and again and again said that you need to go beyond the words, you need to reach for the direct experience. Otherwise, you will not know truth because truth can be known, not through words, not through the most fanciful theory you could ever come up with, but only through that direct experience that some mystics called gnosis, the unity between the knower and the known.

The endless game of arguing

Going a little bit further, what is one possible antidote to the duality consciousness, the division created by the fallen beings, of splitting people up into these groups that are characterized by a label, and therefore, by the definition of that label, set in conflict with each other? We have called it the *essential,* or the *basic* humanity. I called it, twenty five hundred years ago, the Buddha nature. Jesus called it the Christ consciousness, or the kingdom of God. You can have a direct intuitive experience of your own essence, that you are more than the physical body, that you are more than the outer mind, that you are more than your thoughts, your feelings, even your sense of identity.

When you have that experience, it is beyond words and it cannot be counteracted by words, because you will not believe the words that deny the experience. The experience itself was more real than the experience you get by reading or listening to words. This is the connecting link between people, and when you have that connecting link, when you first experience it for yourself and then begin to experience it in others, then you can overcome that division. Now, you realize that your brother is not a Muslim, or a man, or a Democrat, or a Republican, or a German, or an Italian, or this or that. Your brothers and sisters all have the essential nature that you have, that humanity have, that common link that you have. This is really the only way to counteract the division.

Of course, you can do something with words. You can come up with teachings. That is why we give teachings in words, in order to give people something where they can use their critical minds, their critical thinking, they can ask questions, they can find answers, deeper explanations than they have found before. Much can be achieved by this. Ultimately, unless people go beyond the outer teaching, and have that experience and therefore connect at that deeper level, as many of you have connected during this conference, then it will not have the maximum impact. The reason for this is that the fallen beings are very clever at using words, they have a very old momentum on using words. There is hardly any statement made in words that cannot be either counteracted by another statement made with words or put into question by another statement. Or you can do what the fallen beings sometimes do, turn any statement into a label and then come up with a counter label.

There is this entire game that has been played for many, many millennia on this planet where people have been arguing back and forth. They have been attempting to come up with the ultimate argument, the ultimate theory, the ultimate religion. You can see how much energy has been spent on this, how much this has pulled people's attention into fighting this battle of ideas, this battle for the domination of ideas. Consider even today, how many intellectual people are trapped in this almost endless game of arguing back and forth about ideas, instead of focusing on developing some ideas that could actually help society progress and help alleviate suffering.

Do you really need to know what happens in the core of a neutron star 750 million light years away, when there are people that are starving to death every day on this planet? Would it not be more constructive to use your intellectual resources on trying to overcome world hunger than figuring out these rather abstract questions about the universe? Would it not be more constructive that instead of spending billions of dollars building ever more powerful telescopes, or ever more powerful particle accelerators, that you spent that money on alleviating human suffering? I will tell you that if you could get out of your intellectual minds and use your intuitive minds, you could have an intuitive experience of what happens in a neutron star, or what happens at the level of the subatomic, so-called, particles. You could know this intuitively without having to prove it through technology that was released by Saint Germain specifically to address these practical problems of human suffering. Instead of trying to prove Materialism, which is just a label, you could go beyond the labels and actually do something for humanity.

Uniting the people to remove the elite

Now, I wish to give just a few remarks here on the topic of interdependent originations. One of the effects of the duality consciousness is, as we have said, that it produces this illusion that you are a separate being. You experience through the duality consciousness that you are a separate being, you are not connected to anyone else. This is what the fallen beings have used very cleverly because they make themselves believe, as Stalin for example believed, that he could kill millions of people, and because he was separated from them (he was superior in a special category), this would not affect himself. More than that, it also serves to uphold this illusion that humanity can be divided into two classes, the power elite and the population. How will you ultimately overcome this division? How will you ultimately raise the collective consciousness until you reach the point where the fallen beings can no longer embody on the planet? Well, you can do this only by creating that unity between people.

Again, we talk about the basic humanity, but what does the basic humanity mean, what is an aspect of it? Well, one aspect of it, is what has been discovered by science, namely, that everything is interconnected. If you take two subatomic particles and send them off into different directions, near the speed of light, and you can observe that a change in one particle instantly leads to a change in the other, then you must conclude that the particles are connected. If two subatomic particles, the smallest aspect of the material universe or octave, are connected, does it not stand to reason that everything in the physical universe is connected, that all people are connected, that you are all part of the fabric of life, you are all part of the collective consciousness of earth, you are all part of the energy system on earth?

If all people are connected, does it not stand to reason that whatever one person does affects the whole, and that the whole affects every person? When you then realize that there is that connection, you can gain a different perspective on elitism because you realize that the elite is not set apart from the people. They have created the illusion, the appearance, that they are set apart from the people. In other words, they have created the illusion that they belong to a separate category, they are superior to the people, they are separated from the people. The kings live in their castles, the people live in their cottages, there is no connection there, other than the people must do what the kings bid them to do.

When you begin to realize that everything is connected, you realize that the power elite can rule the population in one way only: by dividing you up into all these different factions and keeping you divided. The power elite may seem to have power, they may seem to have authority, but what they do not have is numbers. In any society that is ruled by the elite, the elite is always the minority and the population is the majority. As long as the population is divided, as long as people are even divided in themselves, as long as the population is divided into all these factions, they cannot come together and say: "We have had enough of the elite." Once you begin to overcome that separation and connect, then the elite, the fallen beings, will face a choice: Will they unite with the people or will they leave the planet? Because they cannot remain if the people are united. Of course, the fallen beings cannot unite with the people because they will not get out of the consciousness of separation. In order to get out of the consciousness of separation, they would have to give up the sense of identity that they are the superior elite, and that is what they will not give up. When the people come together, when there is a certain unification, a certain unity, among the people, the elite cannot exist anymore on the planet. You can see how this process was begun with the advent of democracies where the people reached a certain level of unity, and then the power elite that was there during the feudal age, they had to retreat from that country. You may still have remnants in terms of the royal houses of Europe, but they have no power over the people because the people are united to a higher degree than they were before.

Removing the elite by raising consciousness

The other thing you can realize is that if everything is interdependent, everything is connected, where is that connection? Is it in the physical octave? Well, obviously not. You are sitting here all in this room together, but any of you could decide to walk out of here at any moment. Your physical body is not connected to the group with a direct link. Where is the connection? Well, it is in consciousness, it is at the emotional level, at the mental level and at the identity level.

If all people are connected through consciousness, what do you have to do to change the equation on earth? You have to raise your own consciousness because you will pull up on everybody else. When enough people do this, there will be a change even in the physical. That is how democracy was brought into the physical, enough people came to the point where they said: "We have had enough of this dictatorial form of leadership that exploits the population, we want to live in a nation where we all have equal rights and we all have equal opportunity." Then, the power elite had to retreat because the collective consciousness had been raised beyond the level of the consciousness of the elite. What is it that has allowed the fallen beings, as a relatively small number of beings associated with earth, to dominate the population for so long? It is that, in a certain sense, they had a more sophisticated consciousness. I am not hereby talking about in a spiritual sense, of the 144 levels. The fallen beings were low on the scale of the 144 levels, but they were high in another scale in terms of the intellectual sophistication. They also had a certain unity among them where they all wanted to maintain an elitist society and the illusion that an elite was necessary and beneficial. There was a certain sophistication and a certain unification, and because the people had become so divided, then the fallen beings could dominate the people. As the people raise their consciousness, that domination falls away, and that is why democracies emerged and the kings and the noblemen and the clergy had to give way, and give the people greater freedom.

Changing a society without violence

Of course, when you understand the concept of interdependent originations, you realize that nothing in the physical world has a cause that is entirely physical. There are some causes that could be said to be largely physical. But everything in the physical world actually had its origin in these ideal forms or matrices in the emotional, mental and identity realms. You start seeing that there is an alternative to the way society has traditionally changed.

You see the French Revolution, the Bolshevik Revolution where so many times there was the pressure for change because the people were tired of being abused. There were new energies emerging, but then there was a violent revolution that brought some kind of change. You begin to see, and you as spiritual people see, that there is an alternative to this. It is that you realize that everything in the physical is an expression of, a manifestation of, matrices and energies in the three higher realms. When you work on changing those three higher realms, you will, after some time, also change the physical.

This is what did happen before the advent of democracy. There was a change in the identity, mental and emotional bodies of some of these nations that are now democracies, and therefore, the physical form of government had to change accordingly. This was an unconscious process that people were not aware of. Imagine if more people begin to become aware of this and make use of the tools for changing the originations in the identity, mental and emotional levels. There is almost no limit to what could be changed in the physical in this way.

As we have said before, so many things on earth are an expression of the density of the collective consciousness. You raise the collective consciousness, you raise the vibration so you overcome the density, and all of a sudden things can change in the physical that you cannot believe could be changed. There are so many people, returning to the concept of world hunger, who will say: "But the planet only has a finite level of resources, and there are already too many people on the planet to be fed by those resources." Yes, at the current level of density, the planet has a finite number of resources. You change that density just a little bit, you shift the collective consciousness just a little bit up, new technologies will emerge, new ideas will come forth, and suddenly within a few decades, you can produce plenty of food to feed all of the people who are in embodiment.

If you went back to the 1800s and took the farmers in Europe and told them that in 100 years, the land that they had worked with the sweat of their brow with primitive hand tools would be able to produce many times more grain than what they were producing at that time, they would refuse to believe you. With the development of technology, you now have that increased productivity.

The self-reinforcing effect of labels

Why is it, my beloved, that so many people are susceptible to this belief that even though you have seen an incredible increase in the amount of resources that the planet can provide, this will somehow stop, this is in danger of running out? Why do they believe this? Because the fallen beings have made them believe it by creating these labels that the way things are now is the only way they ever could be. This is the self-reinforcing effect of these labels. Once you think God is a certain way, well, you can have a church that maintains that image of God and people believe it for 17 centuries, as the Catholic church has done. Once you have the idea that the earth has limited resources, as has now been projected for a long time by the materialist religion, then you could have a planet that would stagnate at a certain level. This is not going to happen because the earth is in an upward spiral and the collective consciousness is being gradually raised. What I am pointing out is that there is a tension in the collective consciousness, and there is a potential that you, by raising your consciousness, by making the calls, can trigger a breakthrough where many more people begin to accept many of the things we have told you, including that the planet does not have a finite level of resources, that there are technologies that could replace oil completely. I can tell you that if you look back at the last hundred years, and see the technological progress that has happened in those hundred years, in the next hundred years the technological progress will be many times greater. Fossil fuels will be looked at as being as primitive as the Stone Age. The whole idea that energy costs money, and there are people, there are companies, there are corporations who can have a virtual monopoly on the sale of energy, will be seen as being as primitive as the idea of a flat earth. It will become obvious to people that energy should be entirely free and should be available to all people in unlimited quantities. There will come a point where society will never be limited by energy. There will be unlimited energy to create all kinds of progress. What we are asking you to envision and make the calls for, is that people will become free from this emotional level stranglehold, the intellectual level stranglehold and the identity level stranglehold. They will begin to see that nothing on earth is fixed because everything depends on consciousness, and therefore there is the potential to create progress beyond your wildest imaginations.

Due to all the labels that have been projected out there that people have accepted, people have accepted so many limitations that they cannot actually imagine the progress that could be made. As we have said before, go back 200 years, show them the modern age, could they have imagined this kind of progress? They would have denied it, they would have said this could never happen. But it *has* happened, has it not? So why could it not continue? Indeed, it *can,* and indeed it *will.* You can speed up the process whereby people become able to accept the Golden Age of Saint Germain.

With this, the gratitude of all of us who have spoken at this conference, and all of us who have not spoken. Our gratitude for you coming together, giving us this platform for radiating these ideas into the collective consciousness. Therefore, it is my joy to seal you in the peace of the Buddha that I AM.

31 | INVOKING FREEDOM OF IMAGINATION (PART 1)

In the name of the I AM THAT I AM, Jesus Christ, I use the authority that I have as a being in embodiment on earth to call upon Gautama Buddha to reinforce my calls and use my chakras to project the statements in this invocation into the collective consciousness and awaken people to the need to free our imagination from the manipulation of the fallen beings. Awaken people to the reality that we are spiritual beings and that we can co-create a new future by working with the ascended masters. I especially call for …

[Make your own calls here.]

Part 1

1. Gautama Buddha, shatter the energetic matrix that prevents people from seeing that whatever we try to say about the power elite in order to expose them, they will attempt to turn it around and use it against us.

> Gautama, show my mental state
> that does give rise to love and hate,

your exposé I do endure,
so my perception will be pure.

**Gautama, Flame of Cosmic Peace,
unruly thoughts do hereby cease,
we radiate from you and me
the peace to still Samsara's Sea.**

2. Gautama Buddha, shatter the energetic matrix that prevents people from seeing that whenever an individual or group came up with an exposure of the lies and the manipulation of the power elite, the elite would seek to attack that person in return, seek to discredit them, and thereby supposedly counteract what was said.

Gautama, in your Flame of Peace,
the struggling self I now release,
the Buddha Nature I now see,
it is the core of you and me.

**Gautama, Flame of Cosmic Peace,
unruly thoughts do hereby cease,
we radiate from you and me
the peace to still Samsara's Sea.**

3. Gautama Buddha, shatter the energetic matrix that prevents people from seeing that many people subscribe to the concept that certain ideas or certain expressions can be the truth, can be true.

Gautama, I am one with thee,
Mara's demons do now flee,
your Presence like a soothing balm,
my mind and senses ever calm.

**Gautama, Flame of Cosmic Peace,
unruly thoughts do hereby cease,
we radiate from you and me
the peace to still Samsara's Sea.**

4. Gautama Buddha, shatter the energetic matrix that prevents people from seeing that we could make tremendous progress if we asked ourselves the question: "What is my concept of truth, my current concept of truth?"

> Gautama, I now take the vow,
> to live in the eternal now,
> with you I do transcend all time,
> to live in present so sublime.
>
> **Gautama, Flame of Cosmic Peace,**
> **unruly thoughts do hereby cease,**
> **we radiate from you and me**
> **the peace to still Samsara's Sea.**

5. Gautama Buddha, shatter the energetic matrix that prevents people from seeing that our current concept of truth is just a label. In many cases it is a label created by the power elite specifically to deceive us.

> Gautama, I have no desire,
> to nothing earthly I aspire,
> in non-attachment I now rest,
> passing Mara's subtle test.
>
> **Gautama, Flame of Cosmic Peace,**
> **unruly thoughts do hereby cease,**
> **we radiate from you and me**
> **the peace to still Samsara's Sea.**

6. Gautama Buddha, shatter the energetic matrix that prevents people from seeing that the elite create the label, they create a superstructure that supports that label, such as the word "God," they create a structure about how they define God, and then they project with enough force and authority that this is the absolute truth about God.

> Gautama, I melt into you,
> my mind is one, no longer two,
> immersed in your resplendent glow,
> Nirvana is all that I know.

Gautama, Flame of Cosmic Peace,
unruly thoughts do hereby cease,
we radiate from you and me
the peace to still Samsara's Sea.

7. Gautama Buddha, shatter the energetic matrix that prevents people from seeing that this causes us to not question that expression, that label. If we would be willing to question it, we could make tremendous progress.

Gautama, in your timeless space,
I am immersed in Cosmic Grace,
I know the God beyond all form,
to world I will no more conform.

Gautama, Flame of Cosmic Peace,
unruly thoughts do hereby cease,
we radiate from you and me
the peace to still Samsara's Sea.

8. Gautama Buddha, shatter the energetic matrix that prevents people from seeing that labeling everything is the primary tool used by the fallen beings to deceive us, to trap us in some false belief that we cannot get out of because we will not question the label. We think it is the truth.

Gautama, I am now awake,
I clearly see what is at stake,
and thus I claim my sacred right
to be on earth the Buddhic Light.

Gautama, Flame of Cosmic Peace,
unruly thoughts do hereby cease,
we radiate from you and me
the peace to still Samsara's Sea.

9. Gautama Buddha, shatter the energetic matrix that prevents people from seeing that we live on a planet with a high density of matter, a high density of the collective consciousness. This affects everything on earth and causes many limitations that we experience.

Gautama, with your thunderbolt,
we give the earth a mighty jolt,
I know that some will understand,
and join the Buddha's timeless band.

Gautama, Flame of Cosmic Peace,
unruly thoughts do hereby cease,
we radiate from you and me
the peace to still Samsara's Sea.

Part 2

1. Gautama Buddha, shatter the energetic matrix that prevents people from seeing that the density of the planet causes limitations to what we can do with words. Everything else on earth is limited so why would words not also be limited?

Gautama, show my mental state
that does give rise to love and hate,
your exposé I do endure,
so my perception will be pure.

Gautama, Flame of Cosmic Peace,
unruly thoughts do hereby cease,
we radiate from you and me
the peace to still Samsara's Sea.

2. Gautama Buddha, shatter the energetic matrix that prevents people from seeing that the concept that we could formulate a worded statement that was an absolute truth or the word of God, is a limited understanding of the reality of life on this planet.

Gautama, in your Flame of Peace,
the struggling self I now release,
the Buddha Nature I now see,
it is the core of you and me.

**Gautama, Flame of Cosmic Peace,
unruly thoughts do hereby cease,
we radiate from you and me
the peace to still Samsara's Sea.**

3. Gautama Buddha, shatter the energetic matrix that prevents people from seeing that God would never even attempt to give people a worded statement about itself, because it is clear for any ascended being how much words have been misused throughout history, how much words are open to interpretation.

Gautama, I am one with thee,
Mara's demons do now flee,
your Presence like a soothing balm,
my mind and senses ever calm.

**Gautama, Flame of Cosmic Peace,
unruly thoughts do hereby cease,
we radiate from you and me
the peace to still Samsara's Sea.**

4. Gautama Buddha, shatter the energetic matrix that prevents people from seeing that words on a dense planet like earth are a means for communicating practical things. We have a need to communicate about practical everyday matters, and we have the need to have a certain precision.

Gautama, I now take the vow,
to live in the eternal now,
with you I do transcend all time,
to live in present so sublime.

**Gautama, Flame of Cosmic Peace,
unruly thoughts do hereby cease,
we radiate from you and me
the peace to still Samsara's Sea.**

5. Gautama Buddha, shatter the energetic matrix that prevents people from seeing that words have some limitations when it comes to describing more complex ideas. There is a limitation to what can be expressed in words.

Gautama, I have no desire,
to nothing earthly I aspire,
in non-attachment I now rest,
passing Mara's subtle test.

Gautama, Flame of Cosmic Peace,
unruly thoughts do hereby cease,
we radiate from you and me
the peace to still Samsara's Sea.

6. Gautama Buddha, shatter the energetic matrix that prevents people from seeing that the word "soul" has many different meanings. Words should be taken with a grain of salt. We cannot assume that words can precisely express ideas.

Gautama, I melt into you,
my mind is one, no longer two,
immersed in your resplendent glow,
Nirvana is all that I know.

Gautama, Flame of Cosmic Peace,
unruly thoughts do hereby cease,
we radiate from you and me
the peace to still Samsara's Sea.

7. Gautama Buddha, shatter the energetic matrix that prevents people from seeing that we have an entire culture that is based on using words to describe ideas because the fallen beings have created these labels, and they use the labels to stop people from thinking more deeply.

Gautama, in your timeless space,
I am immersed in Cosmic Grace,
I know the God beyond all form,
to world I will no more conform.

Gautama, Flame of Cosmic Peace,
unruly thoughts do hereby cease,
we radiate from you and me
the peace to still Samsara's Sea.

8. Gautama Buddha, shatter the energetic matrix that prevents people from seeing that the label is always a word It is underpinned by some structure of what defines the word, and then it is projected with this energy that causes many people to be overwhelmed by the energy.

Gautama, I am now awake,
I clearly see what is at stake,
and thus I claim my sacred right
to be on earth the Buddhic Light.

Gautama, Flame of Cosmic Peace,
unruly thoughts do hereby cease,
we radiate from you and me
the peace to still Samsara's Sea.

9. Gautama Buddha, shatter the energetic matrix that prevents people from seeing that the purpose of using words in this way is to get us to accept the word at face value. We do not use the faculties we have to investigate deeper, to look behind the word, behind the label, and see what is really there.

Gautama, with your thunderbolt,
we give the earth a mighty jolt,
I know that some will understand,
and join the Buddha's timeless band.

Gautama, Flame of Cosmic Peace,
unruly thoughts do hereby cease,
we radiate from you and me
the peace to still Samsara's Sea.

Part 3

1. Gautama Buddha, shatter the energetic matrix that prevents people from seeing that one of the faculties we have for looking behind words is critical thinking. We look for inconsistencies, we compare this to something else, and we see if there is a consistent definition of a particular word.

Gautama, show my mental state
that does give rise to love and hate,
your exposé I do endure,
so my perception will be pure.

**Gautama, Flame of Cosmic Peace,
unruly thoughts do hereby cease,
we radiate from you and me
the peace to still Samsara's Sea.**

2. Gautama Buddha, shatter the energetic matrix that prevents people from seeing that many people are overpowered by these authoritative labels, and they go into a state of mental paralysis where they do not ask questions. This particularly happens when we have an institution or system, such as a particular religion or the scientific establishment.

Gautama, in your Flame of Peace,
the struggling self I now release,
the Buddha Nature I now see,
it is the core of you and me.

**Gautama, Flame of Cosmic Peace,
unruly thoughts do hereby cease,
we radiate from you and me
the peace to still Samsara's Sea.**

3. Gautama Buddha, shatter the energetic matrix that prevents people from seeing that from childhood we have been discouraged from asking the questions that the authority figures, from parents to teachers, to the leaders of society, could not answer.

Gautama, I am one with thee,
Mara's demons do now flee,
your Presence like a soothing balm,
my mind and senses ever calm.

**Gautama, Flame of Cosmic Peace,
unruly thoughts do hereby cease,**

we radiate from you and me
the peace to still Samsara's Sea.

4. Gautama Buddha, shatter the energetic matrix that prevents people from seeing that another faculty we have is intuition. This is a faculty that gives us an experience.

Gautama, I now take the vow,
to live in the eternal now,
with you I do transcend all time,
to live in present so sublime.

Gautama, Flame of Cosmic Peace,
unruly thoughts do hereby cease,
we radiate from you and me
the peace to still Samsara's Sea.

5. Gautama Buddha, shatter the energetic matrix that prevents people from seeing that the fallen beings do not want us to realize that when it comes to any aspect of life, it is possible to have an intuitive or mystical experience where we directly experience the essence of the phenomenon.

Gautama, I have no desire,
to nothing earthly I aspire,
in non-attachment I now rest,
passing Mara's subtle test.

Gautama, Flame of Cosmic Peace,
unruly thoughts do hereby cease,
we radiate from you and me
the peace to still Samsara's Sea.

6. Gautama Buddha, shatter the energetic matrix that prevents people from seeing that Plato said that beyond the material world is a higher realm of ideal forms. These forms are what become manifest as the things we see in the physical world.

Gautama, I melt into you,
my mind is one, no longer two,

immersed in your resplendent glow,
Nirvana is all that I know.

Gautama, Flame of Cosmic Peace,
unruly thoughts do hereby cease,
we radiate from you and me
the peace to still Samsara's Sea.

7. Gautama Buddha, shatter the energetic matrix that prevents people from seeing that we have a physical thing called an apple, but the apple is a manifestation of this ideal form that exists in a higher realm. It contains the essence of an apple.

Gautama, in your timeless space,
I am immersed in Cosmic Grace,
I know the God beyond all form,
to world I will no more conform.

Gautama, Flame of Cosmic Peace,
unruly thoughts do hereby cease,
we radiate from you and me
the peace to still Samsara's Sea.

8. Gautama Buddha, shatter the energetic matrix that prevents people from seeing that it is possible to have an intuitive experience of that ideal form, the essence of an apple. The same with any complex abstract idea, we can have an intuitive experience of the essence of the idea, the matrix of the idea.

Gautama, I am now awake,
I clearly see what is at stake,
and thus I claim my sacred right
to be on earth the Buddhic Light.

Gautama, Flame of Cosmic Peace,
unruly thoughts do hereby cease,
we radiate from you and me
the peace to still Samsara's Sea.

9. Gautama Buddha, shatter the energetic matrix that prevents people from seeing that we can sharpen our intuition so we know whether an idea came from the emotional realm, the mental realm, the identity realm or the spiritual realm.

Gautama, with your thunderbolt,
we give the earth a mighty jolt,
I know that some will understand,
and join the Buddha's timeless band.

Gautama, Flame of Cosmic Peace,
unruly thoughts do hereby cease,
we radiate from you and me
the peace to still Samsara's Sea.

Part 4

1. Gautama Buddha, shatter the energetic matrix that prevents people from seeing that we can sense the vibration, the vibrational matrix of an idea and know whether it is a valid idea, whether it came from a higher source or a lower source.

Gautama, show my mental state
that does give rise to love and hate,
your exposé I do endure,
so my perception will be pure.

Gautama, Flame of Cosmic Peace,
unruly thoughts do hereby cease,
we radiate from you and me
the peace to still Samsara's Sea.

2. Gautama Buddha, shatter the energetic matrix that prevents people from seeing that by learning to read vibration, we can go beyond the labels that are created by using words and projecting that they have a specific interpretation.

Gautama, in your Flame of Peace,
the struggling self I now release,
the Buddha Nature I now see,
it is the core of you and me.

Gautama, Flame of Cosmic Peace,
unruly thoughts do hereby cease,
we radiate from you and me
the peace to still Samsara's Sea.

3. Gautama Buddha, shatter the energetic matrix that prevents people from seeing that if we cannot know the taste of an apple through words, how could we possibly know the nature of God through words? It is non-constructive to think that any description of the Creator given by words on this dense planet could be accurate or adequate.

Gautama, I am one with thee,
Mara's demons do now flee,
your Presence like a soothing balm,
my mind and senses ever calm.

Gautama, Flame of Cosmic Peace,
unruly thoughts do hereby cease,
we radiate from you and me
the peace to still Samsara's Sea.

4. Gautama Buddha, shatter the energetic matrix that prevents people from seeing that the fallen beings have created these labels, such as "God," and then there is the overlay of what God is.

Gautama, I now take the vow,
to live in the eternal now,
with you I do transcend all time,
to live in present so sublime.

Gautama, Flame of Cosmic Peace,
unruly thoughts do hereby cease,
we radiate from you and me
the peace to still Samsara's Sea.

5. Gautama Buddha, shatter the energetic matrix that prevents people from seeing that there is an intense energy momentum that has been built up over thousands of years that overpowers us so we dare not question what God is. We dare not gainsay God, we dare not challenge. Yet we are not challenging God, we are challenging a worded expression, an interpretation.

Gautama, I have no desire,
to nothing earthly I aspire,
in non-attachment I now rest,
passing Mara's subtle test.

**Gautama, Flame of Cosmic Peace,
unruly thoughts do hereby cease,
we radiate from you and me
the peace to still Samsara's Sea.**

6. Gautama Buddha, shatter the energetic matrix that prevents people from seeing that this prevents us from ever going beyond the label and the understanding of the concept embedded in the label. We simply do not think about it.

Gautama, I melt into you,
my mind is one, no longer two,
immersed in your resplendent glow,
Nirvana is all that I know.

**Gautama, Flame of Cosmic Peace,
unruly thoughts do hereby cease,
we radiate from you and me
the peace to still Samsara's Sea.**

7. Gautama Buddha, shatter the energetic matrix that prevents people from seeing that when we accept this matrix, this process, these labels, we are trapped by those who have defined the labels. We cannot go beyond the minds of the beings who define the label, we are stuck in the label.

Gautama, in your timeless space,
I am immersed in Cosmic Grace,

I know the God beyond all form,
to world I will no more conform.

Gautama, Flame of Cosmic Peace,
unruly thoughts do hereby cease,
we radiate from you and me
the peace to still Samsara's Sea.

8. Gautama Buddha, shatter the energetic matrix that prevents people from seeing that this is why societies, for centuries, can be stuck at a certain level, as Europe was stuck in the Catholic labels for over a thousand years.

Gautama, I am now awake,
I clearly see what is at stake,
and thus I claim my sacred right
to be on earth the Buddhic Light.

Gautama, Flame of Cosmic Peace,
unruly thoughts do hereby cease,
we radiate from you and me
the peace to still Samsara's Sea.

9. Gautama Buddha, shatter the energetic matrix that prevents people from seeing that people could not break out of the stalemate of the kings, the noble class and the Catholic clergy holding the majority of the population as slaves. We see the same thing many times throughout history.

Gautama, with your thunderbolt,
we give the earth a mighty jolt,
I know that some will understand,
and join the Buddha's timeless band.

Gautama, Flame of Cosmic Peace,
unruly thoughts do hereby cease,
we radiate from you and me
the peace to still Samsara's Sea.

Sealing

In the name of the I AM THAT I AM, I accept that Archangel Michael, Astrea and Shiva form an impenetrable shield around myself and all constructive people, sealing us from all fear-based energies in all four octaves. I accept that the Light of God is consuming and transforming all fear-based energies that make up the dark forces working against ending the era of elitism on earth!

32 | INVOKING FREEDOM OF IMAGINATION (PART 2)

In the name of the I AM THAT I AM, Jesus Christ, I use the authority that I have as a being in embodiment on earth to call upon Gautama Buddha to reinforce my calls and use my chakras to project the statements in this invocation into the collective consciousness and awaken people to the need to free our imagination from the manipulation of the fallen beings. Awaken people to the reality that we are spiritual beings and that we can co-create a new future by working with the ascended masters. I especially call for ...

[Make your own calls here.]

Part 1

1. Gautama Buddha, shatter the energetic matrix that prevents people from seeing that we have the same thing today where science is stuck in Materialism, where the economy is stuck in capitalism, thinking we have a free market when we do not.

Gautama, show my mental state
that does give rise to love and hate,

your exposé I do endure,
so my perception will be pure.

**Gautama, Flame of Cosmic Peace,
unruly thoughts do hereby cease,
we radiate from you and me
the peace to still Samsara's Sea.**

2. Gautama Buddha, shatter the energetic matrix that prevents people from seeing that if we really want to know anything, or know about anything, we need to go beyond the word, we need to go beyond the label. We need to have the inner experience where we experience the essence of the idea.

Gautama, in your Flame of Peace,
the struggling self I now release,
the Buddha Nature I now see,
it is the core of you and me.

**Gautama, Flame of Cosmic Peace,
unruly thoughts do hereby cease,
we radiate from you and me
the peace to still Samsara's Sea.**

3. Gautama Buddha, shatter the energetic matrix that prevents people from seeing that this is mental freedom. The only way to mental freedom is to use critical thinking and intuition to free ourselves from these interpretations that are so powerful in the collective consciousness.

Gautama, I am one with thee,
Mara's demons do now flee,
your Presence like a soothing balm,
my mind and senses ever calm.

**Gautama, Flame of Cosmic Peace,
unruly thoughts do hereby cease,
we radiate from you and me
the peace to still Samsara's Sea.**

4. Gautama Buddha, shatter the energetic matrix that prevents people from seeing that the interpretations are often based on assumptions that will later be proven wrong or incomplete.

> Gautama, I now take the vow,
> to live in the eternal now,
> with you I do transcend all time,
> to live in present so sublime.

> **Gautama, Flame of Cosmic Peace,**
> **unruly thoughts do hereby cease,**
> **we radiate from you and me**
> **the peace to still Samsara's Sea.**

5. Gautama Buddha, shatter the energetic matrix that prevents people from seeing that once we have intuitive experiences, we can see beyond the labels and realize that words are not the ultimate expression of truth.

> Gautama, I have no desire,
> to nothing earthly I aspire,
> in non-attachment I now rest,
> passing Mara's subtle test.

> **Gautama, Flame of Cosmic Peace,**
> **unruly thoughts do hereby cease,**
> **we radiate from you and me**
> **the peace to still Samsara's Sea.**

6. Gautama Buddha, shatter the energetic matrix that prevents people from seeing that the ascended masters are not saying that their words represent an absolute truth or that we should blindly believe in the words and never strive to have a direct experience beyond the words.

> Gautama, I melt into you,
> my mind is one, no longer two,
> immersed in your resplendent glow,
> Nirvana is all that I know.

**Gautama, Flame of Cosmic Peace,
unruly thoughts do hereby cease,
we radiate from you and me
the peace to still Samsara's Sea.**

7. Gautama Buddha, shatter the energetic matrix that prevents people from seeing that the ascended masters give a worded teaching because they have to use words, as words can be used, given the density of earth.

Gautama, in your timeless space,
I am immersed in Cosmic Grace,
I know the God beyond all form,
to world I will no more conform.

**Gautama, Flame of Cosmic Peace,
unruly thoughts do hereby cease,
we radiate from you and me
the peace to still Samsara's Sea.**

8. Gautama Buddha, shatter the energetic matrix that prevents people from seeing that the ascended masters always want us to go beyond the words and reach for the direct intuitive experience from within.

Gautama, I am now awake,
I clearly see what is at stake,
and thus I claim my sacred right
to be on earth the Buddhic Light.

**Gautama, Flame of Cosmic Peace,
unruly thoughts do hereby cease,
we radiate from you and me
the peace to still Samsara's Sea.**

9. Gautama Buddha, shatter the energetic matrix that prevents people from seeing that truth can be known, not through words, not through the most fanciful theory, but only through the direct experience of gnosis, the unity between the knower and the known.

Gautama, with your thunderbolt,
we give the earth a mighty jolt,
I know that some will understand,
and join the Buddha's timeless band.

Gautama, Flame of Cosmic Peace,
unruly thoughts do hereby cease,
we radiate from you and me
the peace to still Samsara's Sea.

Part 2

1. Gautama Buddha, shatter the energetic matrix that prevents people from seeing that our essential humanity is one possible antidote to the duality consciousness, the division created by the fallen beings.

Gautama, show my mental state
that does give rise to love and hate,
your exposé I do endure,
so my perception will be pure.

Gautama, Flame of Cosmic Peace,
unruly thoughts do hereby cease,
we radiate from you and me
the peace to still Samsara's Sea.

2. Gautama Buddha, shatter the energetic matrix that prevents people from seeing that the fallen beings always seek to split us up into these groups that are characterized by a label, and therefore, by the definition of that label, the groups are in conflict with each other.

Gautama, in your Flame of Peace,
the struggling self I now release,
the Buddha Nature I now see,
it is the core of you and me.

**Gautama, Flame of Cosmic Peace,
unruly thoughts do hereby cease,
we radiate from you and me
the peace to still Samsara's Sea.**

3. Gautama Buddha, shatter the energetic matrix that prevents people from seeing that the essential humanity is what you called the Buddha nature and which Jesus called the Christ consciousness, or the kingdom of God.

Gautama, I am one with thee,
Mara's demons do now flee,
your Presence like a soothing balm,
my mind and senses ever calm.

**Gautama, Flame of Cosmic Peace,
unruly thoughts do hereby cease,
we radiate from you and me
the peace to still Samsara's Sea.**

4. Gautama Buddha, shatter the energetic matrix that prevents people from seeing that we can have a direct intuitive experience of our own essence. We are more than the physical body, we are more than the outer mind, we are more than our thoughts, our feelings, even our sense of identity.

Gautama, I now take the vow,
to live in the eternal now,
with you I do transcend all time,
to live in present so sublime.

**Gautama, Flame of Cosmic Peace,
unruly thoughts do hereby cease,
we radiate from you and me
the peace to still Samsara's Sea.**

5. Gautama Buddha, shatter the energetic matrix that prevents people from seeing that when we have that experience, it is beyond words and it cannot be counteracted by words, because we will not believe the words that deny the experience. The experience itself was more real than the experience we get through words.

Gautama, I have no desire,
to nothing earthly I aspire,
in non-attachment I now rest,
passing Mara's subtle test.

Gautama, Flame of Cosmic Peace,
unruly thoughts do hereby cease,
we radiate from you and me
the peace to still Samsara's Sea.

6. Gautama Buddha, shatter the energetic matrix that prevents people from seeing that this is the connecting link between people, and when we have that connecting link, when we experience it for ourselves and then begin to experience it in others, then we can overcome the division.

Gautama, I melt into you,
my mind is one, no longer two,
immersed in your resplendent glow,
Nirvana is all that I know.

Gautama, Flame of Cosmic Peace,
unruly thoughts do hereby cease,
we radiate from you and me
the peace to still Samsara's Sea.

7. Gautama Buddha, shatter the energetic matrix that prevents people from seeing that our brother and sisters are not Muslims or Christians, men or women, Democrats or Republicans, Germans or Italians, this or that. Our brothers and sisters all have the essential nature that we have.

Gautama, in your timeless space,
I am immersed in Cosmic Grace,
I know the God beyond all form,
to world I will no more conform.

Gautama, Flame of Cosmic Peace,
unruly thoughts do hereby cease,
we radiate from you and me
the peace to still Samsara's Sea.

8. Gautama Buddha, shatter the energetic matrix that prevents people from seeing that the essential humanity is the common link that we have. It is the only way to counteract the division.

> Gautama, I am now awake,
> I clearly see what is at stake,
> and thus I claim my sacred right
> to be on earth the Buddhic Light.

> **Gautama, Flame of Cosmic Peace,**
> **unruly thoughts do hereby cease,**
> **we radiate from you and me**
> **the peace to still Samsara's Sea.**

9. Gautama Buddha, shatter the energetic matrix that prevents people from seeing that the fallen beings are very clever at using words, they have a very old momentum on using words. There is hardly any statement made in words that cannot be either counteracted by another statement made with words or put into question by another statement.

> Gautama, with your thunderbolt,
> we give the earth a mighty jolt,
> I know that some will understand,
> and join the Buddha's timeless band.

> **Gautama, Flame of Cosmic Peace,**
> **unruly thoughts do hereby cease,**
> **we radiate from you and me**
> **the peace to still Samsara's Sea.**

Part 3

1. Gautama Buddha, shatter the energetic matrix that prevents people from seeing that the fallen beings often turn a statement into a label and then come up with a counter label. There is this entire game that has been played for many millennia where people have been arguing back and forth.

They have been attempting to come up with the ultimate argument, the ultimate theory, the ultimate religion.

> Gautama, show my mental state
> that does give rise to love and hate,
> your exposé I do endure,
> so my perception will be pure.

> **Gautama, Flame of Cosmic Peace,**
> **unruly thoughts do hereby cease,**
> **we radiate from you and me**
> **the peace to still Samsara's Sea.**

2. Gautama Buddha, shatter the energetic matrix that prevents people from seeing how much energy has been spent on this, how much this has pulled people's attention into fighting this battle of ideas, this battle for the domination of ideas.

> Gautama, in your Flame of Peace,
> the struggling self I now release,
> the Buddha Nature I now see,
> it is the core of you and me.

> **Gautama, Flame of Cosmic Peace,**
> **unruly thoughts do hereby cease,**
> **we radiate from you and me**
> **the peace to still Samsara's Sea.**

3. Gautama Buddha, shatter the energetic matrix that prevents people from seeing that even today many intellectual people are trapped in this almost endless game of arguing back and forth about ideas, instead of focusing on developing some ideas that could actually help society progress and help alleviate suffering.

> Gautama, I am one with thee,
> Mara's demons do now flee,
> your Presence like a soothing balm,
> my mind and senses ever calm.

**Gautama, Flame of Cosmic Peace,
unruly thoughts do hereby cease,
we radiate from you and me
the peace to still Samsara's Sea.**

4. Gautama Buddha, shatter the energetic matrix that prevents people from seeing that we really do not need to know what happens in the core of a neutron star 750 million light years away, when it would be more constructive to use our intellectual resources on trying to overcome world hunger or other forms of suffering.

Gautama, I now take the vow,
to live in the eternal now,
with you I do transcend all time,
to live in present so sublime.

**Gautama, Flame of Cosmic Peace,
unruly thoughts do hereby cease,
we radiate from you and me
the peace to still Samsara's Sea.**

5. Gautama Buddha, shatter the energetic matrix that prevents people from seeing that it would be more constructive that instead of spending billions of dollars building ever more powerful telescopes, or ever more powerful particle accelerators, we spent that money on alleviating human suffering.

Gautama, I have no desire,
to nothing earthly I aspire,
in non-attachment I now rest,
passing Mara's subtle test.

**Gautama, Flame of Cosmic Peace,
unruly thoughts do hereby cease,
we radiate from you and me
the peace to still Samsara's Sea.**

6. Gautama Buddha, shatter the energetic matrix that prevents people from seeing that if we could get out of our intellectual minds and use our intuitive minds, we could have an intuitive experience of what happens in

a neutron star, or what happens at the level of the subatomic, so-called, particles.

> Gautama, I melt into you,
> my mind is one, no longer two,
> immersed in your resplendent glow,
> Nirvana is all that I know.

> **Gautama, Flame of Cosmic Peace,**
> **unruly thoughts do hereby cease,**
> **we radiate from you and me**
> **the peace to still Samsara's Sea.**

7. Gautama Buddha, shatter the energetic matrix that prevents people from seeing that we could know this intuitively without having to prove it through technology that was released by Saint Germain specifically to address these practical problems of human suffering.

> Gautama, in your timeless space,
> I am immersed in Cosmic Grace,
> I know the God beyond all form,
> to world I will no more conform.

> **Gautama, Flame of Cosmic Peace,**
> **unruly thoughts do hereby cease,**
> **we radiate from you and me**
> **the peace to still Samsara's Sea.**

8. Gautama Buddha, shatter the energetic matrix that prevents people from seeing that instead of trying to prove Materialism, which is just a label, we could go beyond the labels and actually do something for humanity.

> Gautama, I am now awake,
> I clearly see what is at stake,
> and thus I claim my sacred right
> to be on earth the Buddhic Light.

> **Gautama, Flame of Cosmic Peace,**
> **unruly thoughts do hereby cease,**

**we radiate from you and me
the peace to still Samsara's Sea.**

9. Gautama Buddha, shatter the energetic matrix that prevents people from seeing that one of the effects of the duality consciousness is that it produces this illusion that we are separate beings. We experience through the duality consciousness that we are separate beings, we are not connected to anyone else.

Gautama, with your thunderbolt,
we give the earth a mighty jolt,
I know that some will understand,
and join the Buddha's timeless band.

**Gautama, Flame of Cosmic Peace,
unruly thoughts do hereby cease,
we radiate from you and me
the peace to still Samsara's Sea.**

Part 4

1. Gautama Buddha, shatter the energetic matrix that prevents people from seeing that the fallen beings have used duality to make themselves believe that they could kill millions of people, and because they were separated from them, this would not affect themselves.

Gautama, show my mental state
that does give rise to love and hate,
your exposé I do endure,
so my perception will be pure.

**Gautama, Flame of Cosmic Peace,
unruly thoughts do hereby cease,
we radiate from you and me
the peace to still Samsara's Sea.**

2. Gautama Buddha, shatter the energetic matrix that prevents people from seeing that the fallen beings have also used duality to uphold the illusion that humanity can be divided into two classes, the power elite and the population.

Gautama, in your Flame of Peace,
the struggling self I now release,
the Buddha Nature I now see,
it is the core of you and me.

Gautama, Flame of Cosmic Peace,
unruly thoughts do hereby cease,
we radiate from you and me
the peace to still Samsara's Sea.

3. Gautama Buddha, shatter the energetic matrix that prevents people from seeing that we will ultimately overcome division by raising the collective consciousness until the fallen beings can no longer embody on the planet. We can do this only by creating unity between people.

Gautama, I am one with thee,
Mara's demons do now flee,
your Presence like a soothing balm,
my mind and senses ever calm.

Gautama, Flame of Cosmic Peace,
unruly thoughts do hereby cease,
we radiate from you and me
the peace to still Samsara's Sea.

4. Gautama Buddha, shatter the energetic matrix that prevents people from seeing that the basic humanity means that everything is interconnected, all people are connected. We are all part of the fabric of life, we are all part of the collective consciousness of earth, we are all part of the energy system on earth.

Gautama, I now take the vow,
to live in the eternal now,

with you I do transcend all time,
to live in present so sublime.

**Gautama, Flame of Cosmic Peace,
unruly thoughts do hereby cease,
we radiate from you and me
the peace to still Samsara's Sea.**

5. Gautama Buddha, shatter the energetic matrix that prevents people from seeing that because all people are connected, whatever one person does affects the whole, and the whole affects every person. Therefore, the elite is not set apart from the people.

Gautama, I have no desire,
to nothing earthly I aspire,
in non-attachment I now rest,
passing Mara's subtle test.

**Gautama, Flame of Cosmic Peace,
unruly thoughts do hereby cease,
we radiate from you and me
the peace to still Samsara's Sea.**

6. Gautama Buddha, shatter the energetic matrix that prevents people from seeing that members of the elite have created the illusion, the appearance, that they are set apart from the people. They have created the illusion that they belong to a separate category, they are superior to the people, they are separated from the people.

Gautama, I melt into you,
my mind is one, no longer two,
immersed in your resplendent glow,
Nirvana is all that I know.

**Gautama, Flame of Cosmic Peace,
unruly thoughts do hereby cease,
we radiate from you and me
the peace to still Samsara's Sea.**

7. Gautama Buddha, shatter the energetic matrix that prevents people from seeing that the power elite can rule the population in one way only: by dividing us up into all these different factions and keeping us divided.

> Gautama, in your timeless space,
> I am immersed in Cosmic Grace,
> I know the God beyond all form,
> to world I will no more conform.

> **Gautama, Flame of Cosmic Peace,**
> **unruly thoughts do hereby cease,**
> **we radiate from you and me**
> **the peace to still Samsara's Sea.**

8. Gautama Buddha, shatter the energetic matrix that prevents people from seeing that the power elite may seem to have power, they may seem to have authority, but what they do not have is numbers. In any society that is ruled by the elite, the elite is always the minority and the population is the majority.

> Gautama, I am now awake,
> I clearly see what is at stake,
> and thus I claim my sacred right
> to be on earth the Buddhic Light.

> **Gautama, Flame of Cosmic Peace,**
> **unruly thoughts do hereby cease,**
> **we radiate from you and me**
> **the peace to still Samsara's Sea.**

9. Gautama Buddha, shatter the energetic matrix that prevents people from seeing that as long as the population is divided, as long as people are divided in themselves, we cannot come together and say: "We have had enough of the elite."

> Gautama, with your thunderbolt,
> we give the earth a mighty jolt,
> I know that some will understand,
> and join the Buddha's timeless band.

**Gautama, Flame of Cosmic Peace,
unruly thoughts do hereby cease,
we radiate from you and me
the peace to still Samsara's Sea.**

Sealing

In the name of the I AM THAT I AM, I accept that Archangel Michael, Astrea and Shiva form an impenetrable shield around myself and all constructive people, sealing us from all fear-based energies in all four octaves. I accept that the Light of God is consuming and transforming all fear-based energies that make up the dark forces working against ending the era of elitism on earth!

33 | INVOKING FREEDOM OF IMAGINATION (PART 3)

In the name of the I AM THAT I AM, Jesus Christ, I use the authority that I have as a being in embodiment on earth to call upon Gautama Buddha to reinforce my calls and use my chakras to project the statements in this invocation into the collective consciousness and awaken people to the need to free our imagination from the manipulation of the fallen beings. Awaken people to the reality that we are spiritual beings and that we can co-create a new future by working with the ascended masters. I especially call for …

[Make your own calls here.]

Part 1

1. Gautama Buddha, shatter the energetic matrix that prevents people from seeing that once we begin to overcome that separation and connect, then the fallen beings will face a choice: Will they unite with the people or will they leave the planet? Because they cannot remain if we are united.

> Gautama, show my mental state
> that does give rise to love and hate,

your exposé I do endure,
so my perception will be pure.

**Gautama, Flame of Cosmic Peace,
unruly thoughts do hereby cease,
we radiate from you and me
the peace to still Samsara's Sea.**

2. Gautama Buddha, shatter the energetic matrix that prevents people from seeing that the fallen beings cannot unite with the people because they will not get out of the consciousness of separation. In order to get out of separation, they would have to give up the sense of identity that they are the superior elite, and that is what they will not give up.

Gautama, in your Flame of Peace,
the struggling self I now release,
the Buddha Nature I now see,
it is the core of you and me.

**Gautama, Flame of Cosmic Peace,
unruly thoughts do hereby cease,
we radiate from you and me
the peace to still Samsara's Sea.**

3. Gautama Buddha, shatter the energetic matrix that prevents people from seeing that when we come together, when there is unification among the people, the elite cannot exist anymore on the planet.

Gautama, I am one with thee,
Mara's demons do now flee,
your Presence like a soothing balm,
my mind and senses ever calm.

**Gautama, Flame of Cosmic Peace,
unruly thoughts do hereby cease,
we radiate from you and me
the peace to still Samsara's Sea.**

4. Gautama Buddha, shatter the energetic matrix that prevents people from seeing that this process was begun with the advent of democracies, where the people reached a certain level of unity, and then the power elite of the feudal age had to retreat from the country.

Gautama, I now take the vow,
to live in the eternal now,
with you I do transcend all time,
to live in present so sublime.

Gautama, Flame of Cosmic Peace,
unruly thoughts do hereby cease,
we radiate from you and me
the peace to still Samsara's Sea.

5. Gautama Buddha, shatter the energetic matrix that prevents people from seeing that everything is interdependent, everything is connected, but the connection is not in the physical octave. The connection is in consciousness, it is at the emotional level, at the mental level and at the identity level.

Gautama, I have no desire,
to nothing earthly I aspire,
in non-attachment I now rest,
passing Mara's subtle test.

Gautama, Flame of Cosmic Peace,
unruly thoughts do hereby cease,
we radiate from you and me
the peace to still Samsara's Sea.

6. Gautama Buddha, shatter the energetic matrix that prevents people from seeing that because all of us are connected through consciousness, we can change the equation on earth by raising our own consciousness because we will pull up on everybody else.

Gautama, I melt into you,
my mind is one, no longer two,
immersed in your resplendent glow,
Nirvana is all that I know.

Gautama, Flame of Cosmic Peace,
unruly thoughts do hereby cease,
we radiate from you and me
the peace to still Samsara's Sea.

7. Gautama Buddha, shatter the energetic matrix that prevents people from seeing that when enough people raise their consciousness, there will be a change even in the physical.

Gautama, in your timeless space,
I am immersed in Cosmic Grace,
I know the God beyond all form,
to world I will no more conform.

Gautama, Flame of Cosmic Peace,
unruly thoughts do hereby cease,
we radiate from you and me
the peace to still Samsara's Sea.

8. Gautama Buddha, shatter the energetic matrix that prevents people from seeing that democracy was brought into the physical because enough people came to the point where they said: "We have had enough of this dictatorial form of leadership that exploits the population, we want to live in a nation where we all have equal rights and we all have equal opportunity."

Gautama, I am now awake,
I clearly see what is at stake,
and thus I claim my sacred right
to be on earth the Buddhic Light.

Gautama, Flame of Cosmic Peace,
unruly thoughts do hereby cease,
we radiate from you and me
the peace to still Samsara's Sea.

9. Gautama Buddha, shatter the energetic matrix that prevents people from seeing that the power elite has to retreat when the collective consciousness had been raised beyond the level of consciousness of the elite.

Gautama, with your thunderbolt,
we give the earth a mighty jolt,
I know that some will understand,
and join the Buddha's timeless band.

Gautama, Flame of Cosmic Peace,
unruly thoughts do hereby cease,
we radiate from you and me
the peace to still Samsara's Sea.

Part 2

1. Gautama Buddha, shatter the energetic matrix that prevents people from seeing that what has allowed a relatively small number of fallen beings to dominate the population for so long is that, in a certain sense, they had a more sophisticated consciousness.

Gautama, show my mental state
that does give rise to love and hate,
your exposé I do endure,
so my perception will be pure.

Gautama, Flame of Cosmic Peace,
unruly thoughts do hereby cease,
we radiate from you and me
the peace to still Samsara's Sea.

2. Gautama Buddha, shatter the energetic matrix that prevents people from seeing that the fallen beings were high in terms of intellectual sophistication. They also had a certain unity among them where they all wanted to maintain an elitist society and the illusion that an elite was necessary and beneficial.

Gautama, in your Flame of Peace,
the struggling self I now release,
the Buddha Nature I now see,
it is the core of you and me.

Gautama, Flame of Cosmic Peace,
unruly thoughts do hereby cease,
we radiate from you and me
the peace to still Samsara's Sea.

3. Gautama Buddha, shatter the energetic matrix that prevents people from seeing that there was a certain sophistication and a certain unification, and because the people had become so divided, then the fallen beings could dominate the people.

Gautama, I am one with thee,
Mara's demons do now flee,
your Presence like a soothing balm,
my mind and senses ever calm.

Gautama, Flame of Cosmic Peace,
unruly thoughts do hereby cease,
we radiate from you and me
the peace to still Samsara's Sea.

4. Gautama Buddha, shatter the energetic matrix that prevents people from seeing that as we raise our consciousness, that domination falls away, and that is why democracies emerged and the kings, the noblemen and the clergy had to give the people greater freedom.

Gautama, I now take the vow,
to live in the eternal now,
with you I do transcend all time,
to live in present so sublime.

Gautama, Flame of Cosmic Peace,
unruly thoughts do hereby cease,
we radiate from you and me
the peace to still Samsara's Sea.

5. Gautama Buddha, shatter the energetic matrix that prevents people from seeing that the concept of interdependent originations means that nothing in the physical world has a cause that is entirely physical.

Gautama, I have no desire,
to nothing earthly I aspire,
in non-attachment I now rest,
passing Mara's subtle test.

Gautama, Flame of Cosmic Peace,
unruly thoughts do hereby cease,
we radiate from you and me
the peace to still Samsara's Sea.

6. Gautama Buddha, shatter the energetic matrix that prevents people from seeing that everything in the physical world had its origin in these ideal forms or matrices in the emotional, mental and identity realms. This means there is an alternative to the way society has traditionally changed.

Gautama, I melt into you,
my mind is one, no longer two,
immersed in your resplendent glow,
Nirvana is all that I know.

Gautama, Flame of Cosmic Peace,
unruly thoughts do hereby cease,
we radiate from you and me
the peace to still Samsara's Sea.

7. Gautama Buddha, shatter the energetic matrix that prevents people from seeing that the French Revolution, the Bolshevik Revolution were caused by the pressure for change because the people were tired of being abused. There were new energies emerging, but then there was a violent revolution that brought some kind of change.

Gautama, in your timeless space,
I am immersed in Cosmic Grace,
I know the God beyond all form,
to world I will no more conform.

Gautama, Flame of Cosmic Peace,
unruly thoughts do hereby cease,

**we radiate from you and me
the peace to still Samsara's Sea.**

8. Gautama Buddha, shatter the energetic matrix that prevents people from seeing that there is an alternative to this. Because everything in the physical is a manifestation of matrices in the three higher realms, when we can change those matrices, we will also change the physical.

Gautama, I am now awake,
I clearly see what is at stake,
and thus I claim my sacred right
to be on earth the Buddhic Light.

**Gautama, Flame of Cosmic Peace,
unruly thoughts do hereby cease,
we radiate from you and me
the peace to still Samsara's Sea.**

9. Gautama Buddha, shatter the energetic matrix that prevents people from seeing that this is what did happen before the advent of democracy. There was a change in the identity, mental and emotional bodies of some of these nations that are now democracies, and therefore, the physical form of government had to change accordingly.

Gautama, with your thunderbolt,
we give the earth a mighty jolt,
I know that some will understand,
and join the Buddha's timeless band.

**Gautama, Flame of Cosmic Peace,
unruly thoughts do hereby cease,
we radiate from you and me
the peace to still Samsara's Sea.**

Part 3

1. Gautama Buddha, shatter the energetic matrix that prevents people from seeing that this was an unconscious process that people were not aware of. If we become aware of this and make use of the tools for changing the originations in the identity, mental and emotional levels, there is almost no limit to what could be changed in the physical.

> Gautama, show my mental state
> that does give rise to love and hate,
> your exposé I do endure,
> so my perception will be pure.

> **Gautama, Flame of Cosmic Peace,**
> **unruly thoughts do hereby cease,**
> **we radiate from you and me**
> **the peace to still Samsara's Sea.**

2. Gautama Buddha, shatter the energetic matrix that prevents people from seeing that so many things on earth are an expression of the density of the collective consciousness. When we raise the collective consciousness, raise the vibration so we overcome the density, all of a sudden things can change in the physical that we cannot believe could be changed.

> Gautama, in your Flame of Peace,
> the struggling self I now release,
> the Buddha Nature I now see,
> it is the core of you and me.

> **Gautama, Flame of Cosmic Peace,**
> **unruly thoughts do hereby cease,**
> **we radiate from you and me**
> **the peace to still Samsara's Sea.**

3. Gautama Buddha, shatter the energetic matrix that prevents people from seeing that so many people will say that the planet only has a finite level of resources, and there are already too many people on the planet to be fed by those resources.

Gautama, I am one with thee,
Mara's demons do now flee,
your Presence like a soothing balm,
my mind and senses ever calm.

Gautama, Flame of Cosmic Peace,
unruly thoughts do hereby cease,
we radiate from you and me
the peace to still Samsara's Sea.

4. Gautama Buddha, shatter the energetic matrix that prevents people from seeing that at the current level of density, the planet has a finite number of resources. When we change that density, shift the collective consciousness just a little bit up, new technologies will emerge, new ideas will come forth, and within a few decades, we can produce plenty of food to feed all of the people who are in embodiment.

Gautama, I now take the vow,
to live in the eternal now,
with you I do transcend all time,
to live in present so sublime.

Gautama, Flame of Cosmic Peace,
unruly thoughts do hereby cease,
we radiate from you and me
the peace to still Samsara's Sea.

5. Gautama Buddha, shatter the energetic matrix that prevents people from seeing that the fallen beings have made people believe in the scarcity of resources by creating these labels that the way things are now is the only way they ever could be. This is the self-reinforcing effect of labels.

Gautama, I have no desire,
to nothing earthly I aspire,
in non-attachment I now rest,
passing Mara's subtle test.

Gautama, Flame of Cosmic Peace,
unruly thoughts do hereby cease,

we radiate from you and me
the peace to still Samsara's Sea.

6. Gautama Buddha, shatter the energetic matrix that prevents people from seeing that once we think God is a certain way, we can have a church that maintains that image of God for 17 centuries, as the Catholic church has done.

Gautama, I melt into you,
my mind is one, no longer two,
immersed in your resplendent glow,
Nirvana is all that I know.

**Gautama, Flame of Cosmic Peace,
unruly thoughts do hereby cease,
we radiate from you and me
the peace to still Samsara's Sea.**

7. Gautama Buddha, shatter the energetic matrix that prevents people from seeing that once we accept the idea that the earth has limited resources, as has now been projected for a long time by the materialist religion, then the planet will stagnate at a certain level.

Gautama, in your timeless space,
I am immersed in Cosmic Grace,
I know the God beyond all form,
to world I will no more conform.

**Gautama, Flame of Cosmic Peace,
unruly thoughts do hereby cease,
we radiate from you and me
the peace to still Samsara's Sea.**

8. Gautama Buddha, shatter the energetic matrix that prevents people from having a breakthrough where we begin to accept that the planet does not have a finite level of resources, that there are technologies that could replace oil completely.

Gautama, I am now awake,
I clearly see what is at stake,
and thus I claim my sacred right
to be on earth the Buddhic Light.

**Gautama, Flame of Cosmic Peace,
unruly thoughts do hereby cease,
we radiate from you and me
the peace to still Samsara's Sea.**

9. Gautama Buddha, shatter the energetic matrix that prevents people from seeing that compared to the technological progress that has happened in the last hundred years, in the next hundred years the technological progress will be many times greater.

Gautama, with your thunderbolt,
we give the earth a mighty jolt,
I know that some will understand,
and join the Buddha's timeless band.

**Gautama, Flame of Cosmic Peace,
unruly thoughts do hereby cease,
we radiate from you and me
the peace to still Samsara's Sea.**

Part 4

1. Gautama Buddha, shatter the energetic matrix that prevents people from seeing that fossil fuels will be looked at as being as primitive as the Stone Age.

Gautama, show my mental state
that does give rise to love and hate,
your exposé I do endure,
so my perception will be pure.

**Gautama, Flame of Cosmic Peace,
unruly thoughts do hereby cease,
we radiate from you and me
the peace to still Samsara's Sea.**

2. Gautama Buddha, shatter the energetic matrix that prevents people from seeing that the idea that energy costs money, and there are corporations who can have a virtual monopoly on the sale of energy, will be seen as being as primitive as the idea of a flat earth.

Gautama, in your Flame of Peace,
the struggling self I now release,
the Buddha Nature I now see,
it is the core of you and me.

**Gautama, Flame of Cosmic Peace,
unruly thoughts do hereby cease,
we radiate from you and me
the peace to still Samsara's Sea.**

3. Gautama Buddha, shatter the energetic matrix that prevents people from seeing that energy should be entirely free and should be available to all people in unlimited quantities. There will come a point where society will never be limited by energy. There will be unlimited energy to create all kinds of progress.

Gautama, I am one with thee,
Mara's demons do now flee,
your Presence like a soothing balm,
my mind and senses ever calm.

**Gautama, Flame of Cosmic Peace,
unruly thoughts do hereby cease,
we radiate from you and me
the peace to still Samsara's Sea.**

4. Gautama Buddha, shatter the energetic matrix that prevents people from becoming free from this emotional level stranglehold, the intellectual level stranglehold and the identity level stranglehold, so we begin to see

that nothing on earth is fixed because everything depends on consciousness. Therefore, there is the potential to create progress beyond our wildest imaginations.

> Gautama, I now take the vow,
> to live in the eternal now,
> with you I do transcend all time,
> to live in present so sublime.

> **Gautama, Flame of Cosmic Peace,**
> **unruly thoughts do hereby cease,**
> **we radiate from you and me**
> **the peace to still Samsara's Sea.**

5. Gautama Buddha, shatter the energetic matrix that prevents people from seeing that due to all the labels that have been projected, we have accepted so many limitations that we cannot actually imagine the progress that could be made.

> Gautama, I have no desire,
> to nothing earthly I aspire,
> in non-attachment I now rest,
> passing Mara's subtle test.

> **Gautama, Flame of Cosmic Peace,**
> **unruly thoughts do hereby cease,**
> **we radiate from you and me**
> **the peace to still Samsara's Sea.**

6. Gautama Buddha, shatter the energetic matrix that prevents people from seeing that if we took people who lived 200 years ago and showed them the modern age, they could not have imagined this kind of progress. They would have denied it, they would have said this could never happen.

> Gautama, I melt into you,
> my mind is one, no longer two,
> immersed in your resplendent glow,
> Nirvana is all that I know.

Gautama, Flame of Cosmic Peace,
unruly thoughts do hereby cease,
we radiate from you and me
the peace to still Samsara's Sea.

7. Gautama Buddha, shatter the energetic matrix that prevents people from seeing that progress *has* happened, so why could it not continue? Indeed, it *can,* and indeed it *will.*

Gautama, in your timeless space,
I am immersed in Cosmic Grace,
I know the God beyond all form,
to world I will no more conform.

Gautama, Flame of Cosmic Peace,
unruly thoughts do hereby cease,
we radiate from you and me
the peace to still Samsara's Sea.

8. Gautama Buddha, shatter the energetic matrix that prevents people from seeing that if we are willing to go beyond the labels created by the fallen beings, we can speed up the process whereby we become able to accept the Golden Age of Saint Germain.

Gautama, I am now awake,
I clearly see what is at stake,
and thus I claim my sacred right
to be on earth the Buddhic Light.

Gautama, Flame of Cosmic Peace,
unruly thoughts do hereby cease,
we radiate from you and me
the peace to still Samsara's Sea.

9. Gautama Buddha, shatter the energetic matrix that prevents people from shedding the snakeskin of the labels created by the fallen beings. Help us free our imagination so we can accept that the Golden Age that Saint Germain envisions is indeed a realistic potential.

Gautama, with your thunderbolt,
we give the earth a mighty jolt,
I know that some will understand,
and join the Buddha's timeless band.

**Gautama, Flame of Cosmic Peace,
unruly thoughts do hereby cease,
we radiate from you and me
the peace to still Samsara's Sea.**

Sealing

In the name of the I AM THAT I AM, I accept that Archangel Michael, Astrea and Shiva form an impenetrable shield around myself and all constructive people, sealing us from all fear-based energies in all four octaves. I accept that the Light of God is consuming and transforming all fear-based energies that make up the dark forces working against ending the era of elitism on earth!

34 | EXPOSING THE ELITE'S ATTITUDE TOWARDS THE PEOPLE

I AM the Ascended Master Saint Germain. I wish to take this opportunity to make some remarks about elitism that time and space did not allow me to make at our previous conference on that topic.

What is, in a sense, the one thing that could help people awaken to the problem of elitism, to the existence of an elite? Well, many years ago there was an incident in the United States, which was known as the Watergate scandal. As a part of the process of publicly resolving this matter, some of the tapes that were recorded in the White House of the President talking to some of his closest advisors about this problem were made public. What shocked the public the most was the very coarse, derogatory language used by the President, which many people did not find was fitting for the highest office of the land.

Well, in the same vein, it is not a matter of exposing the language used by the power elite but the way that the power elite talks about the people, about the population. There are various power elite groups of beings in embodiment who have their private meetings, whether it is in a small group of friends or family, or whether it is in some bigger or more organized meeting where they will feel relaxed, they will feel they are alone. Therefore, they will freely talk about their attitude towards the people, towards the population on earth. I can assure you that if people could hear some of these conversations, they would be extremely shocked over the level of arrogance, the level of pride that comes through these people, but also the way they look down upon the people.

Those who are the core members of the elite have a very clear, elitist, superior attitude. They feel they are in a separate class of beings from human beings. They feel they are superhuman beings, they are above and beyond human beings. They consider the general population to be made up of very primitive individuals that they consider to be stupid, unintelligent, unable to make their own decisions, unable to take responsibility for themselves, unable to discern between what is right and wrong. They consider the population to be extremely gullible, extremely naive and extremely easily fooled.

Now, I do not imagine that anyone will make a recording of these meetings, although that of course could happen. What I wish to bring to your attention is that you can make the calls that there are people who can expose what is going on in these meetings, perhaps through books that have a fictional character like the "My Lives" book but nevertheless records how these people talk, so that people can have an opportunity to see what is going on. To some degree this has already been done, but I desire you to make the calls that it can be done in a greater measure so that it can have more of an impact and people can then get a feel for how these people look at the population. This could of course also be the subject of movies, TV series and what have you. Again, some things have already been done, but actually the level of arrogance, the level of looking down upon the people that these elitists have, has never really been exposed the way it needs to be exposed for the people to be shocked enough to say: "We have to do something about this elite."

Diverting attention from the real problem

Now, if you look at it from the perspective of the elite, they see how time and time again, throughout history, they have been able to hide from the people, to fool the people, to divert the attention of the people so that instead of looking at the elite as the problem, they look at some other part of the population as the problem. This is again the divide-and-conquer strategy where, instead of having one division that has some reality to it (namely that between the power elite and the population), they have created all of these sub-divisions in the population that really have no reality to it. They use these to set these groups of people up against each other so that they use another group of people as the scapegoat when things are not going well in their country. They can blame it on someone outside the country, or maybe someone inside the country like the Germans did to the Jews in the 1930s, instead of actually blaming it on the elite who should have the blame because they have the responsibility for things not going well.

Time and time again, they divert the attention in this way so that the people are not seeing the real cause of the problem, namely the elite. They have of course seen this happen so many times in history where people have been fooled, they have believed what they wanted to believe, they have believed what was the easiest to believe and they have taken the easy way out. This has created this growing level of arrogance, this growing sense that, we are not only in a special category of people but we are above the law, we are untouchables. Nobody can touch us because we have so much power, so many connections, so much money, we know we can get away with anything. Or at least, that is what they think.

Once people could realize that this is how they think, then some people would start waking up and saying: "It is really time that we placed responsibility and accountability where it belongs. It is really time that we do not blame other people, other groups in the population, but that we are willing to place blame where it is and realize, it is the power elite in our own country that is creating the problems. Thereby, we also of course need to take responsibility for having allowed this elite to come to power or remain in power."

What the fallen beings, what the power elite, have been using so many times is precisely this unwillingness to make decisions, this fear of making decisions where people think they can only make bad decisions so they do not want to take responsibility. They do not want to make the decisions because they do not want to risk suffering negative consequences.

In a sense, many among the population have been willing to give away responsibility and to let a seemingly benevolent power elite rule them. This, however is not (as many among the power elite believe) an expression of human nature. It is, as we have explained many times, a condition that is artificially created through the manipulation of the fallen beings where they have systematically caused people to make bad decisions that then caused them to go into this state of fearing to make decisions. It is something that the fallen beings behind the power elite have systematically produced. Therefore, it is in a sense complete cognitive dissonance that they use this artificially created condition to reason that people just are that way, they just are incompetent, ignorant, stupid, what have you. What you can make the calls for is that people become aware of this.

Again, there is a tension in the collective consciousness, many people in the modern democracies are ready to step up and take a higher level of responsibility. There are many of the smaller countries in the democratic world where the power elite is no longer as strong as it was, for example, before the advent of democracy, during the feudal age or when you had the almighty kings. Many of the countries have already created a more egalitarian society where the power elite is not as strong, they are not quite as arrogant. Therefore, it will be easier for the people to step up and take responsibility for their country, demand not only a better representation but a more direct influence through direct democracy on the decision making in their countries.

The potential for an economic collapse

As we have said several times, even though the people might fear the consequences of them making the choices, the reality that you can make a call for people to realize, is that the population making decisions could not possibly be worse than the disaster after disaster created by the power elites throughout history. You just look at history and how it is littered with examples. This is again something people are ready to see: That the power elites have made some very, very bad decisions throughout history that have had disastrous consequences. It was not the people who started all these wars—it was the elite. It was not the people who manipulated the economy—it was the elite. It was not the people who created the financial crisis of 2008—it was the financial elite.

The reality is that we are nearing a time where what we have called the second law of thermodynamics, the self-correcting feature of the universe, has reached a point where the power elites will no longer be able to get away with doing what they have been doing. They think they are untouchable, they think they can escape the consequences of their actions, they think they can get the people to bear the consequences. If you look at the financial crisis of 2008, you will see that the economy of the world was on the brink of collapse. This was not something that was engineered by the financial power elite. It was created through their arrogance where they did not accurately assess the risk, therefore without realizing what they were doing, they brought the system to the brink of collapse.

There were some of them that were awakened by this. There were also people who are not part of the power elite in the government, in the media, in academia, who were awakened by this and realized that it would actually be possible for the entire economy to collapse and that it would have very severe consequences. Now, of course there are some among the elite who said: "Yes, yes, we realize we took this too far and we were on the brink of the collapse of the system. But look, the government, the people bailed us out in the end and they will do that again to avoid a collapse." You see, the second law of thermodynamics will bring this to a point where, if another crisis emerges like this, then it will not be stoppable. The government will not be able to bail out the elite. Therefore, the elite will fall, they will suffer the consequences. Of course, we do not desire to see such a collapse although we again allow free will to outplay itself. What you can make the calls for is that the people will wake up, that there will be an ongoing process of gradually higher states of awakening, where people realize that we simply cannot allow a small elite of billionaires to control and manipulate the economy. Why should we, in a democratic nation, allow a small elite of billionaires to manipulate the economy. What sense does it make?

This is what you can make the calls for: That people wake up and realize, what sense does it make that we have a democratic political system but an entirely undemocratic elitist economic system? What sense does that make? There can be one of these dramatic shifts where suddenly it is as if the scales fall from people's eyes and they see this is entirely inconsistent, this is entirely unsustainable. We cannot allow such an undemocratic elitist system to continue in a democratic nation because it undermines democracy. It completely undermines democracy. It undermines the principle of democracy that all people have equal rights, including the equal right to improve their lives through their own effort.

When you create a financial system that concentrates wealth in the hands of those who already have too much, then this undermines people's opportunity to improve their life by making an effort. So much of the money that should be going back to the people who make an effort is stolen away from them and concentrated in the hands of the elite. This simply is unsustainable and it is undemocratic. Many, many people are ready to see this and therefore demand systemic reforms of the economic and financial system.

The elite is afraid of the people

Another thing I want to bring out in order to complete what we want to release about elitism, is that the elite does not only have a derogatory attitude towards the people, they are actually afraid of the people. Whether it is the fallen beings in the identity, mental and emotional realms, or the fallen beings in embodiment, all fallen beings have a fear of the people. This is partly because they realize that there are so many more human beings than fallen beings. Therefore, at any moment where enough human beings decided to rise up against the fallen beings, they would lose their power. The human beings could always win if they saw what was going on. If a critical mass of them could unite, they could always overthrow the power elites, they could always, in the extreme case, kill all of the fallen beings.

What they also realize is that the population does not have to kill the elite for the elite to lose power. They just have to become aware of the existence and the methods of the elite. The moment people become aware, the fallen beings lose a lot of their power because their power is based on deception, manipulation, it is based on the people not knowing what is going on. The moment this was to happen, then they would lose power. That is why they are doing everything, as we have described, to prevent the people from waking up and making that determination: "We want something better, we want a better society."

One thing that also needs to be mentioned here is that the fallen beings, both those in embodiment and those in the higher realms, have a clear desire, a clear strategy, to limit the size of the human population. They are very capable of looking at history, and as we have described before, you had the feudal societies of Europe where the noblemen owned the land, then there were a large number of peasants living on that land who literally belonged to the land and the noblemen. This was a system that could work with a certain number of peasants that could still be sustained by the land, what the land could produce. There came a point where, through better hygiene, better awareness, the population started increasing. Not as many children died, people lived longer and therefore the population grew. There came a point where the population was so big that people could no longer survive by what could be produced on their nobleman's land.

When people were facing starvation, they would no longer submit to the nobleman and therefore the system was overthrown, as you for example saw in the French revolution. Part of this was that the people in Paris did not have the basic necessities to survive. They did not have enough bread, they did not have enough food and this was what caused them to support the uprising. Even though, as we have said before, the French revolution was driven by an aspiring power elite that wanted to overthrow the established power elite, nevertheless, they could not have done this if the people had not been brought to the brink of starvation.

The same thing with the feudal system, it did not get overthrown until the population faced such a severe situation that they could not live with it, they could not ignore it, they could not go on. You see here that it is always the arrogance, the ignorance, of the power elite, the established power elite, where they continue to do the same thing, they continue to hold on to power. This is what brings a society to that point where the population can no longer live with the conditions they have been given by the elite, and then they rise up.

The elite will always hold on to power

In many cases, this leads to the emergence of an aspiring power elite, who make use of the people's anger to overthrow the established elite. Then, in some cases, the people end up being worse off, as was the case after the Bolshevik revolution to some degree, and in many other instances. Nevertheless, what needs to be seen here is that there is always an established power elite and they cannot change their ways until they are faced with a determined population who will no longer accept current conditions, but want some kind of change. In other words the elite will not do it by themselves, unless it is to give them even more power and more privilege, but they will not change the system in favour of the people. This is what the population needs to realize so that people can wake up and say: "We are the ones who can bring change. We are the ones who must take upon ourselves the responsibility to bring change."

What also needs to be seen is that, as I said, the fallen beings had and have had for a long time, an active program of limiting the size of the population. They know when the population reaches a certain level, they cannot control the population, or at least that is what they think. The reality is somewhat more complex because we have told you that your planet exists inside a sphere with many other inhabited planets. On most of these planets, the population is in an upward spiral of raising their consciousness. This has created this upward, accelerating movement in the universe and it is pulling on the earth. When you look at the last several hundred years, of what has happened in societies on earth, you see that there has been a clear progression. There has been an improvement in the area of politics where more and more people have come to live under democratic governments, which I can assure you that the power elite never wanted, the fallen beings never wanted.

There has been greater political freedom, the economy has grown and there has been a more equal distribution of wealth, although it is not equal enough. The economy has improved, there has been a growth, there has been a growth in the size of the population, there has been a growth in people's knowledge, there has been a growth in technology. All of this has been brought about, not just because the population has grown, but also because of that upward pull from the rest of the universe that is pulling on people.

The elite cannot stop progress

The reality here is that many among the population are able to tune in to this upward movement. That is why some people decide that they want to have a better life, they want to have a better political system, they take a stand and demand something better, they educate themselves, they raise their consciousness, they start businesses and start improving their outer situation and so forth. People can tune in to this accelerating movement and this is what actually has brought about change. It is not just the rise in the number of the population, but also the rise in the consciousness of the population, because they are tuned in to that accelerating movement.

Now, the fallen beings do not realize this because they are not able to tune in to that accelerating movement. They know there is something but they do not understand what it is. They are simply too blind to see it. They think they know everything about how the world works. They do not actually see the reality of how the universe functions, and how there is absolutely no chance that the earth can resist that accelerating movement of the rest of the universe. There is nothing they can do to stop it and that is why they have not, with all their manipulation, with all their keeping the people in ignorance, they have not been able to stop the forward progression on this planet.

Now, I know that there are many people who have a negative view and think there are still so many problems, or maybe there are even more and more problems, but it simply is not the case. If you step back, look neutrally at society as it was 500 or a 1,000 years ago, how can you fail to see that there has been so much progression in so many areas? Certainly, for example, technology has created problems but there has still been a progression. This is brought about by the upward movement of the universe. The problems that have been created are a product of the duality consciousness and also the manipulation of the fallen beings, but there has still been an overall progression. Otherwise, all people on earth would still be living in the same kind of societies as you saw in the feudal system in Europe where they were the slaves of a small power elite and they lived their entire lives without having the possibility of improving their condition.

The elite feels threatened by population growth

You realize here that the fallen beings feel threatened. They feel there is change that they cannot hold back but they do not see the real reason. They think it is the increase in population: "That is the problem, we need to limit the size of the population so we can still keep them in a state of slavery." Of course, some of the fallen beings have given up on this because they realize they cannot actually stop population growth, except through perhaps a nuclear war but that will also wipe out their own privileged positions because it is not so fun to be a king if you have no underlings to rule over. There are still many among the fallen beings who believe that the problem is the size of the population. They also believe that the earth simply does not have the resources to sustain the current level of the population.

Nor does it have the resources to give all people on earth a decent standard of living. This of course is, in a sense, correct. The earth does not have the resources right now to give all people a decent standard of living, but that is for two reasons: 1. The fallen beings have manipulated things to the point where there are a lot of resources that are not recognized by science, they do not see this as a resource. So there *is* a limited amount of resources. 2. The real problem is the unequal distribution of resources and wealth. Certainly, with the present distribution of money, for example where 2% of the population in the United States controls over 90% of the wealth, well obviously you cannot give all people in the world a decent standard of living. But with a redistribution of wealth, you certainly could.

Now, the fallen beings of course do not want the redistribution of wealth. They cannot see the potential for technology that could change and increase the level of resources. They cannot really see the potential for free energy technology, which is why they have made such a determined effort to ridicule it and put it down or to stop it if they can. Nevertheless, behind all of this there are still some fallen beings, both in embodiment and in the higher realms, who are actively working on limiting the size of the population. They do this in various ways. We have previously talked about abortion being one of the ways they want to limit the size of the population, but there are more sinister and inhumane ways. Poverty is one of the more inhumane ways to limit the size of the population because it increases of course child mortality, limits the lifespan when people are living in a state of malnutrition. Disease is another where they have tried to create modern medicine in such a way that it cannot cure certain diseases, which then again limit the size of the population.

Another aspect is the entire environmental debate, which they have taken over and manipulated to the point where many among the people actually believe that the problem on earth, the biggest problem on earth, the biggest threat to the survival of humanity, is the increase in population. This has caused millions upon millions of people, especially in the more democratic world, to voluntarily limit the amount of children they have. You do not need to abort the children. You do not need to kill them off with disease or malnutrition because people voluntarily choose not to have as many children.

You see how there is an attempt to create this attitude that humanity needs to do something to limit population growth. What they are trying to do is to create an attitude in the population where they will actually accept some of these more subtle methods that they are working on developing to limit the size of the population, including genetic manipulation that could lower the fertility of women so they could not have as many children. These are some of the topics they are researching. They are even talking about forced sterilization and many other things. Therefore, through the environmental debate they are trying to create an attitude among people where they accept the necessity of limiting the human population.

You will see, if you look at the environmental debate from a neutral standpoint, that much of it, not *all* of it but *much* of it, is not about the environment. It is actually about human beings, it is about creating some kind of attitude that accepts more control with the size of the population. It is not directed at improving the environment. It is directed at limiting the size of the human population. Now, as we have said before: Who is it that creates most of the pollution in the world, the more serious form of pollution? Well, it is the power elite who are driven by their profit motive so that they create these factories that let out more toxins and more toxic substances than what is produced by normal human waste.

Again, you can see that the biggest problem with pollution is created by the power elite, but who are they blaming it on? The people. It is not the little power elite that is the problem with pollution, no it is that there are too many in the population. They say *that* is what creates pollution. Many, many people have believed this, hook, line and sinker. This is a real concern for me as the hierarch of the Aquarian Age and the promoter of the Golden Age.

More concern for people than the environment

Who are the people who believe in this, who are concerned about the environment? Well, they are the people who have a certain level of humanity. Because when you have a basic level of humanity, then you are also concerned about the environment. You should really be primarily concerned about improving the conditions for other people. These people have that tendency but it has been misdirected by the fallen beings where they are more concerned about the environment than they are about people in the third world, for example, who are living near the starvation level.

You see that these people have a high level of humanity. Many of them are very sensitive, very creative, very constructive people. They are the kind of people that I need in order to drive the progress into the Golden Age. The Golden Age is about growth, it is not about limiting growth but they have been deceived into thinking that they should limit growth. They should work towards limiting growth, living a minimalistic lifestyle, consuming as little as possible, all of these things. They are not able to tune in to my Presence and my ideas and bring them forth. It is a huge wasted potential where some of these creative people could play a role in bringing forth the Golden Age.

I can assure you that in the Golden Age, there will not be a problem with pollution because we will bring forth a non-force-based technology that does not pollute. But who is going to bring it forth? There has to be some creative people who can receive it. Who is going to make the changes in society, in the economy, who is going to do all of these things that will manifest the Golden Age? Well, precisely the people who are today so concerned about limiting the size of the population, improving the environment, combating global warming and all of these things that could be transcended by moving into the Golden Age mindset, which is not based on lack, not based on limitations, and bringing forth Golden Age technology.

This is what I would be grateful for you making the calls on: That these people would be awakened, that they would be cut free from this deception of the fallen beings. One of the ways this can happen is when they recognize the arrogance of the fallen beings, how they have no respect, they have no humanity. Therefore, they can be awakened to see that these are not the kind of people we want to be following because it is actually not going to help the environment. I can assure you that what is currently being proposed in order to combat pollution and global warming is not going to be effective.

Transcending force-based technology

There is the need for an entirely new kind of technology that is not forced-based, therefore, what you today call free energy technology, even though it is not free. Free energy is a manipulated terminology, created by the fallen beings to discredit this technology and make people think it is a utopian fantasy. It is not a utopian fantasy because if there was not a realm beyond the physical, if there was not energy in that realm that could be brought into the physical, how would there be a universe? Where would it come from? You have the Big Bang model that claims that in the Big Bang all energy was released. But you know from an explosion that there is only a limited amount of energy released so there comes a point where the expansion stops and things start imploding.

Well, cosmologists tell you that the universe is not only expanding, it is expanding at an accelerated rate. There must be energy to drive this expansion. Since it cannot come from the physical, it must come from beyond the physical. Why could you not make use of this energy to charge your smartphone or even drive your smartphone, drive your car, heat your house, bring light to your house and all of these things? Suddenly, you have a technology that is not burning fossil fuel, it is not polluting.

The technology has to be brought forth, but not only does it have to be brought forth, there has to be a critical mass of people who can accept that this is a realistic possibility. Who could do this? Well, precisely the people who have a level of humanity, precisely the people who are concerned about the environment, but they have been misled into thinking that the only way to save the environment is through control.

In reality, look at history: What has driven positive growth? It is *acceleration,* it is transcending the old ways of looking at things. Transcendence and acceleration is the key to saving the environment, not control. Who wants control? The fallen beings, the power elite, they are the ones who are always wanting control. Control works against the basic forces of the universe. Control creates a closed system that becomes subject to the second law of thermodynamics and therefore will self-destruct.

That is what happened in the Soviet Union, that is what happened in many previous civilizations that became closed systems because there was a small power elite who did all they could to control the population. They wanted to keep the population down, they wanted to keep the creativity of the population down, to lower their consciousness. When you lower the collective consciousness, you create a tension that will eventually cause that society to fall apart.

We have talked about the 144 levels of consciousness. When you go below the 48th level, people become increasingly selfish. Well, if people become more and more selfish, how concerned are they about the environment? How concerned are they about other people? The people who are the most selfish, they do not care about the environment. They do not care about the coral reefs. They do not care about the whales. They do not care about children starving to death in Bangladesh. It is of no concern to them whatsoever, they just want the lifestyle they think they are entitled to. This is precisely the attitude of the power elite. They are not concerned whatsoever about the environment, they only claim to be because they can use it as a means to an end of controlling the population.

Wake up! I say to those of you who are the creative people, who are concerned about the environment. Wake up and realize what will save the environment and what will not! Allowing a small power elite to continue to control the human population will not save the environment. It will only make things worse, as the power elite has been making things gradually worse with the increase in technology. Who has misused technology? Is it the people or is it the power elite? Well, you know my answer to that question. So wake up, look around, educate yourself to what is really going on. Stop being put into thinking you are doing something good for the planet. In reality, you are only doing what is good for the elite. I for one, want a Golden Age where all people can live an abundant, affluent lifestyle without destroying the environment on the planet. This is possible. It is not possible with current technology. It is not possible with the current distribution of wealth. But both of those can be changed.

I cannot do it alone. I have all the ideas for how this could be done. I am willing to release those ideas but there has to be those who can implement them and there has to be those who can accept it. You have the potential. I speak into the collective consciousness to these many well-meaning, enthusiastic, idealistic people. You have the potential to be forerunners for my Golden Age. Wake up and recognize that potential and realize that this is why you are here. This is why you wanted to embody at this particular time, you did not want to embody to take society backwards. You wanted to embody to take it forwards into the Golden Age. Awaken yourselves, educate yourselves, realize the dynamic that the real issue on the planet is the existence of a power elite who are sabotaging absolutely everything, every positive initiative that has ever been taken, they are attempting to sabotage it.

You may say, as many people believe: "But we need to create a new system, a new ideology, a new approach." But whatever you create, the fallen beings will only have one concern: "How can we turn it into a system that serves our cause of getting power and privilege and control?" Many people were enthusiastic about communism, socialism in some form, in previous decades. Well, as we have said, a socialist system with common ownership, could work. But it cannot work when the fallen beings are attempting to manipulate it into setting themselves up with power and privilege. Now, a free market economy, I am not saying a capitalist economy, but a free market economy can also work but not when you have a small elite who are doing everything they can to destroy free competition, to destroy the free market so they can create monopolies that concentrate wealth in the hands of a small group of people.

Raising consciousness is the effective solution

There is no system you could possibly think up that could ever work as long as the population allows a small power elite to manipulate that system. The only way out is to raise consciousness so that the power elite cannot continue to manipulate the population. It is not a matter of just knowledge. It is not a matter of creating websites that expose the power elite, and are then labelled as conspiracy theories by the elite in order to discredit it. It is a matter of raising the general level of awareness, the general level of consciousness.

How do you do it? By raising your own level of consciousness—*that* is how you pull up on the collective. There are many people who came into embodiment because this is what they wanted. They have been misled by a materialistic philosophy that has never given them an inkling of the possibility of raising their consciousness. You can awaken from this, you can come to realize that the greatest potential you have for improving your personal life is to raise your consciousness. Incidentally, that is also the greatest potential you have for improving the environment. Raising of consciousness is the only way out of humankind's problems. This is the one thing that the power elites of the world do not want a critical mass of people to realize. Once a critical mass realizes this, the power elite will be done, they will lose their power very, very quickly once the collective consciousness is raised beyond a certain level. It does not require the entire population to become aware of the power elite, but a critical mass will be enough to pull the collective consciousness up to where people simply will no longer believe all of the illusions that have been spread by the elites.

This is the critical shift that could happen, that could have wide-ranging consequences for every aspect of society. Whatever concern you may have, and many, many people have valid concerns, they have a great desire to improve some aspect of life, but the foundation for fulfilling your aspirations is the raising of consciousness. It is simply the engine that drives growth and you are not going to get out of problems through control, you will only get out of problems through growth, through acceleration. I am not talking about the kind of growth where you get more of the same. In other words, I am not saying that in order to raise the standard of living in third world countries, you need to increase energy production by burning more coal. I am saying you need to bring forth a new kind of technology that does not pollute.

Ask yourself this: If it was possible to increase the standard of living for all people on earth without destroying the environment, would you not want to increase the standard of living of all of these people who are watching their children starve to death, or dying of diseases that could easily be cured? Would you not want this to happen? Well, of course they would, all of these people that I am talking about, who are not awakened, who have the good intentions but who are not seeing how these intentions could actually be carried out. It is, as we have said before, they have a vision of *what* should happen on earth but they do not have a realistic vision of *how* it could be attained. They could be awakened and realize that: "Why shouldn't it be possible to both improve people's standard of living and preserve the environment? Why shouldn't it be possible?" It will require a different kind of technology, a different distribution of wealth, a different approach and attitude to society.

Look how much society in the democratic world has transcended itself in the past thousand years. Why would it not be possible to have another period of very intense accelerated growth so that in a matter of decades there would be a change so dramatic that people's intuitive sense of what is possible suddenly becomes realistic. Because now you do not have just the *what,* you also have the *how.*

My beloved, if you are willing to open your consciousness, I will give you the ideas for *how* you can manifest *what* you know in your hearts is possible on earth. You give me the openness, you give me the acceptance that it is possible and I will give you the *how. That* is my promise and I will stand by it for the next 2,000 years. Will *you* stand by it and the potential for growth?

35 | INVOKING AN EXPOSURE OF THE REAL PROBLEM (PART 1)

In the name of the I AM THAT I AM, Jesus Christ, I use the authority that I have as a being in embodiment on earth to call upon Saint Germain to reinforce my calls and use my chakras to project the statements in this invocation into the collective consciousness and awaken people to the fact that the real problem on earth is that the fallen beings attempt to sabotage any constructive endeavour. Awaken people to the reality that we are spiritual beings and that we can co-create a new future by working with the ascended masters. I especially call for …

[Make your own calls here.]

Part 1

1. Saint Germain, shatter the energetic matrix that prevents people from seeing that the one thing that could help people awaken to the problem of elitism is an exposure of the way that the power elite talks about the people, about the population.

O Saint Germain, you do inspire,
my vision raised forever higher,
with you I form a figure-eight,
your Golden Age I co-create.

O Saint Germain, what love you bring,
it truly makes all matter sing,
your violet flame does all restore,
with you we are becoming more.

2. Saint Germain, shatter the energetic matrix that prevents people from seeing that various power elite groups have their private meetings, where they freely talk about their attitude towards the people, towards the population on earth.

O Saint Germain, what Freedom Flame,
released when we recite your name,
acceleration is your gift,
our planet it will surely lift.

O Saint Germain, what love you bring,
it truly makes all matter sing,
your violet flame does all restore,
with you we are becoming more.

3. Saint Germain, shatter the energetic matrix that prevents people from seeing that if people could hear some of these conversations, they would be extremely shocked over the level of arrogance, the level of pride that comes through these people, but also the way they look down upon the people.

O Saint Germain, in love we claim,
our right to bring your violet flame,
from you Above, to us below,
it is an all-transforming flow.

O Saint Germain, what love you bring,
it truly makes all matter sing,

**your violet flame does all restore,
with you we are becoming more.**

4. Saint Germain, shatter the energetic matrix that prevents people from seeing that those who are the core members of the elite have a very clear elitist, superior attitude. They feel they are in a separate class of beings from human beings.

O Saint Germain, I love you so,
my aura filled with violet glow,
my chakras filled with violet fire,
I am your cosmic amplifier.

**O Saint Germain, what love you bring,
it truly makes all matter sing,
your violet flame does all restore,
with you we are becoming more.**

5. Saint Germain, shatter the energetic matrix that prevents people from seeing that members of the elite feel they are superhuman beings, they are above and beyond human beings.

O Saint Germain, I am now free,
your violet flame is therapy,
transform all hang-ups in my mind,
as inner peace I surely find.

**O Saint Germain, what love you bring,
it truly makes all matter sing,
your violet flame does all restore,
with you we are becoming more.**

6. Saint Germain, shatter the energetic matrix that prevents people from seeing that members of the elite consider the general population to be made up of very primitive individuals that they consider to be stupid, unintelligent, unable to make their own decisions, unable to take responsibility for themselves, unable to discern between what is right and wrong.

O Saint Germain, my body pure,
your violet flame for all is cure,
consume the cause of all disease,
and therefore I am all at ease.

O Saint Germain, what love you bring,
it truly makes all matter sing,
your violet flame does all restore,
with you we are becoming more.

7. Saint Germain, shatter the energetic matrix that prevents people from seeing that members of the elite consider the population to be extremely gullible, extremely naive and extremely easily fooled.

O Saint Germain, I'm karma-free,
the past no longer burdens me,
a brand new opportunity,
I am in Christic unity.

O Saint Germain, what love you bring,
it truly makes all matter sing,
your violet flame does all restore,
with you we are becoming more.

8. Saint Germain, shatter the energetic matrix that prevents people who are in the right position from exposing what is going on in these meetings, perhaps through books that have a fictional character.

O Saint Germain, we are now one,
I am for you a violet sun,
as we transform this planet earth,
your Golden Age is given birth.

O Saint Germain, what love you bring,
it truly makes all matter sing,
your violet flame does all restore,
with you we are becoming more.

9. Saint Germain, shatter the energetic matrix that prevents people from exposing how members of the elite talk, so that people can get a feel for how these people look at the population.

O Saint Germain, the earth is free,
from burden of duality,
in oneness we bring what is best,
your Golden Age is manifest.

**O Saint Germain, what love you bring,
it truly makes all matter sing,
your violet flame does all restore,
with you we are becoming more.**

Part 2

1. Saint Germain, shatter the energetic matrix that prevents people in the right positions from making movies or TV that expose the level of arrogance, the level of looking down upon the people that these elitists have.

O Saint Germain, you do inspire,
my vision raised forever higher,
with you I form a figure-eight,
your Golden Age I co-create.

**O Saint Germain, what love you bring,
it truly makes all matter sing,
your violet flame does all restore,
with you we are becoming more.**

2. Saint Germain, shatter the energetic matrix that prevents the arrogance of the elite from being exposed, so the people will be so shocked that they say: "We have to do something about this elite."

O Saint Germain, what Freedom Flame,
released when we recite your name,

acceleration is your gift,
our planet it will surely lift.

**O Saint Germain, what love you bring,
it truly makes all matter sing,
your violet flame does all restore,
with you we are becoming more.**

3. Saint Germain, shatter the energetic matrix that prevents people from seeing that from the perspective of the elite, they see how time and time again, throughout history, they have been able to hide from the people, to fool the people.

O Saint Germain, in love we claim,
our right to bring your violet flame,
from you Above, to us below,
it is an all-transforming flow.

**O Saint Germain, what love you bring,
it truly makes all matter sing,
your violet flame does all restore,
with you we are becoming more.**

4. Saint Germain, shatter the energetic matrix that prevents people from seeing that the elite has been able to divert the attention of the people, so that instead of looking at the elite as the problem, we look at some other part of the population as the problem.

O Saint Germain, I love you so,
my aura filled with violet glow,
my chakras filled with violet fire,
I am your cosmic amplifier.

**O Saint Germain, what love you bring,
it truly makes all matter sing,
your violet flame does all restore,
with you we are becoming more.**

5. Saint Germain, shatter the energetic matrix that prevents people from seeing that the elite uses the divide-and-conquer strategy where, instead of having one division that has some reality to it, namely that between the power elite and the population, they have created all of these sub-divisions in the population that really have no reality.

> O Saint Germain, I am now free,
> your violet flame is therapy,
> transform all hang-ups in my mind,
> as inner peace I surely find.

> **O Saint Germain, what love you bring,**
> **it truly makes all matter sing,**
> **your violet flame does all restore,**
> **with you we are becoming more.**

6. Saint Germain, shatter the energetic matrix that prevents people from seeing that the elite uses the divisions to set groups of people up against each other so that we use another group of people as the scapegoat when things are not going well for us.

> O Saint Germain, my body pure,
> your violet flame for all is cure,
> consume the cause of all disease,
> and therefore I am all at ease.

> **O Saint Germain, what love you bring,**
> **it truly makes all matter sing,**
> **your violet flame does all restore,**
> **with you we are becoming more.**

7. Saint Germain, shatter the energetic matrix that prevents people from seeing that the elite will blame problems on someone outside the country, or maybe someone inside the country, like the Germans did to the Jews in the 1930s, instead of actually blaming it on the elite who should have the blame because they have the responsibility for things not going well.

> O Saint Germain, I'm karma-free,
> the past no longer burdens me,

a brand new opportunity,
I am in Christic unity.

O Saint Germain, what love you bring,
it truly makes all matter sing,
your violet flame does all restore,
with you we are becoming more.

8. Saint Germain, shatter the energetic matrix that prevents people from seeing that time and time again, the elite has diverted the attention in this way so that the people are not seeing the real cause of the problem, namely the elite.

O Saint Germain, we are now one,
I am for you a violet sun,
as we transform this planet earth,
your Golden Age is given birth.

O Saint Germain, what love you bring,
it truly makes all matter sing,
your violet flame does all restore,
with you we are becoming more.

9. Saint Germain, shatter the energetic matrix that prevents people from seeing that members of the elite have seen this happen so many times in history, where we have been fooled, we have believed what we wanted to believe, we have believed what was the easiest to believe and we have taken the easy way out.

O Saint Germain, the earth is free,
from burden of duality,
in oneness we bring what is best,
your Golden Age is manifest.

O Saint Germain, what love you bring,
it truly makes all matter sing,
your violet flame does all restore,
with you we are becoming more.

Part 3

1. Saint Germain, shatter the energetic matrix that prevents people from seeing that the elite has a growing level of arrogance, a growing sense that, we are not only in a special category of people but we are above the law, we are untouchables. Nobody can touch us because we have so much power, so many connections, so much money, we know we can get away with anything.

> O Saint Germain, you do inspire,
> my vision raised forever higher,
> with you I form a figure-eight,
> your Golden Age I co-create.

> **O Saint Germain, what love you bring,**
> **it truly makes all matter sing,**
> **your violet flame does all restore,**
> **with you we are becoming more.**

2. Saint Germain, shatter the energetic matrix that prevents people from waking up and saying: "It is really time that we placed responsibility and accountability where it belongs. It is really time that we do not blame other people, other groups in the population, but that we are willing to place blame where it is and realize, it is the power elite in our own country that is creating the problems. Thereby, we also need to take responsibility for having allowed this elite to come to power or remain in power."

> O Saint Germain, what Freedom Flame,
> released when we recite your name,
> acceleration is your gift,
> our planet it will surely lift.

> **O Saint Germain, what love you bring,**
> **it truly makes all matter sing,**
> **your violet flame does all restore,**
> **with you we are becoming more.**

3. Saint Germain, shatter the energetic matrix that prevents people from seeing that the fallen beings have been using this unwillingness to make decisions, this fear of making decisions, where we think we can only make bad decisions so we do not want to take responsibility. We do not want to make the decisions because we do not want to risk suffering negative consequences.

O Saint Germain, in love we claim,
our right to bring your violet flame,
from you Above, to us below,
it is an all-transforming flow.

O Saint Germain, what love you bring,
it truly makes all matter sing,
your violet flame does all restore,
with you we are becoming more.

4. Saint Germain, shatter the energetic matrix that prevents people from seeing that many of us have been willing to give away responsibility and to let a seemingly benevolent power elite rule us.

O Saint Germain, I love you so,
my aura filled with violet glow,
my chakras filled with violet fire,
I am your cosmic amplifier.

O Saint Germain, what love you bring,
it truly makes all matter sing,
your violet flame does all restore,
with you we are becoming more.

5. Saint Germain, shatter the energetic matrix that prevents people from seeing that this is not, as many among the power elite believe, an expression of human nature. It is a condition that is artificially created through the manipulation of the fallen beings.

O Saint Germain, I am now free,
your violet flame is therapy,

transform all hang-ups in my mind,
as inner peace I surely find.

**O Saint Germain, what love you bring,
it truly makes all matter sing,
your violet flame does all restore,
with you we are becoming more.**

6. Saint Germain, shatter the energetic matrix that prevents people from seeing that the fallen beings have systematically caused us to make bad decisions that then caused us to go into this state of fearing to make decisions. It is something that the fallen beings behind the power elite have systematically produced.

O Saint Germain, my body pure,
your violet flame for all is cure,
consume the cause of all disease,
and therefore I am all at ease.

**O Saint Germain, what love you bring,
it truly makes all matter sing,
your violet flame does all restore,
with you we are becoming more.**

7. Saint Germain, shatter the energetic matrix that prevents people from seeing that it is cognitive dissonance that the elite uses this artificially created condition to reason that people just are that way, they just are incompetent, ignorant and stupid.

O Saint Germain, I'm karma-free,
the past no longer burdens me,
a brand new opportunity,
I am in Christic unity.

**O Saint Germain, what love you bring,
it truly makes all matter sing,
your violet flame does all restore,
with you we are becoming more.**

8. Saint Germain, shatter the energetic matrix that prevents people from seeing that in many of the smaller countries in the democratic world, the power elite is no longer as strong as it was before the advent of democracy.

O Saint Germain, we are now one,
I am for you a violet sun,
as we transform this planet earth,
your Golden Age is given birth.

O Saint Germain, what love you bring,
it truly makes all matter sing,
your violet flame does all restore,
with you we are becoming more.

9. Saint Germain, shatter the energetic matrix that prevents people from stepping up and taking responsibility for our country, demanding not only a better representation but a more direct influence through direct democracy on the decision making in our countries.

O Saint Germain, the earth is free,
from burden of duality,
in oneness we bring what is best,
your Golden Age is manifest.

O Saint Germain, what love you bring,
it truly makes all matter sing,
your violet flame does all restore,
with you we are becoming more.

Part 4

1. Saint Germain, shatter the energetic matrix that prevents people from seeing that although some people fear the consequences of the population making the choices, the reality is that the population making decisions could not possibly be worse than the disaster after disaster created by the power elites throughout history.

O Saint Germain, you do inspire,
my vision raised forever higher,
with you I form a figure-eight,
your Golden Age I co-create.

**O Saint Germain, what love you bring,
it truly makes all matter sing,
your violet flame does all restore,
with you we are becoming more.**

2. Saint Germain, shatter the energetic matrix that prevents people from seeing that the power elites have made some very bad decisions throughout history that have had disastrous consequences.

O Saint Germain, what Freedom Flame,
released when we recite your name,
acceleration is your gift,
our planet it will surely lift.

**O Saint Germain, what love you bring,
it truly makes all matter sing,
your violet flame does all restore,
with you we are becoming more.**

3. Saint Germain, shatter the energetic matrix that prevents people from seeing that it was not the people who started all these wars—it was the elite. It was not the people who manipulated the economy—it was the elite. It was not the people who created the financial crisis of 2008—it was the financial elite.

O Saint Germain, in love we claim,
our right to bring your violet flame,
from you Above, to us below,
it is an all-transforming flow.

**O Saint Germain, what love you bring,
it truly makes all matter sing,
your violet flame does all restore,
with you we are becoming more.**

4. Saint Germain, shatter the energetic matrix that prevents people from seeing that the self-correcting feature of the universe has reached a point, where the power elites will no longer be able to get away with doing what they have been doing.

O Saint Germain, I love you so,
my aura filled with violet glow,
my chakras filled with violet fire,
I am your cosmic amplifier.

O Saint Germain, what love you bring,
it truly makes all matter sing,
your violet flame does all restore,
with you we are becoming more.

5. Saint Germain, shatter the energetic matrix that prevents people from seeing that members of the elite think they are untouchable, they think they can escape the consequences of their actions, they think they can get the people to bear the consequences.

O Saint Germain, I am now free,
your violet flame is therapy,
transform all hang-ups in my mind,
as inner peace I surely find.

O Saint Germain, what love you bring,
it truly makes all matter sing,
your violet flame does all restore,
with you we are becoming more.

6. Saint Germain, shatter the energetic matrix that prevents people from seeing that during the financial crisis of 2008, the economy of the world was on the brink of collapse. This was not something that was engineered by the financial power elite. It was created through their arrogance where they did not accurately assess the risk, therefore without realizing what they were doing, they brought the system to the brink of collapse.

O Saint Germain, my body pure,
your violet flame for all is cure,

consume the cause of all disease,
and therefore I am all at ease.

O Saint Germain, what love you bring,
it truly makes all matter sing,
your violet flame does all restore,
with you we are becoming more.

7. Saint Germain, shatter the energetic matrix that prevents people from seeing that some members of the elite were awakened by this. Some people who are not part of the power elite in the government, the media and academia were awakened by this. They realized that it would actually be possible for the entire economy to collapse and that it would have very severe consequences.

O Saint Germain, I'm karma-free,
the past no longer burdens me,
a brand new opportunity,
I am in Christic unity.

O Saint Germain, what love you bring,
it truly makes all matter sing,
your violet flame does all restore,
with you we are becoming more.

8. Saint Germain, shatter the energetic matrix that prevents people from seeing that some among the elite said: "Yes, we realize we took this too far and we were on the brink of the collapse of the system. But look, the government, the people bailed us out in the end and they will do that again to avoid a collapse."

O Saint Germain, we are now one,
I am for you a violet sun,
as we transform this planet earth,
your Golden Age is given birth.

O Saint Germain, what love you bring,
it truly makes all matter sing,

your violet flame does all restore,
with you we are becoming more.

9. Saint Germain, shatter the energetic matrix that prevents people from seeing that the self-correcting law of the universe will bring this to a point where, if another crisis emerges like this, then it will not be stoppable. The government will not be able to bail out the elite. The elite will fall.

O Saint Germain, the earth is free,
from burden of duality,
in oneness we bring what is best,
your Golden Age is manifest.

O Saint Germain, what love you bring,
it truly makes all matter sing,
your violet flame does all restore,
with you we are becoming more.

Part 5

1. Saint Germain, shatter the energetic matrix that prevents an ongoing process of gradually higher states of awakening, where people realize that we simply cannot allow a small elite of billionaires to control and manipulate the economy. Why should we, in a democratic nation, allow a small elite of billionaires to manipulate the economy. What sense does it make?

O Saint Germain, you do inspire,
my vision raised forever higher,
with you I form a figure-eight,
your Golden Age I co-create.

O Saint Germain, what love you bring,
it truly makes all matter sing,
your violet flame does all restore,
with you we are becoming more.

2. Saint Germain, shatter the energetic matrix that prevents people from waking up and realizing: What sense does it make that we have a democratic political system but an entirely undemocratic, elitist economic system? What sense does that make?

> O Saint Germain, what Freedom Flame,
> released when we recite your name,
> acceleration is your gift,
> our planet it will surely lift.

> **O Saint Germain, what love you bring,**
> **it truly makes all matter sing,**
> **your violet flame does all restore,**
> **with you we are becoming more.**

3. Saint Germain, shatter the energetic matrix that prevents a dramatic shift, where suddenly it is as if the scales fall from people's eyes and they see this is entirely inconsistent, this is entirely unsustainable.

> O Saint Germain, in love we claim,
> our right to bring your violet flame,
> from you Above, to us below,
> it is an all-transforming flow.

> **O Saint Germain, what love you bring,**
> **it truly makes all matter sing,**
> **your violet flame does all restore,**
> **with you we are becoming more.**

4. Saint Germain, shatter the energetic matrix that prevents people from seeing that we cannot allow such an undemocratic elitist system to continue in a democratic nation because it undermines democracy. It undermines the principle of democracy that all people have equal rights, including the equal right to improve their lives through their own efforts.

> O Saint Germain, I love you so,
> my aura filled with violet glow,
> my chakras filled with violet fire,
> I am your cosmic amplifier.

**O Saint Germain, what love you bring,
it truly makes all matter sing,
your violet flame does all restore,
with you we are becoming more.**

5. Saint Germain, shatter the energetic matrix that prevents people from seeing that when we create a financial system that concentrates wealth in the hands of those who already have too much, then this undermines people's opportunity to improve their lives by making an effort.

O Saint Germain, I am now free,
your violet flame is therapy,
transform all hang-ups in my mind,
as inner peace I surely find.

**O Saint Germain, what love you bring,
it truly makes all matter sing,
your violet flame does all restore,
with you we are becoming more.**

6. Saint Germain, shatter the energetic matrix that prevents people from seeing that so much of the money that should be going back to the people who make an effort, is stolen away from them and concentrated in the hands of the elite. This is unsustainable and it is undemocratic.

O Saint Germain, my body pure,
your violet flame for all is cure,
consume the cause of all disease,
and therefore I am all at ease.

**O Saint Germain, what love you bring,
it truly makes all matter sing,
your violet flame does all restore,
with you we are becoming more.**

7. Saint Germain, shatter the energetic matrix that prevents people from seeing that members of the elite do not only have a derogatory attitude towards the people, they are actually afraid of the people. Whether it is

the fallen beings in the identity, mental and emotional realms, or the fallen beings in embodiment, all fallen beings have a fear of the people.

O Saint Germain, I'm karma-free,
the past no longer burdens me,
a brand new opportunity,
I am in Christic unity.

**O Saint Germain, what love you bring,
it truly makes all matter sing,
your violet flame does all restore,
with you we are becoming more.**

8. Saint Germain, shatter the energetic matrix that prevents people from seeing that this is partly because they realize that there are so many more human beings than fallen beings. Therefore, at any moment where enough human beings decide to rise up against the fallen beings, they would lose their power.

O Saint Germain, we are now one,
I am for you a violet sun,
as we transform this planet earth,
your Golden Age is given birth.

**O Saint Germain, what love you bring,
it truly makes all matter sing,
your violet flame does all restore,
with you we are becoming more.**

9. Saint Germain, shatter the energetic matrix that prevents people from seeing that we human beings could always win if we see what is going on. If a critical mass of us could unite, we could always overthrow the power elites, we could always, in the extreme case, kill all of the fallen beings.

O Saint Germain, the earth is free,
from burden of duality,
in oneness we bring what is best,
your Golden Age is manifest.

O Saint Germain, what love you bring,
it truly makes all matter sing,
your violet flame does all restore,
with you we are becoming more.

Sealing

In the name of the I AM THAT I AM, I accept that Archangel Michael, Astrea and Shiva form an impenetrable shield around myself and all constructive people, sealing us from all fear-based energies in all four octaves. I accept that the Light of God is consuming and transforming all fear-based energies that make up the dark forces working against ending the era of elitism on earth!

36 | INVOKING AN EXPOSURE OF THE REAL PROBLEM (PART 2)

In the name of the I AM THAT I AM, Jesus Christ, I use the authority that I have as a being in embodiment on earth to call upon Saint Germain to reinforce my calls and use my chakras to project the statements in this invocation into the collective consciousness and awaken people to the fact that the real problem on earth is that the fallen beings attempt to sabotage any constructive endeavour. Awaken people to the reality that we are spiritual beings and that we can co-create a new future by working with the ascended masters. I especially call for …

[Make your own calls here.]

Part 1

1. Saint Germain, shatter the energetic matrix that prevents people from seeing that the fallen beings realize that the population does not have to kill the elite for the elite to lose power. We just have to become aware of the existence and the methods of the elite.

O Saint Germain, you do inspire,
my vision raised forever higher,
with you I form a figure-eight,
your Golden Age I co-create.

O Saint Germain, what love you bring,
it truly makes all matter sing,
your violet flame does all restore,
with you we are becoming more.

2. Saint Germain, shatter the energetic matrix that prevents people from seeing that the moment we become aware, the fallen beings lose a lot of their power, because their power is based on deception, manipulation, it is based on the people not knowing what is going on.

O Saint Germain, what Freedom Flame,
released when we recite your name,
acceleration is your gift,
our planet it will surely lift.

O Saint Germain, what love you bring,
it truly makes all matter sing,
your violet flame does all restore,
with you we are becoming more.

3. Saint Germain, shatter the energetic matrix that prevents people from seeing that the fallen beings know that the moment we wake up, they will lose power. That is why they are doing everything to prevent us from waking up and making the determination: "We want something better, we want a better society."

O Saint Germain, in love we claim,
our right to bring your violet flame,
from you Above, to us below,
it is an all-transforming flow.

O Saint Germain, what love you bring,
it truly makes all matter sing,

**your violet flame does all restore,
with you we are becoming more.**

4. Saint Germain, shatter the energetic matrix that prevents people from seeing that the fallen beings, both those in embodiment and those in the higher realms, have a clear desire, a clear strategy, to limit the size of the human population.

O Saint Germain, I love you so,
my aura filled with violet glow,
my chakras filled with violet fire,
I am your cosmic amplifier.

**O Saint Germain, what love you bring,
it truly makes all matter sing,
your violet flame does all restore,
with you we are becoming more.**

5. Saint Germain, shatter the energetic matrix that prevents people from seeing that the fallen beings are very capable of looking at history, and seeing how the feudal system was overthrown because the population became too large, so that people could no longer survive with the uneven distribution of wealth.

O Saint Germain, I am now free,
your violet flame is therapy,
transform all hang-ups in my mind,
as inner peace I surely find.

**O Saint Germain, what love you bring,
it truly makes all matter sing,
your violet flame does all restore,
with you we are becoming more.**

6. Saint Germain, shatter the energetic matrix that prevents people from seeing that the fallen beings know that when people are facing starvation, they will no longer submit to the elite and therefore the system will be overthrown, as we saw in the French revolution.

O Saint Germain, my body pure,
your violet flame for all is cure,
consume the cause of all disease,
and therefore I am all at ease.

O Saint Germain, what love you bring,
it truly makes all matter sing,
your violet flame does all restore,
with you we are becoming more.

7. Saint Germain, shatter the energetic matrix that prevents people from seeing that the French revolution was driven by an aspiring power elite that wanted to overthrow the established power elite, but they could not have done this if the people had not been brought to the brink of starvation.

O Saint Germain, I'm karma-free,
the past no longer burdens me,
a brand new opportunity,
I am in Christic unity.

O Saint Germain, what love you bring,
it truly makes all matter sing,
your violet flame does all restore,
with you we are becoming more.

8. Saint Germain, shatter the energetic matrix that prevents people from seeing the arrogance, the ignorance, of the established power elite, where they continue to do the same thing, they continue to hold on to power. This is what brings a society to that point where the population can no longer live with the conditions they have been given by the elite, and then they rise up.

O Saint Germain, we are now one,
I am for you a violet sun,
as we transform this planet earth,
your Golden Age is given birth.

O Saint Germain, what love you bring,
it truly makes all matter sing,

your violet flame does all restore,
with you we are becoming more.

9. Saint Germain, shatter the energetic matrix that prevents people from seeing that in many cases, this leads to the emergence of an aspiring power elite, who make use of the people's anger to overthrow the established elite. Then, in some cases, the people end up being worse off, as was the case after the Bolshevik revolution.

O Saint Germain, the earth is free,
from burden of duality,
in oneness we bring what is best,
your Golden Age is manifest.

O Saint Germain, what love you bring,
it truly makes all matter sing,
your violet flame does all restore,
with you we are becoming more.

Part 2

1. Saint Germain, shatter the energetic matrix that prevents people from seeing that there is always an established power elite and they cannot change their ways, until they are faced with a determined population who will no longer accept current conditions, but want some kind of change.

O Saint Germain, you do inspire,
my vision raised forever higher,
with you I form a figure-eight,
your Golden Age I co-create.

O Saint Germain, what love you bring,
it truly makes all matter sing,
your violet flame does all restore,
with you we are becoming more.

2. Saint Germain, shatter the energetic matrix that prevents people from seeing that the elite will not change by themselves, unless it is to give them even more power and more privilege, but they will not change the system in favour of the people.

O Saint Germain, what Freedom Flame,
released when we recite your name,
acceleration is your gift,
our planet it will surely lift.

O Saint Germain, what love you bring,
it truly makes all matter sing,
your violet flame does all restore,
with you we are becoming more.

3. Saint Germain, shatter the energetic matrix that prevents people from seeing that: "We are the ones who can bring change. We are the ones who must take upon ourselves the responsibility to bring change."

O Saint Germain, in love we claim,
our right to bring your violet flame,
from you Above, to us below,
it is an all-transforming flow.

O Saint Germain, what love you bring,
it truly makes all matter sing,
your violet flame does all restore,
with you we are becoming more.

4. Saint Germain, shatter the energetic matrix that prevents people from seeing that the fallen beings have for a long time had an active program of limiting the size of the population. They know that when the population reaches a certain level, they cannot control the people.

O Saint Germain, I love you so,
my aura filled with violet glow,
my chakras filled with violet fire,
I am your cosmic amplifier.

**O Saint Germain, what love you bring,
it truly makes all matter sing,
your violet flame does all restore,
with you we are becoming more.**

5. Saint Germain, shatter the energetic matrix that prevents people from seeing that over the last several hundred years, there has been a clear progression in societies on earth. There has been an improvement in the area of politics, where more people have come to live under democratic governments, which the power elite, the fallen beings, never wanted.

O Saint Germain, I am now free,
your violet flame is therapy,
transform all hang-ups in my mind,
as inner peace I surely find.

**O Saint Germain, what love you bring,
it truly makes all matter sing,
your violet flame does all restore,
with you we are becoming more.**

6. Saint Germain, shatter the energetic matrix that prevents people from seeing that the greater political freedom, the better economy, the growth of knowledge and technology has been brought about, not just because the population has grown, but also because of the upward pull from the rest of the universe.

O Saint Germain, my body pure,
your violet flame for all is cure,
consume the cause of all disease,
and therefore I am all at ease.

**O Saint Germain, what love you bring,
it truly makes all matter sing,
your violet flame does all restore,
with you we are becoming more.**

7. Saint Germain, shatter the energetic matrix that prevents people from tuning in to this upward movement and deciding that we want to have a better life, we want to have a better political system.

> O Saint Germain, I'm karma-free,
> the past no longer burdens me,
> a brand new opportunity,
> I am in Christic unity.

> **O Saint Germain, what love you bring,**
> **it truly makes all matter sing,**
> **your violet flame does all restore,**
> **with you we are becoming more.**

8. Saint Germain, shatter the energetic matrix that prevents people from taking a stand and demanding something better, educating ourselves, raising our consciousness, starting businesses and improving our outer situation.

> O Saint Germain, we are now one,
> I am for you a violet sun,
> as we transform this planet earth,
> your Golden Age is given birth.

> **O Saint Germain, what love you bring,**
> **it truly makes all matter sing,**
> **your violet flame does all restore,**
> **with you we are becoming more.**

9. Saint Germain, shatter the energetic matrix that prevents people from tuning in to this accelerating movement and bringing about change. Change is caused not just by the rise in the number of the population, but also the rise in the consciousness of the population, because we are tuned in to the accelerating movement.

> O Saint Germain, the earth is free,
> from burden of duality,
> in oneness we bring what is best,
> your Golden Age is manifest.

**O Saint Germain, what love you bring,
it truly makes all matter sing,
your violet flame does all restore,
with you we are becoming more.**

Part 3

1. Saint Germain, shatter the energetic matrix that prevents people from seeing that the fallen beings are not able to tune in to the accelerating movement. They know there is something but they do not understand what it is. They are too blind to see it.

O Saint Germain, you do inspire,
my vision raised forever higher,
with you I form a figure-eight,
your Golden Age I co-create.

**O Saint Germain, what love you bring,
it truly makes all matter sing,
your violet flame does all restore,
with you we are becoming more.**

2. Saint Germain, shatter the energetic matrix that prevents people from seeing that the fallen beings think they know everything about how the world works. They do not actually see the reality of how the universe functions, and how there is absolutely no chance that the earth can resist the accelerating movement of the rest of the universe.

O Saint Germain, what Freedom Flame,
released when we recite your name,
acceleration is your gift,
our planet it will surely lift.

**O Saint Germain, what love you bring,
it truly makes all matter sing,
your violet flame does all restore,
with you we are becoming more.**

3. Saint Germain, shatter the energetic matrix that prevents people from seeing that there is nothing the fallen beings can do to stop it and that is why they have not, with all their manipulation, with all their keeping the people in ignorance, been able to stop the forward progression on this planet.

O Saint Germain, in love we claim,
our right to bring your violet flame,
from you Above, to us below,
it is an all-transforming flow.

O Saint Germain, what love you bring,
it truly makes all matter sing,
your violet flame does all restore,
with you we are becoming more.

4. Saint Germain, shatter the energetic matrix that prevents people from seeing that compared to society as it was 500 or a 1,000 years ago, there has been much progression in many areas. This is brought about by the upward movement of the universe.

O Saint Germain, I love you so,
my aura filled with violet glow,
my chakras filled with violet fire,
I am your cosmic amplifier.

O Saint Germain, what love you bring,
it truly makes all matter sing,
your violet flame does all restore,
with you we are becoming more.

5. Saint Germain, shatter the energetic matrix that prevents people from seeing that the problems that have been created are a product of the duality consciousness and also the manipulation of the fallen beings, but there has still been an overall progression.

O Saint Germain, I am now free,
your violet flame is therapy,

transform all hang-ups in my mind,
as inner peace I surely find.

O Saint Germain, what love you bring,
it truly makes all matter sing,
your violet flame does all restore,
with you we are becoming more.

6. Saint Germain, shatter the energetic matrix that prevents people from seeing that if there had not been progress, all people on earth would still be living as the slaves of a small power elite, and they would live their entire lives without having the possibility of improving their condition.

O Saint Germain, my body pure,
your violet flame for all is cure,
consume the cause of all disease,
and therefore I am all at ease.

O Saint Germain, what love you bring,
it truly makes all matter sing,
your violet flame does all restore,
with you we are becoming more.

7. Saint Germain, shatter the energetic matrix that prevents people from seeing that the fallen beings feel threatened. They feel there is change that they cannot hold back but they do not see the real reason. They think it is the increase in population.

O Saint Germain, I'm karma-free,
the past no longer burdens me,
a brand new opportunity,
I am in Christic unity.

O Saint Germain, what love you bring,
it truly makes all matter sing,
your violet flame does all restore,
with you we are becoming more.

8. Saint Germain, shatter the energetic matrix that prevents people from seeing that the fallen beings think they need to limit the size of the population so they can still keep us in a state of slavery.

O Saint Germain, we are now one,
I am for you a violet sun,
as we transform this planet earth,
your Golden Age is given birth.

**O Saint Germain, what love you bring,
it truly makes all matter sing,
your violet flame does all restore,
with you we are becoming more.**

9. Saint Germain, shatter the energetic matrix that prevents people from seeing that there are still many among the fallen beings who believe that the problem is the size of the population. They also believe that the earth simply does not have the resources to sustain the current level of population.

O Saint Germain, the earth is free,
from burden of duality,
in oneness we bring what is best,
your Golden Age is manifest.

**O Saint Germain, what love you bring,
it truly makes all matter sing,
your violet flame does all restore,
with you we are becoming more.**

Part 4

1. Saint Germain, shatter the energetic matrix that prevents people from seeing that the fallen beings believe the earth does not have the resources to give all people on earth a decent standard of living. This is correct, but only because resources are not distributed evenly.

O Saint Germain, you do inspire,
my vision raised forever higher,
with you I form a figure-eight,
your Golden Age I co-create.

O Saint Germain, what love you bring,
it truly makes all matter sing,
your violet flame does all restore,
with you we are becoming more.

2. Saint Germain, shatter the energetic matrix that prevents people from
seeing that one problem is that the fallen beings have manipulated things
to the point where there are a lot of resources that are not recognized by
science, they do not see this as a resource. So there *is* a limited amount of
resources.

O Saint Germain, what Freedom Flame,
released when we recite your name,
acceleration is your gift,
our planet it will surely lift.

O Saint Germain, what love you bring,
it truly makes all matter sing,
your violet flame does all restore,
with you we are becoming more.

3. Saint Germain, shatter the energetic matrix that prevents people from
seeing that the real problem is the unequal distribution of resources and
wealth. With the present distribution of money, where 2% of the population in the United States control over 90% of the wealth, obviously we
cannot give all people in the world a decent standard of living. But with a
redistribution of wealth, we certainly could.

O Saint Germain, in love we claim,
our right to bring your violet flame,
from you Above, to us below,
it is an all-transforming flow.

**O Saint Germain, what love you bring,
it truly makes all matter sing,
your violet flame does all restore,
with you we are becoming more.**

4. Saint Germain, shatter the energetic matrix that prevents people from seeing that the fallen beings do not want the redistribution of wealth. They cannot see the potential for technology that could increase the level of resources.

O Saint Germain, I love you so,
my aura filled with violet glow,
my chakras filled with violet fire,
I am your cosmic amplifier.

**O Saint Germain, what love you bring,
it truly makes all matter sing,
your violet flame does all restore,
with you we are becoming more.**

5. Saint Germain, shatter the energetic matrix that prevents people from seeing that the fallen beings cannot see the potential for free energy technology, which is why they have made such a determined effort to ridicule it and put it down or to stop it if they can.

O Saint Germain, I am now free,
your violet flame is therapy,
transform all hang-ups in my mind,
as inner peace I surely find.

**O Saint Germain, what love you bring,
it truly makes all matter sing,
your violet flame does all restore,
with you we are becoming more.**

6. Saint Germain, shatter the energetic matrix that prevents people from seeing that behind all of this, there are still some fallen beings, both in embodiment and in the higher realms, who are actively working on limiting the size of the population. They do this in various ways.

O Saint Germain, my body pure,
your violet flame for all is cure,
consume the cause of all disease,
and therefore I am all at ease.

**O Saint Germain, what love you bring,
it truly makes all matter sing,
your violet flame does all restore,
with you we are becoming more.**

7. Saint Germain, shatter the energetic matrix that prevents people from seeing that abortion is one of the ways they want to limit the size of the population. Poverty is one of the more inhumane ways to limit the size of the population, because it increases child mortality and limits the lifespan when people are living in a state of malnutrition.

O Saint Germain, I'm karma-free,
the past no longer burdens me,
a brand new opportunity,
I am in Christic unity.

**O Saint Germain, what love you bring,
it truly makes all matter sing,
your violet flame does all restore,
with you we are becoming more.**

8. Saint Germain, shatter the energetic matrix that prevents people from seeing that disease is another way, and they have tried to create modern medicine in such a way that it cannot cure certain diseases, which then limit the size of the population.

O Saint Germain, we are now one,
I am for you a violet sun,
as we transform this planet earth,
your Golden Age is given birth.

**O Saint Germain, what love you bring,
it truly makes all matter sing,**

**your violet flame does all restore,
with you we are becoming more.**

9. Saint Germain, shatter the energetic matrix that prevents people from seeing that another aspect is the entire environmental debate, which they have taken over and manipulated to the point, where many among the people actually believe that the biggest problem on earth, the biggest threat to the survival of humanity, is the increase in population.

O Saint Germain, the earth is free,
from burden of duality,
in oneness we bring what is best,
your Golden Age is manifest.

**O Saint Germain, what love you bring,
it truly makes all matter sing,
your violet flame does all restore,
with you we are becoming more.**

Part 5

1. Saint Germain, shatter the energetic matrix that prevents people from seeing that this has caused millions of people, especially in the more democratic world, to voluntarily limit the amount of children they have. The elite does not need to abort the children. They do not need to kill them off with disease or malnutrition, because people voluntarily choose not to have as many children.

O Saint Germain, you do inspire,
my vision raised forever higher,
with you I form a figure-eight,
your Golden Age I co-create.

**O Saint Germain, what love you bring,
it truly makes all matter sing,
your violet flame does all restore,
with you we are becoming more.**

2. Saint Germain, shatter the energetic matrix that prevents people from seeing that there is an attempt to create this attitude that humanity needs to do something to limit population growth.

> O Saint Germain, what Freedom Flame,
> released when we recite your name,
> acceleration is your gift,
> our planet it will surely lift.

> **O Saint Germain, what love you bring,**
> **it truly makes all matter sing,**
> **your violet flame does all restore,**
> **with you we are becoming more.**

3. Saint Germain, shatter the energetic matrix that prevents people from seeing that the fallen beings are trying create an attitude in the population, where we will accept some new methods for limiting the size of the population, including genetic manipulation that could lower the fertility of women so they could not have as many children.

> O Saint Germain, in love we claim,
> our right to bring your violet flame,
> from you Above, to us below,
> it is an all-transforming flow.

> **O Saint Germain, what love you bring,**
> **it truly makes all matter sing,**
> **your violet flame does all restore,**
> **with you we are becoming more.**

4. Saint Germain, shatter the energetic matrix that prevents people from seeing that the fallen beings are talking about forced sterilization. Through the environmental debate, they are trying to create an attitude among people where we will accept the necessity of limiting the human population.

> O Saint Germain, I love you so,
> my aura filled with violet glow,
> my chakras filled with violet fire,
> I am your cosmic amplifier.

O Saint Germain, what love you bring,
it truly makes all matter sing,
your violet flame does all restore,
with you we are becoming more.

5. Saint Germain, shatter the energetic matrix that prevents people from seeing that much of the environmental debate is not about the environment. It is about human beings, it is about creating an attitude that accepts more control with the size of the population.

O Saint Germain, I am now free,
your violet flame is therapy,
transform all hang-ups in my mind,
as inner peace I surely find.

O Saint Germain, what love you bring,
it truly makes all matter sing,
your violet flame does all restore,
with you we are becoming more.

6. Saint Germain, shatter the energetic matrix that prevents people from seeing that this attitude is not directed at improving the environment. It is directed at limiting the size of the population.

O Saint Germain, my body pure,
your violet flame for all is cure,
consume the cause of all disease,
and therefore I am all at ease.

O Saint Germain, what love you bring,
it truly makes all matter sing,
your violet flame does all restore,
with you we are becoming more.

7. Saint Germain, shatter the energetic matrix that prevents people from seeing that it is the power elite that creates most of the pollution in the world, the more serious form of pollution. They are driven by their profit motives, so that they create factories that let out more toxins and more toxic substances than what is produced by normal human waste.

O Saint Germain, I'm karma-free,
the past no longer burdens me,
a brand new opportunity,
I am in Christic unity.

O Saint Germain, what love you bring,
it truly makes all matter sing,
your violet flame does all restore,
with you we are becoming more.

8. Saint Germain, shatter the energetic matrix that prevents people from seeing that the biggest problem with pollution is created by the power elite, but they are blaming it on the people.

O Saint Germain, we are now one,
I am for you a violet sun,
as we transform this planet earth,
your Golden Age is given birth.

O Saint Germain, what love you bring,
it truly makes all matter sing,
your violet flame does all restore,
with you we are becoming more.

9. Saint Germain, shatter the energetic matrix that prevents people from seeing that the fallen beings say it is not the power elite that is the problem with pollution, no it is that there are too many in the population. They say *that* is what creates pollution and many people have believed this.

O Saint Germain, the earth is free,
from burden of duality,
in oneness we bring what is best,
your Golden Age is manifest.

O Saint Germain, what love you bring,
it truly makes all matter sing,
your violet flame does all restore,
with you we are becoming more.

Sealing

In the name of the I AM THAT I AM, I accept that Archangel Michael, Astrea and Shiva form an impenetrable shield around myself and all constructive people, sealing us from all fear-based energies in all four octaves. I accept that the Light of God is consuming and transforming all fear-based energies that make up the dark forces working against ending the era of elitism on earth!

37 | INVOKING AN EXPOSURE OF THE REAL PROBLEM (PART 3)

In the name of the I AM THAT I AM, Jesus Christ, I use the authority that I have as a being in embodiment on earth to call upon Saint Germain to reinforce my calls and use my chakras to project the statements in this invocation into the collective consciousness and awaken people to the fact that the real problem on earth is that the fallen beings attempt to sabotage any constructive endeavour. Awaken people to the reality that we are spiritual beings and that we can co-create a new future by working with the ascended masters. I especially call for …

[Make your own calls here.]

Part 1

1. Saint Germain, shatter the energetic matrix that prevents people from seeing that people who are concerned about the environment are the people who have a certain level of humanity. When we have a basic level of humanity, then we are also concerned about the environment.

O Saint Germain, you do inspire,
my vision raised forever higher,
with you I form a figure-eight,
your Golden Age I co-create.

O Saint Germain, what love you bring,
it truly makes all matter sing,
your violet flame does all restore,
with you we are becoming more.

2. Saint Germain, shatter the energetic matrix that prevents people from seeing that we should be primarily concerned about improving the conditions for other people. Our good intentions have been misdirected by the fallen beings, where we are more concerned about the environment than we are about people in the third world who are living near the starvation level.

O Saint Germain, what Freedom Flame,
released when we recite your name,
acceleration is your gift,
our planet it will surely lift.

O Saint Germain, what love you bring,
it truly makes all matter sing,
your violet flame does all restore,
with you we are becoming more.

3. Saint Germain, shatter the energetic matrix that prevents people from seeing that people with a high level of humanity, those who are sensitive, creative and constructive people, are the kind of people that Saint Germain needs in order to drive the progress into the Golden Age.

O Saint Germain, in love we claim,
our right to bring your violet flame,
from you Above, to us below,
it is an all-transforming flow.

O Saint Germain, what love you bring,
it truly makes all matter sing,

**your violet flame does all restore,
with you we are becoming more.**

4. Saint Germain, shatter the energetic matrix that prevents people from seeing that the Golden Age is about growth, it is not about limiting growth, but we have been deceived into thinking that we should limit growth. We should work towards limiting growth, living a minimalistic lifestyle, consuming as little as possible.

O Saint Germain, I love you so,
my aura filled with violet glow,
my chakras filled with violet fire,
I am your cosmic amplifier.

**O Saint Germain, what love you bring,
it truly makes all matter sing,
your violet flame does all restore,
with you we are becoming more.**

5. Saint Germain, shatter the energetic matrix that prevents people from seeing that too many creative people are not able to tune in to Saint Germain's Presence and his ideas and bring them forth. It is a huge wasted potential where some of these creative people could play a role in bringing forth the Golden Age.

O Saint Germain, I am now free,
your violet flame is therapy,
transform all hang-ups in my mind,
as inner peace I surely find.

**O Saint Germain, what love you bring,
it truly makes all matter sing,
your violet flame does all restore,
with you we are becoming more.**

6. Saint Germain, shatter the energetic matrix that prevents people from seeing that in the Golden Age, there will not be a problem with pollution because you will bring forth a non-force-based technology that does not pollute.

O Saint Germain, my body pure,
your violet flame for all is cure,
consume the cause of all disease,
and therefore I am all at ease.

O Saint Germain, what love you bring,
it truly makes all matter sing,
your violet flame does all restore,
with you we are becoming more.

7. Saint Germain, shatter the energetic matrix that prevents people from seeing that in order to bring forth new technology, you need some creative people who can receive it.

O Saint Germain, I'm karma-free,
the past no longer burdens me,
a brand new opportunity,
I am in Christic unity.

O Saint Germain, what love you bring,
it truly makes all matter sing,
your violet flame does all restore,
with you we are becoming more.

8. Saint Germain, shatter the energetic matrix that prevents people from seeing that the people who can make changes in society, in the economy, who can help manifest the Golden Age, are precisely the people who are today so concerned about limiting the size of the population, improving the environment and combating global warming.

O Saint Germain, we are now one,
I am for you a violet sun,
as we transform this planet earth,
your Golden Age is given birth.

O Saint Germain, what love you bring,
it truly makes all matter sing,
your violet flame does all restore,
with you we are becoming more.

9. Saint Germain, shatter the energetic matrix that prevents people from seeing that all of these problems could be transcended by moving into the Golden Age mindset, which is not based on lack, not based on limitations, but based on bringing forth Golden Age technology.

O Saint Germain, the earth is free,
from burden of duality,
in oneness we bring what is best,
your Golden Age is manifest.

O Saint Germain, what love you bring,
it truly makes all matter sing,
your violet flame does all restore,
with you we are becoming more.

Part 2

1. Saint Germain, shatter the energetic matrix that prevents people from being awakened and becoming free from this deception of the fallen beings.

O Saint Germain, you do inspire,
my vision raised forever higher,
with you I form a figure-eight,
your Golden Age I co-create.

O Saint Germain, what love you bring,
it truly makes all matter sing,
your violet flame does all restore,
with you we are becoming more.

2. Saint Germain, shatter the energetic matrix that prevents people from recognizing the arrogance of the fallen beings, how they have no respect, they have no humanity.

O Saint Germain, what Freedom Flame,
released when we recite your name,

acceleration is your gift,
our planet it will surely lift.

O Saint Germain, what love you bring,
it truly makes all matter sing,
your violet flame does all restore,
with you we are becoming more.

3. Saint Germain, shatter the energetic matrix that prevents people from seeing that these are not the kind of people we want to be following, because it is actually not going to help the environment. What is currently being proposed in order to combat pollution and global warming is not going to be effective.

O Saint Germain, in love we claim,
our right to bring your violet flame,
from you Above, to us below,
it is an all-transforming flow.

O Saint Germain, what love you bring,
it truly makes all matter sing,
your violet flame does all restore,
with you we are becoming more.

4. Saint Germain, shatter the energetic matrix that prevents people from seeing that there is the need for an entirely new kind of technology that is not forced-based, namely what we today call free energy technology, even though it is not free.

O Saint Germain, I love you so,
my aura filled with violet glow,
my chakras filled with violet fire,
I am your cosmic amplifier.

O Saint Germain, what love you bring,
it truly makes all matter sing,
your violet flame does all restore,
with you we are becoming more.

5. Saint Germain, shatter the energetic matrix that prevents people from seeing that free energy is a manipulated terminology, created by the fallen beings to discredit this technology and make people think it is a utopian fantasy.

O Saint Germain, I am now free,
your violet flame is therapy,
transform all hang-ups in my mind,
as inner peace I surely find.

O Saint Germain, what love you bring,
it truly makes all matter sing,
your violet flame does all restore,
with you we are becoming more.

6. Saint Germain, shatter the energetic matrix that prevents people from seeing that if there was not a realm beyond the physical, if there was not energy in that realm that could be brought into the physical, how would there be a universe? Where would the energy come from to drive the Big Bang?

O Saint Germain, my body pure,
your violet flame for all is cure,
consume the cause of all disease,
and therefore I am all at ease.

O Saint Germain, what love you bring,
it truly makes all matter sing,
your violet flame does all restore,
with you we are becoming more.

7. Saint Germain, shatter the energetic matrix that prevents people from seeing that cosmologists know that the universe is not only expanding, it is expanding at an accelerated rate. There must be energy to drive this expansion. Since it cannot come from the physical, it must come from beyond the physical.

O Saint Germain, I'm karma-free,
the past no longer burdens me,

a brand new opportunity,
I am in Christic unity.

O Saint Germain, what love you bring,
it truly makes all matter sing,
your violet flame does all restore,
with you we are becoming more.

8. Saint Germain, shatter the energetic matrix that prevents people from seeing that we can make use of this energy to drive our phones, drive our cars, heat our houses and bring light to our houses. This is a technology that is not burning fossil fuel, it is not polluting.

O Saint Germain, we are now one,
I am for you a violet sun,
as we transform this planet earth,
your Golden Age is given birth.

O Saint Germain, what love you bring,
it truly makes all matter sing,
your violet flame does all restore,
with you we are becoming more.

9. Saint Germain, shatter the energetic matrix that prevents people from seeing that the technology has to be brought forth, but there has to be a critical mass of people who can accept that this is a realistic possibility. The people who could do this are those who are concerned about the environment, but they have been misled into thinking that the only way to save the environment is through control.

O Saint Germain, the earth is free,
from burden of duality,
in oneness we bring what is best,
your Golden Age is manifest.

O Saint Germain, what love you bring,
it truly makes all matter sing,
your violet flame does all restore,
with you we are becoming more.

Part 3

1. Saint Germain, shatter the energetic matrix that prevents people from seeing that what has driven positive growth is *acceleration,* it is transcending the old ways of looking at things. Transcendence and acceleration is the key to saving the environment, not control.

O Saint Germain, you do inspire,
my vision raised forever higher,
with you I form a figure-eight,
your Golden Age I co-create.

O Saint Germain, what love you bring,
it truly makes all matter sing,
your violet flame does all restore,
with you we are becoming more.

2. Saint Germain, shatter the energetic matrix that prevents people from seeing that the fallen beings, the power elite, they are the ones who are always wanting control.

O Saint Germain, what Freedom Flame,
released when we recite your name,
acceleration is your gift,
our planet it will surely lift.

O Saint Germain, what love you bring,
it truly makes all matter sing,
your violet flame does all restore,
with you we are becoming more.

3. Saint Germain, shatter the energetic matrix that prevents people from seeing that control works against the basic forces of the universe. Control creates a closed system that becomes subject to the second law of thermo-dynamics and therefore will self-destruct.

O Saint Germain, in love we claim,
our right to bring your violet flame,

from you Above, to us below,
it is an all-transforming flow.

O Saint Germain, what love you bring,
it truly makes all matter sing,
your violet flame does all restore,
with you we are becoming more.

4. Saint Germain, shatter the energetic matrix that prevents people from seeing that this is what happened in the Soviet Union, this is what happened in many previous civilizations that became closed systems, because there was a small power elite who did all they could to control the population.

O Saint Germain, I love you so,
my aura filled with violet glow,
my chakras filled with violet fire,
I am your cosmic amplifier.

O Saint Germain, what love you bring,
it truly makes all matter sing,
your violet flame does all restore,
with you we are becoming more.

5. Saint Germain, shatter the energetic matrix that prevents people from seeing that the elite wanted to keep the population down, they wanted to keep the creativity of the population down, to lower their consciousness. When they lower the collective consciousness, they create a tension that will eventually cause that society to fall apart.

O Saint Germain, I am now free,
your violet flame is therapy,
transform all hang-ups in my mind,
as inner peace I surely find.

O Saint Germain, what love you bring,
it truly makes all matter sing,
your violet flame does all restore,
with you we are becoming more.

6. Saint Germain, shatter the energetic matrix that prevents people from seeing that when a society goes below a certain level of consciousness, people become increasingly selfish. If people become more and more selfish, how concerned are they about the environment? How concerned are they about other people?

> O Saint Germain, my body pure,
> your violet flame for all is cure,
> consume the cause of all disease,
> and therefore I am all at ease.

> **O Saint Germain, what love you bring,**
> **it truly makes all matter sing,**
> **your violet flame does all restore,**
> **with you we are becoming more.**

7. Saint Germain, shatter the energetic matrix that prevents people from seeing that the people who are the most selfish, they do not care about the environment. They do not care about children starving to death in Bangladesh. It is of no concern to them whatsoever, they just want the lifestyle they think they are entitled to.

> O Saint Germain, I'm karma-free,
> the past no longer burdens me,
> a brand new opportunity,
> I am in Christic unity.

> **O Saint Germain, what love you bring,**
> **it truly makes all matter sing,**
> **your violet flame does all restore,**
> **with you we are becoming more.**

8. Saint Germain, shatter the energetic matrix that prevents people from seeing that this is precisely the attitude of the power elite. They are not concerned whatsoever about the environment, they only claim to be because they can use it as a means to the end of controlling the population.

> O Saint Germain, we are now one,
> I am for you a violet sun,

as we transform this planet earth,
your Golden Age is given birth.

O Saint Germain, what love you bring,
it truly makes all matter sing,
your violet flame does all restore,
with you we are becoming more.

9. Saint Germain, shatter the energetic matrix that prevents the creative people, who are concerned about the environment, from waking up and realizing what will save the environment and what will not!

O Saint Germain, the earth is free,
from burden of duality,
in oneness we bring what is best,
your Golden Age is manifest.

O Saint Germain, what love you bring,
it truly makes all matter sing,
your violet flame does all restore,
with you we are becoming more.

Part 4

1. Saint Germain, shatter the energetic matrix that prevents people from seeing that allowing a small power elite to continue to control the human population will not save the environment. It will only make things worse, as the power elite has been making things gradually worse with the increase in technology.

O Saint Germain, you do inspire,
my vision raised forever higher,
with you I form a figure-eight,
your Golden Age I co-create.

O Saint Germain, what love you bring,
it truly makes all matter sing,

your violet flame does all restore,
with you we are becoming more.

2. Saint Germain, shatter the energetic matrix that prevents people from seeing that it is not the people who have misused technology, it is the power elite.

O Saint Germain, what Freedom Flame,
released when we recite your name,
acceleration is your gift,
our planet it will surely lift.

O Saint Germain, what love you bring,
it truly makes all matter sing,
your violet flame does all restore,
with you we are becoming more.

3. Saint Germain, shatter the energetic matrix that prevents people from waking up and educating ourselves to what is really going on. Help us to stop thinking we are doing something good for the planet, when in reality, we are only doing what is good for the elite.

O Saint Germain, in love we claim,
our right to bring your violet flame,
from you Above, to us below,
it is an all-transforming flow.

O Saint Germain, what love you bring,
it truly makes all matter sing,
your violet flame does all restore,
with you we are becoming more.

4. Saint Germain, shatter the energetic matrix that prevents people from seeing that you want a Golden Age where all people can live an abundant, affluent lifestyle without destroying the environment on the planet. This is possible. It is not possible with current technology. It is not possible with the current distribution of wealth. But both of those things can be changed.

O Saint Germain, I love you so,
my aura filled with violet glow,
my chakras filled with violet fire,
I am your cosmic amplifier.

O Saint Germain, what love you bring,
it truly makes all matter sing,
your violet flame does all restore,
with you we are becoming more.

5. Saint Germain, shatter the energetic matrix that prevents people from seeing that you cannot do it alone. You have all the ideas for how this could be done. You are willing to release those ideas, but there has to be those who can implement them and there has to be those who can accept it. We have that potential.

O Saint Germain, I am now free,
your violet flame is therapy,
transform all hang-ups in my mind,
as inner peace I surely find.

O Saint Germain, what love you bring,
it truly makes all matter sing,
your violet flame does all restore,
with you we are becoming more.

6. Saint Germain, shatter the energetic matrix that prevents the well-meaning, enthusiastic, idealistic people from seeing that we have the potential to be forerunners for your Golden Age. Help us wake up and recognize that potential and realize that this is why we are here.

O Saint Germain, my body pure,
your violet flame for all is cure,
consume the cause of all disease,
and therefore I am all at ease.

O Saint Germain, what love you bring,
it truly makes all matter sing,

**your violet flame does all restore,
with you we are becoming more.**

7. Saint Germain, shatter the energetic matrix that prevents people from seeing that this is why we wanted to embody at this particular time. We did not want to embody to take society backwards. We wanted to embody to take it forwards into the Golden Age.

O Saint Germain, I'm karma-free,
the past no longer burdens me,
a brand new opportunity,
I am in Christic unity.

**O Saint Germain, what love you bring,
it truly makes all matter sing,
your violet flame does all restore,
with you we are becoming more.**

8. Saint Germain, shatter the energetic matrix that prevents people from awakening ourselves, educating ourselves, realizing the dynamic that the real issue on the planet is the existence of a power elite who is sabotaging absolutely everything. Every positive initiative that has ever been taken, they are attempting to sabotage it.

O Saint Germain, we are now one,
I am for you a violet sun,
as we transform this planet earth,
your Golden Age is given birth.

**O Saint Germain, what love you bring,
it truly makes all matter sing,
your violet flame does all restore,
with you we are becoming more.**

9. Saint Germain, shatter the energetic matrix that prevents people from seeing that it is not enough to create a new system, a new ideology, a new approach. Whatever we create, the fallen beings will only have one concern: "How can we turn it into a system that serves our cause of getting power, privilege and control?"

O Saint Germain, the earth is free,
from burden of duality,
in oneness we bring what is best,
your Golden Age is manifest.

O Saint Germain, what love you bring,
it truly makes all matter sing,
your violet flame does all restore,
with you we are becoming more.

Part 5

1. Saint Germain, shatter the energetic matrix that prevents people from seeing that a socialist system with common ownership, could work. But it cannot work when the fallen beings are attempting to manipulate it into setting themselves up with power and privilege.

O Saint Germain, you do inspire,
my vision raised forever higher,
with you I form a figure-eight,
your Golden Age I co-create.

O Saint Germain, what love you bring,
it truly makes all matter sing,
your violet flame does all restore,
with you we are becoming more.

2. Saint Germain, shatter the energetic matrix that prevents people from seeing that a free market economy, not a capitalist economy but a free market economy, can also work, but not when we have a small elite who are doing everything they can to destroy free competition, to destroy the free market so they can create monopolies that concentrate wealth in the hands of a small group of people.

O Saint Germain, what Freedom Flame,
released when we recite your name,

acceleration is your gift,
our planet it will surely lift.

O Saint Germain, what love you bring,
it truly makes all matter sing,
your violet flame does all restore,
with you we are becoming more.

3. Saint Germain, shatter the energetic matrix that prevents people from seeing that there is no system we could possibly think up that could ever work as long as the population allows a small power elite to manipulate that system. The only way out is to raise consciousness so that the power elite cannot continue to manipulate the population.

O Saint Germain, in love we claim,
our right to bring your violet flame,
from you Above, to us below,
it is an all-transforming flow.

O Saint Germain, what love you bring,
it truly makes all matter sing,
your violet flame does all restore,
with you we are becoming more.

4. Saint Germain, shatter the energetic matrix that prevents people from seeing that it is not a matter of just knowledge. It is not a matter of creating websites that expose the power elite, and are then labelled as conspiracy theories by the elite in order to discredit it. It is a matter of raising the general level of awareness, the general level of consciousness.

O Saint Germain, I love you so,
my aura filled with violet glow,
my chakras filled with violet fire,
I am your cosmic amplifier.

O Saint Germain, what love you bring,
it truly makes all matter sing,
your violet flame does all restore,
with you we are becoming more.

5. Saint Germain, shatter the energetic matrix that prevents people from seeing that we do this by raising our own level of consciousness—*that* is how we pull up on the collective.

> O Saint Germain, I am now free,
> your violet flame is therapy,
> transform all hang-ups in my mind,
> as inner peace I surely find.

> **O Saint Germain, what love you bring,**
> **it truly makes all matter sing,**
> **your violet flame does all restore,**
> **with you we are becoming more.**

6. Saint Germain, shatter the energetic matrix that prevents people from seeing that we came into embodiment because this is what we wanted. We have been misled by a materialistic philosophy that has never given us an inkling of the possibility of raising our consciousness.

> O Saint Germain, my body pure,
> your violet flame for all is cure,
> consume the cause of all disease,
> and therefore I am all at ease.

> **O Saint Germain, what love you bring,**
> **it truly makes all matter sing,**
> **your violet flame does all restore,**
> **with you we are becoming more.**

7. Saint Germain, shatter the energetic matrix that prevents people from awakening from this, and realizing that the greatest potential we have for improving our personal life is to raise our consciousness. That is also the greatest potential we have for improving the environment.

> O Saint Germain, I'm karma-free,
> the past no longer burdens me,
> a brand new opportunity,
> I am in Christic unity.

**O Saint Germain, what love you bring,
it truly makes all matter sing,
your violet flame does all restore,
with you we are becoming more.**

8. Saint Germain, shatter the energetic matrix that prevents people from seeing that the raising of consciousness is the only way out of humankind's problems. This is the one thing that the power elites of the world do not want a critical mass of people to realize.

O Saint Germain, we are now one,
I am for you a violet sun,
as we transform this planet earth,
your Golden Age is given birth.

**O Saint Germain, what love you bring,
it truly makes all matter sing,
your violet flame does all restore,
with you we are becoming more.**

9. Saint Germain, shatter the energetic matrix that prevents people from seeing that once a critical mass realizes this, the power elite will be done. They will lose their power very quickly once the collective consciousness is raised beyond a certain level.

O Saint Germain, the earth is free,
from burden of duality,
in oneness we bring what is best,
your Golden Age is manifest.

**O Saint Germain, what love you bring,
it truly makes all matter sing,
your violet flame does all restore,
with you we are becoming more.**

Part 6

1. Saint Germain, shatter the energetic matrix that prevents people from seeing that it does not require the entire population to become aware of the power elite. A critical mass will be enough to pull the collective consciousness up to where people simply will no longer believe all of the illusions that have been spread by the elites.

O Saint Germain, you do inspire,
my vision raised forever higher,
with you I form a figure-eight,
your Golden Age I co-create.

O Saint Germain, what love you bring,
it truly makes all matter sing,
your violet flame does all restore,
with you we are becoming more.

2. Saint Germain, shatter the energetic matrix that prevents people from seeing that this is the critical shift that could happen, and it could have wide-ranging consequences for every aspect of society. Whatever concern we may have, the foundation for fulfilling our aspirations is the raising of consciousness.

O Saint Germain, what Freedom Flame,
released when we recite your name,
acceleration is your gift,
our planet it will surely lift.

O Saint Germain, what love you bring,
it truly makes all matter sing,
your violet flame does all restore,
with you we are becoming more.

3. Saint Germain, shatter the energetic matrix that prevents people from seeing that raising consciousness is the engine that drives growth, and we are not going to get out of problems through control. We will only get out of problems through growth, through acceleration.

O Saint Germain, in love we claim,
our right to bring your violet flame,
from you Above, to us below,
it is an all-transforming flow.

O Saint Germain, what love you bring,
it truly makes all matter sing,
your violet flame does all restore,
with you we are becoming more.

4. Saint Germain, shatter the energetic matrix that prevents people from seeing that this is not the kind of growth where we get more of the same. In order to raise the standard of living in third world countries, we do not need to increase energy production by burning more coal. We need to bring forth a new kind of technology that does not pollute.

O Saint Germain, I love you so,
my aura filled with violet glow,
my chakras filled with violet fire,
I am your cosmic amplifier.

O Saint Germain, what love you bring,
it truly makes all matter sing,
your violet flame does all restore,
with you we are becoming more.

5. Saint Germain, shatter the energetic matrix that prevents people from seeing that if it was possible to increase the standard of living for all people on earth without destroying the environment, we would want this to happen.

O Saint Germain, I am now free,
your violet flame is therapy,
transform all hang-ups in my mind,
as inner peace I surely find.

O Saint Germain, what love you bring,
it truly makes all matter sing,

your violet flame does all restore,
with you we are becoming more.

6. Saint Germain, shatter the energetic matrix that prevents people from seeing that it is possible to both improve people's standard of living and preserve the environment. It will require a different kind of technology, a different distribution of wealth, a different approach and attitude to society.

O Saint Germain, my body pure,
your violet flame for all is cure,
consume the cause of all disease,
and therefore I am all at ease.

O Saint Germain, what love you bring,
it truly makes all matter sing,
your violet flame does all restore,
with you we are becoming more.

7. Saint Germain, shatter the energetic matrix that prevents people from seeing that society in the democratic world has transcended itself so much in the past thousand years. It is possible to have another period of very intense accelerated growth so that our intuitive sense of what is possible suddenly becomes realistic. Because now we do not have just the *what,* we also have the *how.*

O Saint Germain, I'm karma-free,
the past no longer burdens me,
a brand new opportunity,
I am in Christic unity.

O Saint Germain, what love you bring,
it truly makes all matter sing,
your violet flame does all restore,
with you we are becoming more.

8. Saint Germain, shatter the energetic matrix that prevents people from seeing that if we are willing to open our consciousness, you will give us the

ideas for *how* we can manifest *what* we know in our hearts is possible on earth.

O Saint Germain, we are now one,
I am for you a violet sun,
as we transform this planet earth,
your Golden Age is given birth.

O Saint Germain, what love you bring,
it truly makes all matter sing,
your violet flame does all restore,
with you we are becoming more.

9. Saint Germain, shatter the energetic matrix that prevents people from seeing that when we give you the openness, when we give you the acceptance that it is possible, you will give us the *how*. *That* is your promise and you will stand by it for the next 2,000 years. We will also stand by it and the potential for growth.

O Saint Germain, the earth is free,
from burden of duality,
in oneness we bring what is best,
your Golden Age is manifest.

O Saint Germain, what love you bring,
it truly makes all matter sing,
your violet flame does all restore,
with you we are becoming more.

Sealing

In the name of the I AM THAT I AM, I accept that Archangel Michael, Astrea and Shiva form an impenetrable shield around myself and all constructive people, sealing us from all fear-based energies in all four octaves. I accept that the Light of God is consuming and transforming all fear-based energies that make up the dark forces working against ending the era of elitism on earth!

www.ingramcontent.com/pod-product-compliance
Lightning Source LLC
Chambersburg PA
CBHW020307160726
47992CB00004B/1436